Open Resources for Community College Algebra (Part III)

Open Resources for Community College Algebra (Part III)

Portland Community College Faculty

August 19, 2019

Project Leads: Ann Cary, Alex Jordan, Ross Kouzes
Technology Engineer: Alex Jordan
Contributing Authors: Ann Cary, Alex Jordan, Ross Kouzes, Scot Leavitt, Cara Lee, Carl Yao, Ralf Youtz
WeBWorK Problem Coding: Chris Hughes, Alex Jordan, Carl Yao
Significant Contributors: Kara Colley, Wendy Lightheart
Cover Image: Ralf Youtz

Edition: 2.0

Website: pcc.edu/ORCCA

Acknowledgements

This book has been made possible through Portland Community College's Strategic Investment Funding, approved by PCC's Budget Planning Advisory Council and the Board of Directors. Without significant funding to provide the authors with the adequate time, an ambitious project such as this one would not be possible.

The technology that makes it possible to create integrated print, HTML eBook, and WeBWorK content is PreTeXt, created by Rob Beezer. David Farmer and the American Institute of Mathematics deserve credit for the PreTeXt HTML eBook layout being feature-rich, yet easy to navigate. A grant from OpenOregon funded the original bridge between WeBWorK and PreTeXt.

This book uses WeBWorK to provide most of its exercises, which may be used for online homework. WeBWorK was created by Mike Gage and Arnie Pizer, and has benefited from over 25 years of contributions from open source developers. In 2013, Chris Hughes, Alex Jordan, and Carl Yao programmed most of the WeBWorK questions in this book with a PCC curriculum development grant.

The javascript library MathJax, created and maintained by David Cervone, Volker Sorge, Christian Lawson-Perfect, and Peter Krautzberger allows math content to render nicely on screen in the HTML eBook. Additionally, MathJax makes web accessible mathematics possible.

The PDF versions are built using the typesetting software LaTeX, created by Donald Knuth and enhanced by Leslie Lamport.

Each of these open technologies, along with many that we use but have not listed here, has been enhanced by many additional contributors over the past 40 years. We are indebted to these contributors for their many contributions. By releasing this book with an open license, we honor their dedication to open software and open education.

To All

HTML, PDF, and print. This book is freely available as an HTML eBook, a PDF for reading on a screen, and a PDF intended for printing. Additionally, a printed and bound copy is available for purchase at low cost. All versions offer the same content and are synchronized such that cross-references match across versions. They can each be found at pcc.edu/orcca.

There are some differences between the HTML eBook, PDF screen version, and PDF-for-print version.

- The HTML eBook offers interactive elements, easier navigation than print, and its content is accessible in ways that a PDF cannot be. It has content (particularly in appendices) that is omitted from the PDF versions for the sake of economy. It requires no more software than a modern web browser with internet access.

- Two PDF versions can be downloaded and then accessed without the internet. One version is intended to be read on a screen with a PDF viewer. This version retains full color, has its text centered on the page, and includes hyperlinking. The other version is intended for printing on two-sided paper and then binding. Most of its color has been converted with care to gray scale. Text is positioned to the left or right of each page in a manner to support two-sided binding. Hyperlinks have been disabled.

- Printed and bound copies are available for purchase online. Up-to-date information about purchasing a copy should be available at pcc.edu/orcca. Contact orcca-group@pcc.edu if you have trouble finding the latest version online. Any royalties generated from these sales support OER development and maintenance at PCC and/or scholarships to PCC students.

Copying Content. The source files for this book are available through pcc.edu/orca, and openly licensed for use. However, it may be more conveneient to copy certain things directly from the HTML eBook.

The graphs and other images that appear in this manual may be copied in various file formats using the HTML eBook version. Below each image are links to .png, .eps, .svg, .pdf, and .tex files for the image.

Mathematical content can be copied from the HTML eBook. To copy math content into *MS Word*, right-click or control-click over the math content, and click to Show Math As MathML Code. Copy the resulting code, and Paste Special into *Word*. In the Paste Special menu, paste it as Unformatted Text. To copy math content into LaTeX source, right-click or control-click over the math content, and click to Show Math As TeX Commands.

Tables can be copied from the HTML eBook version and pasted into applications like *MS Word*. However, mathematical content within tables will not always paste correctly without a little extra effort as described above.

Accessibility. The HTML eBook version is intended to meet or exceed web accessibility standards. If you encounter an accessibility issue, please report it.

- All graphs and images should have meaningful alt text that communicates what a sighted person would see, without necessarily giving away anything that is intended to be deduced from the image.

- All math content is rendered using MathJax. MathJax has a contextual menu that can be accessed in several ways, depending on what operating system and browser you are using. The most common way is to right-click or control-click on some piece of math content.

- In the MathJax contextual menu, you may set options for triggering a zoom effect on math content, and also by what factor the zoom will be. Also in the MathJax contextual menu, you can enable the Explorer, which allows for sophisticated navigation of the math content.

- A screen reader will generally have success verbalizing the math content from MathJax. With certain screen reader and browser combinations, you may need to set some configuration settings in the MathJax contextual menu.

Tablets and Smartphones. PreTeXt documents like this book are "mobile-friendly." When you view the HTML version, the display adapts to whatever screen size or window size you are using. A math teacher will usually recommend that you do not study from the small screen on a phone, but if it's necessary, the HTML eBook gives you that option.

WeBWorK for Online Homework. Most exercises are available in a ready-to-use collection of WeBWorK problem sets. Visit webwork.pcc.edu/webwork2/orcca-demonstration to see a demonstration WeBWorK course where guest login is enabled. Anyone interested in using these problem sets may contact the project leads. The WeBWorK set defintion files and supporting files should be available for download from pcc.edu/orcca.

Odd Answers. The answers to the odd homework exercises at the end of each section are not printed in the PDF versions for economy. Instead, a separate PDF with the odd answers is available through pcc.edu/orcca. Additionally, the odd answers are printed in an appendix in the HTML eBook.

Interactive and Static Examples. Traditionally, a math textbook has examples throughout each section. This textbook uses two types of "example":

Static These are labeled "Example." Static examples may or may not be subdivided into a "statement" followed by a walk-through solution. This is basically what traditional examples from math textbooks do.

Active These are labeled "Checkpoint." In the HTML version, active examples have WeBWorK answer blanks where a reader may try submitting an answer. In the PDF output, active examples are almost indistinguishable from static examples, but there is a WeBWorK icon indicating that a reader could interact more actively using the eBook. Generally, a walk-through solution is provided immediately following the answer blank.

Some readers using the HTML eBook will skip the opportunity to try an active example and go straight to its solution. That is OK. Some readers will try an active example once and then move on to just read the solution. That is also OK. Some readers will tough it out for a period of time and resist reading the solution until they answer the active example themselves.

For readers of the PDF, the expectation is to read the example and its solution just as they would read a static example.

A reader is *not* required to try submitting an answer to an active example before moving on. A reader *is* expected to read the solution to an active example, even if they succeed on their own at finding an answer.

Reading Questions. Each section has a few "reading questions" immediately before the exercises. These may be treated as regular homework questions, but they are intended to be something more. The intention is that reading questions could be used in certain classroom models as a tool to encourage students to do their assigned reading, and as a tool to measure what basic concepts might have been misunderstood by students following the reading.

At some point it will be possible for students to log in to the HTML eBook and record answers to reading questions for an instructor to review. The infrastructure for that feature is not yet in place at the time of printing this edition, but please check pcc.edu/orcca for updates.

Alternative Video Lessons. Most sections open with an alternative video lesson (that is only visible in the HTML eBook). These video play lists are managed through a YouTube account, and it is possible to swap videos out for better ones at any time, provided that does not disrupt courses at PCC. Please contact us if you would like to submit a different video into these video collections.

x

Pedagogical Decisions

The authors and the greater PCC faculty have taken various stances on certain pedagogical and notational questions that arise in basic algebra instruction. We attempt to catalog these decisions here, although this list is certainly incomplete. If you find something in the book that runs contrary to these decisions, please let us know.

- Basic math is addressed in an appendix. For the course sequence taught at PCC, this content is prerequisite and not within the scope of this book. However it is quite common for students in the basic algebra sequence to have skills deficiencies in these areas, so we include the basic math appendix. It should be understood that the content there does not attempt to teach basic math from first principles. It is itended to be more of a review.

- Interleaving is our preferred approach, compared to a proficiency-based approach. To us, this means that once the book covers a topic, that topic will be appear in subsequent sections and chapters in indirect ways.

- We round decimal results to four significant digits, or possibly fewer leaving out trailing zeros. We do this to maintain consistency with the most common level of precision that WeBWorK uses to assess decimal answers. We generally *round*, not *truncate*, and we use the $\approx$ symbol. For example, $\pi \approx 3.142$ and Portland's population is ≈ 609500. On rare occasions where it is the better option, we truncate and use an ellipsis. For example, $\pi = 3.141\ldots$.

- We offer *alternative* video lessons associated with each section, found at the top of most sections in the HTML eBook. We hope these videos provide readers with an alternative to whatever is in the reading, but there may be discrepancies here and there between the video content and reading content.

- We believe in opening a topic with some level of application rather than abstract examples, whenever that is possible. From applications and practical questions, we move to motivate more abstract definitions and notation. At first this may feel backwards to some instructors, with some easier examples *following* more difficult contextual examples.

- Linear inequalities are not strictly separated from linear equations. The section that teaches how to solve $2x + 3 = 8$ is immediately followed by the section teaching how to solve $2x + 3 < 8$. Our aim is to not treat inequalities as an add-on optional topic, but rather to show how intimately related they are to corresponding equations.

- When issues of "proper formatting" of student work arise, we value that the reader understand *why* such things help the reader to communicate outwardly. We believe that mathematics is about more than understanding a topic, but also about understanding it well enough to communicate results to others. For example we promote progression of equations like

$$1 + 1 + 1 = 2 + 1$$
$$= 3$$

instead of

$$1 + 1 + 1 = 2 + 1 = 3.$$

We want students to understand that the former method makes their work easier for a reader to read. It is not simply a matter of "this is the standard and this is how it's done."

- When solving equations (or systems of linear equations), most examples should come with a check, intended to communicate to students that checking is part of the process. In Chapters 1–4, these checks will be complete simplifications using order of operations one step at a time. The later sections may have more summary checks where steps are skipped or carried out together, or we promote entering expressions into a calculator to check.

- Within a section, any first context-free example of solving some equation (or system) should summarize with some variant of both "the solution is..." and "the solution set is...." Later examples can mix it up, but always offer at least one of these.

- With applications of linear equations (not including linear systems), we limit applications to situations where the setup will be in the form $x +$ expression-in-$x = C$ and also to certain rate problems where the setup will be in the form $at + bt = C$. There are other classes of application problem (mixing problems, interest problems, ...) which can be handled with a system of two equations, and we reserve these until linear systems are covered.

- With simplifications of rational expressions in one variable, we always include domain restrictions that are lost in the simplification. For example, we would write $\frac{x(x+1)}{x+1} = x$, for $x \neq -1$. With *multivariable* rational expressions, we are content to ignore domain restrictions lost during simplification.

Entering WeBWorK Answers

This preface offers some guidance with syntax for WeBWorK answers. WeBWorK answer blanks appear in the active reading examples (called "checkpoints") in the HTML eBook version of the book. If you are using WeBWorK for online homework, then you will also enter answers into WeBWorK answer blanks there.

Basic Arithmetic. The five basic arithmetic operations are: addition, subtraction, multiplication, and raising to a power. The symbols for addition and subtraction are $+$ and $-$, and both of these are directly avialable on most keyboards as + and -.

On paper, multiplication is sometimes written using $\times$ and sometimes written using $\cdot$ (a centered dot). Since these symbols are not available on most keyboards, WeBWorK uses * instead, which is often shift-8 on a full keyboard.

On paper, division is sometimes written using $\div$, sometimes written using a fraction layout like $\frac{4}{2}$, and sometimes written just using a slash, /. The slash is available on most full keyboards, near the question mark. WeBWorK uses / to indicate division.

On paper, raising to a power is written using a two-dimensional layout like 4^2. Since we don't have a way to directly type that with a simple keyboard, calculators and computers use the caret character, ^, as in 4^2. The character is usually shift-6.

Roots and Radicals. On paper, a square root is represented with a radical symbol like $\sqrt{}$. Since a keyboard does not usually have this symbol, WeBWorK and many computer applications use sqrt( ) instead. For example, to enter $\sqrt{17}$, type sqrt(17).

Higher-index radicals are written on paper like $\sqrt[4]{12}$. Again we have no direct way to write this using most keyboards. In *some* WeBWorK problems it is possible to type something like root(4, 12) for the fourth root of twelve. However this is not enabled for all WeBWorK problems.

As an alternative that you may learn about in a later chapter, $\sqrt[4]{12}$ is mathematically equal to $12^{1/4}$, so it can be typed as 12^(1/4). Take note of the parentheses, which very much matter.

Common Hiccups with Grouping Symbols. Suppose you wanted to enter $\frac{x+1}{2}$. You might type x+1/2, but this is not right. The computer will use the order of operations and do your division first, dividing 1 by 2. So the computer will see $x + \frac{1}{2}$. To address this, you would need to use grouping symbols like parentheses, and type something like (x+1)/2.

Suppose you wanted to enter $6^{1/4}$, and you typed 6^1/4. This is not right. The order of operations places a higher priority on exponentiation than division, so it calculates 6^1 first and then divides the result by 4. That is simply not the same as raising 6 to the $\frac{1}{4}$ power. Again the way to address this is to use grouping symbols, like 6^(1/4).

Entering Decimal Answers.   Often you will find a decimal answer with decimal places that go on and on. You are allowed to round, but not by too much. WeBWorK generally looks at how many *significant digits* you use, and generally expects you to use *four or more* correct significant digits.

"Significant digits" and "places past the decimal" are not the same thing. To count significant digits, read the number left to right and look for the first nonzero digit. Then count all the digits to the right including that first one.

The number 102.3 has four significant digits, but only one place past the decimal. This number could be a correct answer to a WeBWorK question. The number 0.0003 has one significant digit and four places past the decimal. This number might cause you trouble if you enter it, because maybe the "real" answer was 0.0003091, and rounding to 0.0003 was too much rounding.

Special Symbols.   There are a handful of special symbols that are easy to write on paper, but it's not clear how to type them. Here are WeBWorK's expectations.

Symbol	Name	How to Type
∞	infinity	infinity or inf
π	pi	pi
$\cup$	union	U
$\mathbb{R}$	the real numbers	R
$\mid$	such that	| (shift-\\, where \\ is above the enter key)
$\leq$	less than or equal to	<=
$\geq$	greater than or equal to	>=
$\neq$	not equal to	!=

Contents

Part III

Preparation for College Algebra

Chapter 10

Factoring

10.1 Factoring Out the Common Factor

In Chapter 5, we learned how to multiply polynomials, such as when you start with $(x+2)(x+3)$ and obtain $x^2 + 5x + 6$. This chapter, starting with this section, is about the *opposite* process—factoring. For example, starting with $x^2 + 5x + 6$ and obtaining $(x + 2)(x + 3)$. We will start with the simplest kind of factoring: for example starting with $x^2 + 2x$ and obtaining $x(x + 2)$.

10.1.1 Motivation for Factoring

When you write $x^2 + 2x$, you have an algebraic expression built with two terms—two parts that are *added* together. When you write $x(x + 2)$, you have an algebraic expression built with two factors—two parts that are *multiplied* together. Factoring is useful, because sometimes (but not always) having your expression written as parts that are *multiplied* together makes it easy to simplify the expression.

You've seen this with fractions. To simplify $\frac{15}{35}$, breaking down the numerator and denominator into factors is useful: $\frac{3 \cdot 5}{7 \cdot 5}$. Now you can see that the factors of 5 cancel.

There are other reasons to appreciate the value in factoring. One reason is that there is a relationship between a factored polynomial and the horizontal intercepts of its graph. For example in the graph of $y = (x + 2)(x - 3)$, the horizontal intercepts are $(-2, 0)$ and $(3, 0)$. Note the x-values are -2 and 3, and think about what happens when you subsitutue those numbers in for x in $y = (x+2)(x-3)$. We will explore this more fully in Section 13.2.

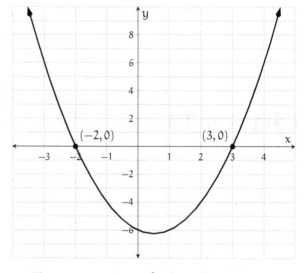

Figure 10.1.2: A graph of $y = (x + 2)(x - 3)$

10.1.2 Identifying the Greatest Common Factor

The most basic technique for factoring involves recognizing the **greatest common factor** between two expressions, which is the largest factor that goes in evenly to both expressions. For example, the greatest common factor between 6 and 8 is 2, since 2 divides nicely into both 6 and 8 and no larger number would divide nicely into both 6 and 8.

Similarly, the greatest common factor between $4x$ and $3x^2$ is x. If you write $4x$ as a product of its factors, you have $2 \cdot 2 \cdot x$. And if you fully factor $3x^2$, you have $3 \cdot x \cdot x$. The only factor they have in common is x, so that is the greatest common factor. No larger expression goes in nicely to both expressions.

Example 10.1.3 Finding the Greatest Common Factor. What is the common factor between $6x^2$ and $70x$? Break down each of these into its factors:

$$6x^2 = 2 \cdot 3 \cdot x \cdot x \qquad\qquad 70x = 2 \cdot 5 \cdot 7 \cdot x$$

And identify the common factors:

$$6x^2 = \overset{\downarrow}{2} \cdot 3 \cdot \overset{\downarrow}{x} \cdot x \qquad\qquad 70x = \overset{\downarrow}{2} \cdot 5 \cdot 7 \cdot \overset{\downarrow}{x}$$

With 2 and x in common, the greatest common factor is 2x.

Checkpoint 10.1.4

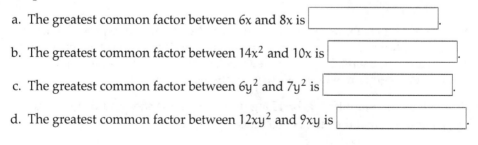

a. The greatest common factor between $6x$ and $8x$ is _____.

b. The greatest common factor between $14x^2$ and $10x$ is _____.

c. The greatest common factor between $6y^2$ and $7y^2$ is _____.

d. The greatest common factor between $12xy^2$ and $9xy$ is _____.

e. The greatest common factor between $6x^3$, $2x^2$, and $8x$ is $\boxed{}$.

Explanation.

a. Since $6x$ completely factors as $\overset{\downarrow}{2} \cdot 3 \cdot \overset{\downarrow}{x}$ ... and $8x$ completely factors as $\overset{\downarrow}{2} \cdot 2 \cdot 2 \cdot \overset{\downarrow}{x}$, ...

   ... the greatest common factor is $2x$.

b. Since $14x^2$ completely factors as $\overset{\downarrow}{2} \cdot 7 \cdot \overset{\downarrow}{x} \cdot x$ ... and $10x$ completely factors as $\overset{\downarrow}{2} \cdot 5 \cdot \overset{\downarrow}{x}$, ...

   ... the greatest common factor is $2x$.

c. Since $6y^2$ completely factors as $2 \cdot 3 \cdot \overset{\downarrow}{y} \cdot \overset{\downarrow}{y}$ ... and $7y^2$ completely factors as $7 \cdot \overset{\downarrow}{y} \cdot \overset{\downarrow}{y}$, ...

   ... the greatest common factor is y^2.

d. Since $12xy^2$ completely factors as $2 \cdot 2 \cdot \overset{\downarrow}{3} \cdot \overset{\downarrow}{x} \cdot \overset{\downarrow}{y} \cdot y$ ... and $9xy$ completely factors as $\overset{\downarrow}{3} \cdot 3 \cdot \overset{\downarrow}{x} \cdot \overset{\downarrow}{y}$, ...

   ... the greatest common factor is $3xy$.

e. Since $6x^3$ completely factors as $\overset{\downarrow}{2} \cdot 3 \cdot \overset{\downarrow}{x} \cdot x \cdot x$ ... $2x^2$ completely factors as $\overset{\downarrow}{2} \cdot \overset{\downarrow}{x} \cdot x$, ...and $8x$ completely factors as $\overset{\downarrow}{2} \cdot 2 \cdot 2 \cdot \overset{\downarrow}{x}$, ...

   ... the greatest common factor is $2x$.

10.1.3 Factoring Out the Greatest Common Factor

We have learned the distributive property: $a(b + c) = ab + ac$. Perhaps you have thought of this as a way to "distribute" the number a to each of b and c. In this section, we will use the distributive property in the opposite way. If you have an expression $ab + ac$, it is equal to $a(b + c)$. In that example, we factored out a, which is the common factor between ab and ac.

The following steps use the distributive property to factor out the greatest common factor between two or more terms.

Process 10.1.5 Factoring Out the Greatest Common Factor.

1. *Identify the greatest common factor in all terms.*

2. *Write the greatest common factor outside a pair of parentheses with the appropriate addition or subtraction signs inside.*

3. *For each term from the original expression, what would you multiply the greatest common factor by to result in that term? Write your answer in the parentheses.*

Example 10.1.6 To factor $12x^2 + 15x$:

1. The greatest common factor between $12x^2$ and $15x$ is $3x$.

2. $3x(\quad + \quad)$

3. $3x(4x + 5)$

Example 10.1.7 Factor the polynomial $3x^3 + 3x^2 - 9$.

1. We identify the greatest common factor as 3, because 3 is the only common factor between $3x^3$, $3x^2$ and 9.

2. We write:
$$3x^3 + 3x^2 - 9 = 3(\quad + \quad - \quad).$$

3. We ask the question "3 times what gives $3x^3$?" The answer is x^3. Now we have:
$$3x^3 + 3x^2 - 9 = 3(x^3 + \quad - \quad).$$

    We ask the question "3 times what gives $3x^2$?" The answer is x^2. Now we have:
$$3x^3 + 3x^2 - 9 = 3(x^3 + x^2 - \quad).$$

    We ask the question "3 times what gives 9?" The answer is 3. Now we have:
$$3x^3 + 3x^2 - 9 = 3(x^3 + x^2 - 3).$$

To check that this is correct, multiplying through $3(x^3 + x^2 - 3)$ should give the original expression $3x^3 + 3x^2 - 9$. We check this, and it does.

Checkpoint 10.1.8 Factor the polynomial $4x^3 + 12x^2 - 12x$.

Explanation.   In this exercise, $4x$ is the greatest common factor. We find

$$\begin{aligned} 4x^3 + 12x^2 - 12x &= 4x(\quad + \quad - \quad) \\ &= 4x(x^2 + \quad - \quad) \\ &= 4x(x^2 + 3x - \quad) \\ &= 4x(x^2 + 3x - 3) \end{aligned}$$

Note that you might fail to recognize that $4x$ is the greatest common factor. At first you might only find that, say, 4 is a common factor. This is OK—you can factor out the 4 and continue from there:

$$\begin{aligned} 4x^3 + 12x^2 - 12x &= 4(\quad + \quad - \quad) \\ &= 4(x^3 + \quad - \quad) \\ &= 4(x^3 + 3x^2 - \quad) \\ &= 4(x^3 + 3x^2 - 3x) \end{aligned}$$

Now examine the second factor here and there is *still* a common factor, x. Factoring this out too.

$$\begin{aligned} &= 4x(\quad + \quad - \quad) \\ &= 4x(x^2 + \quad - \quad) \\ &= 4x(x^2 + 3x - \quad) \\ &= 4x(x^2 + 3x - 3) \end{aligned}$$

So there is more than one way to find the answer.

10.1.4 Visualizing With Rectangles

In Section 5.4, we learned one way to multiply polynomials using rectangle diagrams. Similarly, we can factor a polynomial with a rectangle diagram.

Process 10.1.9 Factoring Out the Greatest Common Factor Using Rectangles.

1. *Put the terms into adjacent rectangles. Think of these as labeling the areas of each rectangle.*

2. *Identify the greatest common factor, and mark the height of the overall rectangle with it.*

3. *Mark the width of each rectangle based on each rectangle's area and height.*

4. *Since the overall rectangle's area equals its width times its height, the height is one factor, and the sum of the widths is another factor.*

Example 10.1.10 We will factor $12x^2 + 15x$, the same polynomial from the example in Algorithm 10.1.5, so that you may compare the two styles.

So $12x^2 + 15x$ factors as $3x(4x + 5)$.

10.1.5 More Examples of Factoring out the Common Factor

Previous examples did not cover every nuance with factoring out the greatest common factor. Here are a few more factoring examples that attempt to do so.

Example 10.1.11 Factor $-35m^5 + 5m^4 - 10m^3$.

First, we identify the common factor. The number 5 is the greatest common factor of the three coefficients (which were -35, 5, and -10) and also m^3 is the largest expression that divides m^5, m^4, and m^3. Therefore the greatest common factor is $5m^3$.

In this example, the leading term is a negative number. When this happens, we will make it common practice to take that negative as part of the greatest common factor. So we will proceed by factoring out $-5m^3$. Note the signs change inside the parentheses.

$$\begin{aligned} -35m^5 + 5m^4 - 10m^3 &= -5m^3(\quad - \quad + \quad) \\ &= -5m^3(7m^2 - \quad + \quad) \\ &= -5m^3(7m^2 - m + \quad) \\ &= -5m^3(7m^2 - m + 2) \end{aligned}$$

Example 10.1.12 Factor $14 - 7n^2 + 28n^4 - 21n$.

Notice that the terms are not in a standard order, with powers of n decreasing as you read left to right. It is usually a best practice to rearrange the terms into the standard order first.

$$14 - 7n^2 + 28n^4 - 21n = 28n^4 - 7n^2 - 21n + 14.$$

The number 7 divides all of the numerical coefficients. Separately, no power of n is part of the greatest common factor because the 14 term has no n factors. So the greatest common factor is just 7. We proceed by factoring that out:

$$14 - 7n^2 + 28n^4 - 21n = 28n^4 - 7n^2 - 21n + 14$$
$$= 7(4n^4 - n^2 - 3n + 2)$$

Example 10.1.13 Factor $24ab^2 + 16a^2b^3 - 12a^3b^2$.

There are two variables in this polynomial, but that does not change the factoring strategy. The greatest numerical factor between the three terms is 4. The variable a divides all three terms, and b^2 divides all three terms. So we have:

$$24ab^2 + 16a^2b^3 - 12a^3b^2 = 4ab^2(6 + 4ab - 3a^2)$$

Example 10.1.14 Factor $4m^2n - 3xy$.

There are no common factors in those two terms (unless you want to count 1 or -1, but we do not count these for the purposes of identifying a greatest common factor). In this situation we can say the polynomial is **prime** or **irreducible**, and leave it as it is.

Example 10.1.15 Factor $-x^3 + 2x + 18$.

There are no common factors in those three terms, and it would be correct to state that this polynomial is prime or irreducible. However, since its leading coefficient is negative, it may be wise to factor out a negative sign. So, it could be factored as $-(x^3 - 2x - 18)$. Note that *every* term is negated as the leading negative sign is extracted.

10.1.6 Reading Questions

1. Given two terms, how would you describe their "greatest common factor?"

2. If a simplified polynomial has four terms, and you factor out its greatest common factor, how many terms will remain inside a set of parentheses?

10.1.7 Exercises

Review and Warmup Multiply the polynomials.

1.	$-4x(x-2)$	**2.**	$-x(x-7)$	**3.**	$-6x(9x-9)$	**4.**	$-7x(4x+9)$
5.	$6x^2(x+8)$	**6.**	$8x^2(x-4)$	**7.**	$10t^2(8t^2-5t)$	**8.**	$7x^2(5x^2-9x)$

Identifying Common Factors Find the greatest common factor of the following terms.

9.	4 and $20x$	**10.**	10 and $90y$	**11.**	$7y$ and $28y^2$
12.	$4r$ and $28r^2$	**13.**	$10r^3$ and $-100r^4$	**14.**	$6t^3$ and $-42t^4$
15.	$3t^{19}$ and $-18t^{15}$	**16.**	$9t^{12}$ and $-81t^{11}$	**17.**	$6x^{17}, -12x^{14}, 30x^2$
18.	$3x^{11}, -15x^{10}, 27x^3$	**19.**	$5x^{16}y^7, -40x^{10}y^{12}, 10x^4y^{13}$	**20.**	$2x^{16}y^{10}, -6x^{11}y^{11}, 10x^7y^{14}$

Factoring out the Common Factor Factor the given polynomial.

21.	$3r + 3$	**22.**	$8r + 8$

23. $5t - 5$

24. $2t - 2$

25. $-8t - 8$

26. $-5x - 5$

27. $2x - 18$

28. $8y + 32$

29. $12y^2 + 32$

30. $90r^2 - 20$

31. $18r^2 + 9r + 72$

32. $60t^2 + 70t + 60$

33. $32t^4 - 12t^3 + 24t^2$

34. $10t^4 + 12t^3 + 4t^2$

35. $20x^5 - 35x^4 + 45x^3$

36. $50x^5 + 10x^4 + 15x^3$

37. $28y - 20y^2 + 20y^3$

38. $72y + 48y^2 + 40y^3$

39. $5r^2 + 11$

40. $16r^2 + 9$

41. $8xy + 8y$

42. $9xy + 9y$

43. $10x^{11}y^5 + 60y^5$

44. $2x^7y^5 + 6y^5$

45. $6x^5y^9 - 18x^4y^9 + 21x^3y^9$

46. $63x^5y^{10} - 35x^4y^{10} + 35x^3y^{10}$

47. $40x^5y^6z^5 - 10x^4y^6z^4 + 25x^3y^6z^3$

48. $24x^5y^4z^9 + 20x^4y^4z^8 + 8x^3y^4z^7$

10.2 Factoring by Grouping

This section covers a technique for factoring polynomials like $x^3 + 3x^2 + 2x + 6$, which factors as $(x^2 + 2)(x + 3)$. If there are *four* terms, the technique in this section *might* help you to factor the polynomial. Additionally, this technique is a stepping stone to a factoring technique in Section 10.3 and Section 10.4.

10.2.1 Factoring out Common Polynomials

Recall that to factor $3x + 6$, we factor out the common factor 3:

$$3x + 6 = \overset{\downarrow}{3}x + \overset{\downarrow}{3} \cdot 2$$
$$= 3(x + 2)$$

The "3" here could have been something more abstract, and it still would be valid to factor it out:

$$xA + 2A = x\overset{\downarrow}{A} + 2\overset{\downarrow}{A} \qquad\qquad x🍎 + 2🍎 = x\overset{\downarrow}{🍎} + 2\overset{\downarrow}{🍎}$$
$$= A(x + 2) \qquad\qquad\qquad = 🍎(x + 2)$$

In fact, even "larger" things can be factored out, as in this example:

$$x(a + b) + 2(a + b) = x\overbrace{(a + b)}^{\downarrow} + 2\overbrace{(a + b)}^{\downarrow}$$
$$= (a + b)(x + 2)$$

In this last example, we factored out the binomial factor $(a + b)$. Factoring out binomials is the essence of this section, so let's see that a few more times:

$$x(x + 2) + 3(x + 2) = x\overbrace{(x + 2)}^{\downarrow} + 3\overbrace{(x + 2)}^{\downarrow}$$
$$= (x + 2)(x + 3)$$

$$z^2(2y + 5) + 3(2y + 5) = z^2\overbrace{(2y + 5)}^{\downarrow} + 3\overbrace{(2y + 5)}^{\downarrow}$$
$$= (2y + 5)(z^2 + 3)$$

And even with an expression like $Q^2(Q - 3) + Q - 3$, if we re-write it in the right way using a 1 and some parentheses, then it too can be factored:

$$Q^2(Q - 3) + Q - 3 = Q^2(Q - 3) + 1(Q - 3)$$
$$= Q^2\overbrace{(Q - 3)}^{\downarrow} + 1\overbrace{(Q - 3)}^{\downarrow}$$
$$= (Q - 3)(Q^2 + 1)$$

The truth is you are unlikely to come upon an expression like $x(x + 2) + 3(x + 2)$, as in these examples. Why wouldn't someone have multiplied that out already? Or factored it all the way? So far in this section, we have only been looking at a stepping stone to a real factoring technique called **factoring by grouping**.

10.2.2 Factoring by Grouping

Factoring by grouping is a factoring technique that *sometimes* works on polynomials with four terms. Here is an example.

Example 10.2.2 Suppose we must factor $x^3 - 3x^2 + 5x - 15$. Note that there are four terms, and they are written in descending order of the powers of x. "Grouping" means to group the first two terms and the last two terms together:

$$x^3 - 3x^2 + 5x - 15 = (x^3 - 3x^2) + (5x - 15)$$

Now, each of these two groups has its own greatest common factor we can factor out:

$$= x^2(x - 3) + 5(x - 3)$$

In a sense, we are "lucky" because we now see matching binomials that can themselves be factored out:

$$= x^2\overbrace{(x - 3)}^{\downarrow} + 5\overbrace{(x - 3)}^{\downarrow}$$
$$= (x - 3)(x^2 + 5)$$

And so we have factored $x^3 - 3x^2 + 5x - 15$ as $(x - 3)(x^2 + 5)$. But to be sure, if we multiply this back out, it should recover the original $x^3 - 3x^2 + 5x - 15$. To confirm your factoring is correct, you should always multiply out your factored result to check that it matches the original polynomial.

Checkpoint 10.2.3 Factor $x^3 + 4x^2 + 2x + 8$.

Explanation. We will break the polynomial into two groups: $x^3 + 4x^2$ and $2x + 8$.

$$x^3 + 4x^2 + 2x + 8 = (x^3 + 4x^2) + (2x + 8)$$
$$= x^2(x + 4) + 2(x + 4)$$
$$= (x + 4)(x^2 + 2)$$

Example 10.2.4 Factor $t^3 - 5t^2 - 3t + 15$. This example has a complication with negative signs. If we try to break up this polynomial into two groups as $(t^3 - 5t^2) - (3t + 15)$, then we've made an error! In that last expression, we are *subtracting* a group with the term 15, so overall it subtracts 15. The original polynomial *added* 15, so we are off course.

One way to handle this is to treat subtraction as addition of a negative:

$$t^3 - 5t^2 - 3t + 15 = t^3 - 5t^2 + (-3t) + 15$$
$$= (t^3 - 5t^2) + (-3t + 15)$$

Now we can proceed to factor out common factors from each group. Since the second group leads with a negative coefficient, we'll factor out -3. This will result in the " $+ 15$" becoming " $- 5$."

$$= t^2(t - 5) + (-3)(t - 5)$$

$$= t^2\overbrace{(t - 5)}^{\downarrow} - 3\overbrace{(t - 5)}^{\downarrow}$$

$$= (t - 5)(t^2 - 3)$$

And remember that we can confirm this is correct by multiplying it out. If we made no mistakes, it should result in the original $t^3 - 5t^2 - 3t + 15$.

Checkpoint 10.2.5 Factor $6q^3 - 9q^2 - 4q + 6$.

Explanation.   We will break the polynomial into two groups: $6q^3 - 9q^2$ and $-4q + 6$.

$$\begin{aligned}
6q^3 - 9q^2 - 4q + 6 &= \left(6q^3 - 9q^2\right) + (-4q + 6) \\
&= 3q^2(2q - 3) - 2(2q - 3) \\
&= (2q - 3)\left(3q^2 - 2\right)
\end{aligned}$$

Example 10.2.6 Factor $x^3 - 3x^2 + x - 3$. To succeed with this example, we will need to "factor out" a trivial number 1 that isn't apparent until we make it so.

$$\begin{aligned}
x^3 - 3x^2 + x - 3 &= \left(x^3 - 3x^2\right) + (x - 3) \\
&= x^2(x - 3) + 1(x - 3) \\
&= x^2\overbrace{(x - 3)}^{\downarrow} + 1\overbrace{(x - 3)}^{\downarrow} \\
&= (x - 3)\left(x^2 + 1\right)
\end{aligned}$$

Notice how we changed $x - 3$ to $+1(x - 3)$, so we wouldn't forget the $+1$ in the final factored form. As always, we should check this is correct by multiplying it out.

Checkpoint 10.2.7 Factor $6t^6 + 9t^4 + 2t^2 + 3$.

Explanation.   We will break the polynomial into two groups: $6t^6 + 9t^4$ and $2t^2 + 3$.

$$\begin{aligned}
6t^6 + 9t^4 + 2t^2 + 3 &= \left(6t^6 + 9t^4\right) + \left(2t^2 + 3\right) \\
&= 3t^4\left(2t^2 + 3\right) + 1\left(2t^2 + 3\right) \\
&= \left(2t^2 + 3\right)\left(3t^4 + 1\right)
\end{aligned}$$

Example 10.2.8 Factor $xy^2 - 10y^2 - 2x + 20$. The technique can work when there are multiple variables too.

$$\begin{aligned}
xy^2 - 10y^2 - 2x + 20 &= \left(xy^2 - 10y^2\right) + (-2x + 20) \\
&= y^2(x - 10) + (-2)(x - 10) \\
&= y^2\overbrace{(x - 10)}^{\downarrow} - 2\overbrace{(x - 10)}^{\downarrow} \\
&= (x - 10)\left(y^2 - 2\right).
\end{aligned}$$

Unfortunately, this technique is not guaranteed to work on every polynomial with four terms. In fact, *most* randomly selected four-term polynomials will not factor using this method and those selected here should be considered "nice." Here is an example that will not factor with grouping:

$$\begin{aligned}
x^3 + 6x^2 + 11x + 6 &= \left(x^3 + 6x^2\right) + (11x + 6) \\
&= x^2 \underbrace{(x + 6)}_{?} + 1 \underbrace{(11x + 6)}_{?}
\end{aligned}$$

In this example, at the step where we hope to see the same binomial appearing twice, we see two different binomials. It doesn't mean that this kind of polynomial can't be factored, but it does mean that "factoring by grouping" is not going to help. This polynomial actually factors as $(x + 1)(x + 2)(x + 3)$. So the fact that grouping fails to factor the polynomial doesn't tell us whether or not it is prime.

10.2.3 Reading Questions

1. Factoring by grouping is a factoring technique for when a polynomial has ☐ terms.

10.2.4 Exercises

Review and Warmup Factor the given polynomial.

1.	$-5t - 5$	**2.**	$-10x - 10$	**3.**	$7x + 14$
4.	$4y - 24$	**5.**	$30y^2 - 100$	**6.**	$21r^2 + 35$

Factoring out Common Polynomials Factor the given polynomial.

7.	$r(r + 4) - 6(r + 4)$	**8.**	$t(t - 10) - 4(t - 10)$
9.	$x(y + 9) + 7(y + 9)$	**10.**	$x(y - 10) + 2(y - 10)$
11.	$2x(x + y) - 9(x + y)$	**12.**	$3x(x + y) + 7(x + y)$
13.	$3y^4(4y + 9) + 4y + 9$	**14.**	$9y^3(8y - 7) + 8y - 7$
15.	$12r^4(r + 10) + 6r^3(r + 10) + 60r^2(r + 10)$	**16.**	$10r^4(r - 15) - 30r^3(r - 15) + 35r^2(r - 15)$

Factoring by Grouping Factor the given polynomial.

17.	$t^2 + 8t + 9t + 72$	**18.**	$t^2 - 5t + 6t - 30$
19.	$t^2 + 2t + 4t + 8$	**20.**	$x^2 - 8x + 10x - 80$
21.	$x^3 + 5x^2 + 7x + 35$	**22.**	$y^3 - 2y^2 + 5y - 10$
23.	$y^3 - 7y^2 + 2y - 14$	**24.**	$r^3 + 5r^2 + 8r + 40$
25.	$xy + 7x + 4y + 28$	**26.**	$xy + 8x - 9y - 72$
27.	$xy - 9x - 3y + 27$	**28.**	$xy + 10x + 6y + 60$
29.	$2x^2 + 4xy + 9xy + 18y^2$	**30.**	$3x^2 + 15xy + 8xy + 40y^2$
31.	$4x^2 + 36xy + 9xy + 81y^2$	**32.**	$5x^2 - 5xy + 7xy - 7y^2$
33.	$x^3 - 6 - 7x^3y + 42y$	**34.**	$x^3 + 7 - 2x^3y - 14y$
35.	$x^3 + 6 + 8x^3y + 48y$	**36.**	$x^3 - 9 - 8x^3y + 72y$
37.	$10t^5 + 20t^4 - 15t^4 - 30t^3 + 25t^3 + 50t^2$	**38.**	$24x^5 + 48x^4 + 16x^4 + 32x^3 + 40x^3 + 80x^2$

10.3 Factoring Trinomials with Leading Coefficient One

In Chapter 5, we learned how to multiply binomials like $(x + 2)(x + 3)$ and obtain the trinomial $x^2 + 5x + 6$. In this section, we will learn how to undo that. So we'll be starting with a trinomial like $x^2 + 5x + 6$ and obtaining its factored form $(x + 2)(x + 3)$. The trinomials that we'll factor in this section all have leading coefficient 1, but Section 10.4 will cover some more general trinomials.

10.3.1 Factoring Trinomials by Listing Factor Pairs

Consider the example $x^2 + 5x + 6 = (x+2)(x+3)$. There are at least three things that are important to notice:

- The leading coefficient of $x^2 + 5x + 6$ is 1.

- The two factors on the right use the numbers 2 and 3, and when you *multiply* these you get the 6.

- The two factors on the right use the numbers 2 and 3, and when you *add* these you get the 5.

So the idea is that if you need to factor $x^2 + 5x + 6$ and you somehow discover that 2 and 3 are special numbers (because $2 \cdot 3 = 6$ and $2 + 3 = 5$), then you can conclude that $(x + 2)(x + 3)$ is the factored form of the given polynomial.

Example 10.3.2 Factor $x^2 + 13x + 40$. Since the leading coefficient is 1, we are looking to write this polynomial as $(x + ?)(x + ?)$ where the question marks are two possibly different, possibly negative, numbers. We need these two numbers to multiply to 40 and add to 13. How can you track these two numbers down? Since the numbers need to multiply to 40, one method is to list all **factor pairs** of 40 in a table just to see what your options are. We'll write every *pair of factors* that multiply to 40.

$1 \cdot 40$	$-1 \cdot (-40)$
$2 \cdot 20$	$-2 \cdot (-20)$
$4 \cdot 10$	$-4 \cdot (-10)$
$5 \cdot 8$	$-5 \cdot (-8)$

We wanted to find *all* factor pairs. To avoid missing any, we started using 1 as a factor, and then slowly increased that first factor. The table skips over using 3 as a factor, because 3 is not a factor of 40. Similarly the table skips using 6 and 7 as a factor. And there would be no need to continue with 8 and beyond, because we already found "large" factors like 8 as the partners of "small" factors like 5.

There is an entire second column where the signs are reversed, since these are also ways to multiply two numbers to get 40. In the end, there are eight factor pairs.

We need a pair of numbers that also *adds* to 13. So we check what each of our factor pairs add up to:

Factor Pair	Sum of the Pair		Factor Pair	Sum of the Pair
$1 \cdot 40$	41		$-1 \cdot (-40)$	(no need to go this far)
$2 \cdot 20$	22		$-2 \cdot (-20)$	(no need to go this far)
$4 \cdot 10$	14		$-4 \cdot (-10)$	(no need to go this far)
$5 \cdot 8$	13 (what we wanted)		$-5 \cdot (-8)$	(no need to go this far)

The winning pair of numbers is 5 and 8. Again, what matters is that $5 \cdot 8 = 40$, and $5 + 8 = 13$. So we can conclude that $x^2 + 13x + 40 = (x + 5)(x + 8)$.

To ensure that we made no mistakes, here are some possible checks.

Multiply it Out. Multiplying out our answer $(x+5)(x+8)$ should give us $x^2 + 13x + 40$.

$$(x+5)(x+8) = (x+5)\cdot x + (x+5)\cdot 8$$
$$= x^2 + 5x + 8x + 40$$
$$\overset{\checkmark}{=} x^2 + 13x + 40$$

We could also use a rectangular area diagram to verify the factorization is correct:

	x	5
x	x^2	$5x$
8	$8x$	40

Evaluating. If the answer really is $(x+5)(x+8)$, then notice how evaluating at -5 would result in 0. So the original expression should also result in 0 if we evaluate at -5. And similarly, if we evaluate it at -8, $x^2 + 13x + 40$ should be 0.

$$(-5)^2 + 13(-5) + 40 \overset{?}{=} 0$$
$$25 - 65 + 40 \overset{?}{=} 0$$
$$0 \overset{\checkmark}{=} 0$$

$$(-8)^2 + 13(-8) + 40 \overset{?}{=} 0$$
$$64 - 104 + 40 \overset{?}{=} 0$$
$$0 \overset{\checkmark}{=} 0.$$

This also gives us evidence that the factoring was correct.

Example 10.3.3 Factor $y^2 - 11y + 24$. The negative coefficient is a small complication from Example 10.3.2, but the process is actually still the same.

Explanation. We need a pair of numbers that multiply to 24 and add to -11. Note that we *do* care to keep track that they sum to a negative total.

Factor Pair	Sum of the Pair
$1 \cdot 24$	25
$2 \cdot 12$	14
$3 \cdot 8$	11 (close; wrong sign)
$4 \cdot 6$	10

Factor Pair	Sum of the Pair
$-1 \cdot (-24)$	-25
$-2 \cdot (-12)$	-14
$-3 \cdot (-8)$	-11 (what we wanted)
$-4 \cdot (-6)$	(no need to go this far)

So $y^2 - 11y + 24 = (y-3)(y-8)$. To confirm that this is correct, we should check. Either by multiplying out the factored form:

$$(y-3)(y-8) = (y-3)\cdot y - (y-3)\cdot 8$$
$$= y^2 - 3y - 8y + 24$$
$$\overset{\checkmark}{=} y^2 - 11y + 24$$

	y	-3
y	y^2	$-3y$
-8	$-8y$	24

Or by evaluating the original expression at 3 and 8:

$$3^2 - 11(3) + 24 \overset{?}{=} 0$$
$$9 - 33 + 24 \overset{?}{=} 0$$
$$0 \overset{\checkmark}{=} 0$$

$$8^2 - 11(8) + 24 \overset{?}{=} 0$$
$$64 - 88 + 24 \overset{?}{=} 0$$
$$0 \overset{\checkmark}{=} 0.$$

Our factorization passes the tests.

Example 10.3.4 Factor $z^2 + 5z - 6$. The negative coefficient is again a small complication from Example 10.3.2, but the process is actually still the same.

Explanation. We need a pair of numbers that multiply to -6 and add to 5. Note that we *do* care to keep track that they multiply to a negative product.

Factor Pair	Sum of the Pair		Factor Pair	Sum of the Pair
$1 \cdot (-6)$	-5 (close; wrong sign)		$-1 \cdot 6$	5 (what we wanted)
$2 \cdot (-3)$	14		$-2 \cdot 3$	(no need to go this far)

So $z^2 + 5z - 6 = (z-1)(z+6)$. To confirm that this is correct, we should check. Either by multiplying out the factored form:

$$(z-1)(z+6) = (z-1) \cdot z + (z-1) \cdot 6$$
$$= z^2 - z + 6z - 6$$
$$\overset{\checkmark}{=} z^2 + 5z - 6$$

	z	-1
z	z^2	$-z$
6	$6z$	-6

Or by evaluating the original expression at 1 and -6:

$$1^2 + 5(1) - 6 \overset{?}{=} 0 \qquad\qquad (-6)^2 + 5(-6) - 6 \overset{?}{=} 0$$
$$1 + 5 - 6 \overset{?}{=} 0 \qquad\qquad 36 - 30 - 6 \overset{?}{=} 0$$
$$0 \overset{\checkmark}{=} 0 \qquad\qquad 0 \overset{\checkmark}{=} 0.$$

Our factorization passes the tests.

Checkpoint 10.3.5 Factor $m^2 - 6m - 40$.

Explanation. We need a pair of numbers that multiply to -40 and add to -6. Note that we *do* care to keep track that they multiply to a negative product and sum to a negative total.

Factor Pair	Sum of the Pair
$1 \cdot (-40)$	-39
$2 \cdot (-20)$	-18
$4 \cdot (-10)$	-6 (what we wanted)
(no need to continue)	...

So $m^2 - 6m - 40 = (m+4)(m-10)$.

10.3.2 Connection to Grouping

The factoring method we just learned is actually taking a shortcut compared to what we will learn in Section 10.4. To prepare yourself for that more complicated factoring technique, you may want to try taking the "scenic route" instead of that shortcut.

Example 10.3.6 Let's factor $x^2 + 13x + 40$ again (the polynomial from Example 10.3.2). As before, it is important to discover that 5 and 8 are important numbers, because they multiply to 40 and add to 13. As before, listing out all of the factor pairs is one way to discover the 5 and the 8.

Instead of jumping to the factored answer, we can show how $x^2 + 13x + 40$ factors in a more step-by-step fashion using 5 and 8. Since they add up to 13, we can write:

$$x^2 + \overset{\downarrow}{13}x + 40 = x^2 + \overbrace{5x + 8x}^{\downarrow} + 40$$

We have intentionally split up the trinomial into an unsimplified polynomial with four terms. In Section 10.2, we handled such four-term polynomials by grouping:

$$= \left(x^2 + 5x\right) + (8x + 40)$$

Now we can factor out each group's greatest common factor:

$$= x(x+5) + 8(x+5)$$

$$= x\overbrace{(x+5)}^{\downarrow} + 8\overbrace{(x+5)}^{\downarrow}$$

$$= (x+5)(x+8)$$

And we have found that $x^2 + 13x + 40$ factors as $(x+5)(x+8)$ without taking the shortcut.

This approach takes more time, and ultimately you may not use it much. However, if you try a few examples this way, it may make you more comfortable with the more complicated technique in Section 10.4.

10.3.3 Trinomials with Higher Powers

So far we have only factored examples of **quadratic** trinomials: trinomials whose highest power of the variable is 2. However, this technique can also be used to factor trinomials where there is a larger highest power of the variable. It only requires that the highest power is even, that the next highest power is half of the highest power, and that the third term is a constant term.

In the four examples below, check:

1. if the highest power is even

2. if the next highest power is half of the highest power

3. if the last term is constant

Factor pairs *will* help with...

- $y^6 - 23y^3 - 50$

- $h^{16} + 22h^8 + 105$

Factor pairs *won't* help with...

- $y^5 - 23y^3 - 50$

- $h^{16} + 22h^8 + 105h^2$

Example 10.3.7 Factor $h^{16} + 22h^8 + 105$. This polynomial is one of the examples above where using factor pairs will help. We find that $7 \cdot 15 = 105$, and $7 + 15 = 22$, so the numbers 7 and 15 can be used:

$$h^{16} + 22h^8 + 105 = h^{16} + \overbrace{7h^8 + 15h^8}^{} + 105$$

$$= \left(h^{16} + 7h^8\right) + \left(15h^8 + 105\right)$$

$$= h^8\left(h^8 + 7\right) + 15\left(h^8 + 7\right)$$

$$= \left(h^8 + 7\right)\left(h^8 + 15\right)$$

Actually, once we settled on using 7 and 15, we could have concluded that $h^{16} + 22h^8 + 105$ factors as $\left(h^8 + 7\right)\left(h^8 + 15\right)$, if we know which power of h to use. We'll always use half the highest power in these factorizations.

In any case, to confirm that this is correct, we should check by multiplying out the factored form:

$$(h^8 + 7)(h^8 + 15) = (h^8 + 7) \cdot h^8 + (h^8 + 7) \cdot 15$$

$$= h^{16} + 7h^8 + 15h^8 + 105$$

$$\overset{\checkmark}{=} h^{16} + 22h^8 + 15$$

	h^8	7
h^8	h^{16}	$7h^8$
15	$15h^8$	105

Our factorization passes the tests.

⭐ **Checkpoint 10.3.8** Factor $y^6 - 23y^3 - 50$.

Explanation.   We need a pair of numbers that multiply to -50 and add to -23. Note that we *do* care to keep track that they multiply to a negative product and sum to a negative total.

Factor Pair	Sum of the Pair
$1 \cdot (-50)$	-49
$2 \cdot (-25)$	-23 (what we wanted)
(no need to continue)	...

So $y^6 - 23y^3 - 50 = \left(y^3 - 25\right)\left(y^3 + 2\right)$.

10.3.4 Factoring in Stages

Sometimes factoring a polynomial will take two or more "stages." Always begin factoring a polynomial by factoring out its greatest common factor, and *then* apply a second stage where you use a technique from this section. The process of factoring a polynomial is not complete until each of the factors cannot be factored further.

Example 10.3.9 Factor $2z^2 - 6z - 80$.

Explanation.   We will first factor out the common factor, 2:

$$2z^2 - 6z - 80 = 2\left(z^2 - 3z - 40\right)$$

Now we are left with a factored expression that might factor more. Looking inside the parentheses, we ask ourselves, "what two numbers multiply to be -40 and add to be -3?" Since 5 and -8 do the job the full factorization is:

$$\begin{aligned} 2z^2 - 6z - 80 &= 2\left(z^2 - 3z - 40\right) \\ &= 2(z + 5)(z - 8) \end{aligned}$$

Example 10.3.10 Factor $-r^2 + 2r + 24$.

Explanation.   The three terms don't exactly have a common factor, but as discussed in Section 10.1, when the leading term has a negative sign, it is often helpful to factor out that negative sign:

$$-r^2 + 2r + 24 = -\left(r^2 - 2r - 24\right).$$

Looking inside the parentheses, we ask ourselves, "what two numbers multiply to be -24 and add to be -2?" Since -6 and 4 work here and the full factorization is shown:

$$\begin{aligned} -r^2 + 2r + 24 &= -\left(r^2 - 2r - 24\right) \\ &= -(r - 6)(r + 4) \end{aligned}$$

Example 10.3.11 Factor $p^2q^3 + 4p^2q^2 - 60p^2q$.

Explanation.   First, always look for the greatest common factor: in this trinomial it is p^2q. After factoring this out, we have

$$p^2q^3 + 4p^2q^2 - 60p^2q = p^2q\left(q^2 + 4q - 60\right).$$

Looking inside the parentheses, we ask ourselves, "what two numbers multiply to be -60 and add to be 4?"

Since 10 and -6 fit the bill, the full factorization can be shown below:

$$p^2q^3 + 4p^2q^2 - 60p^2q = p^2q(q^2 + 4q - 60)$$
$$= p^2q(q + 10)(q - 6)$$

10.3.5 More Trinomials with Two Variables

You might encounter a trinomial with two variables that can be factored using the methods we've discussed in this section. It can be tricky though: $x^2 + 5xy + 6y^2$ has two variables and it *can* factor using the methods from this section, but $x^2 + 5x + 6y^2$ also has two variables and it *cannot* be factored. So in examples of this nature, it is even more important to check that factorizations you find actually work.

Example 10.3.12 Factor $x^2 + 5xy + 6y^2$. This is a trinomial, and the coefficient of x is 1, so maybe we can factor it. We want to write $(x+?)(x+?)$ where the question marks will be *something* that makes it all multiply out to $x^2 + 5xy + 6y^2$.

Since the last term in the polynomial has a factor of y^2, it is natural to wonder if there is a factor of y in each of the two question marks. If there were, these two factors of y would multiply to y^2. So it is natural to wonder if we are looking for $(x + ?y)(x + ?y)$ where now the question marks are just numbers.

At this point we can think like we have throughout this section. Are there some numbers that multiply to 6 and add to 5? Yes, specifically 2 and 3. So we suspect that $(x + 2y)(x + 3y)$ might be the factorization.

To confirm that this is correct, we should check by multiplying out the factored form:

$$(x + 2y)(x + 3y) = (x + 2y) \cdot x + (x + 2y) \cdot 3y$$
$$= x^2 + 2xy + 3xy + 6y^2$$
$$\overset{\checkmark}{=} x^2 + 5xy + 6y^2$$

	x	$2y$
x	x^2	$2xy$
$3y$	$3xy$	$6y^2$

Our factorization passes the tests.

In Section 10.4, there is a more definitive method for factoring polynomials of this form.

10.3.6 Reading Questions

1. To factor $x^2 + bx + c$, you look for two numbers that do what?

2. How many factor pairs are there for the number 6?

10.3.7 Exercises

Review and Warmup Multiply the polynomials.

1.	$(y + 5)(y + 10)$	2.	$(r + 1)(r + 4)$	3.	$(r + 8)(r - 3)$
4.	$(r + 4)(r - 8)$	5.	$(t - 10)(t - 4)$	6.	$(t - 4)(t - 10)$
7.	$3(x + 2)(x + 3)$	8.	$-4(y - 1)(y - 9)$	9.	$2(y - 10)(y - 3)$
10.	$-2(r + 7)(r + 6)$				

Factoring Trinomials with Leading Coefficient One Factor the given polynomial.

11.	$r^2 + 12r + 20$	12.	$r^2 + 13r + 42$	13.	$r^2 + 13r + 30$
14.	$t^2 + 14t + 40$	15.	$t^2 + 3t - 18$	16.	$x^2 + 7x - 30$

17. $x^2 + 2x - 63$

18. $y^2 - y - 30$

19. $y^2 - 7y + 10$

20. $r^2 - 14r + 45$

21. $r^2 - 8r + 15$

22. $r^2 - 10r + 16$

23. $t^2 + 10t + 16$

24. $t^2 + 11t + 30$

25. $x^2 + 11x + 10$

26. $x^2 + 12x + 32$

27. $y^2 - 6y - 40$

28. $y^2 + 6y - 7$

29. $r^2 + 3r - 28$

30. $r^2 - 3r - 4$

31. $r^2 - 6r + 5$

32. $t^2 - 16t + 63$

33. $t^2 - 7t + 12$

34. $x^2 - 18x + 80$

35. $x^2 + x + 6$

36. $y^2 + 3y + 10$

37. $y^2 + 9$

38. $r^2 - 4r + 6$

39. $r^2 + 6r + 9$

40. $r^2 + 22r + 121$

41. $t^2 + 14t + 49$

42. $t^2 + 6t + 9$

43. $x^2 - 20x + 100$

44. $x^2 - 12x + 36$

45. $y^2 - 4y + 4$

46. $y^2 - 20y + 100$

47. $2r^2 - 2r - 40$

48. $2r^2 - 2r - 4$

49. $10r^2 - 10$

50. $2t^2 + 6t - 20$

51. $10t^2 - 30t + 20$

52. $2x^2 - 18x + 16$

53. $3x^2 - 15x + 12$

54. $3y^2 - 21y + 18$

55. $2y^6 + 20y^5 + 18y^4$

56. $2y^7 + 14y^6 + 12y^5$

57. $3r^6 + 24r^5 + 21r^4$

58. $5r^7 + 20r^6 + 15r^5$

59. $10t^7 - 20t^6 - 30t^5$

60. $9t^4 + 9t^3 - 18t^2$

61. $3x^{10} - 12x^8$

62. $5x^6 - 20x^5 - 25x^4$

63. $2y^7 - 8y^6 + 6y^5$

64. $5y^5 - 15y^4 + 10y^3$

65. $3y^7 - 12y^6 + 9y^5$

66. $6r^4 - 18r^3 + 12r^2$

67. $-r^2 - 4r + 45$

68. $-t^2 + 4t + 12$

69. $-t^2 + 5t + 24$

70. $-x^2 - 4x + 5$

71. $x^2 + 12xr + 20r^2$

72. $y^2 + 7yr + 6r^2$

73. $y^2 - 3yt - 10t^2$

74. $y^2 - 4yx - 32x^2$

75. $r^2 - 7rt + 12t^2$

76. $r^2 - 5ry + 4y^2$

77. $t^2 + 16tx + 64x^2$

78. $t^2 + 2tr + r^2$

79. $x^2 - 12xy + 36y^2$

80. $x^2 - 22xt + 121t^2$

81. $4y^2 + 20y + 16$

82. $2y^2 + 18y + 16$

83. $3x^2y + 15xy + 18y$

84. $2x^2y + 6xy + 4y$

85. $7a^2b - 7ab - 14b$

86. $10a^2b + 10ab - 20b$

87. $2x^2y - 22xy + 20y$

88. $9x^2y - 27xy + 18y$

89. $3x^3y + 24x^2y + 21xy$

90. $2x^3y + 16x^2y + 30xy$

91. $x^2y^2 + x^2yz - 20x^2z^2$

92. $x^2y^2 + 8x^2yz - 9x^2z^2$

93. $r^2 + 0.9r + 0.2$

94. $r^2 + 0.9r + 0.14$

95. $t^2x^2 + 6tx + 5$

96. $t^2y^2 + 5ty + 6$

97. $x^2t^2 - 2xt - 24$

98. $x^2r^2 + xr - 20$

99. $y^2t^2 - 8yt + 7$

100. $y^2x^2 - 9yx + 14$

101. $6y^2r^2 + 18yr + 12$

102. $5r^2y^2 + 15ry + 10$

103. $7r^2t^2 - 7$

104. $3t^2r^2 + 6tr - 24$

105. $6x^2y^3 - 18xy^2 + 12y$

106. $6x^2y^3 - 24xy^2 + 18y$

Factor the given polynomial.

107. $(a + b)x^2 + 8(a + b)x + 12(a + b)$

108. $(a + b)y^2 + 9(a + b)y + 18(a + b)$

Challenge

109. What integers can go in the place of b so that the quadratic expression $x^2 + bx + 10$ is factorable?

10.4 Factoring Trinomials with a Nontrivial Leading Coefficient

In Section 10.3, we learned how to factor $ax^2 + bx + c$ when $a = 1$. In this section, we will examine the situation when $a \neq 1$. The techniques are similar to those in the last section, but there are a few important differences that will make-or-break your success in factoring these.

10.4.1 The AC Method

The AC Method is a technique for factoring trinomials like $4x^2 + 5x - 6$, where there is no greatest common factor, and the leading coefficient is not 1.

Please note at this point that if we try the method in the previous section and ask ourselves the question "what two numbers multiply to be -6 and add to be 5?," we might come to the *erroneous* conclusion that $4x^2 + 5x - 6$ factors as $(x + 6)(x - 1)$. If we expand $(x + 6)(x - 1)$, we get

$$(x + 6)(x - 1) = x^2 + 5x - 6$$

This expression is *almost* correct, except for the missing leading coefficient, 4. Dealing with this missing coefficient requires starting over with the AC method. If you are only interested in the steps for using the technique, skip ahead to Algorithm 10.4.3.

The example below explains *why* the "AC Method" works, which will be more carefully outlined a bit later. Understanding all of the details might take a few rereads, and coming back to this example after mastering the algorithm may be the best course of action.

Example 10.4.2 Expand the expression $(px + q)(rx + s)$ and analyze the result to gain insight into factoring $4x^2 + 5x - 6$.

Explanation. Factoring is the opposite process from multiplying polynomials together. We can gain some insight into how to factor complicated polynomials by taking a closer look at what happens when two generic polynomials are multiplied together:

$$\begin{aligned}
(px + q)(rx + s) &= (px + q)(rx) + (px + q)s \\
&= (px)(rx) + q(rx) + (px)s + qs \\
&= (pr)x^2 + qrx + psx + qs \\
&= (pr)x^2 + (qr + ps)x + qs \quad\quad\quad (10.4.1)
\end{aligned}$$

When you encounter a trinomial like $4x^2 + 5x - 6$ and you wish to factor it, the leading coefficient, 4, is the (pr) from Equation (10.4.1). Similarly, the -6 is the qs, and the 5 is the $(qr + ps)$.

Now, if you multiply the leading coefficient and constant term from Equation (10.4.1), you have $(pr)(qs)$, which equals $pqrs$. Notice that if we factor this number in just the right way, $(qr)(ps)$, then we have two factors that add to the middle coefficient from Equation (10.4.1), $(qr + ps)$.

Can we do all this with the example $4x^2 + 5x - 6$? Multiplying 4 and -6 makes -24. Is there some way to factor -24 into two factors which add to 5? We make a table of factor pairs for -24 to see:

Factor Pair	Sum of the Pair		Factor Pair	Sum of the Pair
$-1 \cdot 24$	23		$1 \cdot (-24)$	(no need to go this far)
$-2 \cdot 12$	10		$2 \cdot (-12)$	(no need to go this far)
$-3 \cdot 8$	5 (what we wanted)		$3 \cdot (-8)$	(no need to go this far)
$-4 \cdot 6$	(no need to go this far)		$4 \cdot (-6)$	(no need to go this far)

So that 5 in $4x^2 + 5x - 6$, which is equal to the abstract $(qr + ps)$ from Equation (10.4.1), breaks down as $-3 + 8$.

We can take -3 to be the qr and 8 to be the ps. Once we intentionally break up the 5 this way, factoring by grouping (see Section 10.2) can take over and is guaranteed to give us a factorization.

$$4x^2 \overbrace{+\ 5x}\ -6 = 4x^2 \overbrace{-3x + 8x}\ -6$$

Now that there are four terms, group them and factor out each group's greatest common factor.

$$\begin{aligned} &= \left(4x^2 - 3x\right) + (8x - 6) \\ &= x(4x - 3) + 2(4x - 3) \\ &= (4x - 3)(x + 2) \end{aligned}$$

And this is the factorization of $4x^2 + 5x - 6$. This whole process is known as the "AC method," since it begins by multiplying a and c from the generic $ax^2 + bx + c$.

Here is a summary of the algorithm:

Process 10.4.3 The AC Method. *To factor $ax^2 + bx + c$:*

1. *Multiply $a \cdot c$.*

2. *Make a table of factor pairs for ac. Look for a pair that adds to b. If you cannot find one, the polynomial is irreducible.*

3. *If you did find a factor pair summing to b, replace b with an explicit sum, and distribute x. With the four terms you have at this point, use factoring by grouping to continue. You are guaranteed to find a factorization.*

Example 10.4.4 Factor $10x^2 + 23x + 6$.

1. $10 \cdot 6 = 60$

2. Use a list of factor pairs for 60 to find that 3 and 20 are a pair that sums to 23.

3. Intentionally break up the 23 as $3 + 20$:

$$\begin{aligned} 10x^2 &\overbrace{+\ 23x}\ +6 \\ &= 10x^2 \overbrace{+ 3x + 20x}\ +6 \\ &= \left(10x^2 + 3x\right) + (20x + 6) \\ &= x(10x + 3) + 2(10x + 3) \\ &= (10x + 3)(x + 2) \end{aligned}$$

Example 10.4.5 Factor $2x^2 - 5x - 3$.

Explanation. Always start the factoring process by examining if there is a greatest common factor. Here there is not one. Next, note that this is a trinomial with a leading coefficient that is not 1. So the AC Method may be of help.

1. Multiply $2 \cdot (-3) = -6$.

2. Examine factor pairs that multiply to -6, looking for a pair that sums to -5:

Factor Pair	Sum of the Pair		Factor Pair	Sum of the Pair
$1 \cdot -6$	-5 (what we wanted)		$-1 \cdot 6$	(no need to go this far)
$2 \cdot -3$	(no need to go this far)		$-2 \cdot 3$	(no need to go this far)

3. Intentionally break up the -5 as $1 + (-6)$:

$$2x^2 \overbrace{-5x} -3 = 2x^2 \overbrace{+x - 6x} -3$$
$$= \left(2x^2 + x\right) + (-6x - 3)$$
$$= x(2x + 1) - 3(2x + 1)$$
$$= (2x + 1)(x - 3)$$

So we believe that $2x^2 - 5x - 3$ factors as $(2x + 1)(x - 3)$, and we should check by multiplying out the factored form:

$$(2x + 1)(x - 3) = (2x + 1) \cdot x + (2x + 1) \cdot (-3)$$
$$= 2x^2 + x - 6x - 3$$
$$\overset{\checkmark}{=} 2x^2 - 5x - 3$$

	$2x$	1
x	$2x^2$	x
-3	$-6x$	-3

Our factorization passes the tests.

Example 10.4.6 Factor $6p^2 + 5pq - 6q^2$. Note that this example has two variables, but that does not really change our approach.

Explanation.   There is no greatest common factor. Since this is a trinomial, we try the AC Method.

1. Multiply $6 \cdot (-6) = -36$.

2. Examine factor pairs that multiply to -36, looking for a pair that sums to 5:

Factor Pair	Sum of the Pair		Factor Pair	Sum of the Pair
$1 \cdot -36$	-35		$-1 \cdot 36$	35
$2 \cdot -18$	-16		$-2 \cdot 18$	16
$3 \cdot -12$	-9		$-3 \cdot 12$	9
$4 \cdot -9$	-5 (close; wrong sign)		$-4 \cdot 9$	5 (what we wanted)
$6 \cdot -6$	0			

3. Intentionally break up the 5 as $-4 + 9$:

$$6p^2 \overbrace{+5pq} -6q^2 = 6p^2 \overbrace{-4pq + 9pq} -6q^2$$
$$= \left(6p^2 - 4pq\right) + \left(9pq - 6q^2\right)$$
$$= 2p(3p - 2q) + 3q(3p - 2q)$$
$$= (3p - 2q)(2p + 3q)$$

So we believe that $6p^2 + 5pq - 6q^2$ factors as $(3p - 2q)(2p + 3q)$, and we should check by multiplying out the factored form:

$$(3p - 2q)(2p + 3q) = (3p - 2q) \cdot 2p + (3p - 2q) \cdot 3q$$
$$= 6p^2 - 4pq + 9pq - 6q^2$$
$$\overset{\checkmark}{=} 6p^2 + 5pq - 6q^2$$

	$3p$	$-2q$
$2p$	$6p^2$	$-4pq$
$3q$	$9pq$	$-6q^2$

Our factorization passes the tests.

10.4.2 Factoring in Stages

Sometimes factoring a polynomial will take two or more "stages." For instance you may need to begin factoring a polynomial by factoring out its greatest common factor, and *then* apply a second stage where you use a technique from this section. The process of factoring a polynomial is not complete until each of the factors cannot be factored further.

Example 10.4.7 Factor $18n^2 - 21n - 60$.

Explanation. Notice that 3 is a common factor in this trinomial. We should factor it out first:

$$18n^2 - 21n - 60 = 3\left(6n^2 - 7n - 20\right)$$

Now we are left with two factors, one of which is $6n^2 - 7n - 20$, which might factor further. Using the AC Method:

1. $6 \cdot -20 = -120$

2. Examine factor pairs that multiply to -120, looking for a pair that sums to -7:

Factor Pair	Sum of the Pair		Factor Pair	Sum of the Pair
$1 \cdot -120$	-119		$-1 \cdot 120$	(no need to go this far)
$2 \cdot -60$	-58		$-2 \cdot 60$	(no need to go this far)
$3 \cdot -40$	-37		$-3 \cdot 40$	(no need to go this far)
$4 \cdot -30$	-26		$-4 \cdot 30$	(no need to go this far)
$5 \cdot -24$	-19		$-5 \cdot 24$	(no need to go this far)
$6 \cdot -20$	-14		$-6 \cdot 20$	(no need to go this far)
$8 \cdot -15$	-7 (what we wanted)		$-8 \cdot 15$	(no need to go this far)
$10 \cdot -12$	(no need to go this far)		$-10 \cdot 12$	(no need to go this far)

3. Intentionally break up the -7 as $8 + (-15)$:

$$18n^2 - 21n - 60 = 3\left(6n^2 \overbrace{-7n} - 20\right)$$
$$= 3\left(6n^2 \overbrace{+8n - 15n} - 20\right)$$
$$= 3\left((6n^2 + 8n) + (-15n - 20)\right)$$
$$= 3\left(2n(3n + 4) - 5(3n + 4)\right)$$
$$= 3(3n + 4)(2n - 5)$$

So we believe that $18n^2 - 21n - 60$ factors as $3(3n + 4)(2n - 5)$, and you should check by multiplying out the factored form.

Example 10.4.8 Factor $-16x^3y - 12x^2y + 18xy$.

Explanation. Notice that $2xy$ is a common factor in this trinomial. Also the leading coefficient is negative, and as discussed in Section 10.1, it is wise to factor that out as well. So we find:

$$-16x^3y - 12x^2y + 18xy = -2xy\left(8x^2 + 6x - 9\right)$$

Now we are left with one factor being $8x^2 + 6x - 9$, which might factor further. Using the AC Method:

1. $8 \cdot -9 = -72$

2. Examine factor pairs that multiply to -72, looking for a pair that sums to 6:

Factor Pair	Sum of the Pair		Factor Pair	Sum of the Pair
$1 \cdot -72$	-71		$-1 \cdot 72$	71
$2 \cdot -36$	-34		$-2 \cdot 36$	34
$3 \cdot -24$	-21		$-3 \cdot 24$	21
$4 \cdot -18$	-14		$-4 \cdot 18$	14
$6 \cdot -12$	-6 (close; wrong sign)		$-6 \cdot 12$	6 (what we wanted)
$8 \cdot -9$	-1		$-8 \cdot 9$	(no need to go this far)

3. Intentionally break up the 6 as $-6 + 12$:

$$-16x^3y - 12x^2y + 18xy = -2xy\left(8x^2 \overbrace{+ 6x} - 9\right)$$
$$= -2xy\left(8x^2 \overbrace{- 6x + 12x} - 9\right)$$
$$= -2xy\left(\left(8x^2 - 6x\right) + \left(12x - 9\right)\right)$$
$$= -2xy\left(2x(4x - 3) + 3(4x - 3)\right)$$
$$= -2xy(4x - 3)(2x + 3)$$

So we believe that $-16x^3y - 12x^2y + 18xy$ factors as $-2xy(4x - 3)(2x + 3)$, and you should check by multiplying out the factored form.

10.4.3 Reading Questions

1. The AC Method is really trying to turn a trinomial into a polynomial with ☐ terms so that factoring by grouping may be used.

2. When you are tyring to factor a polynomial and the leading coefficient is not 1, what should you try to do *before* you try the AC Method?

10.4.4 Exercises

Review and Warmup Multiply the polynomials.

1. $(4y + 10)(2y + 9)$
2. $(2r + 9)(4r + 3)$
3. $(6r - 8)(3r - 8)$
4. $(4t - 10)(2t - 7)$
5. $(3t - 10)(t + 9)$
6. $(9x - 6)(x + 2)$
7. $\left(6x^3 + 9\right)\left(x^2 + 3\right)$
8. $\left(2y^3 + 4\right)\left(y^2 + 10\right)$

Factoring Trinomials with a Nontrivial Leading Coefficient Factor the given polynomial.

9. $5y^2 + 6y + 1$

10. $3y^2 + 17y + 10$

11. $2r^2 + 11r - 21$

12. $5r^2 + 23r - 10$

13. $2t^2 - 13t + 15$

14. $3t^2 - 16t + 20$

15. $5x^2 + 6x + 10$

16. $2x^2 + 3x + 6$

17. $4x^2 + 13x + 9$

18. $6y^2 + 23y + 15$

19. $4y^2 - 11y - 3$

20. $8r^2 - r - 7$

21. $6r^2 - 13r + 7$

22. $4t^2 - 17t + 18$

23. $6t^2 + 19t + 10$

24. $8x^2 + 18x + 9$

25. $10x^2 - x - 24$

26. $10x^2 + 3x - 27$

27. $6y^2 - 29y + 9$

28. $10y^2 - 17y + 6$

29. $18r^2 + 27r + 9$

30. $4r^2 + 34r + 16$

31. $35t^2 + 28t - 7$

32. $14t^2 - 7t - 21$

33. $4x^2 - 26x + 12$

34. $15x^2 - 24x + 9$

35. $4x^9 + 18x^8 + 14x^7$

36. $14y^9 + 21y^8 + 7y^7$

37. $16y^6 - 8y^5 - 24y^4$

38. $8r^9 - 12r^8 - 20r^7$

39. $6r^7 - 8r^6 + 2r^5$

40. $10t^9 - 35t^8 + 15t^7$

41. $3t^2r^2 + 13tr + 12$

42. $3x^2y^2 + 14xy + 16$

43. $2x^2t^2 + 3xt - 2$

44. $2x^2r^2 - 3xr - 2$

45. $5y^2x^2 - 23yx + 12$

46. $5y^2t^2 - 14yt + 8$

47. $3r^2 + 13rx + 4x^2$

48. $5r^2 + 17rx + 14x^2$

49. $3t^2 - 26ty - 9y^2$

50. $5t^2 - 6tr - 8r^2$

51. $3x^2 - 11xr + 8r^2$

52. $5x^2 - 9xt + 4t^2$

53. $4x^2 + 11xy + 7y^2$

54. $4y^2 + 25yx + 6x^2$

55. $8y^2 - 17yt - 21t^2$

56. $4r^2 - 9ry - 9y^2$

57. $6r^2 - 31rx + 5x^2$

58. $8t^2 - 17tr + 2r^2$

59. $12t^2 + 25ty + 12y^2$

60. $12x^2 + 17xt + 6t^2$

61. $9x^2 - 9xr - 28r^2$

62. $15x^2 - 7xy - 2y^2$

63. $4y^2 - 16yt + 7t^2$

64. $12y^2 - 23yr + 10r^2$

65. $18r^2y^2 + 27ry + 9$

66. $15r^2t^2 + 20rt + 5$

67. $21t^2r^2 - 7tr - 28$

68. $15t^2x^2 + 12tx - 36$

69. $6x^9t^2 - 26x^8t + 24x^7$

70. $10x^7r^2 - 18x^6r + 8x^5$

71. $10x^2 + 22xy + 12y^2$

72. $8x^2 + 28xy + 20y^2$

73. $6a^2 + 10ab - 4b^2$

74. $10a^2 + 8ab - 2b^2$

75. $10x^2 - 24xy + 8y^2$

76. $9x^2 - 12xy + 3y^2$

77. $10x^2y + 32xy^2 + 6y^3$

78. $9x^2y + 21xy^2 + 6y^3$

Factor the given polynomial.

79. $12x^2(y+6) + 28x(y+6) + 16(y+6)$

80. $4x^2(y-6) + 18x(y-6) + 8(y-6)$

81. $9x^2(y+9) + 21x(y+9) + 6(y+9)$

82. $25x^2(y+2) + 30x(y+2) + 5(y+2)$

83. a. Factor the given polynomial.$3x^2 + 19x + 6$

   b. Use your previous answer to factor$3(y-7)^2 + 19(y-7) + 6$

84. a. Factor the given polynomial.$2x^2 + 19x + 9$

   b. Use your previous answer to factor$2(y+3)^2 + 19(y+3) + 9$

Challenge

85. What integers can go in the place of b so that the quadratic expression $3x^2 + bx + 8$ is factorable?

10.5 Factoring Special Polynomials

Certain polynomials have patterns that you can train yourself to recognize. And when they have these patterns, there are formulas you can use to factor them, much more quickly than using the techniques from Section 10.3 and Section 10.4.

10.5.1 Difference of Squares

If b is some positive integer, then when you multiply $(x - b)(x + b)$:

$$(x - b)(x + b) = x^2 - bx + bx - b^2$$
$$= x^2 - b^2.$$

The $-bx$ and the $+bx$ cancel each other out. So this is telling us that

$$x^2 - b^2 = (x - b)(x + b).$$

And so if we ever encounter a polynomial of the form $x^2 - b^2$ (a "difference of squares") then we have a quick formula for factoring it. Just identify what "b" is, and use that in $(x - b)(x + b)$.

To use this formula, it's important to recognize which numbers are perfect squares, as in Figure 6.1.4.

Example 10.5.2 Factor $x^2 - 16$.

Explanation. The "16" being subtracted here is a perfect square. It is the same as 4^2. So we can take $b = 4$ and write:

$$x^2 - 16 = (x - b)(x + b)$$
$$= (x - 4)(x + 4)$$

Checkpoint 10.5.3 Try to factor one yourself:

Factor $x^2 - 49$.

Explanation. The "49" being subtracted here is a perfect square. It is the same as 7^2. So we can take $b = 7$ and write:

$$x^2 - 49 = (x - b)(x + b)$$
$$= (x - 7)(x + 7)$$

We can do a little better. There is nothing special about starting with "x^2" in these examples. In full generality:

Fact 10.5.4 The Difference of Squares Formula. *If A and B are any algebraic expressions, then:*

$$A^2 - B^2 = (A - B)(A + B).$$

Example 10.5.5 Factor $1 - p^2$.

Explanation. The "1" at the beginning of this expression is a perfect square; it's the same as 1^2. The "p^2" being subtracted here is also perfect square. We can take $A = 1$ and $B = p$, and use The Difference of Squares Formula:

$$1 - p^2 = (A - B)(A + B)$$
$$= (1 - p)(1 + p)$$

Example 10.5.6 Factor $m^2n^2 - 4$.

Explanation.   Is the "m^2n^2" at the beginning of this expression a perfect square? By the rules for exponents, it is the same as $(mn)^2$, so yes, it is a perfect square and we may take $A = mn$. The "4" being subtracted here is also perfect square. We can take $B = 2$. The Difference of Squares Formula tells us:

$$m^2n^2 - 4 = (A - B)(A + B)$$
$$= (mn - 2)(mn + 2)$$

Checkpoint 10.5.7 Try to factor one yourself:

Factor $4z^2 - 9$.

Explanation.   The "$4z^2$" at the beginning here is a perfect square. It is the same as $(2z)^2$. So we can take $A = 2z$. The "9" being subtracted is also a perfect square, so we can take $B = 3$:

$$4z^2 - 9 = (A - B)(A + B)$$
$$= (2z - 3)(2z + 3)$$

Example 10.5.8 Factor $x^6 - 9$.

Explanation.   Is the "x^6" at the beginning of this expression is a perfect square? It may appear to be a *sixth* power, but it is *also* a perfect square because we can write $x^6 = \left(x^3\right)^2$. So we may take $A = x^3$. The "9" being subtracted here is also perfect square. We can take $B = 3$. The Difference of Squares Formula tells us:

$$x^6 - 9 = (A - B)(A + B)$$
$$= (x^3 - 3)(x^3 + 3)$$

Warning 10.5.9 It's a common mistake to write something like $x^2 + 16 = (x + 4)(x - 4)$. This is not what The Difference of Squares Formula allows you to do, and this is in fact incorrect. The issue is that $x^2 + 16$ is a *sum* of squares, not a *difference*. And it happens that $x^2 + 16$ is actually prime. In fact, any sum of squares without a common factor will always be prime.

10.5.2 Perfect Square Trinomials

If we expand $(A + B)^2$:

$$(A + B)^2 = (A + B)(A + B)$$
$$= A^2 + BA + AB + B^2$$
$$= A^2 + 2AB + B^2.$$

The BA and the AB equal each other and double up when added together. So this is telling us that

$$A^2 + 2AB + B^2 = (A + B)^2.$$

And so if we ever encounter a polynomial of the form $A^2 + 2AB + B^2$ (a "perfect square trinomial") then we have a quick formula for factoring it.

The tricky part is recognizing when a trinomial you have encountered is in this special form. Ask yourself:

1. Are the first and last terms perfect square? If so, jot down what A and B would be.

2. When you multiply 2 with what you wrote down for A and B, i.e. 2AB, do you have the middle term? If you have this middle term exactly, then your polynomial factors as $(A + B)^2$. If the middle term is the negative of 2AB, then the sign on your B can be reversed, and your polynomial factors as $(A - B)^2$.

Fact 10.5.10 The Perfect Square Trinomial Formula. *If A and B are any algebraic expressions, then:*

$$A^2 + 2AB + B^2 = (A + B)^2 \qquad and \qquad A^2 - 2AB + B^2 = (A - B)^2$$

Example 10.5.11 Factor $x^2 + 6x + 9$.

Explanation. The first term, x^2, is clearly a perfect square. So we could take $A = x$. The last term, 9, is also a perfect square since it is equal to 3^2. So we could take $B = 3$. Now we multiply $2AB = 2 \cdot x \cdot 3$, and the result is $6x$. This is the middle term, which is what we hope to see.

So we can use The Perfect Square Trinomial Formula:

$$x^2 + 6x + 9 = (A + B)^2$$
$$= (x + 3)^2$$

Example 10.5.12 Factor $4x^2 - 20xy + 25y^2$.

Explanation. The first term, $4x^2$, is a perfect square because it equals $(2x)^2$. So we could take $A = 2x$. The last term, $25y^2$, is also a perfect square since it is equal to $(5y)^2$. So we could take $B = 5y$. Now we multiply $2AB = 2 \cdot (2x) \cdot (5y)$, and the result is $20xy$. This is the *negative* of the middle term, which we can work with. The factored form will be $(A - B)^2$ instead of $(A + B)^2$.

So we can use The Perfect Square Trinomial Formula:

$$4x^2 - 20xy + 25y^2 = (A - B)^2$$
$$= (2x - 5y)^2$$

Checkpoint 10.5.13 Try to factor one yourself:

Factor $16q^2 + 56q + 49$.

Explanation. The first term, $16q^2$, is a perfect square because it equals $(4q)^2$. So we could take $A = 4q$. The last term, 49, is also a perfect square since it is equal to 7^2. So we could take $B = 7$. Now we multiply $2AB = 2 \cdot (4q) \cdot 7$, and the result is $56q$. This is the middle term, which is what we hope to see.

So we can use The Perfect Square Trinomial Formula:

$$16q^2 + 56q + 49 = (A + B)^2$$
$$= (4q + 7)^2$$

Warning 10.5.14 It is not enough to just see that the first and last terms are perfect squares. For example, $9x^2 + 10x + 25$ has its first term equal to $(3x)^2$ and its last term equal to 5^2. But when you examine $2 \cdot (3x) \cdot 5$ the result is $30x$, *not* equal to the middle term. So The Perfect Square Trinomial Formula doesn't apply here. In fact, this polynomial doesn't factor at all.

Remark 10.5.15 To factor these perfect square trinomials, we *could* use methods from Section 10.3 and Section 10.4. As an exercise for yourself, try to factor each of the three previous examples using those methods. The advantage to using The Perfect Square Trinomial Formula is that it is much faster. With some practice, all of the work for using it can be done mentally.

10.5.3 Factoring in Stages

Sometimes factoring a polynomial will take two or more "stages." You might use one of the special patters to factor something into two factors, and then those factors might factor even more. When the task is to *factor* a polynomial, the intention is that you *fully* factor it, breaking down the pieces into even smaller pieces when that is possible.

Example 10.5.16 Factor out any greatest common factor. Factor $12z^3 - 27z$.

Explanation.   The two terms of this polynomial have greatest common factor $3z$, so the first step in factoring should be to factor this out:

$$3z\left(4z^2 - 9\right).$$

Now we have two factors. There is nothing for us to do with $3z$, but we should ask if $\left(4z^2 - 9\right)$ can factor further. And in fact, that is a difference of squares. So we can apply The Difference of Squares Formula. The full process would be:

$$\begin{aligned}
12z^3 - 27z &= 3z\left(4z^2 - 9\right) \\
&= 3z(2z - 3)(2z + 3)
\end{aligned}$$

Example 10.5.17 Recognize a *second* special pattern. Factor $p^4 - 1$.

Explanation.   Since p^4 is the same as $\left(p^2\right)^2$, we have a difference of squares here. We can apply The Difference of Squares Formula:

$$p^4 - 1 = \left(p^2 - 1\right)\left(p^2 + 1\right)$$

It doesn't end here. Of the two factors we found, $\left(p^2 + 1\right)$ cannot be factored further. But the other one, $\left(p^2 - 1\right)$ is *also* a difference of squares. So we should apply The Difference of Squares Formula again:

$$= (p - 1)(p + 1)\left(p^2 + 1\right)$$

Example 10.5.18 Factor $32x^6y^2 - 48x^5y + 18x^4$.

Explanation.   The first step of factoring any polynomial is to factor out the common factor if possible. For this trinomial, the common factor is $2x^4$, so we write

$$32x^6y^2 - 48x^5y + 18x^4 = 2x^4(16x^2y^2 - 24xy + 9).$$

The square numbers 16 and 9 in $16x^2y^2 - 24xy + 9$ hint that maybe we could use The Perfect Square Trinomial Formula. Taking $A = 4xy$ and $B = 3$, we multiply $2AB = 2 \cdot (4xy) \cdot 3$. The result is $24xy$, which is the negative of our middle term. So the whole process is:

$$\begin{aligned}
32x^6y^2 - 48x^5y + 18x^4 &= 2x^4(16x^2y^2 - 24xy + 9) \\
&= 2x^4(4xy - 3)^2
\end{aligned}$$

10.5.4 Reading Questions

1. Describe two special patterns where it is possible to memorize a quick factoring shortcut as discussed in this section.

10.5.5 Exercises

Review and Warmup Expand the square of a *bi*nomial.

1. $(10x + 1)^2$ **2.** $(7y + 5)^2$ **3.** $(y - 8)^2$

4. $(r - 2)^2$ **5.** $(r^8 + 1)^2$ **6.** $(t^4 - 8)^2$

Multiply the polynomials.

7. $(t + 10)(t - 10)$ **8.** $(t + 13)(t - 13)$ **9.** $(2x - 2)(2x + 2)$

10. $(6x + 7)(6x - 7)$ **11.** $(4y^9 - 7)(4y^9 + 7)$ **12.** $(2y^6 + 4)(2y^6 - 4)$

Factoring Factor the given polynomial.

13. $r^2 - 100$ **14.** $r^2 - 36$ **15.** $t^2 - 144$

16. $81t^2 - 25$ **17.** $t^2y^2 - 100$ **18.** $x^2t^2 - 121$

19. $64x^2r^2 - 49$ **20.** $16y^2x^2 - 121$ **21.** $36 - y^2$

22. $1 - r^2$ **23.** $49 - 16r^2$ **24.** $1 - 144t^2$

25. $t^4 - 64$ **26.** $t^4 - 49$ **27.** $121x^4 - 144$

28. $64x^4 - 25$ **29.** $y^{14} - 100$ **30.** $y^6 - 121$

31. $49x^4 - 64y^4$ **32.** $81x^4 - 4y^4$ **33.** $x^{14} - 100y^{12}$

34. $x^{10} - 121y^{14}$ **35.** $t^2 + 4t + 4$ **36.** $x^2 + 20x + 100$

37. $x^2 - 12x + 36$ **38.** $y^2 - 2y + 1$ **39.** $100y^2 + 20y + 1$

40. $36r^2 + 12r + 1$ **41.** $4r^2 - 4r + 1$ **42.** $81t^2 - 18t + 1$

43. $64t^2y^2 - 16ty + 1$ **44.** $64t^2x^2 - 16tx + 1$ **45.** $x^2 + 12xr + 36r^2$

46. $x^2 + 22xy + 121y^2$ **47.** $y^2 - 8yt + 16t^2$ **48.** $y^2 - 18yr + 81r^2$

49. $9r^2 + 24ry + 16y^2$ **50.** $64r^2 + 48rt + 9t^2$ **51.** $36t^2 - 60tr + 25r^2$

52. $25t^2 - 60tx + 36x^2$ **53.** $81t^4 - 16$ **54.** $16x^4 - 1$

55. $8x^2 - 72$ **56.** $6y^2 - 96$ **57.** $6y^3 - 6y$

58. $11r^3 - 44r$ **59.** $5r^3t^3 - 125rt$ **60.** $5t^4y^4 - 20t^2y^2$

61. $3 - 3t^2$ **62.** $125 - 5t^2$ **63.** $27x^2 + 18x + 3$

64. $20x^2 + 20x + 5$ **65.** $32y^2r^2 + 32yr + 8$ **66.** $90y^2x^2 + 60yx + 10$

67. $64r^2 - 32r + 4$ **68.** $45r^2 - 30r + 5$ **69.** $25t^7 + 10t^6 + t^5$

70. $144t^9 + 24t^8 + t^7$ **71.** $64t^5 - 16t^4 + t^3$ **72.** $16x^8 - 8x^7 + x^6$

73. $12x^4 + 12x^3 + 3x^2$ **74.** $75y^{10} + 30y^9 + 3y^8$ **75.** $12y^6 - 12y^5 + 3y^4$

76. $90r^{10} - 60r^9 + 10r^8$ **77.** $5r^4 - 80$ **78.** $7r^4 - 7$

79. $t^2 + 100$ **80.** $t^2 + 36$ **81.** $6x^3 + 24x$

82. $2x^3 + 8x$ **83.** $0.25y - y^3$ **84.** $0.01y - y^3$

Challenge

85. Select the expression which is equivalent to $555^2 - 666^2$.

⊙ $1221(1221)$

⊙ $1221(-111)$

⊙ $-111(-111)$

⊙ none of the above

10.6 Factoring Strategies

10.6.1 Factoring Strategies

Deciding which method to use when factoring a random polynomial can seem like a daunting task. Understanding all of the techniques that we have learned and how they fit together can be done using a decision tree.

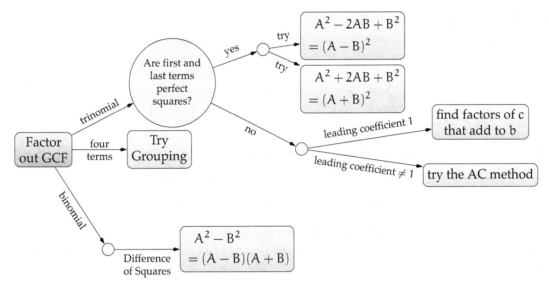

Figure 10.6.2: Factoring Decision Tree

Using the decision tree can guide us when we are given an expression to factor.

Example 10.6.3 Factor the expression $4k^2 + 12k - 40$ completely.

Explanation. Start by noting that the GCF is 4. Factoring this out, we get

$$4k^2 + 12k - 40 = 4\left(k^2 + 3k - 10\right).$$

Following the decision tree, we now have a trinomial where the leading coefficient is 1 and we need to look for factors of -10 that add to 3. We find that -2 and 5 work. So, the full factorization is:

$$4k^2 + 12k - 40 = 4\left(k^2 + 3k - 10\right)$$
$$= 4(k - 2)(k + 5)$$

Example 10.6.4 Factor the expression $64d^2 + 144d + 81$ completely.

Explanation. Start by noting that the GCF is 1, and there is no GCF to factor out. We continue along the decision tree for a trinomial. Notice that both 64 and 81 are perfect squares and that this expression might factor using the pattern $A^2 + 2AB + B^2 = (A + B)^2$. To find A and B, take the square roots of the first and last terms, so $A = 8d$ and $B = 9$. We have to check that the middle term is correct: since $2AB = 2(8d)(9) = 144d$ matches our middle term, the expression must factor as

$$64d^2 + 144d + 81 = (8d + 9)^2.$$

Example 10.6.5 Factor the expression $10x^2y - 12xy^2$ completely.

Explanation.   Start by noting that the GCF is $2xy$. Factoring this out, we get

$$10x^2y - 12xy^2 = 2xy(5x - 6y).$$

Since we have a binomial inside the parentheses, the only options on the decision tree for a binomial involve squares or cubes. Since there are none, we conclude that $2xy(5x - 6y)$ is the complete factorization.

Example 10.6.6 Factor the expression $9b^2 - 25y^2$ completely.

Explanation.   Start by noting that the GCF is 1, and there is no GCF to factor out. We continue along the decision tree for a binomial and notice that we now have a difference of squares, $A^2 - B^2 = (A - B)(A + B)$. To find the values for A and B that fit the patterns, just take the square roots. So $A = 3b$ since $(3b)^2 = 9b^2$ and $B = 5y$ since $(5y)^2 = 25y^2$. So, the expression must factor as

$$9b^2 - 25y^2 = (3b - 5y)(3b + 5y).$$

Example 10.6.7 Factor the expression $24w^3 + 6w^2 - 9w$ completely.

Explanation.   Start by noting that the GCF is $3w$. Factoring this out, we get

$$24w^3 + 6w^2 - 9w = 3w\left(8w^2 + 2w - 3\right).$$

Following the decision tree, we now have a trinomial inside the parentheses where $a \neq 1$. We should try the AC method because neither 8 nor -3 are perfect squares. In this case, $ac = -24$ and we must find two factors of -24 that add to be 2. The numbers 6 and -4 work in this case. The rest of the factoring process is:

$$24w^3 + 6w^2 - 9w = 3w\left(8w^2 \overbrace{+ 2w}\, -3\right)$$
$$= 3w\left(8w^2 \overbrace{+ 6w - 4w}\, -3\right)$$
$$= 3w\left((8w^2 + 6w) + (-4w - 3)\right)$$
$$= 3w\left(2w(4w + 3) - 1(4w + 3)\right)$$
$$= 3w(4w + 3)(2w - 1)$$

Example 10.6.8 Factor the expression $-6xy + 9y + 2x - 3$ completely.

Explanation.   Start by noting that the GCF is 1, and there is no GCF to factor out. We continue along the decision tree. Since we have a four-term polynomial, we should try to factor by grouping. The full process is:

$$-6xy + 9y + 2x - 3 = (-6xy + 9y) + (2x - 3)$$
$$= -3y(2x - 3) + 1(2x - 3)$$
$$= (2x - 3)(-3y + 1)$$

Note that the negative sign in front of the $3y$ can be factored out if you wish. That would look like:

$$= -(2x - 3)(3y - 1)$$

Example 10.6.9 Factor the expression $4w^3 - 20w^2 + 24w$ completely.

Explanation. Start by noting that the GCF is $4w$. Factoring this out, we get

$$4w^3 - 20w^2 + 24w = 4w\left(w^2 - 5w + 6\right).$$

Following the decision tree, we now have a trinomial with $a = 1$ inside the parentheses. So, we can look for factors of 6 that add up to -5. Since -3 and -2 fit the requirements, the full factorization is:

$$
\begin{aligned}
4w^3 - 20w^2 + 24w &= 4w\left(w^2 - 5w + 6\right) \\
&= 4w(w - 3)(w - 2)
\end{aligned}
$$

Example 10.6.10 Factor the expression $9 - 24y + 16y^2$ completely.

Explanation. Start by noting that the GCF is 1, and there is no GCF to factor out. Continue along the decision tree. We now have a trinomial where both the first term, 9, and last term, $16y^2$, look like perfect squares. To use the perfect squares difference pattern, $A^2 - 2AB + B^2 = (A - B)^2$, recall that we need to mentally take the square roots of these two terms to find A and B. So, $A = 3$ since $3^2 = 9$, and $B = 4y$ since $(4y)^2 = 16y^2$. Now we have to check that $2AB$ matches $24y$:

$$2AB = 2(3)(4y) = 24y.$$

So the full factorization is:

$$9 - 24y + 16y^2 = (3 - 4y)^2.$$

Example 10.6.11 Factor the expression $9 - 25y + 16y^2$ completely.

Explanation. Start by noting that the GCF is 1, and there is no GCF to factor out. Since we now have a trinomial where both the first term and last term are perfect squares in exactly the same way as in Example 10. However, we cannot apply the perfect squares method to this problem because it worked when $2AB = 24y$. Since our middle term is $25y$, we can be certain that it won't be a perfect square.

Continuing on with the decision tree, our next option is to use the AC method. You might be tempted to rearrange the order of the terms, but that is unnecessary. In this case, $ac = 144$ and we need to come up with two factors of 144 that add to be -25. After a brief search, we conclude that those values are -16 and -9. The remainder of the factorization is:

$$
\begin{aligned}
9 \overbrace{- 25y} + 16y^2 = 9 \overbrace{- 16y - 9y} + 16y^2 \\
= (9 - 16y) + \left(-9y + 16y^2\right) \\
= 1(9 - 16y) - y(9 + 16y) \\
= (9 - 16y)(1 - y)
\end{aligned}
$$

Example 10.6.12 Factor the expression $20x^4 + 13x^3 - 21x^2$ completely.

Explanation. Start by noting that the GCF is x^2. Factoring this out, we get

$$20x^4 + 13x^3 - 21x^2 = x^2\left(20x^2 + 13x - 21\right).$$

Following the decision tree, we now have a trinomial inside the parentheses where $a \neq 1$ and we should try the AC method. In this case, $ac = -420$ and we need factors of -420 that add to 13.

Factor Pair	Sum		Factor Pair	Sum		Factor Pair	Sum
$1 \cdot -420$	-419		$5 \cdot -84$	-79		$12 \cdot -35$	-23
$2 \cdot -210$	-208		$6 \cdot -70$	-64		$14 \cdot -30$	-16
$3 \cdot -140$	-137		$7 \cdot -60$	-53		$15 \cdot -28$	-13
$4 \cdot -105$	-101		$10 \cdot -42$	-32		$20 \cdot -21$	-1

In the table of the factor pairs of -420 we find $15 + (-28) = -13$, the opposite of what we want, so we want the opposite numbers: -15 and 28. The rest of the factoring process is shown:

$$20x^4 + 13x^3 - 21x^2 = x^2 \left(20x^2 \overbrace{+ 13x} -21 \right)$$
$$= x^2 \left(20x^2 \overbrace{-15x + 28x} -21 \right)$$
$$= x^2 \left((20x^2 - 15x) + (28x - 21) \right)$$
$$= x^2 \left(5x(4x - 3) + 7(4x - 3) \right)$$
$$= x^2 (4x - 3)(5x + 7)$$

10.6.2 Reading Questions

1.   Do you find a factoring flowchart helpful?

10.6.3 Exercises

Strategies Which factoring techniques/tools will be useful for factoring the polynomial below? Check all that apply.
☐ Factoring out a GCF   ☐ Factoring by grouping   ☐ Finding two numbers that multiply to the constant term and sum to the linear coefficient   ☐ The AC Method   ☐ Difference of Squares
☐ Difference of Cubes   ☐ Sum of Cubes   ☐ Perfect Square Trinomial   ☐ None of the above

1. $64B^2 - 216Bb + 140b^2$ **2.** $6m^6 + 384m^3x^3$

3. $49n^3 - 35n^2 - 28n + 20$ **4.** $4q^4 - 2916q$

5. $9y^2 - 24y + 16$ **6.** $3r^4 - 39r^3 + 120r^2$

7. $40x^2 - 408xa + 432a^2$ **8.** $b^3 - b^2 - 2b + 2$

9. $54A^6 - 686A^3B^3$ **10.** $63n - 81$

11. $32m^3 - 50mp^2$ **12.** $n^3 + 64A^3$

13. $210q^3t - 168q^3 - 270q^2t + 216q^2$ **14.** $4y^5 - 2916y^2p^3$

Factoring Factor the given polynomial.

15. $6x + 6$ **16.** $-3y - 3$

17. $36y^2 + 27$ **18.** $30r^4 - 12r^3 + 42r^2$

19. $6r + 12r^2 + 15r^3$ **20.** $8xy + 8y$

21. $54x^5y^8 - 6x^4y^8 + 42x^3y^8$ **22.** $t^2 - 2t + 3t - 6$

23. $xy + 2x + 8y + 16$ **24.** $x^3 - 3 + 2x^3y - 6y$

25. $y^2 - 3y - 4$

26. $5y^2 - 2y - 7$

27. $2r^2y^2 + 3ry - 9$

28. $2r^2 - 6r + 5$

29. $4r^2 - 7r - 2$

30. $8t^2 + 22t + 15$

31. $12t^2 - 23t + 10$

32. $3x^2 + 10xr + 3r^2$

33. $3x^2 - 13xy + 12y^2$

34. $4y^2 + 3yt - 7t^2$

35. $8y^2 + 22yr + 9r^2$

36. $8r^2 - 18rx + 9x^2$

37. $12r^2 - 8r - 4$

38. $15r^2t^2 - 3rt - 12$

39. $10t^9 + 25t^8 + 15t^7$

40. $6t^{10} - 9t^9 + 3t^8$

41. $6x^2 + 20xy + 14y^2$

42. $10x^2 - 34xy + 12y^2$

43. $y^2 + 9y + 8$

44. $y^2 - 6y + 5$

45. $r^2 + 10rx + 16x^2$

46. $r^2y^2 - 4ry - 12$

47. $r^2 - 10ry + 24y^2$

48. $4t^2x^2 + 12tx + 8$

49. $2t^2 + 8t - 10$

50. $3x^4 + 18x^3 + 24x^2$

51. $7x^9 - 28x^8 + 21x^7$

52. $2x^2y + 6xy + 4y$

53. $2x^2y - 18xy + 28y$

54. $2x^2y^3 - 10xy^2 + 8y$

55. $x^2y^2 + 6x^2yz - 7x^2z^2$

56. $r^2 + 0.9r + 0.2$

57. $t^2 - 144$

58. $t^2r^2 - 16$

59. $9 - x^2$

60. $x^4 - 121$

61. $y^{12} - 49$

62. $x^6 - 36y^{14}$

63. $81y^4 - 16$

64. $3r^3 - 147r$

65. $r^2 + 4$

66. $32 - 8t^2$

67. $t^2 + 12t + 36$

68. $x^2 - 12xy + 36y^2$

69. $x^2 - 18x + 81$

70. $36y^2 - 12y + 1$

71. $y^2 + 18yx + 81x^2$

72. $9y^2 + 30yr + 25r^2$

73. $98r^2y^2 + 28ry + 2$

74. $4r^{10} + 4r^9 + r^8$

75. $98t^8 + 28t^7 + 2t^6$

76. $0.16t - t^3$

77. $2x^4 - 162$

78. $x^2 - 14x + 49 - 64y^2$

10.7 Solving Quadratic Equations by Factoring

10.7.1 Introduction

We have learned how to factor trinomials like $x^2 + 5x + 6$ into $(x+2)(x+3)$. This skill can be used to solve an equation like $x^2 + 5x + 6 = 0$, which is a quadratic equation. Note that we solved equations like this in Chapter 7, but here we will use factoring, a new method.

Definition 10.7.1 Quadratic Equation. A **quadratic equation** is is an equation in the form $ax^2 + bx + c = 0$ with $a \neq 0$. We also consider equations such as $x^2 = x + 3$ and $5x^2 + 3 = (x+1)^2 + (x+1)(x-3)$ to be quadratic equations, because we can expand any multiplication, add or subtract terms from both sides, and combine like terms to get the form $ax^2 + bx + c = 0$. The form $ax^2 + bx + c = 0$ is called the **standard form** of a quadratic equation. $\Diamond$

Before we begin exploring the method of solving quadratic equations by factoring, we'll identify what types of equations are quadratic and which are not.

Checkpoint 10.7.3 Identify which of the items are quadratic equations.

   a. The equation $2x^2 + 5x = 7$ ($\square$ is $\square$ is not)   a quadratic equation.

   b. The equation $5 - 2x = 3$ ($\square$ is $\square$ is not)   a quadratic equation.

   c. The equation $15 - x^3 = 3x^2 + 9x$ ($\square$ is $\square$ is not)   a quadratic equation.

   d. The equation $(x+3)(x-4) = 0$ ($\square$ is $\square$ is not)   a quadratic equation.

   e. The equation $x(x+1)(x-1) = 0$ ($\square$ is $\square$ is not)   a quadratic equation.

   f. The expression $x^2 - 5x + 6$ ($\square$ is $\square$ is not)   a quadratic equation.

   g. The equation $(2x-3)(x+5) = 12$ ($\square$ is $\square$ is not)   a quadratic equation.

Explanation.

   a. The equation $2x^2 + 5x = 7$ *is* a quadratic equation. To write it in standard form, simply subtract 7 from both sides.

   b. The equation $5 - 2x = 3$ *is not* quadratic. It is a linear equation.

   c. The equation $15 + x^3 = 3x^2 + 9x$ *is not* a quadratic equation because of the x^3 term.

   d. The equation $(x+3)(x-4) = 0$ *is* a quadratic equation. If we expand the left-hand side of the equation, we would get something in standard form.

   e. The equation $x(x+1)(x-1) = 0$ *is not* a quadratic equation. If we expanded the left-hand side of the equation, we would have an expression with an x^3 term, which automatically makes it not quadratic.

   f. The expression $x^2 - 5x + 6$ *is not* a quadratic equation; it's not an *equation* at all. Instead, this is a quadratic *expression*.

   g. The equation $(2x-3)(x+5) = 12$ *is* a quadratic equation. Multiplying out the left-hand side, and subtracting 12 form both sides, we would have a quadratic equation in standard form.

Now we'll look at an application that demonstrates the need and method for solving a quadratic equation by factoring.

Nita is in a physics class that launches a tennis ball from a rooftop 80 feet above the ground. They fire it directly upward at a speed of 64 feet per second and measure the time it takes for the ball to hit the ground below. We can model the height of the tennis ball, h, in feet, with the quadratic equation

$$h = -16t^2 + 64t + 80,$$

where t represents the time in seconds after the launch. Using the model we can predict when the ball will hit the ground.

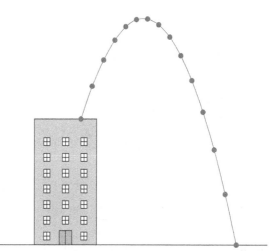

Figure 10.7.4: A Diagram of the Ball Thrown from the Roof

The ground has a height of 0, or $h = 0$. We will substitute 0 for h in the equation and we have

$$-16t^2 + 64t + 80 = 0$$

We need to solve this quadratic equation for t to find when the ball will hit the ground.

The key strategy for solving a *linear* equation is to separate the variable terms from the constant terms on either side of the equal sign. It turns out that this same method *will not work* for quadratic equations. Fortunately, we already have spent a good amount of time discussing a method that *will* work: factoring. If we can factor the polynomial on the left-hand side, we will be on the home stretch to solving the whole equation.

We will look for a common factor first, and see that we can factor out -16. Then we can finish factoring the trinomial:

$$-16t^2 + 64t + 80 = 0$$
$$-16(t^2 - 4t - 5) = 0$$
$$-16(t + 1)(t - 5) = 0$$

In order to finish solving the equation, we need to understand the following property. This property explains why it was *incredibly important* to not move the 80 in our example over to the other side of the equation before trying to factor.

Fact 10.7.5 Zero Product Property. *If the product of two or more numbers is equal to zero, then at least one of the numbers must be zero.*

One way to understand this property is to think about the equation $a \cdot b = 0$. Maybe $b = 0$, because that would certainly cause the equation to be true. But suppose that $b \neq 0$. Then it is safe to divide both sides by b, and the resulting equation says that $a = 0$. So no matter what, either $a = 0$ or $b = 0$.

To understand this property more, let's look at a few products:

$$4 \cdot 7 = 28 \qquad\qquad 4 \cdot 0 = 0 \qquad\qquad 4 \cdot 7 \cdot 3 = 84$$

$$0 \cdot 7 = 0 \qquad\qquad\qquad -4 \cdot 0 = 0 \qquad\qquad\qquad 4 \cdot 0 \cdot 3 = 0$$

When none of the factors are 0, the result is never 0. The only way to get a product of 0 is when one of the factors is 0. This property is unique to the number 0 and can be used no matter how many numbers are multiplied together.

Now we can see the value of factoring. We have three factors in our equation

$$-16(t+1)(t-5) = 0.$$

The first factor is the number -16. The second and third factors, $t+1$ and $t-5$, are expressions that represent numbers. Since the product of the three factors is equal to 0, one of the factors must be zero.

Since -16 is not 0, either $t+1$ or $t-5$ must be 0. This gives us two equations to solve:

$$
\begin{array}{ccc}
t + 1 = 0 & \text{or} & t - 5 = 0 \\
t + 1 - 1 = 0 - 1 & \text{or} & t - 5 + 5 = 0 + 5 \\
t = -1 & \text{or} & t = 5
\end{array}
$$

We have found two solutions, -1 and 5. A quadratic expression will have at most two linear factors, not including any constants, so it can have up to two solutions.

Let's check each of our two solutions -1 and 5:

$$
\begin{array}{rclcrcl}
-16t^2 + 64t + 80 &=& 0 & \qquad & -16t^2 + 64t + 80 &=& 0 \\
-16(-1)^2 + 64(-1) + 80 &\overset{?}{=}& 0 & & -16(5)^2 + 64(5) + 80 &\overset{?}{=}& 0 \\
-16(1) - 64 + 80 &\overset{?}{=}& 0 & & -16(25) + 320 + 80 &\overset{?}{=}& 0 \\
-16 - 64 + 80 &\overset{?}{=}& 0 & & -400 + 320 + 80 &\overset{?}{=}& 0 \\
0 &\overset{\checkmark}{=}& 0 & & 0 &\overset{\checkmark}{=}& 0
\end{array}
$$

We have verified our solutions. While there are two solutions to the equation, the solution -1 is not relevant to this physics model because it is a negative time which would tell us something about the ball's height *before* it was launched. The solution 5 does make sense. According to the model, the tennis ball will hit the ground 5 seconds after it is launched.

10.7.2 Further Examples

We'll now look at further examples of solving quadratic equations by factoring. The general process is outlined here:

Process 10.7.6 Solving Quadratic Equations by Factoring.

Simplify *Simplify the equation using distribution and by combining like terms.*

Isolate *Move all terms onto one side of the equation so that the other side has 0.*

Factor *Factor the quadratic expression.*

Apply the Zero Product Property *Apply the Zero Product Property.*

Solve *Solve the equation(s) that result after the zero product property was applied.*

Example 10.7.7 Solve $x^2 - 5x - 14 = 0$ by factoring.

Explanation.

$$x^2 - 5x - 14 = 0$$
$$(x - 7)(x + 2) = 0$$

$x - 7 = 0$	or	$x + 2 = 0$
$x - 7 + 7 = 0 + 7$	or	$x + 2 - 2 = 0 - 2$
$x = 7$	or	$x = -2$

The solutions are -2 and 7, so the solution set is written as $\{-2, 7\}$.

Example 10.7.8 Solve $x^2 - 5x - 14 = 0$ by using graphing technology.

Explanation. We have already solved the equation $x^2 - 5x - 14 = 0$ by factoring in Example 10.7.7, and now we can analyze the significance of the solutions graphically. What will -2 and 7 mean on the graph?

To solve this equation graphically, we first make a graph of $y = x^2 - 5x - 14$ and of $y = 0$. Both of these graphs are shown in Figure 10.7.9 in an appropriate window.

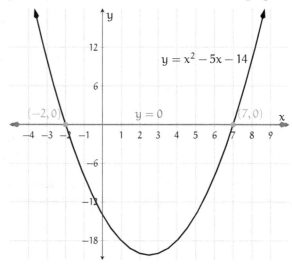

Figure 10.7.9: A graph of $y = x^2 - 5x - 14$ and $y = 0$.

From the graph provided we can see that the solutions (the x-values where the graphs intersect) are -2 and 7.

If the two factors of a polynomial happen to be the same, the equation will only have one solution. Let's look at an example of that.

Example 10.7.10 A Quadratic Equation with Only One Solution. Solve $x^2 - 10x + 25 = 0$ by factoring.

Explanation.

$$x^2 - 10x + 25 = 0$$
$$(x - 5)(x - 5) = 0$$
$$(x - 5)^2 = 0$$
$$x - 5 = 0$$

$$x - 5 + 5 = 0 + 5$$
$$x = 5$$

The solution is 5, so the solution set is written as $\{5\}$.

While we are examining this problem, let's compare the algebraic solution to a graphical solution.

To solve this equation graphically, we first make a graph of $y = x^2 - 10x + 25$ and of $y = 0$. Both of these graphs are shown in Figure 10.7.11 in an appropriate window.

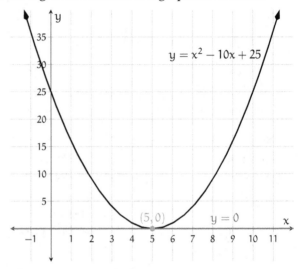

Figure 10.7.11: A graph of $y = x^2 - 10x + 25$ and $y = 0$.

From the graph provided, we can see that the reason that the equation $x^2 - 10x + 25 = 0$ has only one solution is that the parabola $y = x^2 - 10x + 25$ touches the line $y = 0$ only once. So again, the solution is 5.

Example 10.7.12 Factor Out a Common Factor. Solve $5x^2 + 55x + 120 = 0$ by factoring.

Explanation.   Note that the terms are all divisible by 5, so we can factor that out to start.

$$5x^2 + 55x + 120 = 0$$
$$5(x^2 + 11x + 24) = 0$$
$$5(x + 8)(x + 3) = 0$$

$$x + 8 = 0 \qquad\qquad \text{or} \qquad\qquad x + 3 = 0$$
$$x = -8 \qquad\qquad \text{or} \qquad\qquad x = -3$$

The solution set is $\{-8, -3\}$.

Example 10.7.13 Factoring Using the AC Method. Solve $3x^2 - 7x + 2 = 0$ by factoring.

Explanation.   Recall that we multiply $3 \cdot 2 = 6$ and find a factor pair that multiplies to 6 and adds to -7. The factors are -6 and -1. We use the two factors to replace the middle term with $-6x$ and $-x$.

$$3x^2 - 7x + 2 = 0$$
$$3x^2 - 6x - x + 2 = 0$$
$$(3x^2 - 6x) + (-x + 2) = 0$$

$$3x(x-2) - 1(x-2) = 0$$
$$(3x-1)(x-2) = 0$$

$3x - 1 = 0$	or	$x - 2 = 0$
$3x = 1$	or	$x = 2$
$x = \dfrac{1}{3}$	or	$x = 2$

The solution set is $\left\{\frac{1}{3}, 2\right\}$.

So far the equations have been written in standard form, which is

$$ax^2 + bx + c = 0$$

If an equation is not given in standard form then we must rearrange it in order to use the Zero Product Property.

Example 10.7.14 Writing in Standard Form. Solve $x^2 - 10x = 24$ by factoring.

Explanation.   There is nothing like the Zero Product Property for the number 24. We must have a 0 on one side of the equation to solve quadratic equations using factoring.

$$x^2 - 10x = 24$$
$$x^2 - 10x - 24 = 24 - 24$$
$$x^2 - 10x - 24 = 0$$
$$(x - 12)(x + 2) = 0$$

$x - 12 = 0$	or	$x + 2 = 0$
$x = 12$	or	$x = -2$

The solution set is $\{-2, 12\}$.

Example 10.7.15 Writing in Standard Form. Solve $(x + 4)(x - 3) = 18$ by factoring.

Explanation.   Again, there is nothing like the Zero Product Property for a number like 18. We must expand the left side and subtract 18 from both sides.

$$(x + 4)(x - 3) = 18$$
$$x^2 + x - 12 = 18$$
$$x^2 + x - 12 - 18 = 18 - 18$$
$$x^2 + x - 30 = 0$$
$$(x + 6)(x - 5) = 0$$

$x + 6 = 0$	or	$x - 5 = 0$
$x = -6$	or	$x = 5$

The solution set is $\{-6, 5\}$.

Example 10.7.16 A Quadratic Equation with No Constant Term. Solve $2x^2 = 5x$ by factoring.

Explanation. It may be tempting to divide both sides of the equation by x. But x is a variable, and for all we know, maybe $x = 0$. So it is not safe to divide by x. As a general rule, never divide an equation by a variable in the solving process. Instead, we will put the equation in standard form.

$$2x^2 = 5x$$
$$2x^2 - 5x = 5x - 5x$$
$$2x^2 - 5x = 0$$

We can factor out x.

$$x(2x - 5) = 0$$

$x = 0$	or	$2x - 5 = 0$
$x = 0$	or	$2x = 5$
$x = 0$	or	$x = \dfrac{5}{2}$

The solution set is $\left\{0, \frac{5}{2}\right\}$. In general, if a quadratic equation does not have a constant term, then 0 will be one of the solutions.

While we are examining this problem, let's compare the algebraic solution to a graphical solution.

To solve this equation graphically, we first make a graph of $y = 2x^2$ and of $y = 5x$. Both of these graphs are shown in Figure 10.7.17 in an appropriate window.

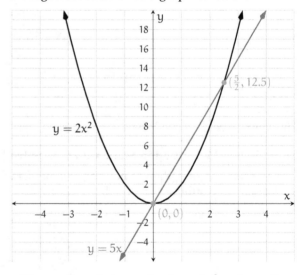

Figure 10.7.17: A graph of $y = 2x^2$ and $y = 5x$.

From the graph provided, we can see that the equation $2x^2 = 5x$ has two solutions because the graph of $y = 2x^2$ crosses the graph of $y = 5x$ twice. Those solutions, the x-values where the graphs cross, appear to be 0 and $\frac{5}{2} = 2.5$.

Example 10.7.18 Factoring a Special Polynomial. Solve $x^2 = 9$ by factoring.

Explanation. We can put the equation in standard form and use factoring. In this case, we find a difference of squares.

$$x^2 = 9$$
$$x^2 - 9 = 0$$
$$(x + 3)(x - 3) = 0$$

$x + 3 = 0$	or	$x - 3 = 0$
$x = -3$	or	$x = 3$

The solution set is $\{-3, 3\}$.

Example 10.7.19 Solving an Equation with a Higher Degree. Solve $2x^3 - 10x^2 - 28x = 0$ by factoring.

Explanation. Although this equation is not quadratic, it does factor so we can solve it by factoring.

$$2x^3 - 10x^2 - 28x = 0$$
$$2x(x^2 - 5x - 14) = 0$$
$$2x(x - 7)(x + 2) = 0$$

$2x = 0$	or	$x - 7 = 0$	or	$x + 2 = 0$
$x = 0$	or	$x = 7$	or	$x = -2$

The solution set is $\{-2, 0, 7\}$.

10.7.3 Applications

Example 10.7.20 Kicking it on Mars.
Some time in the recent past, Filip traveled to Mars for a vacation with his kids, Henrik and Karina, who wanted to kick a soccer ball around in the comparatively reduced gravity. Karina stood at point K and kicked the ball over her dad standing at point F to Henrik standing at point H. The height of the ball off the ground, h in feet, can be modeled by the equation $h = -0.01 \left(x^2 - 70x - 1800 \right)$, where x is how far to the right the ball is from Filip. Note that distances to the left of Filip will be negative.

a. Find out how high the ball was above the ground when it passed over Filip's head.

b. Find the distance from Karina to Henrik.

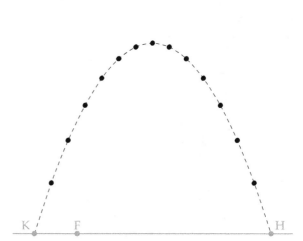

Figure 10.7.21: A Soccer Kick on Mars

Explanation.

a. The ball was neither left nor right of Filip when it went over him, so $x = 0$. Plugging that value into our equation for x,

$$h = -0.01 \left(0^2 - 70(0) - 1800\right)$$
$$= -0.01(-1800)$$
$$= 18$$

It seems that the soccer ball was 18 feet above the ground when it flew over Filip.

b. The distance from Karina to Henrik is the same as the distance from point K to point H. These are the horizontal intercepts of the graph of the given formula: $h = -0.01 \left(x^2 - 70x - 1800\right)$. To find the horizontal intercepts, set $h = 0$ and solve for x.

$$0 = -0.01 \left(x^2 - 70x - 1800\right)$$

Note that we can divide by -0.01 on both sides of the equation to simplify.

$$0 = x^2 - 70x - 1800$$
$$0 = (x - 90)(x + 20)$$

So, either:

$$x - 90 = 0 \qquad \text{or} \qquad x + 20 = 0$$
$$x = 90 \qquad \text{or} \qquad x = -20$$

Since the x-values are how far right or left the points are from Filip, Karina is standing 20 feet left of Filip and Henrik is standing 90 feet right of Filip. Thus, the two kids are 110 feet apart.

It is worth noting that if this same kick, with same initial force at the same angle, took place on Earth, the ball would have traveled less than 30 feet from Karina before landing!

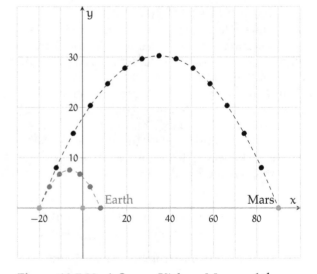

Figure 10.7.22: A Soccer Kick on Mars and the Same Kick on Earth

Example 10.7.23 An Area Application. Rajesh has a hot tub and he wants to build a deck around it. The hot tub is 7 ft by 5 ft and it is covered by a roof that is 99 ft². How wide can he make the deck so that it will be covered by the roof?

Explanation. We will define x to represent the width of the deck (in feet). Here is a diagram to help us understand the scenario.

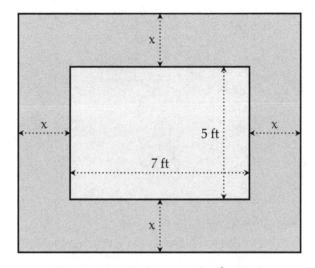

Figure 10.7.24: Diagram for the Deck

The overall length is $7 + 2x$ feet, because Rajesh is adding x feet on each side. Similarly, the overall width is $5 + 2x$ feet.

The formula for the area of a rectangle is area = length · width. Since the total area of the roof is 99 ft², we can write and solve the equation:

$$(7 + 2x)(5 + 2x) = 99$$
$$4x^2 + 24x + 35 = 99$$
$$4x^2 + 24x + 35 - 99 = 99 - 99$$
$$4x^2 + 24x - 64 = 0$$
$$4(x^2 + 6x - 16) = 0$$
$$4(x + 8)(x - 2) = 0$$

$$x + 8 = 0 \qquad \text{or} \qquad x - 2 = 0$$
$$x = -8 \qquad \text{or} \qquad x = 2$$

Since a length cannot be negative, we take $x = 2$ as the only applicable solution. Rajesh should make the deck 2 ft wide on each side to fit under the roof.

10.7.4 Reading Questions

1. If you use factoring to solve a polynomial equation, what number should be the only thing on one side of the equation?

2. When you are tyring to solve a quadratic equation where the leading coefficient is not 1m and you want to use factoring, and you have moved all terms to one side so that the other side is 0, what should you look for before trying anything else?

10.7.5 Exercises

Warmup and Review Factor the given polynomial.

1. $10y - 60$	**2.** $7y + 63$	**3.** $r^2 + 3r - 18$
4. $r^2 + 6r - 27$	**5.** $3t^2 - 4t + 1$	**6.** $2t^2 - 11t + 15$
7. $30x^2 + 12x + 42$	**8.** $27x^2 - 72x + 72$	**9.** $9y^4 - 100$
10. $100y^4 - 9$		

Solve Quadratic Equations by Factoring Solve the equation.

11. $(x-1)(x+3) = 0$	**12.** $(x+2)(x-10) = 0$	**13.** $89(x+4)(16x-5) = 0$
14. $90(x+7)(9x-5) = 0$	**15.** $x^2 + 11x + 10 = 0$	**16.** $x^2 + 9x + 8 = 0$
17. $x^2 - 3x - 28 = 0$	**18.** $x^2 - 4x - 5 = 0$	**19.** $x^2 - 11x + 28 = 0$
20. $x^2 - 13x + 42 = 0$	**21.** $x^2 + 16x = -60$	**22.** $x^2 + 15x = -56$
23. $x^2 + 4x = 21$	**24.** $x^2 - x = 90$	**25.** $x^2 - 15x = -50$
26. $x^2 - 17x = -72$	**27.** $x^2 = 5x$	**28.** $x^2 = 3x$
29. $6x^2 = 36x$	**30.** $7x^2 = -49x$	**31.** $8x^2 = 3x$
32. $9x^2 = 7x$	**33.** $x^2 - 24x + 144 = 0$	**34.** $x^2 - 2x + 1 = 0$
35. $x^2 = 4x - 4$	**36.** $x^2 = 8x - 16$	**37.** $36x^2 = -60x - 25$
38. $49x^2 = -14x - 1$	**39.** $4x^2 = -25x - 36$	**40.** $4x^2 = -37x - 40$
41. $x^2 - 36 = 0$	**42.** $x^2 - 81 = 0$	**43.** $25x^2 - 144 = 0$
44. $25x^2 - 9 = 0$	**45.** $81x^2 = 121$	**46.** $25x^2 = 16$
47. $x(x+11) = 12$	**48.** $x(x-6) = 16$	**49.** $x(4x+33) = 70$
50. $x(3x+20) = 63$	**51.** $(x-5)(x+2) = -6$	**52.** $(x-1)(x+4) = -6$
53. $(x-1)(3x+4) = 2x^2 - 2$	**54.** $(x-1)(4x+7) = 3x^2 - 9$	**55.** $x(x-12) = -3(2x+3)$
56. $x(x-4) = -(2x+1)$	**57.** $49x^2 + 84x + 36 = 0$	**58.** $9x^2 + 24x + 16 = 0$
59. $(x+3)(x^2 + 17x + 72) = 0$	**60.** $(x-9)(x^2 + 15x + 50) = 0$	**61.** $x(x^2 - 1) = 0$
62. $x(x^2 - 4) = 0$	**63.** $x^3 - 8x^2 + 15x = 0$	**64.** $x^3 - 13x^2 + 30x = 0$

Quadratic Equation Application Problems

65. Two numbers' sum is 2, and their product is −35. Find these two numbers.

These two numbers are ☐.

66. Two numbers' sum is −2, and their product is −35. Find these two numbers.

These two numbers are ☐.

67. A rectangle's base is 9 cm longer than its height. The rectangle's area is 136 cm². Find this rectangle's dimensions.

The rectangle's height is [＿＿＿＿＿].

The rectangle's base is [＿＿＿＿＿].

68. A rectangle's base is 8 cm longer than its height. The rectangle's area is 128 cm². Find this rectangle's dimensions.

The rectangle's height is [＿＿＿＿＿].

The rectangle's base is [＿＿＿＿＿].

69. A rectangle's base is 8 in shorter than three times its height. The rectangle's area is 35 in². Find this rectangle's dimensions.

The rectangle's height is [＿＿＿＿＿].

The rectangle's base is [＿＿＿＿＿].

70. A rectangle's base is 2 in shorter than five times its height. The rectangle's area is 16 in². Find this rectangle's dimensions.

The rectangle's height is [＿＿＿＿＿].

The rectangle's base is [＿＿＿＿＿].

71. There is a rectangular lot in the garden, with 9 ft in length and 3 ft in width. You plan to expand the lot by an equal length around its four sides, and make the area of the expanded rectangle 55 ft². How long should you expand the original lot in four directions?

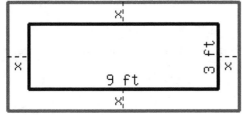

You should expand the original lot by [＿＿＿＿＿] in four directions.

72. There is a rectangular lot in the garden, with 6 ft in length and 4 ft in width. You plan to expand the lot by an equal length around its four sides, and make the area of the expanded rectangle 48 ft². How long should you expand the original lot in four directions?

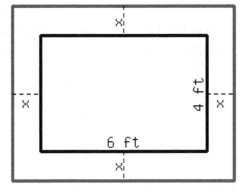

You should expand the original lot by [＿＿＿＿＿] in four directions.

Challenge

73. Give an example of a cubic equation that has three solutions: one solution is $x = 4$, the second solution is $x = -2$, and the third solution is $x = \frac{2}{3}$.

74. Solve for x in the equation $48x^{46} - 3x^{44} = 0$.

10.8 Factoring Chapter Review

10.8.1 Factoring out the GCF

In Section 10.1 we covered how to factor out the greatest common factor. Recall that the **greatest common factor** between two expressions is the largest factor that goes in evenly to both expressions.

Example 10.8.1 Finding the Greatest Common Factor. What is the greatest common factor between $12x^3y$ and $42x^2y^2$?

Explanation.   Break down each of these into its factors:

$$12x^3y = (2 \cdot 2) \cdot 3 \cdot (x \cdot x \cdot x) \cdot y \qquad\qquad 42x^2y^2 = 2 \cdot 3 \cdot 7 \cdot (x \cdot x) \cdot (y \cdot y)$$

Identify the common factors:

$$12x^3y = \overset{\downarrow}{2} \cdot 2 \cdot \overset{\downarrow}{3} \cdot \overset{\downarrow}{x} \cdot \overset{\downarrow}{x} \cdot x \cdot \overset{\downarrow}{y} \qquad\qquad 42x^2y^2 = \overset{\downarrow}{2} \cdot \overset{\downarrow}{3} \cdot 7 \cdot \overset{\downarrow}{x} \cdot \overset{\downarrow}{x} \cdot \overset{\downarrow}{y} \cdot y$$

With 2, 3, two x's and a y in common, the greatest common factor is $6x^2y$.

Example 10.8.2 What is the greatest common factor between $18c^3y^2$ and $27y^3c$?

Explanation.   Break down each into factors. You can definitely do this mentally with practice.

$$18c^3y^2 = 2 \cdot 3 \cdot 3 \cdot c \cdot c \cdot c \cdot y \cdot y \qquad\qquad 27y^3c = 3 \cdot 3 \cdot 3 \cdot y \cdot y \cdot y \cdot c$$

And take note of the common factors.

$$18c^3y^2 = 2 \cdot \overset{\downarrow}{3} \cdot \overset{\downarrow}{3} \cdot \overset{\downarrow}{c} \cdot c \cdot c \cdot \overset{\downarrow}{y} \cdot \overset{\downarrow}{y} \qquad\qquad 27y^3c = \overset{\downarrow}{3} \cdot \overset{\downarrow}{3} \cdot 3 \cdot \overset{\downarrow}{y} \cdot \overset{\downarrow}{y} \cdot y \cdot c$$

And so the GCF is $9y^2c$

Example 10.8.3 Factoring out the Greatest Common Factor.   Factor out the GCF from the expression $32mn^2 - 24m^2n - 12mn$.

Explanation.   To factor out the GCF from the expression $32mn^2 - 24m^2n - 12mn$, first note that the GCF to all three terms is $4mn$. Begin by writing that in front of a blank pair of parentheses and fill in the missing pieces.

$$32mn^2 - 24m^2n - 12mn = 4mn(\quad - \quad - \quad)$$
$$= 4mn(8n - 6m - 3)$$

Example 10.8.4 Factor out the GCF from the expression $14x^3 - 35x^2$.

Explanation.   First note that the GCF of the terms in $14x^3 - 35x^2$ is $7x^2$. Factoring this out, we have:

$$14x^3 - 35x^2 = 7x^2 (\quad - \quad)$$
$$= 7x^2 (2x - 5)$$

Example 10.8.5 Factor out the GCF from the expression $36m^3n^2 - 18m^2n^5 + 24mn^3$.

Explanation. First note that the GCF of the terms in $36m^3n^2 - 18m^2n^5 + 24mn^3$ is $6mn^2$. Factoring this out, we have:

$$36m^3n^2 - 18m^2n^5 + 24mn^3 = 6mn^2 \left(\quad - \quad + \quad \right)$$
$$= 6mn^2 \left(6m^2 - 3mn^3 + 4n \right)$$

Example 10.8.6 Factor out the GCF from the expression $42f^3w^2 - 8w^2 + 9f^3$.

Explanation. First note that the GCF of the terms in $42f^3w^2 - 8w^2 + 9f^3$ is 1, so we call the expression prime. The only way to factor the GCF out of this expression is:

$$42f^3w^2 - 8w^2 + 9f^3 = 1 \left(42f^3w^2 - 8w^2 + 9f^3 \right)$$

10.8.2 Factoring by Grouping

In Section 10.2 we covered how to factor by grouping. Recall that factoring using grouping is used on four-term polynomials, and also later in the AC method in Section 10.4. Begin by grouping two pairs of terms and factoring out their respective GCF; if all is well, we should be left with two matching pieces in parentheses that can be factored out in their own right.

Example 10.8.7 Factor the expression $2x^3 + 5x^2 + 6x + 15$ using grouping.

Explanation.

$$2x^3 + 5x^2 + 6x + 15 = \left(2x^3 + 5x^2 \right) + (6x + 15)$$
$$= x^2 (2x + 5) + 3 (2x + 5)$$
$$= \left(x^2 + 3 \right) (2x + 5)$$

Example 10.8.8 Factor the expression $2xy - 3x - 8y + 12$ using grouping.

Explanation.

$$2xy - 3x + 8y - 12 = (2xy - 3x) + (-8y + 12)$$
$$= x (2y - 3) - 4 (2y - 3)$$
$$= (x - 4)(2y - 3)$$

Example 10.8.9 Factor the expression $xy - 2 - 2x + y$ using grouping.

Explanation. This is a special example because if we try to follow the algorithm without considering the bigger context, we will fail:

$$xy - 2 - 2x + y = (xy - 2) + (-2x + y)$$

Note that there is no common factor in either grouping, besides 1, but the groupings themselves don't match. We should now recognize that whatever we are doing isn't working and try something else. It turns out that this polynomial *isn't* prime; all we need to do is rearrange the polynomial into standard form where the degrees decrease from left to right before grouping.

$$xy - 2 - 2x + y = xy - 2x + y - 2$$
$$= (xy - 2x) + (y - 2)$$
$$= x (y - 2) + 1 (y - 2)$$

$$= (x+1)(y-2)$$

Example 10.8.10 Factor the expression $15m^2 - 3m - 10mn + 2n$ using grouping.

Explanation.

$$\begin{aligned}
15m^2 - 3m - 10mn + 2n &= \left(15m^2 - 3m\right) + \left(-10mn + 2n\right) \\
&= 3m\left(5m - 1\right) - 2n\left(5m - 1\right) \\
&= (3m - 2n)(5m - 1)
\end{aligned}$$

10.8.3 Factoring Trinomials with Leading Coefficient 1

In Section 10.3 we covered factoring expressions that look like $x^2 + bx + c$. The trick was to look for two numbers whose product was c and whose sum was b. Always remember to look for a greatest common factor first, before looking for factor pairs.

Example 10.8.11 Answer the questions to practice for the factor pairs method.

   a. What two numbers multiply to be 6 and add to be 5?

   b. What two numbers multiply to be −6 and add to be 5?

   c. What two numbers multiply to be −6 and add to be −1?

   d. What two numbers multiply to be 24 and add to be −10?

   e. What two numbers multiply to be −24 and add to be 2?

   f. What two numbers multiply to be −24 and add to be −5?

   g. What two numbers multiply to be 420 and add to be 44?

   h. What two numbers multiply to be −420 and add to be −23?

   i. What two numbers multiply to be 420 and add to be −41?

Explanation.

   a. What two numbers multiply to be 6 and add to be 5? The numbers are 2 and 3.

   b. What two numbers multiply to be −6 and add to be 5? The numbers are 6 and −1.

   c. What two numbers multiply to be −6 and add to be −1? The numbers are −3 and 2.

   d. What two numbers multiply to be 24 and add to be −10? The numbers are −6 and −4.

   e. What two numbers multiply to be −24 and add to be 2? The numbers are 6 and −4.

   f. What two numbers multiply to be −24 and add to be −5? The numbers are −8 and 3.

   g. What two numbers multiply to be 420 and add to be 44? The numbers are 30 and 14.

   h. What two numbers multiply to be −420 and add to be −23? The numbers are −35 and 12.

   i. What two numbers multiply to be 420 and add to be −41? The numbers are −20 and −21.

Note that for parts g–i, the factors of 420 are important. Below is a table of factors of 420 which will make it much clearer how the answers were found. To generate a table like this, we start with 1, and we work our way up the factors of 420.

Factor Pair	Factor Pair	Factor Pair
$1 \cdot 420$	$5 \cdot 84$	$12 \cdot 35$
$2 \cdot 210$	$6 \cdot 70$	$14 \cdot 30$
$3 \cdot 140$	$7 \cdot 60$	$15 \cdot 28$
$4 \cdot 105$	$10 \cdot 42$	$20 \cdot 21$

It is now much easier to see how to find the numbers in question. For example, to find two numbers that multiply to be -420 and add to be -23, look in the table for two factors that are 23 apart and assign a negative sign appropriately. As we found earlier, the numbers that are 23 apart are 12 and 35, and making the larger one negative, we have our answer: 12 and -35.

Example 10.8.12 Factor the expression $x^2 - 3x - 28$

Explanation. To factor the expression $x^2 - 3x - 28$, think of two numbers that multiply to be -28 and add to be -3. In the Section 10.3, we created a table of all possibilities of factors, like the one shown, to be sure that we never missed the right numbers; however, we encourage you to try this mentally for most problems.

Factor Pair	Sum of the Pair	Factor Pair	Sum of the Pair
$-1 \cdot 28$	27	$1 \cdot (-28)$	-27
$-2 \cdot 14$	12	$2 \cdot (-14)$	-12
$-4 \cdot 7$	3 (close; wrong sign)	$4 \cdot (-7)$	-3 (what we wanted)

Since the two numbers in question are 4 and -7 that means that

$$x^2 - 3x - 28 = (x + 4)(x - 7)$$

Remember that you can always multiply out your factored expression to verify that you have the correct answer. We will use the FOIL expansion.

$$(x + 4)(x - 7) = x^2 - 7x + 4x - 28$$
$$\overset{\checkmark}{=} x^2 - 3x - 28$$

Example 10.8.13 Factoring in Stages. Completely factor the expression $4x^3 - 4x^2 - 120x$.

Explanation. Remember that some expressions require more than one step to completely factor. To factor $4x^3 - 4x^2 - 120x$, first, always look for any GCF; after that is done, consider other options. Since the GCF is $4x$, we have that

$$4x^3 - 4x^2 - 120x = 4x\left(x^2 - x - 30\right).$$

Now the factor inside parentheses might factor further. The key here is to consider what two numbers multiply to be -30 and add to be -1. In this case, the answer is -6 and 5. So, to completely write the factorization, we have:

$$4x^3 - 4x^2 - 120x = 4x\left(x^2 - x - 30\right)$$
$$= 4x(x - 6)(x + 5)$$

Example 10.8.14 Factoring Expressions with Higher Powers. Completely factor the expression $p^{10} - 6p^5 - 72$.

Explanation. If we have a trinomial with an even exponent on the leading term, and the middle term has an exponent that is half the leading term exponent, we can still use the factor pairs method. To factor $p^{10} - 6p^5 - 72$, we note that the middle term exponent 5 is half of the leading term exponent 10, and that two numbers that multiply to be -72 and add to be -6 are -12 and 6. So the factorization of the expression is

$$p^{10} - 6p^5 - 72 = \left(p^5 - 12\right)\left(p^5 + 6\right)$$

Example 10.8.15 Factoring Expressions with Two Variables. Completely factor the expression $x^2 - 3xy - 70y^2$.

Explanation. If an expression has two variables, like $x^2 - 3xy - 70y^2$, we pretend for a moment that the expression is $x^2 - 3x - 70$. To factor this expression we ask ourselves "what two numbers multiply to be -70 and add to be -3?" The two numbers in question are 7 and -10. So $x^2 - 3x - 70$ factors as $(x + 7)(x - 10)$.

To go back to the original problem now, make the two numbers $7y$ and $-10y$. So, the full factorization is

$$x^2 - 3xy - 70y^2 = (x + 7y)(x - 10y)$$

With problems like this, it is important to verify the your answer to be sure that all of the variables ended up where they were supposed to. So, to verify, FOIL your answer.

$$(x + 7y)(x - 10y) = x^2 - 10xy + 7yx - 70y^2$$
$$= x^2 - 10xy + 7xy - 70y^2$$
$$\overset{\checkmark}{=} x^2 - 3xy - 70y^2$$

Example 10.8.16 Completely factor the expressions.

a. $x^2 - 11x + 30$ c. $g^2 - 3g - 24$ e. $z^8 + 2z^4 - 63$

b. $-s^2 + 3s + 28$ d. $w^2 - wr - 30r^2$

Explanation.

a. $x^2 - 11x + 30 = (x - 6)(x - 5)$

b. $-s^2 + 3s + 28 = -\left(s^2 - 3s - 28\right)$
$$= -(s - 7)(s + 4)$$

c. $g^2 - 3g - 24$ is prime. No two integers multiply to be -24 and add to be -3.

d. $w^2 - wr - 30r^2 = (w - 6r)(w + 5r)$

e. $z^8 + 2z^4 - 63 = \left(z^4 - 7\right)\left(z^4 + 9\right)$

10.8.4 Factoring Trinomials with Non-Trivial Leading Coefficient

In Section 10.4 we covered factoring trinomials of the form $ax^2 + bx + c$ when $a \neq 1$ using the AC method.

Example 10.8.17 Using the AC Method. Completely factor the expression $9x^2 - 6x - 8$.

Explanation. To factor the expression $9x^2 - 6x - 8$, we first find ac:

1. $9 \cdot (-8) = -72$.

2. Examine factor pairs that multiply to -72, looking for a pair that sums to -6:

Factor Pair	Sum of the Pair		Factor Pair	Sum of the Pair
$1 \cdot -72$	-71		$-1 \cdot 72$	(no need to go this far)
$2 \cdot -36$	-34		$-2 \cdot 36$	(no need to go this far)
$3 \cdot -24$	-21		$-3 \cdot 24$	(no need to go this far)
$4 \cdot -18$	-14		$-4 \cdot 18$	(no need to go this far)
$6 \cdot -12$	-6		$-6 \cdot 12$	(no need to go this far)
$8 \cdot -9$	(no need to go this far)		$-8 \cdot 9$	(no need to go this far)

3. Intentionally break up the -6 as $6 + (-12)$ and then factor using grouping:

$$
\begin{aligned}
9x^2 \overbrace{-6x} - 8 = 9x^2 \overbrace{+ 6x - 12x} - 8 \\
= \left(9x^2 + 6x\right) + (-12x - 8) \\
= 3x(3x + 2) - 4(3x + 2) \\
= (3x + 2)(3x - 4)
\end{aligned}
$$

Example 10.8.18 Completely factor the expression $3x^2 + 5x - 6$.

Explanation. First note that there is no GCF besides 1 and that $ac = -18$. To look for two factors of -18 that add up to 5, we will make a factor pair table.

Factor Pair	Sum of the Pair		Factor Pair	Sum of the Pair
$1 \cdot -18$	-17		$-1 \cdot 18$	17
$2 \cdot -9$	-7		$-2 \cdot 9$	7
$3 \cdot -6$	-3		$-3 \cdot 6$	3

Since none of the factor pairs of -18 sum to 5, we must conclude that this trinomial is prime. The only way to factor it is $3x^2 + 5x - 6 = 1\left(3x^2 + 5x - 6\right)$.

Example 10.8.19 Completely factor the expression $3y^2 + 20y - 63$.

Explanation. First note that $ac = -189$. Looking for two factors of -189 that add up to 20, we find 27 and -7. Breaking up the $+20$ into $+27 - 7$, we can factor using grouping.

$$
\begin{aligned}
3y^2 \overbrace{+ 20y} - 63 = 3y^2 \overbrace{+ 27y - 7y} - 63 \\
= \left(3y^2 + 27y\right) + (-7y - 63) \\
= 3y(y + 9) - 7(y + 9) \\
= (y + 9)(3y - 7)
\end{aligned}
$$

Example 10.8.20 Factoring in Stages with the AC Method. Completely factor the expression $8y^3 + 54y^2 + 36y$.

Explanation. Recall that some trinomials need to be factored in stages: the first stage is always to factor out the GCF. To factor $8y^3 + 54y^2 + 36y$, first note that the GCF of the three terms in the expression is $2y$. Then apply the AC method:

$$
8y^3 + 54y^2 + 36y = 2y \left(4y^2 + 27y + 18\right)
$$

Now we find $ac = 4 \cdot 18 = 72$. What two factors of 72 add up to 27? After checking a few numbers, we find that 3 and 24 fit the requirements. So:

$$= 2y \left(4y^2 \overbrace{+27y} +18 \right)$$
$$= 2y \left(4y^2 \overbrace{+3y + 24y} +18 \right)$$
$$= 2y \left((4y^2 + 3y) + (24y + 18) \right)$$
$$= 2y \left(y(4y + 3) + 6(4y + 3) \right)$$
$$= 2y(4y + 3)(y + 6)$$

Example 10.8.21 Completely factor the expression $18x^3 + 26x^2 + 4x$.

Explanation. First note that there is a GCF of $2x$ which should be factored out first. Doing this leaves us with $18x^3 + 26x^2 + 8x = 2x \left(9x^2 + 13x + 4 \right)$. Now we apply the AC method on the factor in the parentheses. So, $ac = 36$, and we must find two factors of 36 that sum to be 13. These two factors are 9 and 4. Now we can use grouping.

$$18x^3 + 26x^2 + 8x = 2x \left(9x^2 \overbrace{+ 13x} +4 \right)$$
$$= 2x \left(9x^2 \overbrace{+ 9x + 4x} +4 \right)$$
$$= 2x \left((9x^2 + 9x) + (4x + 4) \right)$$
$$= 2x \left(9x(x + 1) + 4(x + 1) \right)$$
$$= 2x(x + 1)(9x + 4)$$

10.8.5 Factoring Special Forms

In Section 10.5 we covered how to factor binomials and trinomials using formulas. Using these formulas, when appropriate, often drastically increased the speed of factoring. Below is a summary of the formulas covered. For each, consider that A and B could be any algebraic expressions.

Difference of Squares $A^2 - B^2 = (A + B)(A - B)$

Perfect Square Sum $A^2 + 2AB + B^2 = (A + B)^2$

Perfect Square Difference $A^2 - 2AB + B^2 = (A + B)^2$

Example 10.8.22 Factoring the Form $A^2 - 2AB + B^2$. Completely factor the expression $16y^2 - 24y + 9$.

Explanation. To factor $16y^2 - 24y + 9$ we notice that the expression might be of the form $A^2 - 2AB + B^2$. To find A and B, we mentally take the square root of both the first and last terms of the original expression. The square root of $16y^2$ is $4y$ since $(4y)^2 = 4^2y^2 = 16y^2$. The square root of 9 is 3. So, we conclude that $A = 4y$ and $B = 3$. Recall that we now need to check that the $24y$ matches our $2AB$. Using our values for A and B, we indeed see that $2AB = -2(4y)(3) = 24y$. So, we conclude that

$$16y^2 - 24y + 9 = (4y - 3)^2.$$

Example 10.8.23 Mixed Special Forms Factoring.

    a. Completely factor the expression $9w^2 + 12w + 4$.

    b. Completely factor the expression $4q^2 - 81$.

    c. Completely factor the expression $9p^2 + 25$.

    d. Completely factor the expression $121b^2 - 36$.

    e. Completely factor the expression $25u^2 - 70u + 49$.

Explanation. The first step for each problem is to try to fit the expression to one of the special factoring forms.

    a. To factor $9w^2 + 12w + 4$ we notice that the expression might be of the form $A^2 + 2AB + B^2$ where $A = 3w$ and $B = 2$. With this formula we need to check the value of $2AB$ which in this case is $2AB = 2(3w)(2) = 12w$. Since the value of $2AB$ is correct, the expression must factor as

$$9w^2 + 12w + 4 = (3w + 2)^2$$

    b. To factor $4q^2 - 81$ we notice that the expression is of the form $A^2 - B^2$ where $A = 2q$ and $B = 9$. Thus, the expression must factor as
$$4q^2 - 81 = (2q - 9)(2q + 9)$$

    c. To factor $9p^2 + 25$ we notice that the expression is of the form $A^2 + B^2$. This is called a sum of squares. If you recall from the section, the sum of squares is always prime. So $9p^2 + 25$ is prime.

    d. To completely factor the expression $121b^2 - 36$ first note that the expression is of the form $A^2 - B^2$ where $A = 11b$ and $B = 6$. So, the expression factors as

$$121b^2 - 36 = (11b + 6)(11b - 6).$$

    e. To completely factor the expression $25u^2 - 70u + 49$ first note that the expression might be of the form $A^2 - 2AB + B^2$ where $A = 5u$ and $B = 7$. Now, we check that $2AB$ matches the middle term: $2AB = 2(5u)(7) = 70u$. So, the expression factors as

$$25u^2 - 70u + 49 = (5u - 7)^2.$$

10.8.6 Factoring Strategies

In Section 10.6 we covered a factoring decision tree to help us decide what methods to try when factoring a given expression. Remember to always factor out the GCF first.

Example 10.8.24 Factor the expressions using an effective method.

    a. $24xy - 20x - 18y + 15$.   c. $8u^2 + 14u - 9$.

    b. $12t^2 + 36t + 27$.   d. $18c^2 - 98p^2$.

Explanation.

    a. To factor the expression $24xy - 20x - 18y + 15$, we first look for a GCF. Since the GCF is 1, we can move further on the flowchart. Since this is a four-term polynomial, we will try grouping.

$$24xy - 20x - 18y + 15 = 24xy + (-20x) + (-18y) + 15$$
$$= (24xy - 20x) + (-18y + 15)$$
$$= 4x(6y - 5) + (-3)(6y - 5)$$
$$= 4x\overbrace{(6x - 5)} - 3\overbrace{(6x - 5)}$$
$$= (6x - 5)(4x - 3)$$

b. To factor the expression $12t^2 + 36t + 27$, we first look for a GCF. Since the GCF is 3, first we will factor that out.

$$12t^2 + 36t + 27 = 3\left(4t^2 + 12t + 9\right)$$

Next, we can note that the first and last terms are perfect squares where $A^2 = 4t^2$ and $B = 9$; so $A = 2t$ and $B = 3$. To check the middle term, $2AB = 12t$. So the expression factors as a perfect square.

$$12t^2 + 36t + 27 = 3\left(4t^2 + 12t + 9\right)$$
$$= 3(2t + 3)^2$$

c. To factor the expression $8u^2 + 14u - 9$, we first look for a GCF. Since the GCF is 1, we can move further on the flowchart. Since the expression is a trinomial with leading coefficient other than 1, we should try the AC method. Note that $AC = -72$ and factor pairs of -72 that add up to 14 are 18 and -4.

$$8u^2 + 14u - 9 = 8u^2 + 18u - 4u - 9$$
$$= \left(8u^2 + 18\right) + (-4u - 9)$$
$$= 2u(4u + 9) - 1(4u + 9)$$
$$= (2u - 1)(4u + 9)$$

d. To factor the expression $18c^2 - 98p^2$, we first look for a GCF. Since the GCF is 2, first we will factor that out.

$$18c^2 - 98p^2 = 2\left(9c^2 - 49p^2\right)$$

Now we notice that we have a binomial where both the first and second terms can be written as squares: $9c^2 = (3c)^2$ and $49p^2 = (7p)^2$.

$$18c^2 - 98p^2 = 2\left(9c^2 - 49p^2\right)$$
$$= 2(3c - 7p)(3c + 7p)$$

10.8.7 Solving Quadratic Equations by Factoring

In Section 10.7 we covered the zero product property and learned an algorithm for solving quadratic equations by factoring.

Example 10.8.25 Solving Using Factoring. Solve the quadratic equations using factoring.

a. $x^2 - 2x - 15 = 0$ c. $6x^2 + x - 12 = 0$ e. $x^3 - 64x = 0$

b. $4x^2 - 40x = -96$ d. $(x - 3)(x + 2) = 14$

Explanation.

a. Use factor pairs.

$$x^2 - 2x - 15 = 0$$
$$(x - 5)(x + 3) = 0$$

$x - 5 = 0$	or	$x + 3 = 0$
$x = 5$	or	$x = -3$

So the solution set is $\{5, -3\}$.

b. Start by putting the equation in standard form and factoring out the greatest common factor.

$$4x^2 - 40x = -96$$
$$4x^2 - 40x + 96 = 0$$
$$4\left(x^2 - 10x + 24\right) = 0$$
$$4(x - 6)(x - 4) = 0$$

$x - 6 = 0$	or	$x - 4 = 0$
$x = 6$	or	$x = 4$

So the solution set is $\{4, 6\}$.

c. Use the AC method.

$$6x^2 + x - 12 = 0$$

Note that $a \cdot c = -72$ and that $9 \cdot -8 = -72$ and $9 - 8 = 1$

$$6x^2 + 9x - 8x - 12 = 0$$
$$\left(6x^2 + 9x\right) + (-8x - 12) = 0$$
$$3x\left(2x + 3\right) - 4\left(2x + 3\right) = 0$$
$$\left(2x + 3\right)\left(3x - 4\right) = 0$$

$2x + 3 = 0$	or	$3x - 4 = 0$
$x = -\dfrac{3}{2}$	or	$x = \dfrac{4}{3}$

So the solution set is $\left\{-\frac{3}{2}, \frac{4}{3}\right\}$.

d. Start by putting the equation in standard form.

$$(x - 3)(x + 2) = 14$$
$$x^2 - x - 6 = 14$$
$$x^2 - x - 20 = 0$$
$$(x - 5)(x + 4) = 0$$

$x - 5 = 0$ or $x + 4 = 0$

$x = 5$ or $x = -4$

So the solution set is $\{5, -4\}$.

e. Even though this equation has a power higher than 2, we can still find all of its solutions by following the algorithm. Start by factoring out the greatest common factor.

$$x^3 - 64x = 0$$
$$x\left(x^2 - 64\right) = 0$$
$$x(x - 8)(x + 8) = 0$$

$x = 0$ or $x - 8 = 0$ or $x + 8 = 0$

$x = 0$ or $x = 8$ or $x = -8$

So the solution set is $\{0, 8, -8\}$.

10.8.8 Exercises

Factoring out the Common Factor

1. Find the greatest common factor of the following terms.
   $3r$ and $15r^2$

2. Find the greatest common factor of the following terms.
   $9r$ and $72r^2$

3. Find the greatest common factor of the following terms.
   $6t^{11}$ and $-60t^{10}$

4. Find the greatest common factor of the following terms.
   $3t^{16}$ and $-12t^{15}$

5. Find the greatest common factor of the following terms.
   $6x^{20}y^8, -18x^{17}y^9,$
   $12x^{12}y^{10}$

6. Find the greatest common factor of the following terms.
   $3x^{20}y^4, -21x^{18}y^9,$
   $15x^{17}y^{11}$

7. Factor the given polynomial.
   $90x^2 - 40x + 10$

8. Factor the given polynomial.
   $80y^2 - 60y + 30$

9. Factor the given polynomial.
   $28y^2 - 27$

10. Factor the given polynomial.
    $4r^2 - 3$

11. Factor the given polynomial.
    $r(r - 8) + 9(r - 8)$

12. Factor the given polynomial.
    $t(t + 5) + 6(t + 5)$

Factoring by Grouping Factor the given polynomial.

13. $t^2 - 2t + 4t - 8$ **14.** $x^2 + 8x + 10x + 80$ **15.** $x^3 - 5x^2 + 8x - 40$

16. $x^3 + 10x^2 + 6x + 60$ **17.** $xy + 5x - 10y - 50$ **18.** $xy - 6x + 5y - 30$

19. $7x^2 + 63xy + 8xy + 72y^2$ **20.** $8x^2 - 16xy + 5xy - 10y^2$

Factoring Trinomials with Leading Coefficient One Factor the given polynomial.

21. $t^2 + 10t + 21$ **22.** $t^2 + 10t + 9$ **23.** $x^2 - x - 30$

24. $x^2 - 5x - 24$ **25.** $x^2 + x + 4$ **26.** $y^2 + 5$

27. $y^2 - 4y + 4$ **28.** $r^2 - 20r + 100$ **29.** $6r^2 - 24r + 18$

30. $6t^2 - 18t + 12$ **31.** $-t^2 - 5t + 24$ **32.** $-x^2 + 4x + 5$

33. $x^2 - xr - 6r^2$ **34.** $x^2 + 5xr - 6r^2$ **35.** $y^2 - 8yx + 15x^2$

36. $y^2 - 7yx + 10x^2$

Factoring Trinomials with a Nontrivial Leading Coefficient Factor the given polynomial.

37. $3r^2 + 23r - 8$ **38.** $3r^2 + 5r - 28$ **39.** $3t^2 + 6t + 7$

40. $3t^2 + t + 6$ **41.** $4x^2 - 8x + 3$ **42.** $6x^2 - 17x + 5$

43. $18x^2 - 30x + 12$ **44.** $8y^2 - 12y + 4$ **45.** $4y^9 - 22y^8 + 24y^7$

46. $4r^{10} - 22r^9 + 18r^8$ **47.** $6r^2x^2 - 21rx - 27$ **48.** $20t^2r^2 + 10tr - 30$

49. $6x^2 + 20xy + 16y^2$ **50.** $10x^2 + 35xy + 15y^2$

Factoring Special Polynomials Factor the given polynomial.

51. $x^2 - 100$ **52.** $x^2 - 36$ **53.** $4y^2 - 9$

54. $100y^2 - 121$ **55.** $r^{14} - 36$ **56.** $r^6 - 4$

57. $100t^2 - 20t + 1$ **58.** $36t^2 - 12t + 1$ **59.** $49t^2 - 56tx + 16x^2$

60. $121x^2 - 88xr + 16r^2$ **61.** $16x^4 - 1$ **62.** $81y^4 - 16$

63. $4y^3 - 100y$ **64.** $8r^3 - 128r$ **65.** $6r^3t^4 - 150rt^2$

66. $3t^3r^3 - 108tr$ **67.** $48 - 3t^2$ **68.** $3 - 3t^2$

69. $x^2 + 49$ **70.** $x^2 + 9$

Factoring Strategies Which factoring techniques/tools will be useful for factoring the polynomial below? Check all that apply.

☐ Factoring out a GCF   ☐ Factoring by grouping   ☐ Finding two numbers that multiply to the constant term and sum to the linear coefficient   ☐ The AC Method   ☐ Difference of Squares ☐ Difference of Cubes   ☐ Sum of Cubes   ☐ Perfect Square Trinomial   ☐ None of the above

71. $49a^2 - 70ap + 25p^2$ **72.** $9c^2 - 81cA + 72A^2$

Factor the given polynomial.

73. $6r - 8r^2 + 6r^3$ **74.** $7xy + 7y$

75. $4t^2 - 16ty + 7y^2$ **76.** $t^2 - 7t - 18$

77. $4t^2 + 36tr + 81r^2$ **78.** $x^2y^2 + 4x^2yz - 5x^2z^2$

79. $15x^2 + 26xt + 7t^2$ **80.** $y^2 - 11y + 24$

81. $16y^4 - 81$ **82.** $2r^3 - 2r$

Solving Quadratic Equations by Factoring Solve the equation.

83. $x^2 - 4x - 21 = 0$ **84.** $x^2 + 2x - 24 = 0$ **85.** $x^2 + 19x = -90$

86. $x^2 + 17x = -70$ **87.** $x^2 = 8x$ **88.** $x^2 = 6x$

89. $x^2 - 8x + 16 = 0$ **90.** $x^2 - 12x + 36 = 0$ **91.** $4x^2 = -27x - 44$

92. $4x^2 = -23x - 28$

93. A rectangle's base is 1 in shorter than twice its height. The rectangle's area is 45 in^2. Find this rectangle's dimensions.

     The rectangle's height is ⬚.

     The rectangle's base is ⬚.

94. A rectangle's base is 1 in shorter than five times its height. The rectangle's area is 120 in^2. Find this rectangle's dimensions.

     The rectangle's height is ⬚.

     The rectangle's base is ⬚.

Chapter 11

Functions

11.1 Function Basics

In this section, we will introduce a topic that will be essential for continued mathematical learning: functions. Functions should be thought of as machines that turn one number into another number, much like a cash register can turn a number of pounds of fruit into a price.

11.1.1 Informal Definition of a Function

We are familiar with the $\sqrt{}$ symbol. This symbol is used to turn numbers into their square roots. Sometimes it's simple to do this on paper or in our heads, and sometimes it helps to have a calculator. We can see some calculations in Figure 11.1.2.

$$\sqrt{9} = 3$$
$$\sqrt{1/4} = 1/2$$
$$\sqrt{2} \approx 1.41$$

Figure 11.1.2: Values of $\sqrt{x}$

The $\sqrt{}$ symbol represents a *process*; it's a way for us to turn numbers into other numbers. This idea of having a process for turning numbers into other numbers is the fundamental topic of this chapter.

Definition 11.1.3 Function (Informal Definition). A **function** is a process for turning numbers into (potentially) different numbers. The process must be *consistent*, in that whenever you apply it to some particular number, you always get the same result. ◇

Section 11.5 covers a more technical definition for functions, and covers topics that are more appropriate when using that definition. Definition 11.1.3 is so broad that you probably use functions all the time.

Example 11.1.4 In each of these examples, some process is used for turning one number into another.

- If you convert a person's birth year into their age, you are using a function.

- If you look up the Kelly Blue Book value of a Honda Odyssey based on how old it is, you are using a function.

- If you use the expected guest count for a party to determine how many pizzas you should order, you are using a function.

The $\sqrt{\ }$ function is consistent; for example, every time you evaluate $\sqrt{9}$, you always get 3. One interesting fact is that $\sqrt{\ }$ is not found on most keyboards, and yet computers can still find square roots. Computer technicians write sqrt( ) when they want to compute a square root, as we see in Figure 11.1.5.

sqrt(9)	= 3
sqrt(1/4)	= 1/2
sqrt(2)	≈ 1.41

Figure 11.1.5: Values of sqrt(x)

The parentheses in sqrt( ) are very important. To see why, try to put yourself in the "mind" of a computer. The computer will recognize sqrt and know that it needs to compute a square root but without parentheses it will think that it needs to compute sqrt4 and then put a 9 on the end, which would produce a final result of 29. This is probably not what was intended. And so the purpose of the parentheses in sqrt(49) is to be deliberately clear.

Functions have their own names. We've seen a function named sqrt, but any name you can imagine is allowable. In the sciences, it is common to name functions with whole words, like weight or health_index. In math, we often abbreviate such function names to w or h. And of course, since the word "function" itself starts with "f," we will often name a function f.

Warning 11.1.6 Notation Ambiguity. In some contexts, the symbol t might represent a variable (a number that is represented by a letter) and in other contexts, t might represent a function (a process for changing numbers into other numbers). By staying conscious of the *context* of an investigation, we avoid confusion.

Next we need to discuss how we go about using a function's name.

Definition 11.1.7 Function Notation. The standard notation for referring to functions involves giving the function itself a name, and then writing:

$$\underset{\text{function}}{\overset{\text{name}}{\text{of}}} \left(\text{input} \right)$$

◊

Example 11.1.8 $f(13)$ is pronounced "f of 13." The word "of" is very important, because it reminds us that f is a process and we are about to apply that process to the input value 13. So f is the function, 13 is the input, and $f(13)$ is the output we'd get from using 13 as input.

$f(x)$ is pronounced "f of x." This is just like the previous example, except that the input is not any specific number. The value of x could be 13 or any other number. Whatever x's value, $f(x)$ means the corresponding output from the function f.

BudgetDeficit(2017) is pronounced "BudgetDeficit of 2017." This is probably about a function that takes a year as input, and gives that year's federal budget deficit as output. The process here of changing a year into a dollar amount might not involve any mathematical formula, but rather looking up information from the Congressional Budget Office's website.

Note 11.1.9 While a function has a name like f, and the input to that function often has a variable name like x, the expression $f(x)$ represents the output of the function. To be clear, $f(x)$ is *not* a function. Rather, f is a function, and $f(x)$ its output when the number x was used as input.

Checkpoint 11.1.10 Suppose you see the sentence, "If x is the number of software licenses you buy for your office staff, then $c(x)$ is the total cost of the licenses."

a. In the function notation, what represents input? [   ].

b. What is the function here? [   ] .

c. What represents output? [   ] .

Explanation. The input is x, the function is c, and c(x) is the output from c when the input is x.

Warning 11.1.11 More Notation Ambiguity. As mentioned in Warning 11.1.6, we need to remain conscious of the context of any symbol we are using. Consider the expression a(b). This could easily mean the output of a function a with input b. It could also mean that two numbers a and b need to be multiplied. It all depends on the context in which these symbols are being used.

Sometimes it's helpful to think of a function as a machine, as in Figure 11.1.12. A *function* has the capacity to take in all kinds of different numbers into it's hopper (feeding tray) as inputs and transform them into their outputs.

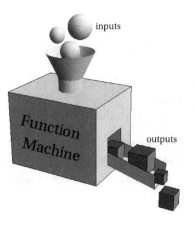

Figure 11.1.12: Imagining a function as a machine. (Image by Duane Nykamp using Mathematica.)

11.1.2 Tables and Graphs

Since functions are potentially complicated, we want ways to understand them more easily. Two basic tools for understanding a function better are tables and graphs.

Example 11.1.13 A Table for the Budget Deficit Function. Consider the function BudgetDeficit, that takes a year as its input and outputs the US federal budget deficit for that year. For example, the Congressional Budget Office's website tells us that BudgetDeficit(2009) is $1.41 trillion. If we'd like to understand this function better, we might make a table of all the inputs and outputs we can find. Using the CBO's website (www.cbo.gov/topics/budget), we can put together Table 11.1.14.

input x (year)	output BudgetDeficit(x) ($trillion)
2007	0.16
2008	0.46
2009	1.4
2010	1.3
2011	1.3
2012	1.1
2013	0.68
2014	0.48
2015	0.44
2016	0.59
2017	0.67
2018	0.78

Table 11.1.14: The Federal Budget Deficit

How is this table helpful? There are things about the function that we can see now by looking at the numbers in this table.

- We can see that the budget deficit had a spike between 2008 and 2009.

- And it fell again between 2012 and 2013.

- It appears to stay roughly steady for several years at a time, with occasional big jumps or drops.

These observations help us understand the function BudgetDeficit a little better.

Checkpoint 11.1.15 According to Table 11.1.14, what is the value of BudgetDeficit(2015)?

Explanation. Table 11.1.14 shows that when the input is 2015, the output is 0.44. So BudgetDeficit(2015) = 0.44. In context, that means that in 2015 the budget deficit was $0.44 trillion.

Example 11.1.16 A Table for the Square Root Function. Let's return to our example of the function sqrt. Tabulating some inputs and outputs reveals Figure 11.1.17.

input, x	output, sqrt(x)
0	0
1	1
2	≈ 1.41
3	≈ 1.73
4	2
5	≈ 2.24
6	≈ 2.45
7	≈ 2.65
8	≈ 2.83
9	3

Figure 11.1.17

How is this table helpful? Here are some observations that we can make now.

- We can see that when input numbers increase, so do output numbers.

- We can see even though outputs are increasing, they increase by less and less with each step forward in x.

These observations help us understand sqrt a little better. For instance, based on these observations which do you think is larger: the difference between sqrt(23) and sqrt(24), or the difference between sqrt(85) and sqrt(86)?

Checkpoint 11.1.18 According to Figure 11.1.17, what is the value of sqrt(6)?

Explanation. Figure 11.1.17 shows that when the input is 6, the output is about 2.45. So sqrt(6) ≈ 2.45.

Another powerful tool for understanding a function better is a graph. Given a function f, one way to make its graph is to take a table of input and output values, and read each row as the coordinates of a point in the xy-plane.

Example 11.1.19 A Graph for the Budget Deficit Function. Returning to the function BudgetDeficit that we studied in Example 11.1.13, in order to make a graph of this function we view Table 11.1.14 as a list of points with x and y coordinates, as in Figure 11.1.20. We then plot these points on a set of coordinate axes, as in Figure 11.1.21. The points have been connected with a curve so that we can see the overall pattern given by the progression of points. Since there was not any actual data for inputs in between any two years, the curve is dashed. That is, this curve is dashed because it just represents someone's best guess as to how to connect the plotted points. Only the plotted points themselves are precise.

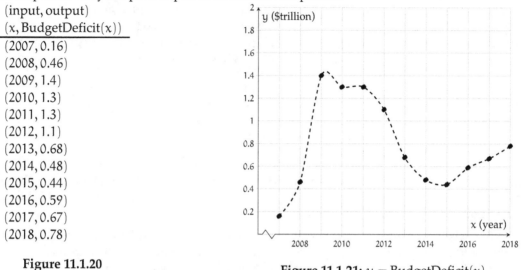

(input, output)
$(x, \text{BudgetDeficit}(x))$
$(2007, 0.16)$
$(2008, 0.46)$
$(2009, 1.4)$
$(2010, 1.3)$
$(2011, 1.3)$
$(2012, 1.1)$
$(2013, 0.68)$
$(2014, 0.48)$
$(2015, 0.44)$
$(2016, 0.59)$
$(2017, 0.67)$
$(2018, 0.78)$

Figure 11.1.20

Figure 11.1.21: $y = \text{BudgetDeficit}(x)$

How has this graph helped us to understand the function better? All of the observations that we made in Example 11.1.13 are perhaps even more clear now. For instance, the spike in the deficit between 2008 and 2009 is now visually apparent. Seeking an explanation for this spike, we recall that there was a financial crisis in late 2008. Revenue from income taxes dropped at the same time that federal money was spent to prevent further losses.

Example 11.1.22 A Graph for the Square Root Function. Let's now construct a graph for sqrt. Tabulating inputs and outputs gives the points in Figure 11.1.23, which in turn gives us the graph in Figure 11.1.24.

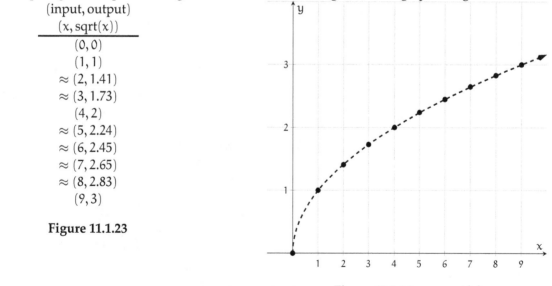

(input, output)
$(x, \text{sqrt}(x))$
$(0, 0)$
$(1, 1)$
$\approx (2, 1.41)$
$\approx (3, 1.73)$
$(4, 2)$
$\approx (5, 2.24)$
$\approx (6, 2.45)$
$\approx (7, 2.65)$
$\approx (8, 2.83)$
$(9, 3)$

Figure 11.1.23

Figure 11.1.24: $y = \text{sqrt}(x)$

Just as in the previous example, we've plotted points where we have concrete coordinates, and then we have made our best attempt to connect those points with a curve. Unlike the previous example, here we believe that points will continue to follow the same pattern indefinitely to the right, and so we have added an arrowhead to the graph.

What has this graph done to improve our understanding of sqrt? As inputs (x-values) increase, the outputs (y-values) increase too, although not at the same rate. In fact we can see that our graph is steep on its left, and less steep as we move to the right. This confirms our earlier observation in Example 11.1.16 that outputs increase by smaller and smaller amounts as the input increases.

Remark 11.1.25 Graph of a Function. Given a function f, when we refer to a **graph of** f we are *not* referring to an entire picture, like Figure 11.1.24. A graph of f is only *part* of that picture—the curve and the points that it connects. Everything else (axes, tick marks, the grid, labels, and the surrounding white space) is just useful decoration so that we can read the graph more easily.

Remark 11.1.26 A Common Wording Misunderstanding. It is common to refer to the graph of f as the **graph of the equation** $y = f(x)$. However, we should avoid saying "the graph of $f(x)$." That would indicate a misunderstanding of our notation. Since $f(x)$ is the output for a certain input x. That means that $f(x)$ is just a number and not worthy of a two-dimensional picture.

While it is important to be able to make a graph of a function f, we also need to be capable of looking at a graph and reading it well. A graph of f provides us with helpful specific information about f; it tells us what f does to its input values. When we were making graphs, we plotted points of the form

$$(\text{input}, \text{output})$$

Now given a graph of f, we interpret coordinates in the same way.

Example 11.1.27 In Figure 11.1.28 we have a graph of a function f. If we wish to find $f(1)$, we recognize that 1 is being used as an input. So we would want to find a point of the form $(1, \ )$. Seeking out x-coordinate 1 in Figure 11.1.28, we find that the only such point is $(1, 2)$. Therefore the output for 1 is 2; in other words $f(1) = 2$.

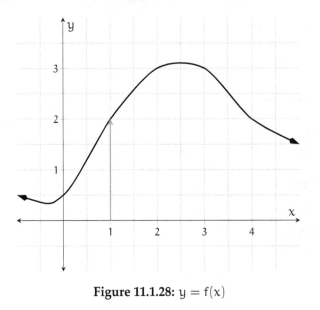

Figure 11.1.28: $y = f(x)$

Checkpoint 11.1.29 Use the graph of f in Figure 11.1.28 to find f(0), f(3), and f(4).

a. f(0)   b. f(3)   c. f(4)

Explanation.

a. $f(0) = 0.5$, since $(0, 0.5)$ is on the graph.

b. $f(3) = 3$, since $(3, 3)$ is on the graph.

c. $f(4) = 2$, since $(4, 2)$ is on the graph.

Example 11.1.30 Unemployment Rates.
Suppose that u is the unemployment function of time. That is, $u(t)$ is the unemployment rate in the United States in year t. The graph of the equation $y = u(t)$ is given in Figure 11.1.31 (data.bls.gov/timeseries/LNS14000000).

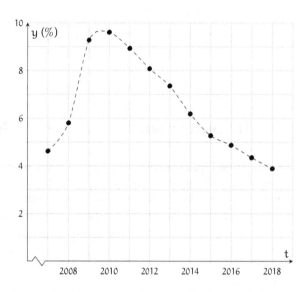

Figure 11.1.31: Unemployment in the United States

What was the unemployment in 2008? It is a straightforward matter to use Figure 11.1.31 to find that unemployment was almost 6% in 2008. Asking this question is exactly the same thing as asking to find u(2008). That is, we have one question that can either be asked in an everyday-English way or which can be asked in a terse, mathematical notation-heavy way:

"What was unemployment in 2008?"   "Find u(2008)."

If we use the table to establish that $u(2009) \approx 9.25$, then we should be prepared to translate that into everyday-English using the context of the function: In 2009, unemployment in the U.S. was about 9.25%.

If we ask the question "when was unemployment at 5%," we can read the graph and see that there were two such times: mid-2007 and about 2016. But there is again a more mathematical notation-heavy way to ask this question. Namely, since we are being told that the output of u is 5, we are being asked to solve the equation $u(t) = 5$. So the following communicate the same thing:

"When was unemployment at 5%?"   "Solve the equation $u(t) = 5$."

And our answer to this question is:

"Unemployment was at 5% in mid-2007 and about 2016."   "$t \approx 2007.5$ or $t \approx 2016$."

Checkpoint 11.1.32 Use the graph of u in Figure 11.1.31 to answer the following.

a. Find u(2011) and interpret it.

Interpretation:

b. Solve the equation $u(t) = 6$ and interpret your solution(s).

$t \approx$ [   ] or $t \approx$ [   ]

Interpretation:

Explanation.

a. $u(2011) \approx 9$; In 2011 the US unemployment rate was about 9%.

b. $t \approx 2008$ or $t \approx 2014$; The points at which unemployment was 6% were in early 2008 and early 2014.

11.1.3 Translating Between Four Descriptions of the Same Function

We have noted that functions are complicated, and we want ways to make them easier to understand. It's common to find a problem involving a function and not know how to find a solution to that problem. Most functions have at least four standard ways to think about them, and if we learn how to translate between these four perspectives, we often find that one of them makes a given problem easier to solve.

The four modes for working with a given function are

- a verbal description

- a table of inputs and outputs

- a graph of the function

- a formula for the function

This has been visualized in Figure 11.1.33.

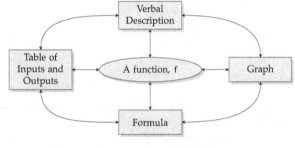

Figure 11.1.33: Function Perspectives

Example 11.1.34 Consider a function f that squares its input and then adds 1. Translate this verbal description of f into a table, a graph, and a formula.

Explanation.

To make a table for f, we'll have to select some input x-values. These choices are left entirely up to us, so we might as well choose small, easy-to-work-with values. However we shouldn't shy away from negative input values. Given the verbal description, we should be able to compute a column of output values. Figure 11.1.35 is one possible table that we might end up with.

x	$f(x)$
-2	$(-2)^2 + 1 = 5$
-1	$(-1)^2 + 1 = 2$
0	$0^2 + 1 = 1$
1	$1^2 + 1 = 2$
2	5
3	10
4	17

Figure 11.1.35

Once we have a table for f, we can make a graph for
f as in Figure 11.1.36, using the table to plot points.

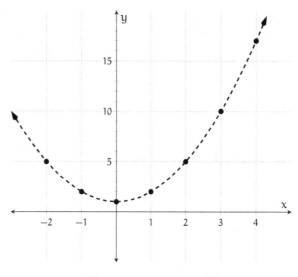

Figure 11.1.36: $y = f(x)$

Lastly, we must find a formula for f. This means we need to write an algebraic expression that says the
same thing about f as the verbal description, the table, and the graph. For this example, we can focus on the
verbal description. Since f takes its input, squares it, and adds 1, we have that

$$f(x) = x^2 + 1.$$

Example 11.1.37 Let F be the function that takes a Celsius temperature as input and outputs the corresponding Fahrenheit temperature. Translate this verbal description of F into a table, a graph, and a formula.

Explanation.   To make a table for F, we will need to rely on what we know about Celsius and Fahrenheit
temperatures. It is a fact that the freezing temperature of water at sea level is 0 °C, which equals 32 °F.
Also, the boiling temperature of water at sea level is 100 °C, which is the same as 212 °F. One more piece
of information we might have is that standard human body temperature is 37 °C, or 98.6 °F. All of this is
compiled in Figure 11.1.38. Note that we tabulated inputs and outputs by working with the context of the
function, not with any computations.

C	F(C)
0	32
37	98.6
100	212

Figure 11.1.38

Once a table is established, making
a graph by plotting points is a simple matter, as in Figure 11.1.39. The
three plotted points seem to be in a
straight line, so we think it is reasonable to connect them in that way.

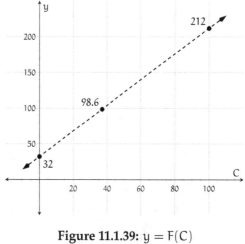

Figure 11.1.39: $y = F(C)$

To find a formula for F, the verbal definition is not of much direct help. But F's graph does seem to be a straight line. And linear equations are familiar to us. This line has a y-intercept at $(0, 32)$ and a slope we can calculate: $\frac{212-32}{100-0} = \frac{180}{100} = \frac{9}{5}$. So the equation of this line is $y = \frac{9}{5}C + 32$. On the other hand, the equation of this graph is $y = F(C)$, since it is a graph of the function F. So evidently,

$$F(C) = \frac{9}{5}C + 32.$$

11.1.4 Reading Questions

1.   When g is a function, how should you say out loud "$g(x)$?"

2.   There are four main ways to communicate how a function turns its inputs into its outputs. What are they?

3.   What is usually an acceptable way to type "the square root of x" if you have to type it using a regular keyboard?

11.1.5 Exercises

Review and Warmup

1.   Locate each point in the graph:

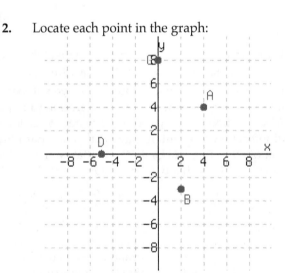

Write each point's position as an ordered pair, like $(1, 2)$.

A = _____   B = _____
C = _____   D = _____

2.   Locate each point in the graph:

Write each point's position as an ordered pair, like $(1, 2)$.

A = _____   B = _____
C = _____   D = _____

3.   Evaluate $\dfrac{2t-1}{8t}$ for $t = -4$.

4.   Evaluate $\dfrac{6t-4}{8t}$ for $t = 10$.

5.   a. Evaluate $2x^2$ when $x = 4$.

   b. Evaluate $(2x)^2$ when $x = 4$.

6.   a. Evaluate $3x^2$ when $x = 2$.

   b. Evaluate $(3x)^2$ when $x = 2$.

Function Formulas and Evaluation Evaluate the function at the given values.

7. $H(x) = x - 4$
   a. $H(5)$
   b. $H(-2)$
   c. $H(0)$

8. $G(x) = x - 1$
   a. $G(3)$
   b. $G(-5)$
   c. $G(0)$

9. $F(x) = 4x$
   a. $F(3)$
   b. $F(-4)$
   c. $F(0)$

10. $G(x) = 10x$
    a. $G(1)$
    b. $G(-5)$
    c. $G(0)$

11. $H(x) = -3x + 5$
    a. $H(4)$
    b. $H(-2)$
    c. $H(0)$

12. $K(x) = -5x + 9$
    a. $K(3)$
    b. $K(-2)$
    c. $K(0)$

13. $K(x) = -x + 9$
    a. $K(2)$
    b. $K(-5)$
    c. $K(0)$

14. $f(x) = -x + 6$
    a. $f(4)$
    b. $f(-1)$
    c. $f(0)$

15. $g(x) = x^2 - 8$
    a. $g(4)$
    b. $g(-2)$
    c. $g(0)$

16. $h(t) = t^2 - 3$
    a. $h(4)$
    b. $h(-4)$
    c. $h(0)$

17. $F(y) = -y^2 + 9$
    a. $F(1)$
    b. $F(-2)$
    c. $F(0)$

18. $F(x) = -x^2 - 3$
    a. $F(5)$
    b. $F(-2)$
    c. $F(0)$

19. $G(t) = 6$
    a. $G(3)$
    b. $G(6)$
    c. $G(0)$

20. $H(y) = -7$
    a. $H(2)$
    b. $H(-7)$
    c. $H(0)$

21. $K(x) = \dfrac{7x}{2x + 10}$
    a. $K(5)$
    b. $K(-1)$

22. $K(x) = \dfrac{7x}{-10x + 4}$
    a. $K(5)$
    b. $K(-6)$

23. $f(x) = \dfrac{3}{x - 2}$.
    a. $f(1)$
    b. $f(2)$

24. $g(x) = -\dfrac{70}{x - 7}$.
    a. $g(14)$
    b. $g(7)$

25. $h(x) = -3x - 4$
    a. $h(7)$
    b. $h(-4)$

26. $F(x) = -6x + 3$
    a. $F(5)$
    b. $F(-5)$

27. $F(x) = x^2 + 5x - 5$
    a. $F(1)$
    b. $F(-3)$

28. $G(x) = x^2 + 2x$
    a. $G(0)$
    b. $G(-3)$

29. $H(x) = -3x^2 + 5x + 3$
    a. $H(2)$
    b. $H(-2)$

30. $K(x) = -2x^2 - 2x - 1$
    a. $K(1)$
    b. $K(-3)$

31. $K(x) = \sqrt{x}$.
    a. $K(49)$
    b. $K\left(\frac{64}{9}\right)$
    c. $K(-6)$

32. $f(x) = \sqrt{x}$.
    a. $f(16)$
    b. $f\left(\frac{4}{9}\right)$
    c. $f(-6)$

33. $g(x) = \sqrt[3]{x}$
    a. $g(-1)$
    b. $g\left(\frac{64}{27}\right)$

34. $h(x) = \sqrt[3]{x}$
    a. $h(-27)$
    b. $h\left(\frac{1}{27}\right)$

35. $F(x) = -12$
    a. $F(4)$
    b. $F(-8)$

36. $F(x) = 15$
    a. $F(7)$
    b. $F(-2)$

Function Formulas and Solving Equations

37. Solve for x, where $G(x) = 12x + 6$.

   a. $G(x) = -42$

   b. $G(x) = -3$

38. Solve for x, where $H(x) = -8x - 5$.

   a. $H(x) = 19$

   b. $H(x) = 7$

39. Solve for x, where $K(x) = x^2 + 7$.

   a. $K(x) = 8$

   b. $K(x) = 6$

40. Solve for x, where $K(x) = x^2 - 1$.

   a. $K(x) = 8$

   b. $K(x) = -4$

41. Solve for x, where $f(x) = x^2 + x - 73$.
$f(x) = -1$

42. Solve for x, where $g(x) = x^2 + 3x - 25$.
$g(x) = -7$

43. If h is a function defined by $h(y) = 4y + 9$,

   a. Find $h(0)$.

   b. Solve $h(y) = 0$.

44. If f is a function defined by $f(y) = -4y + 2$,

   a. Find $f(0)$.

   b. Solve $f(y) = 0$.

45. If H is a function defined by $H(r) = 4r^2 - 4$,

   a. Find $H(0)$.

   b. Solve $H(r) = 0$.

46. If h is a function defined by $h(r) = r^2 - 1$,

   a. Find $h(0)$.

   b. Solve $h(r) = 0$.

47. If f is a function defined by
$f(t) = t^2 - 9t + 18$,

   a. Find $f(0)$.

   b. Solve $f(t) = 0$.

48. If G is a function defined by
$G(t) = t^2 + 2t - 35$,

   a. Find $G(0)$.

   b. Solve $G(t) = 0$.

Functions and Points on a Graph

49. a. If $K(4) = 2$, then the point ⬚ is on the graph of K.

   b. If $(3, 0)$ is on the graph of K, then $K(3) =$ ⬚ .

50. a. If $f(10) = 12$, then the point ⬚ is on the graph of f.

   b. If $(10, 7)$ is on the graph of f, then $f(10) =$ ⬚ .

51. If $g(r) = x$, then the point ⬚ is on the graph of g.

52. If $h(y) = r$, then the point ⬚ is on the graph of h.

53. If (t, x) is on the graph of h, then $h(t) =$ ⬚ .

54. If (r, y) is on the graph of F, then $F(r) =$ ⬚ .

55. For the function G, when $x = 1$, the output is 0.
   Choose all true statements.
   ☐ $G(1) = 0$ ☐ $G(0) = 1$ ☐ The function's value is 1 at 0.   ☐ The point $(1, 0)$ is
   on the graph of the function.   ☐ The function's value is 0 at 1.   ☐ The point $(0, 1)$ is
   on the graph of the function.

56. For the function H, when x = −2, the output is −11.

    Choose all true statements.

☐ The function's value is −2 at −11.   ☐ The point (−11, −2) is on the graph of the function.

☐ H(−11) = −2   ☐ The point (−2, −11) is on the graph of the function.   ☐ The function's
value is −11 at −2.   ☐ H(−2) = −11

Function Graphs

57. Use the graph of K below to evaluate the given expressions. (Estimates are OK.)

58. Use the graph of K below to evaluate the given expressions. (Estimates are OK.)

59. Use the graph of f below to evaluate the given expressions. (Estimates are OK.)

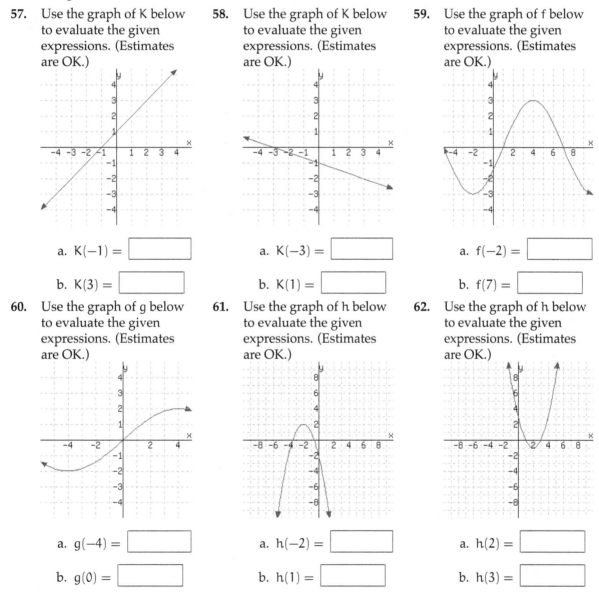

a. K(−1) = ☐

b. K(3) = ☐

a. K(−3) = ☐

b. K(1) = ☐

a. f(−2) = ☐

b. f(7) = ☐

60. Use the graph of g below to evaluate the given expressions. (Estimates are OK.)

61. Use the graph of h below to evaluate the given expressions. (Estimates are OK.)

62. Use the graph of h below to evaluate the given expressions. (Estimates are OK.)

a. g(−4) = ☐

b. g(0) = ☐

a. h(−2) = ☐

b. h(1) = ☐

a. h(2) = ☐

b. h(3) = ☐

63. Function f is graphed.

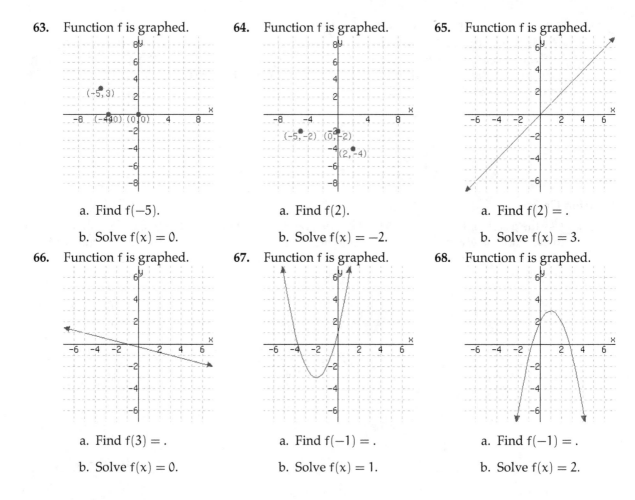

a. Find f(−5).

b. Solve f(x) = 0.

64. Function f is graphed.

a. Find f(2).

b. Solve f(x) = −2.

65. Function f is graphed.

a. Find f(2) = .

b. Solve f(x) = 3.

66. Function f is graphed.

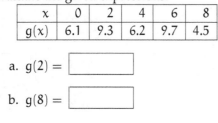

a. Find f(3) = .

b. Solve f(x) = 0.

67. Function f is graphed.

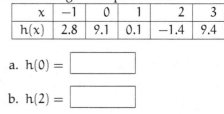

a. Find f(−1) = .

b. Solve f(x) = 1.

68. Function f is graphed.

a. Find f(−1) = .

b. Solve f(x) = 2.

Function Tables

69. Use the table of values for g below to evaluate the given expressions.

x	0	2	4	6	8
g(x)	6.1	9.3	6.2	9.7	4.5

a. g(2) = [ ]

b. g(8) = [ ]

70. Use the table of values for h below to evaluate the given expressions.

x	−1	0	1	2	3
h(x)	2.8	9.1	0.1	−1.4	9.4

a. h(0) = [ ]

b. h(2) = [ ]

71. Make a table of values for the function G, defined by $G(x) = -2x^2$. Based on values in the table, sketch a graph of G.

x	G(x)

72. Make a table of values for the function H, defined by $H(x) = \dfrac{2^x + 2}{x^2 + 3}$. Based on values in the table, sketch a graph of H.

x	H(x)

Translating Between Different Representations of a Function

73. Here is a verbal description of a function G. "Cube the input x to obtain the output y."

   a. Give a numeric representation of G.

x	0	1	2	3	4
G(x)					

   b. Give a formula for G.

74. Here is a verbal description of a function H. "Cube the input x to obtain the output y."

   a. Give a numeric representation of H.

x	0	1	2	3	4
H(x)					

   b. Give a formula for H.

75. Here is a verbal description of a function K. "Double the input x and then subtract three to obtain the output y."

   a. Give a numeric representation of K:

x	0	1	2	3	4
K(x)					

   b. Give a formula for K.

76. Here is a verbal description of a function K. "Quadruple the input x and then subtract seven to obtain the output y."

   a. Give a numeric representation of K:

x	0	1	2	3	4
K(x)					

   b. Give a formula for K.

77. Express the function f numerically with the table.

$$f(x) = 2x^3 - \frac{1}{2}x^2$$

x	−3	−2	−1	0	1	2	3
f(x)							

On graphing paper, you should be able to give a graphical representation of f too.

78. Express the function g numerically with the table.

$$g(x) = x^2 - \frac{1}{2}x$$

x	−3	−2	−1	0	1	2	3
g(x)							

On graphing paper, you should be able to give a graphical representation of g too.

79. Express the function h numerically with the table.

$$h(x) = \frac{8 - x}{7 + x}$$

x	−3	−2	−1	0	1	2	3
h(x)							

On graphing paper, you should be able to give a graphical representation of h too.

80. Express the function h numerically with the table.

$$h(x) = \frac{5 - x}{4 + x}$$

x	−3	−2	−1	0	1	2	3
h(x)							

On graphing paper, you should be able to give a graphical representation of h too.

Functions in Context

81. Phil started saving in a piggy bank on his birthday. The function $f(x) = 2x + 2$ models the amount of money, in dollars, in Phil's piggy bank. The independent variable represents the number of days passed since his birthday.
    Interpret the meaning of $f(4) = 10$.

    ⊙ *A.* Four days after Phil started his piggy bank, there were $10 in it.

    ⊙ *B.* The piggy bank started with $10 in it, and Phil saves $4 each day.

    ⊙ *C.* The piggy bank started with $4 in it, and Phil saves $10 each day.

    ⊙ *D.* Ten days after Phil started his piggy bank, there were $4 in it.

82. An arcade sells multi-day passes. The function $g(x) = \frac{1}{3}x$ models the number of days a pass will work, where x is the amount of money paid, in dollars.
    Interpret the meaning of $g(12) = 4$.

    ⊙ *A.* Each pass costs $12, and it works for 4 days.

    ⊙ *B.* If a pass costs $4, it will work for 12 days.

    ⊙ *C.* If a pass costs $12, it will work for 4 days.

    ⊙ *D.* Each pass costs $4, and it works for 12 days.

83. Maygen will spend $175 to purchase some bowls and some plates. Each bowl costs $3, and each plate costs $5. The function $p(b) = -\frac{3}{5}b + 35$ models the number of plates Maygen will purchase, where b represents the number of bowls Maygen will purchase.
    Interpret the meaning of $p(45) = 8$.

    ⊙ *A.* If 45 bowls are purchased, then 8 plates will be purchased.

    ⊙ *B.* $8 will be used to purchase bowls, and $45 will be used to purchase plates.

    ⊙ *C.* If 8 bowls are purchased, then 45 plates will be purchased.

    ⊙ *D.* $45 will be used to purchase bowls, and $8 will be used to purchase plates.

84. Carly will spend $450 to purchase some bowls and some plates. Each plate costs $2, and each bowl costs $9. The function $q(x) = -\frac{2}{9}x + 50$ models the number of bowls Carly will purchase, where x represents the number of plates to be purchased.
    Interpret the meaning of $q(27) = 44$.

    ⊙ *A.* 44 plates and 27 bowls can be purchased.

    ⊙ *B.* $44 will be used to purchase bowls, and $27 will be used to purchase plates.

    ⊙ *C.* $27 will be used to purchase bowls, and $44 will be used to purchase plates.

    ⊙ *D.* 27 plates and 44 bowls can be purchased.

85. Find a formula for the function f that gives the number of hours in x years.

86. Find a formula for the function f that gives the number of minutes in x days.

87. Suppose that M is the function that computes how many miles are in x feet. Find the formula for M. If you do not know how many feet are in one mile, you can look it up on Google.

Evaluate $M(13000)$ and interpret the result.

There are about [   ] miles in [   ] feet.

88. Suppose that K is the function that computes how many kilograms are in x pounds. Find the formula for K. If you do not know how many pounds are in one kilogram, you can look it up on Google.

Evaluate $K(159)$ and interpret the result.

Something that weighs [   ] pounds would weigh about [   ] kilograms.

89. Suppose that f is the function that the phone company uses to determine what your bill will be (in dollars) for a long-distance phone call that lasts t minutes. Each call costs a fixed price of $2.65 plus 11 cents per minute. Write a formula for this linear function f.

90. Suppose that f is the function that gives the total cost (in dollars) of downhill skiing x times during a season with a $500 season pass. Write a formula for f.

91. Suppose that f is the function that tells you how many dimes are in x dollars. Write a formula for f.

92. The function C models the the number of customers in a store t hours since the store opened.

t	0	1	2	3	4	5	6	7
C(t)	0	40	78	95	99	78	39	0

a. Find $C(6)$.

b. Interpret the meaning of $C(6)$.

⊙ **A.** There were 39 customers in the store 6 hours after the store opened.

⊙ **B.** In 6 hours since the store opened, the store had an average of 39 customers per hour.

⊙ **C.** There were 6 customers in the store 39 hours after the store opened.

⊙ **D.** In 6 hours since the store opened, there were a total of 39 customers.

c. Solve $C(t) = 78$ for t. t = [   ]

d. Interpret the meaning of Part c's solution(s).

⊙ **A.** There were 78 customers in the store 2 hours after the store opened.

⊙ **B.** There were 78 customers in the store 2 hours after the store opened, and again 5 hours after the store opened.

⊙ **C.** There were 78 customers in the store 5 hours after the store opened.

⊙ **D.** There were 78 customers in the store either 2 hours after the store opened, or 5 hours after the store opened.

93. Let $s(t) = 13t^2 - 3t + 200$, where s is the position (in mi) of a car driving on a straight road at time t (in hr). The car's velocity (in mi/hr) at time t is given by $v(t) = 26t - 3$.

a. *Using function notation*, express the car's position after 1.5 hours. The answer here is not a formula, it's just something using function notation like $f(8)$.

b. Where is the car then? The answer here is a number with units.

c. *Use function notation* to express the question, "When is the car going 59 $\frac{mi}{hr}$?" The answer is an equation that uses function notation; something like f(x)=23. You are not being asked to actually solve the equation, just to write down the equation.

d. Where is the car when it is going 75 $\frac{mi}{hr}$? The answer here is a number with units. You are being asked a question about its position, but have been given information about its speed.

94. Let $s(t) = 13t^2 + t + 100$, where s is the position (in mi) of a car driving on a straight road at time t (in hr). The car's velocity (in mi/hr) at time t is given by $v(t) = 26t + 1$.

a. *Using function notation*, express the car's position after 3.4 hours. The answer here is not a formula, it's just something using function notation like f(8).

b. Where is the car then? The answer here is a number with units.

c. *Use function notation* to express the question, "When is the car going 58 $\frac{mi}{hr}$?" The answer is an equation that uses function notation; something like f(x)=23. You are not being asked to actually solve the equation, just to write down the equation.

d. Where is the car when it is going 27 $\frac{mi}{hr}$? The answer here is a number with units. You are being asked a question about its position, but have been given information about its speed.

95. Describe your own example of a function that has real context to it. You will need some kind of input variable, like "number of years since 2000" or "weight of the passengers in my car." You will need a process for using that number to bring about a different kind of number. The process does not need to involve a formula; a verbal description would be great, as would a formula.

    Give your function a name. Write the symbol(s) that you would use to represent input. Write the symbol(s) that you would use to represent output.

96. The following figure has the graph $y = d(t)$, which models a particle's distance from the starting line in feet, where t stands for time in seconds since timing started.

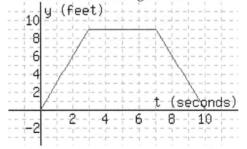

a. Find d(7).

b. Interpret the meaning of d(7).

  ⊙ **A.** In the first 7 seconds, the particle moved a total of 9 feet.

  ⊙ **B.** The particle was 9 feet away from the starting line 7 seconds since timing started.

  ⊙ **C.** In the first 9 seconds, the particle moved a total of 7 feet.

  ⊙ **D.** The particle was 7 feet away from the starting line 9 seconds since timing started.

c. Solve $d(t) = 6$ for t. t = [   ]

d. Interpret the meaning of part c's solution(s).

      ⊙ **A**. The particle was 6 feet from the starting line 2 seconds since timing started, or 8 seconds since timing started.

      ⊙ **B**. The particle was 6 feet from the starting line 2 seconds since timing started, and again 8 seconds since timing started.

      ⊙ **C**. The particle was 6 feet from the starting line 2 seconds since timing started.

      ⊙ **D**. The particle was 6 feet from the starting line 8 seconds since timing started.

97. The following figure has the graph $y = d(t)$, which models a particle's distance from the starting line in feet, where t stands for time in seconds since timing started.

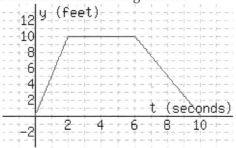

a. Find $d(9)$.

b. Interpret the meaning of $d(9)$.

      ⊙ **A**. The particle was 2.5 feet away from the starting line 9 seconds since timing started.

      ⊙ **B**. The particle was 9 feet away from the starting line 2.5 seconds since timing started.

      ⊙ **C**. In the first 9 seconds, the particle moved a total of 2.5 feet.

      ⊙ **D**. In the first 2.5 seconds, the particle moved a total of 9 feet.

c. Solve $d(t) = 5$ for t. t = [   ]

d. Interpret the meaning of part c's solution(s).

      ⊙ **A**. The particle was 5 feet from the starting line 1 seconds since timing started.

      ⊙ **B**. The particle was 5 feet from the starting line 1 seconds since timing started, and again 8 seconds since timing started.

      ⊙ **C**. The particle was 5 feet from the starting line 1 seconds since timing started, or 8 seconds since timing started.

      ⊙ **D**. The particle was 5 feet from the starting line 8 seconds since timing started.

98. Use the graph of h in the figure to fill in the table.

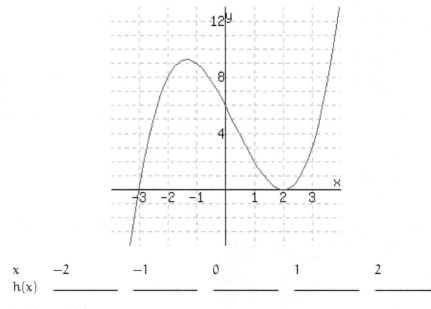

x	−2	−1	0	1	2
h(x)					

a. Evaluate $h(3) - h(0)$.

b. Evaluate $h(2) - h(-1)$.

c. Evaluate $2h(-1)$.

d. Evaluate $h(0) + 3$.

99. Use the given graph of a function f, along with a, b, c, d, e, and h to answer the following questions. Some answers are points, and should be entered as ordered pairs. Some answers ask you to solve for x, so the answer should be in the form *x=...*

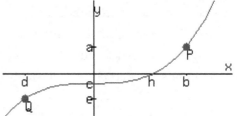

a. What are the coordinates of the point P?

b. What are the coordinates of the point Q?

c. Evaluate $f(b)$. (The answer is symbolic, not a specific number.)

d. Solve $f(x) = e$ for x. (The answer is symbolic, not a specific number.)

e. Suppose $c = f(z)$. Solve the equation $z = f(x)$ for x.

11.2 Domain and Range

A function is a process for turning input values into output values. Occasionally a function f will have input values for which the process breaks down.

11.2.1 Domain

Example 11.2.2 Let P be the population of Portland as a function of the year. According to Google[1] we can say that:

$$P(2016) = 639863 \qquad\qquad P(1990) = 487849$$

But what if we asked to find P(1600)? The question doesn't really make sense anymore. The Multnomah tribe lived in villages in the area, but the city of Portland was not incorporated until 1851. We say that P(1600) is *undefined*.

Example 11.2.3 If m is a person's mass in kg, let $w(m)$ be their weight in lb. There is an approximate formula for w:

$$w(m) \approx 2.2m$$

From this formula we can find:

$$w(50) \approx 110 \qquad\qquad w(80) \approx 176$$

which tells us that a 50- kg person weighs 110 lb, and an 80- kg person weighs 176 lb.

What if we asked for $w(-100)$? In the context of this example, we would be asking for the weight of a person whose mass is -100 kg. This is clearly nonsense. That means that $w(-100)$ is *undefined*. Note that the *context* of the example is telling us that $w(-100)$ is undefined even though the formula alone might suggest that $w(-100) = -220$.

Example 11.2.4 Let g have the formula

$$g(x) = \frac{x}{x-7}.$$

For most x-values, $g(x)$ is perfectly computable:

$$g(2) = -\frac{2}{5} \qquad\qquad g(14) = 2.$$

But if we try to compute $g(7)$, we run into an issue of arithmetic.

$$g(7) = \frac{7}{7-7}$$
$$= \frac{7}{0}$$

The expression $\frac{7}{0}$ is *undefined*. There is no number that this could equal.

---

[1] https://www.google.com/publicdata/explore?ds=kf7tgg1uo9ude_&met_y=population&hl=en&dl=en#!ctype=l&strail=false &bcs=d&nselm=h&met_y=population&scale_y=lin&ind_y=false&rdim=country&idim=place:4159000&ifdim=country &hl=en_US&dl=en&ind=false

Checkpoint 11.2.5 If $f(x) = \dfrac{x+2}{x+8}$, find an input for f that would cause an undefined output.

The number [   ] would cause an undefined output.

Explanation. Trying -8 as an input value would not work out; it would lead to division by 0.

These examples should motivate the following definition.

Definition 11.2.6 Domain. The **domain** of a function f is the collection of all of its valid input values.   ◊

Example 11.2.7 Referring to the functions from Examples 11.2.2–11.2.4

- The domain of P is all years starting from 1851 and later. It would also be reasonable to say that the domain is actually all years from 1851 up to the current year, since we cannot guarantee that Portland will exist forever.

- The domain of w is all positive real numbers. It is nonsensical to have a person with negative mass or even one with zero mass. While there is some lower bound for the smallest mass a person could have, and also an upper bound for the largest mass a person could have, these boundaries are gray. We can say for sure that non-positive numbers should never be used as inputs for w.

- The domain of g is all real numbers except 7. This is the only number that causes a breakdown in g's formula.

11.2.2 Interval, Set, and Set-Builder Notation

Communicating the domain of a function can be wordy. In mathematics, we can communicate the same information using concise notation that is accepted for use almost everywhere. Table 11.2.8 contains example functions from this section and their domains, and demonstrates *interval notation* for these domains. Basic interval notation is covered in Section 1.3, but some of our examples here go beyond what that section covers.

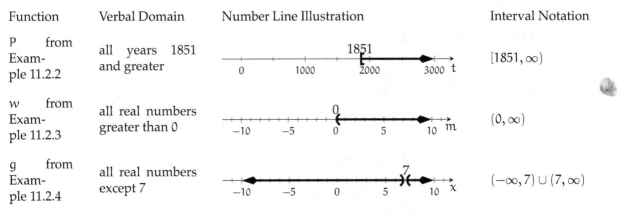

Function	Verbal Domain	Number Line Illustration	Interval Notation
P from Example 11.2.2	all years 1851 and greater		$[1851, \infty)$
w from Example 11.2.3	all real numbers greater than 0		$(0, \infty)$
g from Example 11.2.4	all real numbers except 7		$(-\infty, 7) \cup (7, \infty)$

Figure 11.2.8: Domains from Earlier Examples

Again, basic interval notation is covered in Section 1.3, but one thing appears in Table 11.2.8 that is not explained in that earlier section: the ∪ symbol, which we see in the domain of g.

Occasionally there is a need to consider number line pictures such as Figure 11.2.9, where two or more intervals appear.

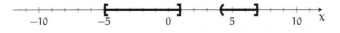

Figure 11.2.9: A number line with a union of two intervals

This picture is trying to tell you to consider numbers that are between −5 and 1, together with numbers that are between 4 and 7. That word "together" is related to the word "union," and in math the **union symbol**, ∪, captures this idea. It means to combine two ideas together, even if they are separate ideas. Think of it as putting everything from two baskets into one basket: a basket of oranges and a basket of apples combined into one big basket still contains oranges and apples, but now it can be thought of as a single idea. So we can write the numbers in this picture as

$$[-5, 1] \cup (4, 7]$$

(which uses interval notation).

   With the domain of g in Table 11.2.8, the number line picture shows us another "union" of two intervals. They are very close together, but there are still two separated intervals in that picture: $(-\infty, 7)$ and $(7, \infty)$. Their union is represented by $(-\infty, 7) \cup (7, \infty)$.

Checkpoint 11.2.10 What is the domain of the function sqrt, where $\text{sqrt}(x) = \sqrt{x}$, using interval notation?

Explanation. The function sqrt cannot take a negative number as an input. It can however take any positive number as input, or the number 0 as input. Representing this on a number line, we find the domain is $[0, \infty)$ in interval notation.

Checkpoint 11.2.11 What is the domain of the function ℓ where $\ell(x) = \frac{2}{x-3}$, using interval notation?

Explanation. The function ℓ cannot take a 3 as an input. It can however take any other number as input. Representing this on a number line, we have an interval $(-\infty, 3)$ to the left of 3, and $(3, \infty)$ to the right of 3. So we find the domain is $(-\infty, 3) \cup (3, \infty)$.

Sometimes we will consider collections of only a short list of numbers. In those cases, we use **set notation** (first introduced in Section A.6). With set notation, we have a list of numbers in mind, and we simply list all of those numbers. Curly braces are standard for surrounding the list. Table 11.2.12 illustrates set notation in use.

Picture of Set   Set Notation

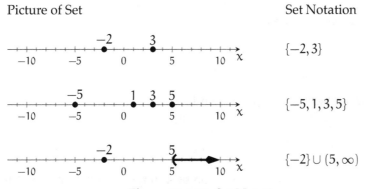

Figure 11.2.12: Set Notation

Checkpoint 11.2.13 A change machine lets you put in an x-dollar bill, and gives you $f(x)$ nickels in return equal in value to x dollars. Any current, legal denomination of US paper money can be fed to the change machine. What is the domain of f?

Explanation. The current, legal denominations of US paper money are $1, $2, $5, $10, $20, $50, and $100. So the domain of f is the set $\{1, 2, 5, 10, 20, 50, 100\}$.

While most collections of numbers that we will encounter can be described using a combination of interval notation and set notation, there is another commonly used notation that is very useful in algebra: **set-builder notation**, which was introduced in Section 1.3. Set-builder notation also uses curly braces. Set-builder notation provides a template for what a number that is under consideration might look like, and then it gives you restrictions on how to use that template. A very basic example of set-builder notation is

$$\{x \mid x \geq 3\}.$$

Verbally, this is "the set of all x such that x is greater than or equal to 3." Table 11.2.14 gives more examples of set-builder notation in use.

Picture of Set   Set Notation

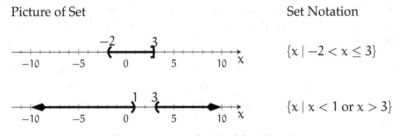

$\{x \mid -2 < x \leq 3\}$

$\{x \mid x < 1 \text{ or } x > 3\}$

Figure 11.2.14: Set-Builder Notation

Checkpoint 11.2.15 What is the domain of the function sqrt, where $\text{sqrt}(x) = \sqrt{x}$, using set-builder notation?

Explanation. The function sqrt cannot take a negative number as an input. It can however take any positive number as input, or the number 0 as input. Representing this on a number line, we find the domain is $\{x \mid x \geq 0\}$ in set-builder notation.

Example 11.2.16 What is the domain of the function A, where $A(x) = \frac{2x+1}{x^2-2x-8}$?

Note that if you plugged in some value for x, the only thing that might go wrong is if the denominator equals 0. So a *bad* value for x would be when

$$x^2 - 2x - 8 = 0$$
$$(x + 2)(x - 4) = 0$$

Here, we used a basic factoring technique from Section 10.3. To continue, either

$$x + 2 = 0 \qquad\qquad \text{or} \qquad\qquad x - 4 = 0$$
$$x = -2 \qquad\qquad \text{or} \qquad\qquad x = 4.$$

These are the *bad* x-values because they lead to division by 0 in the formula for A. So on a number line, if we wanted to picture the domain of A, we would make a sketch like:

So the domain is the union of three intervals: $(-\infty, -2) \cup (-2, 4) \cup (4, \infty)$.

Example 11.2.17 What is the domain of the function B, where $B(x) = \sqrt{7-x} + 3$?

Note that if you plugged in some value for x, the only thing that might go wrong is if the value in the radical is negative. So the *good* values for x would be when

$$7 - x \geq 0$$
$$7 \geq x$$
$$x \leq 7$$

So on a number line, if we wanted to picture the domain of B, we would make a sketch like:

So the domain is the interval $(-\infty, 7]$.

There are three main properties of functions that cause numbers to be excluded from a domain, which are summarized here.

List 11.2.18: Summary of Domain Restrictions

> **Denominators** Division by zero is undefined. So if a function contains an expression in a denominator, it will only be defined where that expression is not equal to zero.
>
> Example 11.2.16 demonstrates this.
>
> **Square Roots** The square root of a negative number is undefined. So if a function contains a square root, it will only be defined when the expression inside that radical is greater than or equal to zero. (This is actually true for any even nth radical.)
>
> Example 11.2.17 demonstrates this.
>
> **Context** Some numbers are nonsensical in context. If a function has real-world context, then this may add additional restrictions on the input values.
>
> Example 11.2.3 demonstrates this.

11.2.3 Range

The domain of a function is the collection of its valid inputs; there is a similar notion for *output*.

Definition 11.2.19 Range. The **range** of a function f is the collection of all of its possible output values. ◇

Example 11.2.20 Let f be the function defined by the formula $f(x) = x^2$. Finding f's *domain* is straightforward. Any number anywhere can be squared to produce an output, so f has domain $(-\infty, \infty)$. What is the *range* of f?

Explanation. We would like to describe the collection of possible numbers that f can give as output. We will use a graphical approach. Figure 11.2.21 displays a graph of f, and the visualization that reveals f's range.

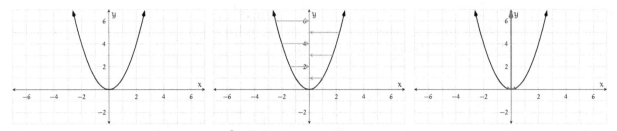

Figure 11.2.21: $y = f(x)$ where $f(x) = x^2$. The second graph illustrates how to visualize the range. In the third graph, the range is marked as an interval on the y-axis.

Output values are the y-coordinates in a graph. If we "slide the ink" left and right over to the y-axis to emphasize what the y-values in the graph are, we have y-values that start from 0 and continue upward forever. Therefore the range is $[0, \infty)$.

Example 11.2.22 Given the function g graphed in Figure 11.2.23, find the domain and range of g.

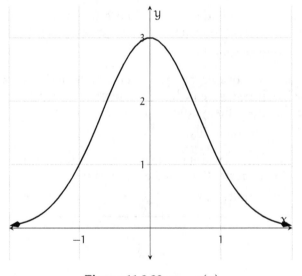

Figure 11.2.23: $y = g(x)$

Explanation.   To find the domain, we can visualize all of the x-values that are valid inputs for this function by "sliding the ink" down onto the x-axis. The arrows at the far left and far right of the curve indicate that whatever pattern we see in the graph continues off to the left and right. Here, we see that the arms of the graph appear to be tapering down to the x-axis and extending left and right forever. Every x-value can be used to get an output for the function, so the domain is $(-\infty, \infty)$.

If we visualize the possible *outputs* by "sliding the ink" sideways onto the y-axis, we find that outputs as high as 3 are possible (including 3 itself). The outputs appear to get very close to 0 when x is large, but they aren't quite equal to 0. So the range is $(0, 3]$.

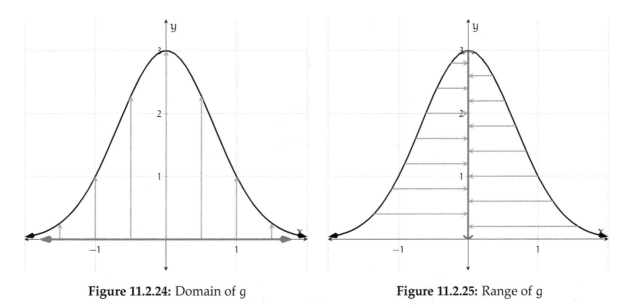

Figure 11.2.24: Domain of g   **Figure 11.2.25:** Range of g

Checkpoint 11.2.26 Given the function h graphed below, find the domain and range of h. Note there is an invisible vertical line at $x = 2$, and the two arms of the graph are extending downward (and upward) forever, getting arbitrarily close to that vertical line, but never touching it. Also note that the two arms extend forever to the left and right, getting arbitrarily close to the x-axis, but never touching it.

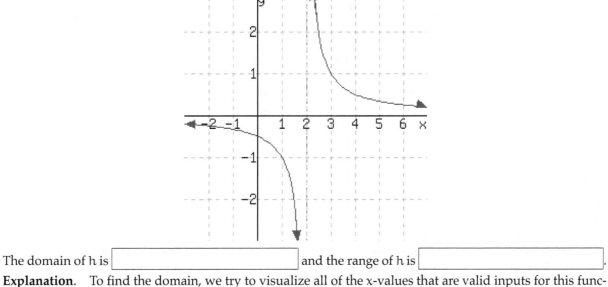

The domain of h is ☐ and the range of h is ☐.

Explanation.   To find the domain, we try to visualize all of the x-values that are valid inputs for this function. The arrows pointing left and right on the curve indicate that whatever pattern we see in the graph continues off to the left and right. So for x-values far to the right or left, we will be able to get an output for h.

The arrows pointing up and down are supposed to indicate that the curve will get closer and closer to the vertical line $x = 2$ after the curve leaves the viewing window we are using. So even when x is some number very close to 2, we will be able to get an output for h.

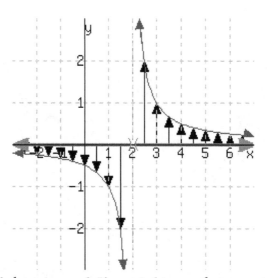

The one x-value that doesn't behave is $x = 2$. If we tried to use that as an input, there is no point on the graph directly above or below that on the x-axis. So the domain is $(-\infty, 2) \cup (2, \infty)$.

To find the range, we try to visualize all of the y-values that are possible outputs for this function. Sliding the ink of the curve left/right onto the y-axis reveals that $y = 0$ is the only y-value that we could never obtain as an output. So the range is $(-\infty, 0) \cup (0, \infty)$.

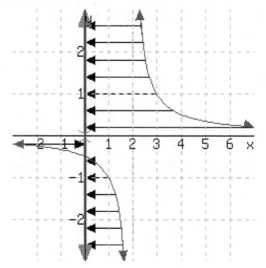

The examples of finding domain and range so far have all involved either a verbal description of a function, a formula for that function, or a graph of that function. Recall that there is a fourth perspective on functions: a table. In the case of a table, we have very limited information about the function's inputs and outputs. If the table is all that we have, then there are a handful of input values listed in the table for which we know outputs. For any other input, the output is undefined.

Example 11.2.27 Consider the function k given in Figure 11.2.28. What is the domain and range of k?

x	k(x)
3	4
8	5
10	5

Figure 11.2.28

Explanation. All that we know about k is that $k(3) = 4$, $k(8) = 5$, and $k(10) = 5$. Without any other information such as a formula for k or a context for k that tells us its verbal description, we must assume that its domain is $\{3, 8, 10\}$; these are the only valid input for k. Similarly, k's range is $\{4, 5\}$.

Note that we have used set notation, not interval notation, since the answers here were *lists* of x-values (for the domain) and y-values (for the range). Also note that we could graph the information that we have about k in Figure 11.2.29, and the visualization of "sliding ink" to determine domain and range still works.

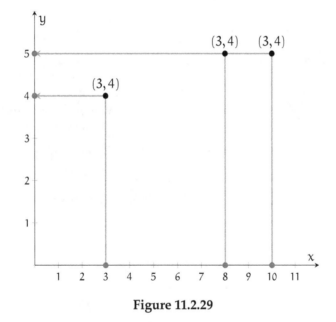

Figure 11.2.29

Warning 11.2.30 Finding Range from a Formula. Sometimes it is possible to find the range of a function using its formula without seeing its graph or a table. However, this often requires advanced techniques learned in calculus. Therefore when you are asked to find the range of a function based on its formula alone, your approach should be to examine a graph.

11.2.4 Reading Questions

1. Use a complete sentence to describe what is the domain of a function.

2. When you have a formula for a function, what is one thing that might tell you a number that is excluded from the domain?

3. To find the range of a function, it's more helpful to have its ☐ than its formula.

11.2.5 Exercises

Review and Warmup

1. For the interval expressed in the number line, write it using set-builder notation and interval notation.

2. For the interval expressed in the number line, write it using set-builder notation and interval notation.

3. For the interval expressed in the number line, write it using set-builder notation and interval notation.

4. For the interval expressed in the number line, write it using set-builder notation and interval notation.

5. Solve this compound inequality, and write your answer in *interval notation*.
$x \geq -2$ and $x \leq -1$

6. Solve this compound inequality, and write your answer in *interval notation*.
$x \geq 2$ and $x < 4$

7. Solve this compound inequality, and write your answer in *interval notation*.
$x \geq 2$ or $x \leq -2$

8. Solve this compound inequality, and write your answer in *interval notation*.
$x > -1$ or $x < -5$

Domain and Range From a Graph A function is graphed. Find its domain and range.

9.

10.

11.

12.

13.

14.

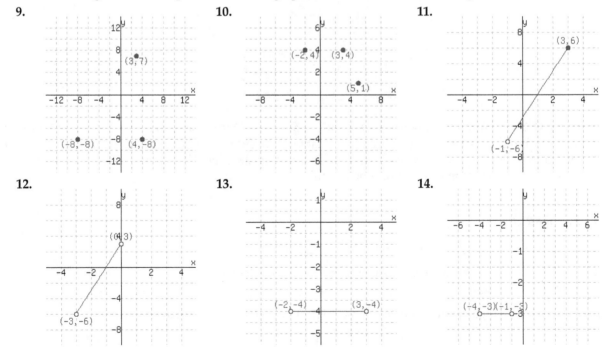

15.

16.

17.

18.

19.

20.

21.

22.

23.

24.

25.

26.

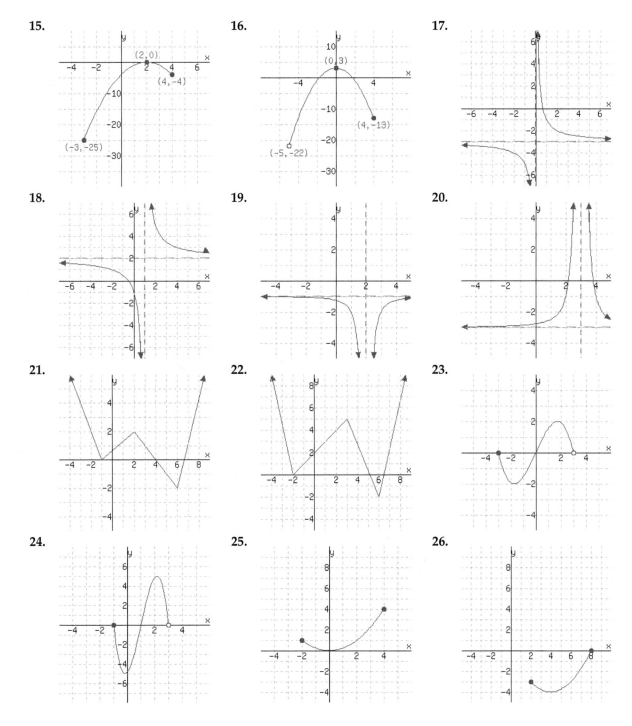

27. **28.** **29.**

30. **31.** **32.**

33. **34.** **35.**

36.

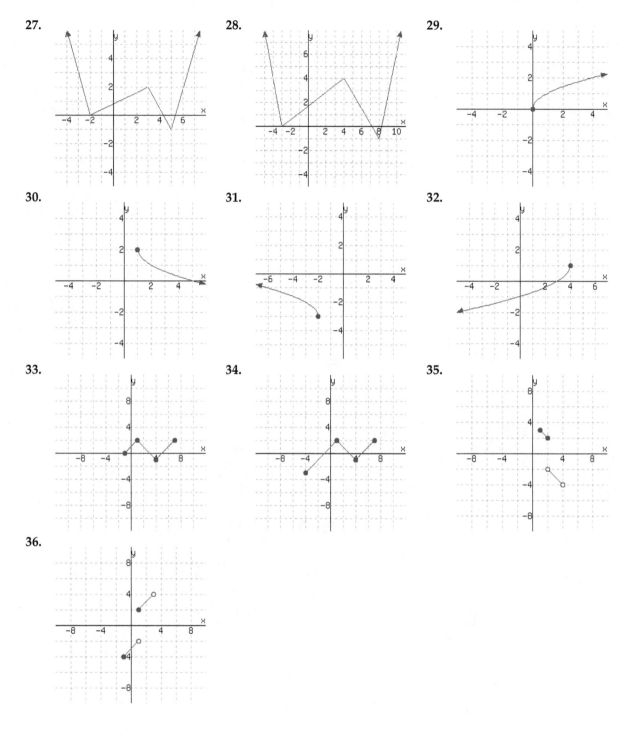

Domain From a Formula

37. Find the domain of H where
H(x) = −7x + 4.

38. Find the domain of K where K(x) = 7x − 8.

39. Find the domain of K where $K(x) = \frac{5}{6}x^4$.

40. Find the domain of f where $f(x) = \frac{2}{5}x^3$.

41. Find the domain of g where $g(x) = |6x - 3|$.

42. Find the domain of h where $h(x) = |-2x + 6|$.

43. Find the domain of h where $h(x) = \frac{2x}{x + 9}$.

44. Find the domain of F where $F(x) = \frac{5x}{x - 5}$.

45. Find the domain of G where $G(x) = \frac{x}{2x + 3}$.

46. Find the domain of H where $H(x) = \frac{4x}{7x + 10}$.

47. Find the domain of K where $K(x) = \frac{4x + 8}{x^2 - 11x + 30}$.

48. Find the domain of K where $K(x) = -\frac{3x + 5}{x^2 - x - 30}$.

49. Find the domain of f where $f(x) = \frac{10x + 4}{x^2 + 9x}$.

50. Find the domain of g where $g(x) = \frac{3x - 8}{x^2 + 3x}$.

51. Find the domain of h where $h(x) = \frac{1 - 4x}{x^2 - 49}$.

52. Find the domain of h where $h(x) = \frac{9x + 9}{x^2 - 81}$.

53. Find the domain of F where $F(x) = \frac{2x - 3}{16x^2 - 49}$.

54. Find the domain of G where $G(x) = \frac{6 - 5x}{81x^2 - 4}$.

55. Find the domain of H where $H(x) = \frac{8x - 6}{x^2 + 3}$.

56. Find the domain of K where $K(x) = \frac{x + 2}{x^2 + 10}$.

57. Find the domain of the function.
$K(x) = -\frac{6}{\sqrt{x-10}}$

58. Find the domain of the function.
$f(x) = \frac{8}{\sqrt{x-1}}$

59. Find the domain of the function.
$g(x) = \sqrt{6 - x}$

60. Find the domain of the function.
$h(x) = \sqrt{3 - x}$

61. Find the domain of the function.
$h(x) = \sqrt{9 + 13x}$

62. Find the domain of the function.
$F(x) = \sqrt{6 + 11x}$

63. Find the domain of A where $A(x) = \frac{x + 13}{x^2 - 9}$.

64. Find the domain of m where $m(x) = \frac{x + 16}{x^2 - 361}$.

65. Find the domain of b where $b(x) = \frac{16x - 2}{x^2 + 7x - 98}$.

66. Find the domain of m where $m(x) = \frac{16x - 11}{x^2 + 7x - 98}$.

67. Find the domain of r where $r(x) = \frac{\sqrt{2 + x}}{8 - x}$.

68. Find the domain of B where $B(x) = \frac{\sqrt{4 + x}}{4 - x}$.

Domain and Range Using Context

69. Thanh bought a used car for $7,800. The car's value decreases at a constant rate each year. After 5 years, the value decreased to $6,300.

Use a function to model the car's value as the number of years increases. Find this function's domain and range in this context.

The function's domain in this context is .

The function's range in this context is ▭.

70. Carmen bought a used car for $8,400. The car's value decreases at a constant rate each year. After 10 years, the value decreased to $5,400.

    Use a function to model the car's value as the number of years increases. Find this function's domain and range in this context.

    The function's domain in this context is [＿＿＿＿＿＿] .

    The function's range in this context is [＿＿＿＿＿＿] .

71. Assume a car uses gas at a constant rate. After driving 25 miles since a full tank of gas was purchased, there was 9 gallons of gas left; after driving 65 miles since a full tank of gas was purchased, there was 7.4 gallons of gas left.

    Use a function to model the amount of gas in the tank (in gallons). Let the independent variable be the number of miles driven since a full tank of gas was purchased. Find this function's domain and range in this context.

    The function's domain in this context is [＿＿＿＿＿＿] .

    The function's range in this context is [＿＿＿＿＿＿] .

72. Assume a car uses gas at a constant rate. After driving 30 miles since a full tank of gas was purchased, there was 13.2 gallons of gas left; after driving 60 miles since a full tank of gas was purchased, there was 11.4 gallons of gas left.

    Use a function to model the amount of gas in the tank (in gallons). Let the independent variable be the number of miles driven since a full tank of gas was purchased. Find this function's domain and range in this context.

    The function's domain in this context is [＿＿＿＿＿＿] .

    The function's range in this context is [＿＿＿＿＿＿] .

73. Joseph inherited a collection of coins when he was 14 years old. Ever since, he has been adding into the collection the same number of coins each year. When he was 20 years old, there were 510 coins in the collection. When he was 30 years old, there were 910 coins in the collection. At the age of 51, Joseph donated all his coins to a museum.

    Use a function to model the number of coins in Joseph's collection, starting in the year he inherited the collection, and ending in the year the collection was donated. Find this function's domain and range in this context.

    The function's domain in this context is [＿＿＿＿＿＿] .

    The function's range in this context is [＿＿＿＿＿＿] .

74. Virginia inherited a collection of coins when she was 15 years old. Ever since, she has been adding into the collection the same number of coins each year. When she was 20 years old, there were 330 coins in the collection. When she was 30 years old, there were 530 coins in the collection. At the age of 57, Virginia donated all her coins to a museum.

    Use a function to model the number of coins in Virginia's collection, starting in the year she inherited the collection, and ending in the year the collection was donated. Find this function's domain and range in this context.

    The function's domain in this context is [＿＿＿＿＿＿] .

    The function's range in this context is [＿＿＿＿＿＿] .

75. Assume a tree grows at a constant rate. When the tree was planted, it was 4 feet tall. After 8 years, the tree grew to 10.4 feet tall.

    Use a function to model the tree's height as years go by. Assume the tree can live 190 years, find this function's domain and range in this context.

    The function's domain in this context is ⬚ .

    The function's range in this context is ⬚ .

76. Assume a tree grows at a constant rate. When the tree was planted, it was 2.1 feet tall. After 10 years, the tree grew to 8.1 feet tall.

    Use a function to model the tree's height as years go by. Assume the tree can live 170 years, find this function's domain and range in this context.

    The function's domain in this context is ⬚ .

    The function's range in this context is ⬚ .

77. An object was shot up into the air at an initial vertical speed of 384 feet per second. Its height as time passes can be modeled by the quadratic function f, where $f(t) = -16t^2 + 384t$. Here t represents the number of seconds since the object's release, and $f(t)$ represents the object's height in feet.

    Find the function's domain and range in this context.

    The function's domain in this context is ⬚ .

    The function's range in this context is ⬚ .

78. An object was shot up into the air at an initial vertical speed of 416 feet per second. Its height as time passes can be modeled by the quadratic function f, where $f(t) = -16t^2 + 416t$. Here t represents the number of seconds since the object's release, and $f(t)$ represents the object's height in feet.

    Find the function's domain and range in this context.

    The function's domain in this context is ⬚ .

    The function's range in this context is ⬚ .

79. From a clifftop over the ocean 376.32 m above sea level, an object was shot straight up into the air with an initial vertical speed of 110.74 $\frac{m}{s}$. On its way down it missed the cliff and fell into the ocean, where it floats on the surface. Its height (above sea level) as time passes can be modeled by the quadratic function f, where $f(t) = -4.9t^2 + 110.74t + 376.32$. Here t represents the number of seconds since the object's release, and $f(t)$ represents the object's height (above sea level) in meters.

    Find the function's domain and range in this context.

    The function's domain in this context is ⬚ .

    The function's range in this context is ⬚ .

80. From a clifftop over the ocean 324.87 m above sea level, an object was shot straight up into the air with an initial vertical speed of 93.59 $\frac{m}{s}$. On its way down it missed the cliff and fell into the ocean, where it floats on the surface. Its height (above sea level) as time passes can be modeled by the quadratic function f, where $f(t) = -4.9t^2 + 93.59t + 324.87$. Here t represents the number of seconds since the object's release, and $f(t)$ represents the object's height (above sea level) in meters.

    Find the function's domain and range in this context.

The function's domain in this context is ☐.

The function's range in this context is ☐.

81. You will build a rectangular sheep pen next to a river. There is no need to build a fence along the river, so you only need to build three sides. You have a total of 460 feet of fence to use. Find the dimensions of the pen such that you can enclose the maximum area.

   Use a function to model the area of the rectangular pen, with respect to the length of the width (the two sides perpendicular to the river). Find the function's domain and range in this context.

   The function's domain is ☐.

   The function's range is ☐.

82. You will build a rectangular sheep pen next to a river. There is no need to build a fence along the river, so you only need to build three sides. You have a total of 480 feet of fence to use. Find the dimensions of the pen such that you can enclose the maximum area.

   Use a function to model the area of the rectangular pen, with respect to the length of the width (the two sides perpendicular to the river). Find the function's domain and range in this context.

   The function's domain is ☐.

   The function's range is ☐.

83. A student's first name is a function of their student identification number.

   (a) Describe the domain for this function in a sentence. Specifics are not needed.

   (b) Describe the range for this function in a sentence. Specifics are not needed.

84. The year a car was made is a function of its VIN (Vehicle Identification Number).

   (a) Describe the domain for this function in a sentence. Specifics are not needed.

   (b) Describe the range for this function in a sentence. Specifics are not needed.

Challenge

85. For each part, sketch the graph of a function with the given domain and range.

   a. The domain is $(0, \infty)$ and the range is $(-\infty, 0)$.

   b. The domain is $(1, 2)$ and the range is $(3, 4)$.

   c. The domain is $(0, \infty)$ and the range is $[2, 3]$.

   d. The domain is $(1, 2)$ and the range is $(-\infty, \infty)$.

   e. The domain is $(-\infty, \infty)$ and the range is $(-1, 1)$.

   f. The domain is $(0, \infty)$ and the range is $[0, \infty)$.

11.3 Using Technology to Explore Functions

Graphing technology allows us to explore the properties of functions more deeply than we can with only pencil and paper. It can quickly create a table of values, and quickly plot the graph of a function. Such technology can also evaluate functions, solve equations with functions, find maximum and minimum values, and explore other key features.

There are many graphing technologies currently available, including (but not limited to) physical (hand-held) graphing calculators, *Desmos*, *GeoGebra*, *Sage*, and *WolframAlpha*.

This section will focus on *how* technology can be used to explore functions and their key features. Although the choice of particular graphing technology varies by each school and curriculum, the main ways in which technology is used to explore functions is the same and can be done with each of the technologies above.

11.3.1 Finding an Appropriate Window

With a simple linear equation like $y = 2x + 5$, most graphing technologies will show this graph in a good window by default. A common default window goes from $x = -10$ to $x = 10$ and $y = -10$ to $y = 10$.

What if we wanted to graph something with a much larger magnitude though, such as $y = 2000x + 5000$? If we tried to view this for $x = -10$ to $x = 10$ and $y = -10$ to $y = 10$, the function would appear as an almost vertical line since it has such a steep slope.

Using technology, we will create a table of values for this function as shown in Figure 11.3.2(a). Then we will set the x-values for which we view the function to go from $x = -5$ to $x = 5$ and the y-values from $y = -20,000$ to $y = 20,000$. The graph is shown in Figure 11.3.2(b).

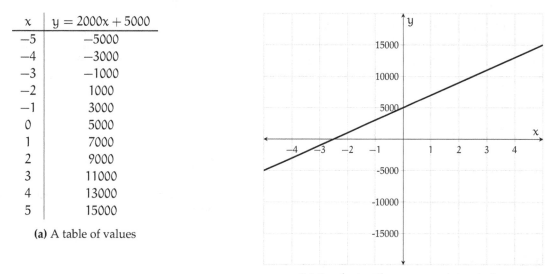

x	$y = 2000x + 5000$
-5	-5000
-4	-3000
-3	-1000
-2	1000
-1	3000
0	5000
1	7000
2	9000
3	11000
4	13000
5	15000

(a) A table of values

(b) Graphed with an appropriate window

Figure 11.3.2: Creating a table of values to determine an appropriate graphing window

Now let's practice finding an appropriate viewing window with a less familiar function.

Example 11.3.3 Find an appropriate window for $q(x) = \frac{x^3}{100} - 2x + 1$. Entering this function into graphing technology, we input q(x)=(x^3)/100-2x+1. A default window will generally give us something like this:

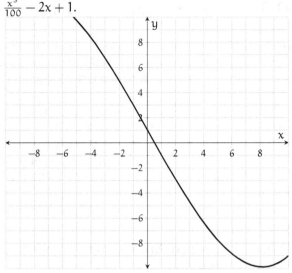

Figure 11.3.4: Function q graphed in the default window.

We can tell from the lower right corner of Figure 11.3.4 that we're not quite viewing all of the important details of this function. To determine a better window, we could use technology to make a table of values. Another more rudimentary option is to double the viewing constraints for x and y, as shown in Figure 11.3.5. Many graphing technologies have the ability to zoom in and out quickly.

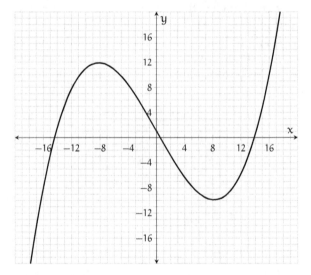

Figure 11.3.5: Function q graphed in an expanded window.

11.3.2 Using Technology to Determine Key Features of a Graph

The key features of a graph can be determined using graphing technology. Here, we'll show how to determine the x-intercepts, y-intercepts, and maximum/minimum values using technology.

Example 11.3.6 Graph the function given by $p(x) = -1000x^2 - 100x + 40$. Determine an appropriate viewing window, and then use graphing technology to determine the following:

    a. Determine the x-intercepts of the function.

    b. Determine the y-intercept of the function.

    c. Determine the maximum function value and where it occurs.

Explanation.

To start, we'll take a quick view of this function in a default window. We can see that we need to zoom in on the x-values, but we need to zoom out on the y-values.

From the graph we see that the x-values might as well run from about -0.5 to 0.5, so we will look at x-values in that window in increments of 0.1, as shown in Table 11.3.8(a). This table allows us to determine an appropriate viewing window for $y = p(x)$ which is shown in Figure 11.3.8(b). The table suggests we should go a little higher than 40 on the y-axis, and it would be OK to go the same distance in the negative direction to keep the x-axis centered.

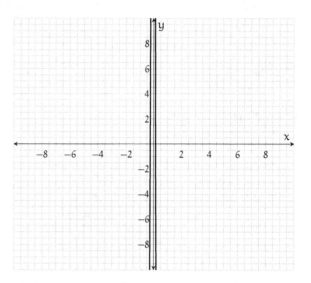

Figure 11.3.7: Graph of $y = p(x)$ in an inappropriate window

x	$p(x)$
-0.5	-160
-0.4	-80
-0.3	-20
-0.2	20
-0.1	40
0	40
0.1	20
0.2	-20
0.3	-80
0.4	-160
0.5	-260

(a) Function values for $y = p(x)$

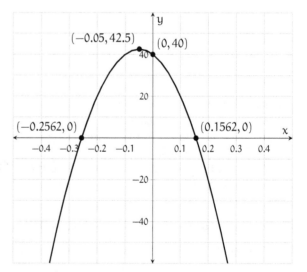

(b) Graph of $y = p(x)$ in an appropriate window showing key features

Figure 11.3.8: Creating a table of values to determine an appropriate graphing window

We can now use Figure 11.3.8(b) to determine the x-intercepts, the y-intercept, and the maximum function value.

a. To determine the x-intercepts, we will find the points where y is zero. These are about $(-0.2562, 0)$ and $(0.1562, 0)$.

b. To determine the y-intercept, we need the point where x is zero. This point is $(0, 40)$.

c. The highest point on the graph is the vertex, which is about $(-0.05, 42.5)$. So the maximum function value is 42.5 and occurs at -0.05.

d. We can see that the function is defined for all x-values, so the domain is $(-\infty, \infty)$. The maximum function value is 42.5, and there is no minimum function value. Thus the range is $(-\infty, 42.5]$.

Example 11.3.9 Graphing Technology Limitations.
If we use graphing technology to graph the function g where $g(x) = 0.0002x^2 + 0.00146x + 0.00266$, we may be mislead by the way values are rounded. Without technology, we know that this function is a quadratic function and therefore has at most two x-intercepts and has a vertex that will determine the minimum function value. However, using technology we could obtain a graph with the following key points:

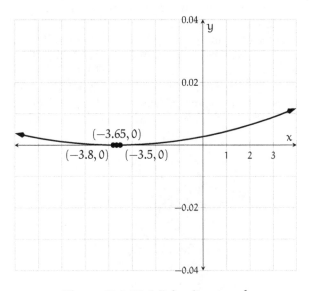

Figure 11.3.10: Misleading graph

This *looks* like there are three x-intercepts, which we know is not possible for a quadratic function. We can evaluate g at $x = -3.65$ and determine that $g(-3.65) = -0.0000045$, which is *approximately* zero when rounded. So the true vertex of this function is $(-3.65, -0.0000045)$, and the minimum value of this function is -0.0000045 (not zero).

Every graphing tool generally has some type of limitation like this one, and it's good to be aware that these limitations exist.

11.3.3 Solving Equations and Inequalities Graphically Using Technology

To *algebraically* solve an equation like $h(x) = v(x)$ for

$$h(x) = -0.01(x - 90)(x + 20) \qquad \text{and} \qquad v(x) = -0.04(x - 10)(x - 80),$$

we'd start by setting up

$$-0.01(x - 90)(x + 20) = -0.04(x - 10)(x - 80)$$

To solve this, we'd then simplify each side of the equation, set it equal to zero, and finally use the quadratic formula like we did in Section 7.2.

An alternative is to *graphically* solve this equation, which is done by graphing

$$y = -0.01(x - 90)(x + 20) \qquad \text{and} \qquad y = -0.04(x - 10)(x - 80).$$

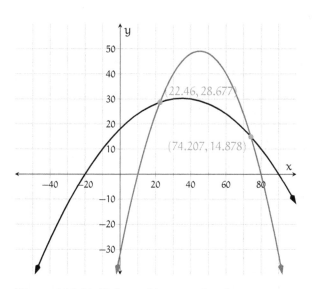

The points of intersection, $(22.46, 28.677)$ and $(74.207, 14.878)$, show where these functions are equal. This means that the x-values give the solutions to the equation $-0.01(x - 90)(x + 20) = -0.04(x - 10)(x - 80)$. So the solutions are approximately 22.46 and 74.207, and the solution set is approximately $\{22.46, 74.207\}$.

Figure 11.3.11: Points of intersection for $h(x) = v(x)$

Similarly, to *graphically* solve an equation like $h(x) = 25$ for

$$h(x) = -0.01(x - 90)(x + 20),$$

we can graph

$$y = -0.01(x - 90)(x + 20) \qquad \text{and} \qquad y = 25$$

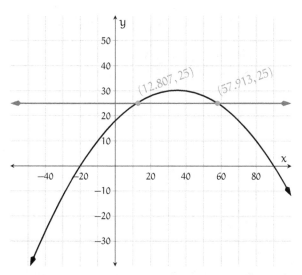

The points of intersection are $(12.807, 25)$ and $(57.913, 25)$, which tells us that the solutions to $h(x) = 25$ are approximately 12.807 and 57.913. The solution set is approximately $\{12.807, 57.913\}$.

Figure 11.3.12: Points of intersection for $h(x) = 25$

Example 11.3.13 Use graphing technology to solve the following inequalities:

    a. $-20t^2 - 70t + 300 \geq -5t + 300$ b. $-20t^2 - 70t + 300 < -5t + 300$

Explanation. To solve these inequalities graphically, we will start by graphing the equations $y = -20t^2 - 70t + 300$ and $y = -5t + 300$ and determining the points of intersection:

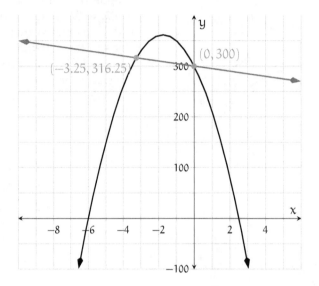

Figure 11.3.14: Points of intersection for $y = -20t^2 - 70t + 300$ and $y = -5t + 300$

  a. To solve $-20t^2 - 70t + 300 \geq -5t + 300$, we need to determine where the y-values of the graph of $y = -20t^2 - 70t + 300$ are *greater* than the y-values of the graph of $y = -5t + 300$ in addition to the values where the y-values are equal. This region is highlighted in Figure 11.3.15.

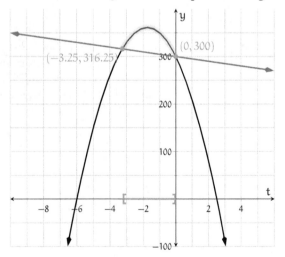

We can see that this region includes all values of t between, and including, $t = -3.25$ and $t = 0$. So the solutions to this inequality include all values of t for which $-3.25 \leq t \leq 0$. We can write this solution set in interval notation as $[-3.25, 0]$ or in set-builder notation as $\{t \mid -3.25 \leq t \leq 0\}$.

Figure 11.3.15

  b. To now solve $-20t^2 - 70t + 300 < -5t + 300$, we will need to determine where the y-values of the graph of $y = -20t^2 - 70t + 300$ are *less than* the y-values of the graph of $y = -5t + 300$. This region is highlighted in Figure 11.3.16.

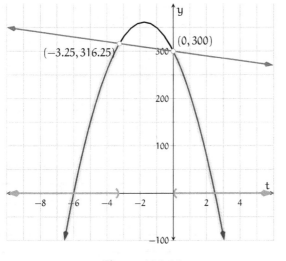

We can see that $-20t^2 - 70t + 300 < -5t + 300$ for all values of t where $t < -3.25$ or $t > 0$. We can write this solution set in interval notation as $(-\infty, -3.25) \cup (0, \infty)$ or in set-builder notation as $\{t \mid t < -3.25 \text{ or } t > 0\}$.

Figure 11.3.16

11.3.4 Reading Questions

1. If you use technology to create a graph of a function, you will have to choose a good ⬚ to capture all of its features.

2. Describe the process to graphically solve an equation in the form $f(x) = g(x)$.

11.3.5 Exercises

Using Technology to Create a Table of Function Values Use technology to make a table of values for the function.

1. $H(x) = -3x^2 + 14x + 3$

x	H(x)

2. $K(x) = 3x^2 - 8x - 3$

x	K(x)

3. $f(x) = -0.2x^2 + 80x + 93$

x	f(x)
-------	-------
-------	-------
-------	-------
-------	-------
-------	-------

4. $g(x) = -3x^2 - 160x + 38$

x	g(x)
-------	-------
-------	-------
-------	-------
-------	-------
-------	-------

5. $h(x) = 7x^3 + 10x - 18$

x	h(x)
-------	-------
-------	-------
-------	-------
-------	-------
-------	-------

6. $h(x) = -2x^3 + 190x - 74$

x	h(x)
-------	-------
-------	-------
-------	-------
-------	-------
-------	-------

Determining Appropriate Windows

7. Let $f(x) = -5670x + 4316$. Choose an appropriate window for graphing f that shows its key features.

The x-interval could be [＿＿＿] and the y-interval could be [＿＿＿].

8. Let $f(x) = 633x + 787$. Choose an appropriate window for graphing f that shows its key features.

The x-interval could be [＿＿＿] and the y-interval could be [＿＿＿].

9. Let $f(x) = -742x^2 - 210x - 6418$. Choose an appropriate window for graphing f that shows its key features.

The x-interval could be [＿＿＿] and the y-interval could be [＿＿＿].

10. Let $f(x) = -852x^2 - 622x + 6289$. Choose an appropriate window for graphing f that shows its key features.

The x-interval could be [＿＿＿] and the y-interval could be [＿＿＿].

11. Let $f(x) = 0.00049x^2 + 0.0011x - 0.59$. Choose an appropriate window for graphing f that shows its key features.

The x-interval could be [＿＿＿] and the y-interval could be [＿＿＿].

12. Let $f(x) = -0.00012x^2 - 0.0028x + 0.58$. Choose an appropriate window for graphing f that shows its key features.

The x-interval could be [＿＿＿] and the y-interval could be [＿＿＿].

Finding Points of Intersection

13. Use technology to determine how many times the equations
$y = (370 - 13x)(-307 + 20x)$ and $y = 4000$
intersect. They intersect   (☐ zero times   ☐ one time   ☐ two times   ☐ three times)
.

14. Use technology to determine how many times the equations
$y = (-214 - 8x)(416 + 6x)$ and $y = 3000$
intersect. They intersect   (☐ zero times   ☐ one time   ☐ two times   ☐ three times)
.

15. Use technology to determine how many times the equations $y = -2x^3 - x^2 + 4x$ and $y = 3x + 1$ intersect. They intersect (□ zero times □ one time □ two times □ three times) .

16. Use technology to determine how many times the equations $y = 9x^3 - 3x^2 - 3x$ and $y = x + 2$ intersect. They intersect (□ zero times □ one time □ two times □ three times) .

17. Use technology to determine how many times the equations $y = 0.1(6x^2 + 1)$ and $y = -0.74(6x - 8)$ intersect. They intersect (□ zero times □ one time □ two times □ three times) .

18. Use technology to determine how many times the equations $y = 0.2(7x^2 + 9)$ and $y = 0.57(3x + 6)$ intersect. They intersect (□ zero times □ one time □ two times □ three times) .

19. Use technology to determine how many times the equations $y = 1.4(x - 8)^2 - 2.35$ and $y = 0.1x$ intersect. They intersect (□ zero times □ one time □ two times □ three times) .

20. Use technology to determine how many times the equations $y = 1.85(x - 1)^2 + 5.2$ and $y = -x$ intersect. They intersect (□ zero times □ one time □ two times □ three times) .

Using Technology to Find Key Features of a Graph

21. For the function j defined by

$$j(x) = -\frac{2}{5}(x - 3)^2 + 6,$$

use technology to determine the following. Round answers as necessary.

 a. Any intercepts.

 b. The vertex.

 c. The domain.

 d. The range.

22. For the function k defined by

$$k(x) = 2(x + 1)^2 + 10,$$

use technology to determine the following. Round answers as necessary.

 a. Any intercepts.

 b. The vertex.

 c. The domain.

 d. The range.

23. For the function L defined by

$$L(x) = 3000x^2 + 10x + 4,$$

use technology to determine the following. Round answers as necessary.

 a. Any intercepts.

 b. The vertex.

 c. The domain.

 d. The range.

24. For the function M defined by

$$M(x) = -(300x - 2950)^2,$$

use technology to determine the following. Round answers as necessary.

 a. Any intercepts.

 b. The vertex.

 c. The domain.

 d. The range.

25. For the function N defined by

$$N(x) = (300x - 1.05)^2,$$

use technology to determine the following. Round answers as necessary.

   a. Any intercepts.

   b. The vertex.

   c. The domain.

   d. The range.

26. For the function B defined by

$$B(x) = x^2 - 0.05x + 0.0006,$$

use technology to determine the following. Round answers as necessary.

   a. Any intercepts.

   b. The vertex.

   c. The domain.

   d. The range.

Solving Equations and Inequalities Graphically Using Technology

27. Let $s(x) = \frac{1}{5}x^2 - 2x + 10$ and $t(x) = -x + 40$. Use graphing technology to determine the following.

   a. What are the points of intersection for these two functions?

   b. Solve $s(x) = t(x)$.

   c. Solve $s(x) > t(x)$.

   d. Solve $s(x) \leq t(x)$.

28. Let $w(x) = \frac{1}{4}x^2 - 3x - 8$ and $m(x) = x + 12$. Use graphing technology to determine the following.

   a. What are the points of intersection for these two functions?

   b. Solve $w(x) = m(x)$.

   c. Solve $w(x) > m(x)$.

   d. Solve $w(x) \leq m(x)$.

29. Let $f(x) = 4x^2 + 5x - 1$ and $g(x) = 5$. Use graphing technology to determine the following.

   a. What are the points of intersection for these two functions?

   b. Solve $f(x) = g(x)$.

   c. Solve $f(x) < g(x)$.

   d. Solve $f(x) \geq g(x)$.

30. Let $p(x) = 6x^2 - 3x + 4$ and $k(x) = 7$. Use graphing technology to determine the following.

   a. What are the points of intersection for these two functions?

   b. Solve $p(x) = k(x)$.

   c. Solve $p(x) < k(x)$.

   d. Solve $p(x) \geq k(x)$.

31. Let $q(x) = -4x^2 - 24x + 10$ and $r(x) = 2x + 22$. Use graphing technology to determine the following.

   a. What are the points of intersection for these two functions?

   b. Solve $q(x) = r(x)$.

   c. Solve $q(x) > r(x)$.

   d. Solve $q(x) \leq r(x)$.

32. Let $h(x) = -10x^2 - 5x + 3$ and $j(x) = -3x - 9$. Use graphing technology to determine the following.

   a. What are the points of intersection for these two functions?

   b. Solve $h(x) = j(x)$.

   c. Solve $h(x) > j(x)$.

   d. Solve $h(x) \leq j(x)$.

33. Use graphing technology to solve the equation $0.4x^2 + 0.5x - 0.2 = 2.4$. Approximate the solution(s) if necessary.

34. Use graphing technology to solve the equation $-0.25x^2 - 2x + 1.75 = 4.75$. Approximate the solution(s) if necessary.

35. Use graphing technology to solve the equation $(200 + 5x)(100 - 2x) = 15000$. Approximate the solution(s) if necessary.

36. Use graphing technology to solve the equation $(200 - 5x)(100 + 10x) = 20000$. Approximate the solution(s) if necessary.

37. Use graphing technology to solve the equation $2x^3 - 5x + 1 = -\frac{1}{2}x + 1$. Approximate the solution(s) if necessary.

38. Use graphing technology to solve the equation $-x^3 + 8x = -4x + 16$. Approximate the solution(s) if necessary.

39. Use graphing technology to solve the equation $-0.05x^2 - 2.03x - 19.6 = 0.05x^2 + 1.97x + 19.4$. Approximate the solution(s) if necessary.

40. Use graphing technology to solve the equation $-0.02x^2 + 1.97x - 51.5 = 0.05(x - 50)^2 - 0.03(x - 50)$. Approximate the solution(s) if necessary.

41. Use graphing technology to solve the equation $-200x^2 + 60x - 55 = -20x - 40$. Approximate the solution(s) if necessary.

42. Use graphing technology to solve the equation $150x^2 - 20x + 50 = 100x + 40$. Approximate the solution(s) if necessary.

43. Use graphing technology to solve the inequality $2x^2 + 5x - 3 > -5$. State the solution set using interval notation, and approximate if necessary.

44. Use graphing technology to solve the inequality $-x^2 + 4x - 7 > -12$. State the solution set using interval notation, and approximate if necessary.

45. Use graphing technology to solve the inequality $10x^2 - 11x + 7 \leq 7$. State the solution set using interval notation, and approximate if necessary.

46. Use graphing technology to solve the inequality $-10x^2 - 15x + 4 \leq 9$. State the solution set using interval notation, and approximate if necessary.

47. Use graphing technology to solve the inequality $-x^2 - 6x + 1 > x + 5$. State the solution set using interval notation, and approximate if necessary.

48. Use graphing technology to solve the inequality $3x^2 + 5x - 4 > -2x + 1$. State the solution set using interval notation, and approximate if necessary.

49. Use graphing technology to solve the inequality $-10x + 4 \leq 20x^2 - 34x + 6$. State the solution set using interval notation, and approximate if necessary.

50. Use graphing technology to solve the inequality $-15x^2 - 6 \leq 10x - 4$. State the solution set using interval notation, and approximate if necessary.

51. Use graphing technology to solve the inequality $\frac{1}{2}x^2 + \frac{3}{2}x \geq \frac{1}{2}x - \frac{3}{2}$. State the solution set using interval notation, and approximate if necessary.

52. Use graphing technology to solve the inequality $\frac{3}{4}x \geq \frac{1}{4}x^2 - 3x$. State the solution set using interval notation, and approximate if necessary.

11.4 Simplifying Expressions with Function Notation

In this section, we will discuss algebra simplification that will appear in many facets of education. Simplification is a skill, like cooking noodles or painting a wall. It may not always be exciting, but it does serve a purpose. Also like cooking noodles or painting a wall, it isn't usually difficult, and yet there are common avoidable mistakes that people make. With practice from this section, you'll have experience to prevent yourself from overcooking the noodles or ruining your paintbrush.

11.4.1 Negative Signs in and out of Function Notation

Let's start by reminding ourselves about the meaning of function notation. When we write $f(x)$, we have a process f that is doing something to an input value x. Whatever is inside those parentheses is the input to the function. What if we use something for input that is not quite as simple as "x?"

Example 11.4.2 Find and simplify a formula for $f(-x)$, where $f(x) = x^2 + 3x - 4$.

Explanation.   Those parentheses encase "$-x$," so we are meant to treat "$-x$" as the input. The rule that we have been given for f is

$$f(x) = x^2 + 3x - 4.$$

But the x's that are in this formula are just place-holders. What f does to a number can just as easily be communicated with

$$f(\ ) = (\ )^2 + 3(\ ) - 4.$$

So now that we are meant to treat "$-x$" as the input, we will insert "$-x$" into those slots, after which we can do more familiar algebraic simplification:

$$f(\ \ ) = (\ \ )^2 + 3(\ \ ) - 4$$
$$f(-x) = (-x)^2 + 3(-x) - 4$$
$$= x^2 - 3x - 4$$

The previous example contrasts nicely with this one:

Example 11.4.3 Find and simplify a formula for $-f(x)$, where $f(x) = x^2 + 3x - 4$.

Explanation.   Here, the parentheses only encase "x." The negative sign is on the outside. So the way to see this expression is that first f will do what it does to x, and then that result will be negated:

$$-f(x) = -(x^2 + 3x - 4)$$
$$= -x^2 - 3x + 4$$

Note that the answer to this exercise, which was to simplify $-f(x)$, is different from the answer to Example 11.4.2, which was to simplify $f(-x)$. In general you cannot pass a negative sign in and out of function notation and still have the same quantity.

In Example 11.4.2 and Example 11.4.3, we are working with the expressions $f(-x)$ and $-f(x)$, and trying to find "simplified" formulas. If it seems strange to be doing these things, perhaps this applied example will help.

Checkpoint 11.4.4 The NASDAQ Composite Index measures how well a portion of the stock market is doing. Suppose $N(t)$ is the value of the index t days after January 1, 2018. A formula for N is $N(t) =$

$3.34t^2 + 26.2t + 6980$.

What if you wanted a new function, B, that gives the value of the NASDAQ index t days *before* January 1, 2018? Technically, t days *before* is the same as *negative* t days after. So $B(t)$ is the same as $N(-t)$, and now the expression $N(-t)$ means something. Find a simplified formula for $N(-t)$.

$N(-t)$

Explanation.

$$N(\quad) = 3.34(\quad)^2 + 26.2(\quad) + 6980$$
$$N(-t) = 3.34(-t)^2 + 26.2(-t) + 6980$$
$$= 3.34t^2 - 26.2t + 6980$$

11.4.2 Other Nontrivial Simplifications

Example 11.4.5 Find and simplify a formula for $h(5x)$, where $h(x) = \frac{x}{x-2}$.

Explanation. The parentheses encase "5x," so we are meant to treat "5x" as the input.

$$h(\quad) = \frac{(\quad)}{(\quad) - 2}$$
$$h(5x) = \frac{5x}{5x - 2}$$
$$= \frac{5x}{5x - 2}$$

Example 11.4.6 Find and simplify a formula for $\frac{1}{3}g(3x)$, where $g(x) = 2x^2 + 8$.

Explanation. Do the $\frac{1}{3}$ and the 3 cancel each other? No. The 3 is part of the input, affecting x right away. Then g does whatever it does to 3x, and *then* we multiply the result by $\frac{1}{3}$. Since the function g acts "in between," we don't have the chance to cancel the 3 with the $\frac{1}{3}$. Let's see what actually happens:

Those parentheses encase "3x," so we are meant to treat "3x" as the input. We will keep the $\frac{1}{3}$ where it is until it is possible to simplify:

$$\frac{1}{3}g(\quad) = \frac{1}{3}\left(2(\quad)^2 + 8\right)$$
$$\frac{1}{3}g(3x) = \frac{1}{3}\left(2(3x)^2 + 8\right)$$
$$= \frac{1}{3}\left(2\left(9x^2\right) + 8\right)$$
$$= \frac{1}{3}\left(18x^2 + 8\right)$$
$$= 6x^2 + \frac{8}{3}$$

Example 11.4.7 If $k(x) = x^2 - 3x$, find and simplify a formula for $k(x-4)$.

Explanation. This type of exercise is often challenging for algebra students. But let's focus on those parentheses one more time. They encase "x − 4," so we are meant to treat "x − 4" as the input.

$$k(\quad) = (\quad)^2 - 3(\quad)$$
$$k(x-4) = (x-4)^2 - 3(x-4)$$

$$= x^2 - 8x + 16 - 3x + 12$$
$$= x^2 - 11x + 28$$

Checkpoint 11.4.8 If $q(x) = x + \sqrt{x+8}$, find and simplify a formula for $q(x+5)$.
   $q(x+5)$

Explanation.   Starting with the generic formula for q:

$$q(\quad) = (\quad) + \sqrt{(\quad) + 8}$$
$$q(x+5) = x + 5 + \sqrt{x + 5 + 8}$$
$$= x + 5 + \sqrt{x + 13}$$

Example 11.4.9 If $f(x) = \frac{1}{x}$, find and simplify a formula for $f(x+3) + 2$.

Explanation.   Do not be tempted to add the 3 and the 2. The 3 is added to input *before* the function f does its work. The 2 is added to the result *after* f has done its work.

$$f(\quad) + 2 = \frac{1}{(\quad)} + 2$$
$$f(x+3) + 2 = \frac{1}{x+3} + 2$$

This last expression is considered fully simplified. However you might combine the two terms using a technique from Section 12.3.

The tasks we have practiced in this section are the kind of tasks that will make it easier to understand interesting and useful material in college algebra and calculus.

11.4.3 Reading Questions

1.   Explain how $f(x+2)$ probably does *not* mean that f is being multiplied by $x + 2$.

11.4.4 Exercises .

Review and Warmup

1.   Use the distributive property to write an equivalent expression to $5(n+5)$ that has no grouping symbols.

2.   Use the distributive property to write an equivalent expression to $2(q+9)$ that has no grouping symbols.

3.   Use the distributive property to write an equivalent expression to $-4(x-6)$ that has no grouping symbols.

4.   Use the distributive property to write an equivalent expression to $-7(r+3)$ that has no grouping symbols.

5.   Multiply the polynomials.
   $2(y+1)^2$

6.   Multiply the polynomials.
   $4(y+7)^2$

7.   Expand the square of a *bi*nomial.
   $(4y+9)^2$

8.   Expand the square of a *bi*nomial.
   $(10r+3)^2$

Simplifying Function Expressions

9. Simplify $G(r+7)$, where $G(r) = 7 - 3r$.

10. Simplify $g(t+2)$, where $g(t) = 7 - 7t$.

11. Simplify $K(-t)$, where $K(t) = 5 + t$.

12. Simplify $F(-x)$, where $F(x) = 7 + 8x$.

13. Simplify $g(x+4)$, where $g(x) = 6 - 4.4x$.

14. Simplify $K(y+8)$, where $K(y) = 6 + 7.3y$.

15. Simplify $F(y - \frac{5}{7})$, where $F(y) = -\frac{3}{4} + \frac{7}{9}y$.

16. Simplify $g(y + \frac{3}{5})$, where $g(y) = -\frac{1}{7} + \frac{7}{5}y$.

17. Simplify $H(r) + 1$, where $H(r) = -6r + 6$.

18. Simplify $F(r) + 5$, where $F(r) = 6r + 5$.

19. Simplify $f(t) + 8$, where $f(t) = 5 + 1.1t$.

20. Simplify $H(t) + 3$, where $H(t) = 5 - 3.4t$.

21. Simplify $F(7x)$, where $F(x) = -8x^2 + 5x + 7$.

22. Simplify $f(3x)$, where $f(x) = 4x^2 + 4x - 1$.

23. Simplify $H(-y)$, where $H(y) = y^2 - y + 4$.

24. Simplify $h(-y)$, where $h(y) = 8y^2 - 5y + 4$.

25. Simplify $5f(y)$, where $f(y) = 7y^2 + 4y + 7$.

26. Simplify $8G(r)$, where $G(r) = 2r^2 + 4r - 1$.

27. Simplify $h(r-5)$, where $h(r) = -2.4r^2 + 3r + 7$.

28. Simplify $f(t+3)$, where $f(t) = -6.9t^2 + 3t - 2$.

29. Simplify $G(t) + 2$, where $G(t) = 5t^2 + 3t + 7$.

30. Simplify $h(x) + 5$, where $h(x) = 3x^2 - 2x + 3$.

31. Simplify $g(x+9)$, where $g(x) = \sqrt{3 - 7x}$.

32. Simplify $g(x+6)$, where $g(x) = \sqrt{2 + 2x}$.

33. Simplify $h(x) + 3$, where $h(x) = \sqrt{2 + 6x}$.

34. Simplify $F(x) + 9$, where $F(x) = \sqrt{2 - x}$.

35. Simplify $G(x+6)$, where $G(x) = 7x + \sqrt{2 - 5x}$.

36. Simplify $G(x+3)$, where $G(x) = -2x + \sqrt{1 + 7x}$.

37. Simplify $K(t+4)$, where $K(t) = \frac{7}{t+1}$.

38. Simplify $G(t+8)$, where $G(t) = -\frac{2}{-3t+1}$.

39. Simplify $h(-3x)$, where $h(x) = \frac{5x}{x^2+6}$.

40. Simplify $K(7x)$, where $K(x) = \frac{6x}{x^2-2}$.

41. Let f be a function given by $f(x) = -4x - 8$. Find and simplify the following:

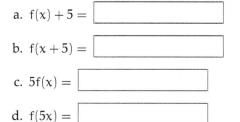

a. $f(x) + 5 =$

b. $f(x + 5) =$

c. $5f(x) =$

d. $f(5x) =$

42. Let f be a function given by $f(x) = -4x - 1$. Find and simplify the following:

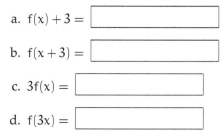

a. $f(x) + 3 =$

b. $f(x + 3) =$

c. $3f(x) =$

d. $f(3x) =$

43. Let f be a function given by $f(x) = 3x^2 + 4x$. Find and simplify the following:

a. $f(x) - 2 =$

b. $f(x - 2) =$

c. $-2f(x) =$

d. $f(-2x) =$

44. Let f be a function given by $f(x) = -4x^2 - 2x$. Find and simplify the following:

a. $f(x) - 3 =$

b. $f(x - 3) =$

c. $-3f(x) =$

d. $f(-3x) =$

Applications

45. A circular oil slick is expanding with radius, r in feet, at time t in hours given by $r = 18t - 0.3t^2$, for t in hours, $0 \le t \le 10$.

Find a formula for $A = f(t)$, the area of the oil slick as a function of time.

$A = f(t)$

with

(Be sure to include units!)

46. Suppose $T(t)$ represents the temperature outside, in Fahrenheit, at t hours past noon, and a formula for T is $T(t) = \frac{28t}{t^2+1} + 56$.

If we introduce $F(t)$ as the temperature outside, in Fahrenheit, at t hours past 1:00pm, then $F(t) = T(t + 1)$. Find a simplified formula for $T(t + 1)$.

$T(t + 1)$

47. Suppose $G(t)$ represents how many gigabytes of data has been downloaded t minutes after you started a download, and a formula for G is $G(t) = 20 - \frac{80}{t+4}$.

If we introduce $M(t)$ as how many megabytes of data has been downloaded t minutes after you started a download, then $M(t) = 1024G(t)$. Find a simplified formula for $1024G(t)$.

$1024G(t)$

11.5 Technical Definition of a Function

In Section 11.1, we discussed a conceptual understanding of functions and Definition 11.1.3. In this section we'll start with a more technical definition of what is a function, consistent with the ideas from Section 11.1.

11.5.1 Formally Defining a Function

Definition 11.5.2 Function (Technical Definition). A **function** is a collection of ordered pairs (x, y) such that any particular value of x is paired with at most one value for y. ◊

How is this definition consistent with the informal Definition 11.1.3, which describes a function as a *process*? Well, if you have a collection of ordered pairs (x, y), you can choose to view the left number as an input, and the right value as the output. If the function's name is f and you want to find $f(x)$ for a particular number x, look in the collection of ordered pairs to see if x appears among the first coordinates. If it does, then $f(x)$ is the (unique) y-value it was paired with. If it does not, then that x is just not in the domain of f, because you have no way to determine what $f(x)$ would be.

Example 11.5.3 Using Definition 11.5.1, a function f could be given by $\{(1, 4), (2, 3), (5, 3), (6, 1)\}$.

    a. What is $f(1)$? Since the ordered pair $(1, 4)$ appears in the collection of ordered pairs, $f(1) = 4$.

    b. What is $f(2)$? Since the ordered pair $(2, 3)$ appears in the collection of ordered pairs, $f(2) = 3$.

    c. What is $f(3)$? None of the ordered pairs in the collection start with 3, so $f(3)$ is undefined, and we would say that 3 is not in the domain of f.

Example 11.5.4 A Function Given as a Table.
Consider the function g expressed by Figure 11.5.5. How is this "a collection of ordered pairs?" With tables the connection is most easily apparent. Pair off each x-value with its y-value.

x	g(x)
12	0.16
15	3.2
18	1.4
21	1.4
24	0.98

Figure 11.5.5

In this case, we can view this function as:

$$\{(12, 0.16), (15, 3.2), (18, 3.2), (21, 1.4), (24, 0.98)\}.$$

Example 11.5.6 A Function Given as a Formula. Consider the function h expressed by the formula $h(x) = x^2$. How is this "a collection of ordered pairs?"

This time, the collection is *really big*. Imagine an x-value, like $x = 2$. We can calculate that $f(2) = 2^2 = 4$. So the input 2 pairs with the output 4 and the ordered pair $(2, 4)$ is part of the collection.

You could move on to *any* x-value, like say $x = 2.1$. We can calculate that $f(2.1) = 2.1^2 = 4.41$. So the input 2.1 pairs with the output 4.41 and the ordered pair $(2.1, 4.41)$ is part of the collection.

The collection is so large that we cannot literally list all the ordered pairs as was done in Example 11.5.3 and Example 11.5.4. We just have to imagine this giant collection of ordered pairs. And if it helps to conceptualize it, we know that the ordered pairs $(2, 4)$ and $(2.1, 4.41)$ are included.

Example 11.5.7 A Function Given as a Graph. Consider the functions p and q expressed in Figure 11.5.8 and Figure 11.5.9. How is each of these "a collection of ordered pairs?"

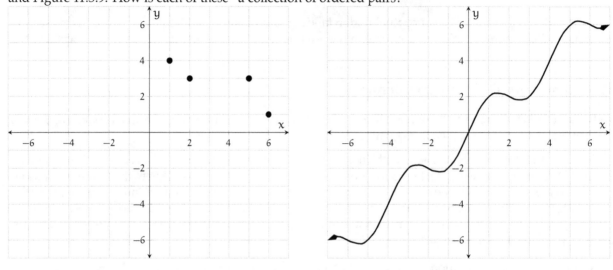

Figure 11.5.8: $y = p(x)$ **Figure 11.5.9:** $y = q(x)$

In Figure 11.5.8, we see that $p(1) = 4$, $p(2) = 3$, $p(5) = 3$, and $p(6) = 1$. The graph *literally is* the collection

$$\{(1, 4), (2, 3), (5, 3), (6, 1)\}.$$

In Figure 11.5.9, we can see a few whole number function values, like $q(0) = 0$ and $q(1) = 2$. But the entire curve has infinitely many points on it and we'd never be able to list them all. We just have to imagine the giant collection of ordered pairs. And if it helps to conceptualize it, we know that the ordered pairs $(0, 0)$ and $(1, 2)$ are included.

Checkpoint 11.5.10 The graph below is of $y = f(x)$.

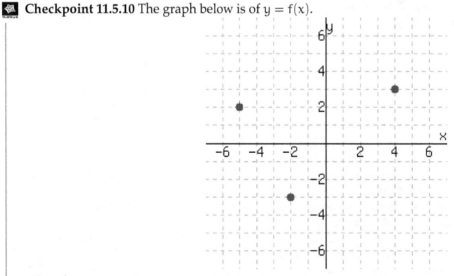

Write the function f as a set of ordered pairs.

Explanation. The function can be expressed as the set $\{(-5, 2), (-2, -3), (4, 3)\}$.

11.5.2 Identifying What is *Not* a Function

Just because you have a set of order pairs, a table, a graph, or an equation, it does not necessarily mean that you have a function. Conceptually, whatever you have needs to give consistent outputs if you feed it the same input. More technically, the set of ordered pairs is not allowed to have two ordered pairs that have the same x-value but different y-values.

Example 11.5.11 Consider each set of ordered pairs. Does it make a function?

a. $\left\{(5,9),(3,2),\left(\frac{1}{2},0.6\right),(5,1)\right\}$

c. $\left\{(5,9),(3,9),\left(4.2,\sqrt{2}\right),\left(\frac{4}{3},\frac{1}{2}\right)\right\}$

b. $\left\{(-5,12),(3,7),\left(\sqrt{2},1\right),(-0.9,4)\right\}$

d. $\left\{(5,9),(0.7,2),\left(\sqrt{25},3\right),\left(\frac{2}{3},\frac{3}{2}\right)\right\}$

Explanation.

a. This set of ordered pairs is *not* a function. The problem is that it has both $(5,9)$ and $(5,1)$. It uses the same x-value paired with two different y-values. We have no clear way to turn the input 5 into an output.

b. This set of ordered pairs *is* a function. It is a collection of ordered pairs, and the x-values are never reused.

c. This set of ordered pairs *is* a function. It is a collection of ordered pairs, and the x-values are never reused. You might note that the *output* value 9 appears twice, but that doesn't matter. That just tells us that the function turns 5 into 9 and it also turns 3 into 9.

d. This set of ordered pairs is *not* a function, but it's a little tricky. One of the ordered pairs uses $\sqrt{25}$ as an input value. But that is the same as 5, which is also used as an input value.

Now that we understand how some sets of ordered pairs might not be functions, what about tables, graphs, and equations? If we are handed one of these things, can we tell whether or not it is giving us a function?

Checkpoint 11.5.12 Does This Table Make a Function? Which of these tables make y a function of x?

a.

x	y
2	1
3	1
4	2
5	2
6	2

This table (□ does □ does not) make y a function of x.

b.

x	y
8	3
9	2
5	1
2	0
8	1

This table (□ does □ does not) make y a function of x.

c.

x	y
5	9
5	9
6	2
6	2
6	2

This table (□ does □ does not) make y a function of x.

Explanation.

a. This table does make y a function of x. In the table, no x-value is repeated.

b. This table does not make y a function of x. In the table, the x-value 8 is repeated, and it is paired with two different y-values, 3 and 1.

c. This table does make y a function of x, but you have to think carefully. It's true that the x-value 5 is used more than once in the table. But in both places, the y-value is the same, 9. So there is no conceptual issue with asking for f(5); it would definitely be 9. Similarly, the repeated use of 6 as an x-value is not a problem since it is always paired with output 2.

Example 11.5.13 Does This Graph Make a Function? Which of these graphs make y a function of x?

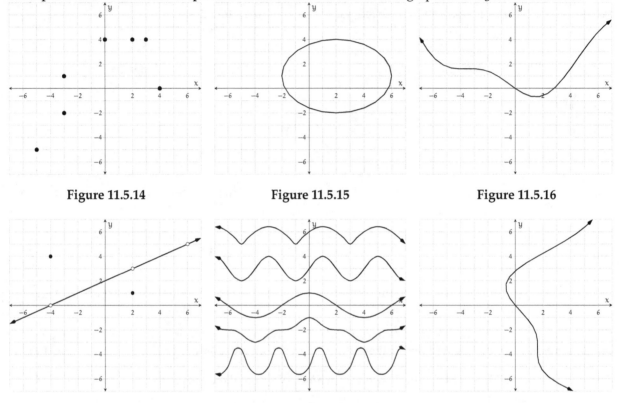

Figure 11.5.14   Figure 11.5.15   Figure 11.5.16

Figure 11.5.17   Figure 11.5.18   Figure 11.5.19

Explanation. The graph in Figure 11.5.14 does *not* make y a function of x. Two ordered pairs on that graph are $(-3, 1)$ and $(-3, -2)$, so an input value is used twice with different output values.

The graph in Figure 11.5.15 does *not* make y a function of x. There are many ordered pairs with the same input value but different output values. For example, $(2, -2)$ and $(2, 4)$.

The graph in Figure 11.5.16 *does* make y a function of x. It appears that no matter what x-value you choose on the x-axis, there is exactly one y-value paired up with it on the graph.

The graph in Figure 11.5.17 *does* make y a function of x, but we should discuss. The hollow dots on the line indicate that the line goes right up to that point, but never reaches it. We say there is a "hole" in the graph at these places. For two of these holes, there is a separate ordered pair immediately above or below the hole. The graph has the ordered pair $(-4, 4)$. It *also* has ordered pairs like (very close to -4, very close to 0), but it does not have $(-4, 0)$. Overall, there is no x-value that is used twice with different y-values, so this graph does make y a function of x

The graph in Figure 11.5.15 does *not* make y a function of x. There are many ordered pairs with the same input value but different output values. For example, $(0, 1)$, $(0, 3)$, $(0, -1)$, $(0, 5)$, and $(0, -6)$ all use $x = 0$.

The graph in Figure 11.5.15 does *not* make y a function of x. There are many ordered pairs with the same input value but different output values. For example at $x = 2$, there is both a positive and a negative associated y-value. It's hard to say exactly what these y-values are, but we don't have to.

This last set of examples might reveal something to you. For instance in Figure 11.5.15, the issue is that there are places on the graph with the same x-value, but different y-values. Visually, what that means is there are places on the graph that are directly above/below each other. Thinking about this leads to a quick visual "test" to determine if a graph gives y as a function of x.

Fact 11.5.20 Vertical Line Test. *Given a graph in the xy-plane, if a vertical line ever touches it in more than one place, the graph does* not *give y as a function of x. If vertical lines only ever touch the graph once or never at all, then the graph* does *give y as a function of x.*

Example 11.5.21 In each graph from Example 11.5.13, we can apply the Vertical Line Test.

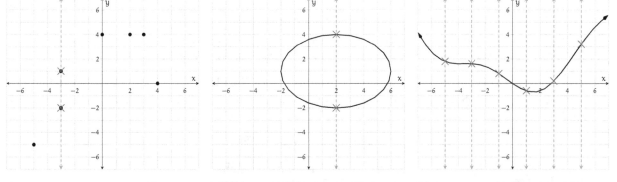

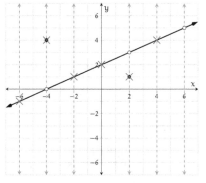

Figure 11.5.22: A vertical line touching the graph twice makes this graph not give y as a function of x.

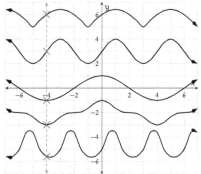

Figure 11.5.23: A vertical line touching the graph twice makes this graph not give y as a function of x.

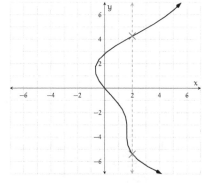

Figure 11.5.24: All vertical lines only touch the graph once, so this graph does give y as a function of x.

Figure 11.5.25: All vertical lines only touch the graph once, or not at all, so this graph does give y as a function of x.

Figure 11.5.26: A vertical line touching the graph more than once makes this graph not give y as a function of x.

Figure 11.5.27: A vertical line touching the graph more than once makes this graph not give y as a function of x.

Lastly, we come to equations. Certain equations with variables x and y clearly make y a function of x. For example, $y = x^2 + 1$ says that if you have an x-value, all you have to do is substitute it into that equation and you will have determined an output y-value. You could then name the function f and give a formula for it: $f(x) = x^2 + 1$.

With other equations, it may not be immediately clear whether or not they make y a function of x.

Example 11.5.28 Do each of these equations make y a function of x?

a. $2x + 3y = 5$ b. $y = \pm\sqrt{x+4}$ c. $x^2 + y^2 = 9$

Explanation.

a. The equation $2x + 3y = 5$ *does* make y a function of x. Here are three possible explanations.

     i. You recognize that the graph of this equation would be a non-vertical line, and so it would pass the Vertical Line Test.

     ii. Imagine that you have a specific value for x and you substitute it in to $2x + 3y = 5$. Will you be able to use algebra to solve for y? All you will need is to simplify, subtract from both sides, and divide on both sides, so you will be able to determine y.

     iii. Can you just isolate y in terms of x? Yes, a few steps of algebra can turn $2x + 3y = 5$ into $y = \frac{5-2x}{3}$. Now you have an explicit formula for y in terms of x, so y is a function of x.

b. The equation $y = \pm\sqrt{x+4}$ does *not* make y a function of x. Just having the $\pm$ (plus *or* minus) in the equation immediately tells you that for almost any valid x-value, there would be *two* associated y-values.

c. The equation $x^2 + y^2 = 9$ does *not* make y a function of x. Here are three possible explanations.

     i. Imagine that you have a specific value for x and you substitute it in to $x^2 + y^2 = 9$. Will you be able to use algebra to solve for y? For example, if you substitute in $x = 1$, then you have $1 + y^2 = 9$, which simplifies to $y^2 = 8$. Can you really determine what y is? No, because it could be $\sqrt{8}$ or it could be $-\sqrt{8}$. So this equation does not provide you with a way to turn x-values into y-values.

     ii. Can you just isolate y in terms of x? You might get started and use algebra to convert $x^2 + y^2 = 9$ into $y^2 = 9 - x^2$. But what now? The best you can do is acknowledge that y is either the positive or the negative square root of $9 - x^2$. You might write $y = \pm\sqrt{9-x^2}$. But now for almost any valid x-value, there are *two* associated y-values.

     iii. You recognize that the graph of this equation would be a circle with radius 3, and so it would not pass the Vertical Line Test.

Checkpoint 11.5.29 Do each of these equations make y a function of x?

a. $5x^2 - 4y = 12$ b. $5x - 4y^2 = 12$ c. $x = \sqrt{y}$

This equation (☐ does ☐ does not) make y a function of x.

This equation (☐ does ☐ does not) make y a function of x.

This equation (☐ does ☐ does not) make y a function of x.

Explanation.

a. The equation $5x^2 - 4y = 12$ *does* make y a function of x. You can isolate y in terms of x. A few steps of algebra can turn $5x^2 - 4y = 12$ into $y = \frac{5x^2 - 12}{4}$. Now you have an explicit formula for y in terms of x, so y is a function of x.

b. The equation $5x - 4y^2 = 12$ does *not* make y a function of x. You cannot isolate y in terms of x. You might get started and use algebra to convert $5x - 4y^2 = 12$ into $y^2 = \frac{5x-12}{4}$. But what now? The best you can do is acknowledge that y is either the positive or the negative square root of $\frac{5x-12}{4}$. You might write $y = \pm\sqrt{\frac{5x-12}{4}}$. But now for almost any valid x-value, there are *two* associated y-values.

c. The equation $x = \sqrt{y}$ *does* make y a function of x. If you try substituting a non-negative x-value, then you can square both sides and you know exactly what the value of y is.

If you try substituting a negative x-value, then you are saying that $\sqrt{y}$ is negative which is impossible. So for negative x, there are no y-values. This is not a problem for the equation giving you a function. This just means that the domain of that function does not include negative numbers. Its domain would be $[0, \infty)$.

11.5.3 Reading Questions

1. Suppose you have a "relation". That is, a set of order pairs, a table of x- and y-values, a graph, or an equation in x and y. What is the one thing that could happen that would make the relation *not* be a function?

2. Explain how to use the vertical line test.

11.5.4 Exercises

Determining If Sets of Ordered Pairs Are Functions

1. Do these sets of ordered pairs make functions of x? What are their domains and ranges?

   a. $\left\{(-10, 10), (2, 0)\right\}$

   This set of ordered pairs ($\square$ describes $\square$ does not describe) a function of x. This set of ordered pairs has domain [____] and range [____].

   b. $\left\{(-9, 3), (-6, 2), (-4, 6)\right\}$

   This set of ordered pairs ($\square$ describes $\square$ does not describe) a function of x. This set of ordered pairs has domain [____] and range [____].

   c. $\left\{(3, 9), (10, 0), (3, 0), (3, 4)\right\}$

   This set of ordered pairs ($\square$ describes $\square$ does not describe) a function of x. This set of ordered pairs has domain [____] and range [____].

   d. $\left\{(-8, 6), (-10, 10), (-8, 7), (3, 10), (8, 3)\right\}$

   This set of ordered pairs ($\square$ describes $\square$ does not describe) a function of x. This set of ordered pairs has domain [____] and range [____].

2. Do these sets of ordered pairs make functions of x? What are their domains and ranges?

   a. $\left\{(0, 7), (3, 4)\right\}$

   This set of ordered pairs ($\square$ describes $\square$ does not describe) a function of x. This set of ordered pairs has domain [   ] and range [   ].

b. $\{(-3,3),(3,3),(6,0)\}$

This set of ordered pairs   ($\square$ describes $\square$ does not describe)   a function of x. This set of
ordered pairs has domain [   ] and range [   ].

c. $\{(9,9),(6,2),(8,6),(9,10)\}$

This set of ordered pairs   ($\square$ describes $\square$ does not describe)   a function of x. This set of
ordered pairs has domain [   ] and range [   ].

d. $\{(-8,0),(0,5),(1,7),(4,9),(0,8)\}$

This set of ordered pairs   ($\square$ describes $\square$ does not describe)   a function of x. This set of
ordered pairs has domain [   ] and range [   ].

3.   Does the following set of ordered pairs make for a function of x?
     $\{(-1,2),(-1,5),(-7,6),(-6,2),(8,9)\}$
     This set of ordered pairs   ($\square$ describes $\square$ does not describe)   a function of x. This set of
     ordered pairs has domain [   ] and range [   ].

4.   Does the following set of ordered pairs make for a function of x?
     $\{(-10,9),(6,4),(-8,5),(1,2),(-9,9)\}$
     This set of ordered pairs   ($\square$ describes $\square$ does not describe)   a function of x. This set of
     ordered pairs has domain [   ] and range [   ].

Domain and Range

5.   Below is all of the information that exists about a function H.
     $H(1)=3$ $H(3)=1$ $H(6)=4$
     Write H as a set of ordered pairs.

     H has domain [   ] and range [   ].

6.   Below is all of the information about a function K.
     $K(a)=2$ $K(b)=1$
     $K(c)=-2$ $K(d)=2$
     Write K as a set of ordered pairs.

     K has domain [   ] and range [   ].

Determining If Graphs Are Functions

7. Decide whether each graph shows a relationship where y is a function of x.

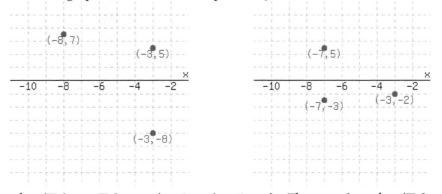

The first graph (□ does □ does not) give a function of x. The second graph (□ does □ does not) give a function of x.

8. Decide whether each graph shows a relationship where y is a function of x.

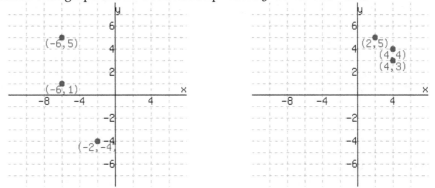

The first graph (□ does □ does not) give a function of x. The second graph (□ does □ does not) give a function of x.

9. The following graphs show two relationships. Decide whether each graph shows a relationship where y is a function of x.

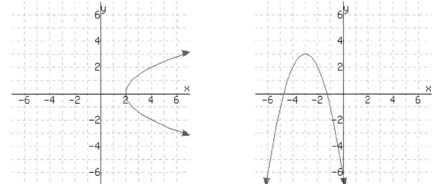

The first graph (□ does □ does not) give a function of x. The second graph (□ does □ does not) give a function of x.

10. The following graphs show two relationships. Decide whether each graph shows a relationship where y is a function of x.

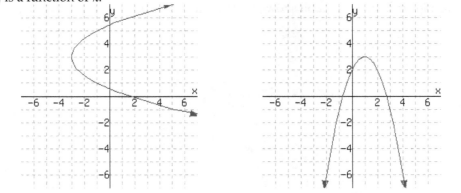

The first graph   (□ does   □ does not)   give a function of x. The second graph   (□ does   □ does not)   give a function of x.

Determining If Tables Are Functions Determine whether or not the following table could be the table of values of a function. If the table can not be the table of values of a function, give an input that has more than one possible output.

11.

Input	Output
2	−1
4	1
6	−4
8	18
−2	−10

Could this be the table of values for a function?   (□ yes   □ no)
If not, which input has more than one possible output?   (□ -2   □ 2   □ 4   □ 6   □ 8   □ None, the table represents a function.)

12.

Input	Output
2	4
4	−13
6	13
8	6
−2	−11

Could this be the table of values for a function?   (□ yes   □ no)
If not, which input has more than one possible output?   (□ -2   □ 2   □ 4   □ 6   □ 8   □ None, the table represents a function.)

13.

Input	Output
−4	13
−3	2
−2	11
−3	13
−1	−18

Could this be the table of values for a function?   (□ yes   □ no)
If not, which input has more than one possible output?   (□ -4   □ -3   □ -2   □ -1   □ None, the table represents a function.)

14.

Input	Output
−4	−8
−3	4
−2	−14
−3	19
−1	0

Could this be the table of values for a function?   (□ yes   □ no)
If not, which input has more than one possible output?   (□ -4   □ -3   □ -2   □ -1   □ None, the table represents a function.)

Determining If Equations Are Functions

15. Select all of the following relations that make y a function of x. There are several correct answers.
    □ $y = \pm\sqrt{81 - x^2}$ □ $y = x^2$ □ $x = y^3$ □ $y = \sqrt[3]{x}$ □ $y = \frac{1}{x^2}$ □ $y = |x|$
    □ $x^2 + y^2 = 81$ □ $5x + 4y = 1$ □ $y = \frac{x+7}{8-x}$ □ $|y| = x$ □ $y = \sqrt{81 - x^2}$
    □ $x = y^2$

16. Select all of the following relations that make y a function of x. There are several correct answers.
    □ $x = y^2$ □ $5x + 5y = 1$ □ $x^2 + y^2 = 16$ □ $y = \frac{1}{x^3}$ □ $|y| = x$
    □ $x = y^3$ □ $y = \sqrt{36 - x^2}$ □ $y = x^5$ □ $y = \pm\sqrt{36 - x^2}$ □ $y = |x|$
    □ $y = \frac{x+2}{4-x}$ □ $y = \sqrt[8]{x}$

17. Some equations involving x and y define y as a function of x, and others do not. For example, if
    $x + y = 1$, we can solve for y and obtain $y = 1 - x$. And we can then think of $y = f(x) = 1 - x$.
    On the other hand, if we have the equation $x = y^2$ then y is not a function of x, since for a given
    positive value of x, the value of y could equal $\sqrt{x}$ or it could equal $-\sqrt{x}$. Select all of the following
    relations that make y a function of x. There are several correct answers.
    □ $|y| - x = 0$ □ $y + x^2 = 1$ □ $y^2 + x^2 = 1$ □ $3x + 5y + 9 = 0$ □ $y - |x| = 0$
    □ $x + y = 1$ □ $y^6 + x = 1$ □ $y^3 + x^4 = 1$

    On the other hand, some equations involving x and y define x as a function of y (the other way
    round).

    Select all of the following relations that make x a function of y. There are several correct answers.
    □ $y^2 + x^2 = 1$ □ $3x + 5y + 9 = 0$ □ $|y| - x = 0$ □ $y - |x| = 0$ □ $y^4 + x^5 = 1$

18. Some equations involving x and y define y as a function of x, and others do not. For example, if
    $x + y = 1$, we can solve for y and obtain $y = 1 - x$. And we can then think of $y = f(x) = 1 - x$.
    On the other hand, if we have the equation $x = y^2$ then y is not a function of x, since for a given
    positive value of x, the value of y could equal $\sqrt{x}$ or it could equal $-\sqrt{x}$. Select all of the following
    relations that make y a function of x. There are several correct answers.
    □ $y^6 + x = 1$ □ $y - |x| = 0$ □ $|y| - x = 0$ □ $y + x^2 = 1$ □ $4x + 2y + 4 = 0$
    □ $y^3 + x^4 = 1$ □ $x + y = 1$ □ $y^2 + x^2 = 1$

    On the other hand, some equations involving x and y define x as a function of y (the other way
    round).

    Select all of the following relations that make x a function of y. There are several correct answers.
    □ $y^4 + x^5 = 1$ □ $y - |x| = 0$ □ $y^2 + x^2 = 1$ □ $|y| - x = 0$ □ $4x + 2y + 4 = 0$

11.6 Functions Chapter Review

11.6.1 Function Basics

In Section 11.1 we defined functions informally, as well as function notation. We saw functions in four forms: verbal descriptions, formulas, graphs and tables.

Example 11.6.1 Informal Definition of a Function. Determine whether each example below describes a function.
   a. The area of a circle given its radius.   b. The number you square to get 9.

Explanation.

   a. The area of a circle given its radius is a function because there is a set of steps or a formula that changes the radius into the area of the circle. We could write $A(r) = \pi r^2$.

   b. The number you square to get 9 is not a function because the process we would apply to get the result does not give a single answer. There are two different answers, -3 and 3. A function must give a single output for a given input.

Example 11.6.2 Tables and Graphs. Make a table and a graph of the function f, where $f(x) = x^2$.

Explanation.

First we will set up a table with negative and positive inputs and calculate the function values. The values are shown in Figure 11.6.3, which in turn gives us the graph in Figure 11.6.4.

input, x	output, f(x)
-3	9
-2	4
-1	1
0	0
1	2
2	4
3	9

Figure 11.6.3

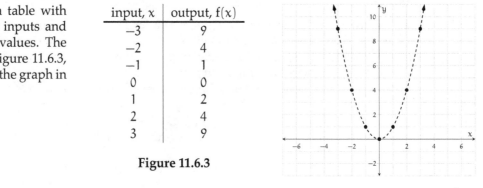

Figure 11.6.4: $y = f(x) = x^2$

Example 11.6.5 Translating between Four Descriptions of the Same Function. Consider a function f that triples its input and then adds 4. Translate this verbal description of f into a table, a graph, and a formula.

Explanation.

To make a table for f, we'll have to select some input x-values so we will choose some small negative and positive values that are easy to work with. Given the verbal description, we should be able to compute a column of output values. Table 11.6.6 is one possible table that we might end up with.

x	f(x)
-2	$3(-2) + 4 = -2$
-1	$3(-1) + 4 = 1$
0	$3(0) + 4 = 4$
1	$3(1) + 4 = 7$
2	$3(2) + 4 = 10$

Figure 11.6.6

Once we have a table for f, we can make a graph for f as in Figure 11.6.7, using the table to plot points. Lastly, we must find a formula for f. This means we need to write an algebraic expression that says the same thing about f as the verbal description, the table, and the graph. For this example, we can focus on the verbal description. Since f takes its input, triples it, and adds 4, we have the formula

$$f(x) = 3x + 4.$$

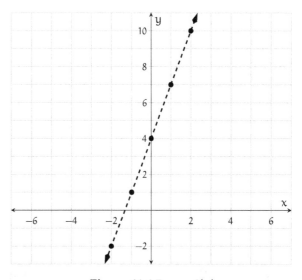

Figure 11.6.7: $y = f(x)$

11.6.2 Domain and Range

In Section 11.2 we saw the definition of domain and range, and three types of domain restrictions. We also learned how to write the domain and range in interval and set-builder notation.

Example 11.6.8 Determine the domain of p, where $p(x) = \dfrac{x}{2x - 1}$.

Explanation. This is an example of the first type of domain restriction, when you have a variable in the denominator. The denominator cannot equal 0 so a *bad* value for x would be when

$$2x - 1 = 0$$
$$2x = 1$$
$$x = \frac{1}{2}$$

The domain is all real numbers except $\frac{1}{2}$.

Example 11.6.9 What is the domain of the function C, where $C(x) = \sqrt{2x - 3} - 5$?

Explanation. This is an example of the second type of domain restriction where the value inside the radical cannot be negative. So the *good* values for x would be when

$$2x - 3 \geq 0$$
$$2x \geq 3$$
$$x \geq \frac{3}{2}$$

So on a number line, if we wanted to picture the domain of C, we would make a sketch like:

The domain is the interval $\left[\frac{3}{2}, \infty\right)$.

Example 11.6.10 Range.
Find the range of the function q using its graph shown in Figure 11.6.11.

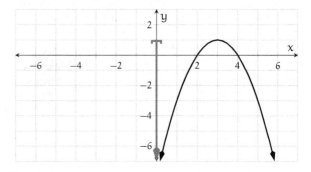

Figure 11.6.11: $y = q(x)$. The range is marked as an interval on the y-axis.

Explanation. The range is the collection of possible numbers that q can give for output. Figure 11.6.11 displays a graph of q, with the range shown as an interval on the y-axis.

The output values are the y-coordinates so we can see that the y-values start from 1 and continue downward forever. Therefore the range is $(-\infty, 1]$.

11.6.3 Using Technology to Explore Functions

In Section 11.3 we covered how to find a good graphing window and use it to identify all of the key features of a function. We also learned how to solve equations and inequalities using a graph. Here are some examples for review.

Example 11.6.12 Finding an Appropriate Window. Graph the function t, where $t(x) = (x + 10)^2 - 15$, using technology and find a good viewing window.

Explanation.

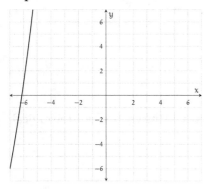

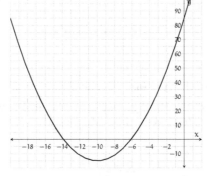

After some trial and error we found this window that goes from -20 to 2 on the x-axis and -20 to 100 on the y-axis.

Figure 11.6.13: $y = t(x)$ in the viewing window of -7 to 7 on the x and y axes. We need to zoom out and move our window to the left.

Figure 11.6.14: $y = t(x)$ in a good viewing window.

Now we can see the vertex and all of the intercepts and we will identify them in the next example.

Example 11.6.15 Using Technology to Determine Key Features of a Graph. Use the previous graph in figure 11.6.14 to identify the intercepts, minimum or maximum function value, and the domain and range of the function t, where $t(x) = (x + 10)^2 - 15$.

Explanation.

From our graph we can now identify the vertex at $(-10, -15)$, the y-intercept at $(0, 85)$, and the x-intercepts at approximately $(-13.9, 0)$ and $(-6.13, 0)$.

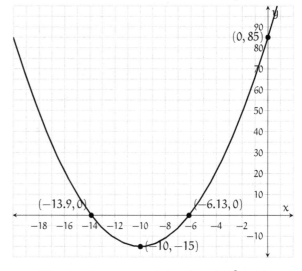

Figure 11.6.16: $y = t(x) = (x + 10)^2 - 15$.

Example 11.6.17 Solving Equations and Inequalities Graphically Using Technology. Use graphing technology to solve the equation $t(x) = 40$, where $t(x) = (x + 10)^2 - 15$.

Explanation.

To solve the equation $t(x) = 40$, we need to graph $y = t(x)$ and $y = 40$ on the same axes and find the x-values where they intersect.

From the graph we can see that the intersection points are approximately $(-17.4, 40)$ and $(-2.58, 40)$. The solution set is $\{-17.4, -2.58\}$.

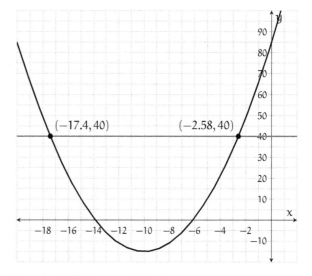

Figure 11.6.18: $y = t(x)$ where $t(x) = (x + 10)^2 - 15$ and $y = 40$.

11.6.4 Simplifying Expressions with Function Notation

In Section 11.4 we learned about the difference between $f(-x)$ and $-f(x)$ and how to simplify them. We also learned how to simplify other changes to the input and output like $f(3x)$ and $\frac{1}{3}f(x)$. Here are some examples.

Example 11.6.19 Negative Signs in and out of Function Notation. Find and simplify a formula for $f(-x)$ and $-f(x)$, where $f(x) = -3x^2 - 7x + 1$.

Explanation. To find $f(-x)$, we use an input of $-x$ in our function f and simplify to get:

$$f(-x) = -3(-x)^2 - 7(-x) + 1$$
$$= -3x^2 + 7x + 1$$

To find $-f(x)$, we take the opposite of the function f and simplify to get:

$$-f(x) = -(-3x^2 - 7x + 1)$$
$$= 3x^2 + 7x - 1$$

Example 11.6.20 Other Nontrivial Simplifications. If $g(x) = 2x^2 - 3x - 5$, find and simplify a formula for $g(x - 1)$.

Explanation. To find $g(x - 1)$, we put in $(x - 1)$ for the input. It is important to keep the parentheses because we have exponents and negative signs in the function.

$$g(x - 1) = 2(x - 1)^2 - 3(x - 1) - 5$$
$$= 2(x^2 - 2x + 1) - 3x + 3 - 5$$
$$= 2x^2 - 4x + 2 - 3x - 2$$
$$= 2x^2 - 7x$$

11.6.5 Technical Definition of a Function

In Section 11.5 we gave a formal definition of a function 11.5.2 and learned to identify what is and is not a function with sets or ordered pairs, tables and graphs. We also used the vertical line test 11.5.20.

Example 11.6.21 Formally Defining a Function. We learned that sets of ordered pairs, tables and graphs can meet the formal definition of a function. Here is an example that shows a function in all three forms. We can verify that each input has at most one output.

$\{(1,4),(2,4),(3,3),(4,6),(5,-2)\}$

Figure 11.6.22: The function f represented as a collection of ordered pairs.

x	f(x)
1	4
2	4
3	3
4	6
5	-2

Figure 11.6.23: The function f represented as a table.

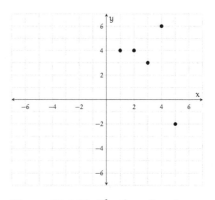

Figure 11.6.24: The function f represented as a graph.

Example 11.6.25 Identifying What is _Not_ a Function. Identify whether each graph represents a function using the vertical line test 11.5.20.

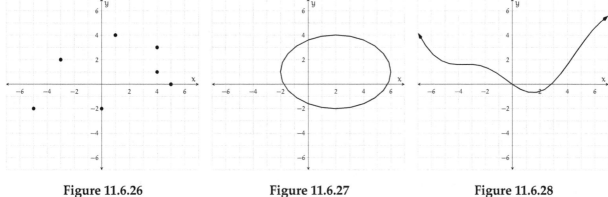

Figure 11.6.26   Figure 11.6.27   Figure 11.6.28

Explanation.

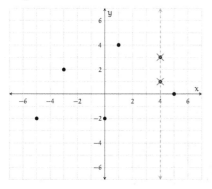 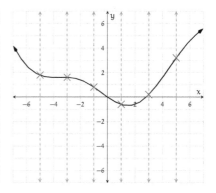

Figure 11.6.29: A vertical line touching the graph twice makes this graph not give y as a function of x.

Figure 11.6.30: A vertical line touching the graph twice makes this graph not give y as a function of x.

Figure 11.6.31: All vertical lines only touch the graph once, so this graph does give y as a function of x.

11.6.6 Exercises

Function Basics

1.   Randi will spend $225 to purchase some bowls and some plates. Each plate costs $8, and each bowl costs $5. The function $q(x) = -\frac{8}{5}x + 45$ models the number of bowls Randi will purchase, where x represents the number of plates to be purchased.
     Interpret the meaning of $q(35) = -11$.

     ⊙ **A.** −$11 will be used to purchase bowls, and $35 will be used to purchase plates.

     ⊙ **B.** −11 plates and 35 bowls can be purchased.

     ⊙ **C.** 35 plates and −11 bowls can be purchased.

     ⊙ **D.** $35 will be used to purchase bowls, and −$11 will be used to purchase plates.

2.   Douglas will spend $150 to purchase some bowls and some plates. Each plate costs $5, and each bowl costs $6. The function $q(x) = -\frac{5}{6}x + 25$ models the number of bowls Douglas will purchase, where x represents the number of plates to be purchased.
     Interpret the meaning of $q(12) = 15$.

     ⊙ **A.** $15 will be used to purchase bowls, and $12 will be used to purchase plates.

     ⊙ **B.** 12 plates and 15 bowls can be purchased.

     ⊙ **C.** 15 plates and 12 bowls can be purchased.

     ⊙ **D.** $12 will be used to purchase bowls, and $15 will be used to purchase plates.

3.   Evaluate the function at the given values.
     $$G(x) = -\frac{9}{x-7}.$$

     a. $G(8)$

     b. $G(7)$

4.   Evaluate the function at the given values.
     $$G(x) = \frac{40}{x+8}.$$

     a. $G(2)$

     b. $G(-8)$

5. Use the graph of H below to evaluate the given expressions. (Estimates are OK.)

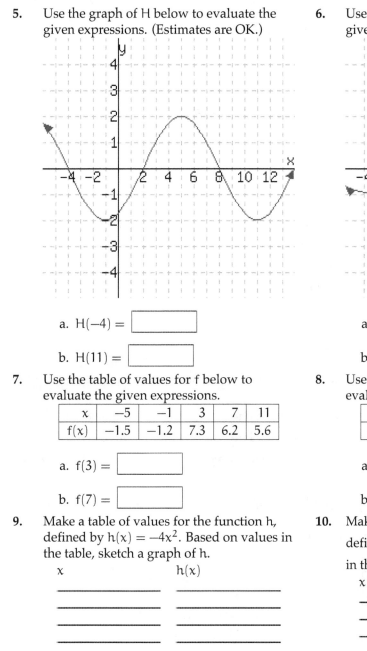

  a. H(−4) = [   ]

  b. H(11) = [   ]

6. Use the graph of K below to evaluate the given expressions. (Estimates are OK.)

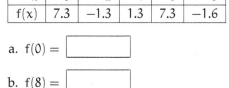

  a. K(−3) = [   ]

  b. K(5) = [   ]

7. Use the table of values for f below to evaluate the given expressions.

x	−5	−1	3	7	11
f(x)	−1.5	−1.2	7.3	6.2	5.6

  a. f(3) = [   ]

  b. f(7) = [   ]

8. Use the table of values for f below to evaluate the given expressions.

x	0	2	4	6	8
f(x)	7.3	−1.3	1.3	7.3	−1.6

  a. f(0) = [   ]

  b. f(8) = [   ]

9. Make a table of values for the function h, defined by $h(x) = -4x^2$. Based on values in the table, sketch a graph of h.

x   h(x)

_____   _____
_____   _____
_____   _____
_____   _____
_____   _____

10. Make a table of values for the function H, defined by $H(x) = \dfrac{2^x - 3}{x^2 + 3}$. Based on values in the table, sketch a graph of H.

x   H(x)

_____   _____
_____   _____
_____   _____
_____   _____
_____   _____

11. The following figure has the graph $y = d(t)$, which models a particle's distance from the starting line in feet, where t stands for time in seconds since timing started.

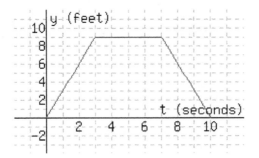

a. Find d(7).

b. Interpret the meaning of d(7).

  ⊙ *A*. The particle was 9 feet away from the starting line 7 seconds since timing started.

  ⊙ *B*. The particle was 7 feet away from the starting line 9 seconds since timing started.

  ⊙ *C*. In the first 9 seconds, the particle moved a total of 7 feet.

  ⊙ *D*. In the first 7 seconds, the particle moved a total of 9 feet.

c. Solve d(t) = 3 for t. t = [   ]

d. Interpret the meaning of part c's solution(s).

  ⊙ *A*. The particle was 3 feet from the starting line 1 seconds since timing started, and again 9 seconds since timing started.

  ⊙ *B*. The particle was 3 feet from the starting line 9 seconds since timing started.

  ⊙ *C*. The particle was 3 feet from the starting line 1 seconds since timing started.

  ⊙ *D*. The particle was 3 feet from the starting line 1 seconds since timing started, or 9 seconds since timing started.

12. The following figure has the graph y = d(t), which models a particle's distance from the starting line in feet, where t stands for time in seconds since timing started.

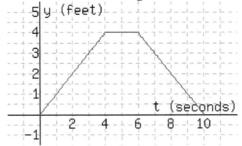

a. Find d(8).

b. Interpret the meaning of d(8).

  ⊙ *A*. In the first 2 seconds, the particle moved a total of 8 feet.

  ⊙ *B*. The particle was 8 feet away from the starting line 2 seconds since timing started.

⊙ **C.** In the first 8 seconds, the particle moved a total of 2 feet.

⊙ **D.** The particle was 2 feet away from the starting line 8 seconds since timing started.

c. Solve $d(t) = 3$ for t. $t = \boxed{}$

d. Interpret the meaning of part c's solution(s).

⊙ **A.** The particle was 3 feet from the starting line 3 seconds since timing started, or 7 seconds since timing started.

⊙ **B.** The particle was 3 feet from the starting line 3 seconds since timing started.

⊙ **C.** The particle was 3 feet from the starting line 7 seconds since timing started.

⊙ **D.** The particle was 3 feet from the starting line 3 seconds since timing started, and again 7 seconds since timing started.

Domain and Range A function is graphed.

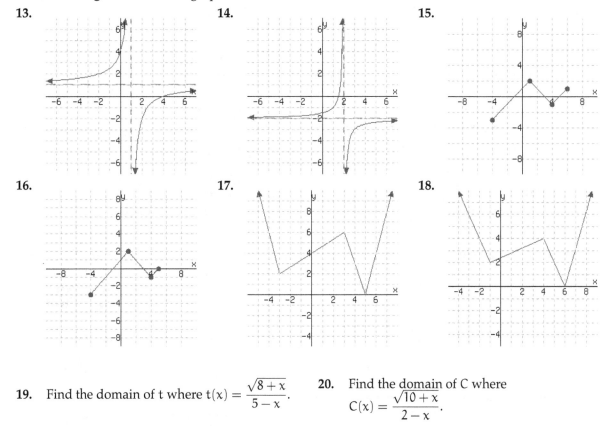

13.   **14.**   **15.**

16.   **17.**   **18.**

19. Find the domain of t where $t(x) = \dfrac{\sqrt{8+x}}{5-x}$.

20. Find the domain of C where $C(x) = \dfrac{\sqrt{10+x}}{2-x}$.

21. An object was shot up into the air at an initial vertical speed of 512 feet per second. Its height as time passes can be modeled by the quadratic function f, where $f(t) = -16t^2 + 512t$. Here t represents the number of seconds since the object's release, and $f(t)$ represents the object's height in feet.

Find the function's domain and range in this context.

The function's domain in this context is $\boxed{}$.

The function's range in this context is [   ].

22. An object was shot up into the air at an initial vertical speed of 544 feet per second. Its height as time passes can be modeled by the quadratic function f, where $f(t) = -16t^2 + 544t$. Here t represents the number of seconds since the object's release, and $f(t)$ represents the object's height in feet.

Find the function's domain and range in this context.

The function's domain in this context is [   ].

The function's range in this context is [   ].

Using Technology to Explore Functions

23. Use technology to make a table of values for the function H defined by
$H(x) = -4x^2 + 16x + 1$.

x	H(x)
___	___
___	___
___	___
___	___
___	___
___	___

24. Use technology to make a table of values for the function K defined by
$K(x) = 2x^2 - 7x - 2$.

x	K(x)
___	___
___	___
___	___
___	___
___	___

25. Choose an appropriate window for graphing the function f defined by $f(x) = -1184x - 7607$ that shows its key features.

The x-interval could be [   ] and

the y-interval could be [   ].

26. Choose an appropriate window for graphing the function f defined by $f(x) = -139x + 159$ that shows its key features.

The x-interval could be [   ] and

the y-interval could be [   ].

27. Use technology to determine how many times the equations $y = -5x^3 + 2x^2 + x$ and $y = 6x + 4$ intersect. They intersect
(☐ zero times   ☐ one time   ☐ two times
☐ three times) .

28. Use technology to determine how many times the equations $y = -3x^3 - x^2 + 9x$ and $y = -5x + 6$ intersect. They intersect
(☐ zero times   ☐ one time   ☐ two times
☐ three times) .

29. For the function L defined by

$$L(x) = 3000x^2 + 10x + 4,$$

use technology to determine the following. Round answers as necessary.

  a. Any intercepts.

  b. The vertex.

  c. The domain.

  d. The range.

30. For the function M defined by

$$M(x) = -(300x - 2950)^2,$$

use technology to determine the following. Round answers as necessary.

  a. Any intercepts.

  b. The vertex.

  c. The domain.

  d. The range.

31. Let $f(x) = 4x^2 + 5x - 1$ and $g(x) = 5$. Use graphing technology to determine the following.

    a. What are the points of intersection for these two functions?

    b. Solve $f(x) = g(x)$.

    c. Solve $f(x) < g(x)$.

    d. Solve $f(x) \geq g(x)$.

32. Let $p(x) = 6x^2 - 3x + 4$ and $k(x) = 7$. Use graphing technology to determine the following.

    a. What are the points of intersection for these two functions?

    b. Solve $p(x) = k(x)$.

    c. Solve $p(x) < k(x)$.

    d. Solve $p(x) \geq k(x)$.

33. Use graphing technology to solve the equation $-0.02x^2 + 1.97x - 51.5 = 0.05(x - 50)^2 - 0.03(x - 50)$. Approximate the solution(s) if necessary.

34. Use graphing technology to solve the equation $-200x^2 + 60x - 55 = -20x - 40$. Approximate the solution(s) if necessary.

35. Use graphing technology to solve the inequality $-15x^2 - 6 \leq 10x - 4$. State the solution set using interval notation, and approximate if necessary.

36. Use graphing technology to solve the inequality $\frac{1}{2}x^2 + \frac{3}{2}x \geq \frac{1}{2}x - \frac{3}{2}$. State the solution set using interval notation, and approximate if necessary.

Simplifying Expressions with Function Notation

37. Let f be a function given by
$f(x) = -3x^2 + 3x$. Find and simplify the
following:

    a. $f(x) - 3 =$ ⬚

    b. $f(x - 3) =$ ⬚

    c. $-3f(x) =$ ⬚

    d. $f(-3x) =$ ⬚

38. Let f be a function given by $f(x) = 3x^2 - 4x$.
Find and simplify the following:

    a. $f(x) - 4 =$ ⬚

    b. $f(x - 4) =$ ⬚

    c. $-4f(x) =$ ⬚

    d. $f(-4x) =$ ⬚

39. Simplify $F(r) + 6$, where $F(r) = 3 - 5.1r$.

40. Simplify $g(r) + 9$, where $g(r) = 2 + 6.5r$.

Technical Definition of a Function

41. Does the following set of ordered pairs make for a function of x?
$$\left\{(-3,3), (-5,9), (-5,0), (1,7), (-6,3)\right\}$$
This set of ordered pairs   (☐ describes ☐ does not describe) a function of x. This set of
ordered pairs has domain ⬚ and range ⬚ .

42. Does the following set of ordered pairs make for a function of x?
$$\left\{(-8,9), (5,5), (-3,9), (-1,2), (-8,10)\right\}$$
This set of ordered pairs   (☐ describes ☐ does not describe) a function of x. This set of
ordered pairs has domain ⬚ and range ⬚ .

43. Below is all of the information that exists about a function f.
    $f(-2) = 1$ $f(0) = 5$ $f(1) = 2$
    Write f as a set of ordered pairs.
      f has domain ⬚ and range ⬚ .

44. Below is all of the information about a function f.
    $f(a) = 5$ $f(b) = 6$
    $f(c) = 3$ $f(d) = 6$
    Write f as a set of ordered pairs.
      f has domain ⬚ and range ⬚ .

45. The following graphs show two relationships. Decide whether each graph shows a relationship
where y is a function of x.

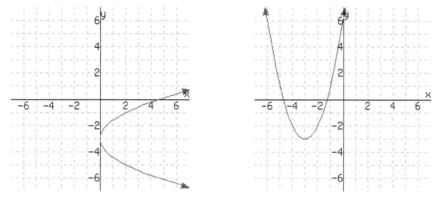

The first graph (□ does □ does not) give a function of x. The second graph (□ does □ does not) give a function of x.

46. The following graphs show two relationships. Decide whether each graph shows a relationship where y is a function of x.

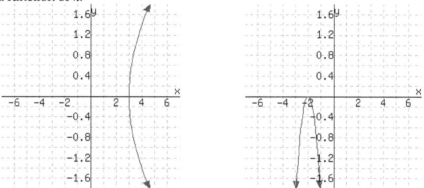

The first graph (□ does □ does not) give a function of x. The second graph (□ does □ does not) give a function of x.

47. Some equations involving x and y define y as a function of x, and others do not. For example, if $x + y = 1$, we can solve for y and obtain $y = 1 - x$. And we can then think of $y = f(x) = 1 - x$. On the other hand, if we have the equation $x = y^2$ then y is not a function of x, since for a given positive value of x, the value of y could equal $\sqrt{x}$ or it could equal $-\sqrt{x}$. Select all of the following relations that make y a function of x. There are several correct answers.

□ $y^3 + x^4 = 1$ □ $y + x^2 = 1$ □ $y^2 + x^2 = 1$ □ $y^6 + x = 1$ □ $y - |x| = 0$
□ $5x + 8y + 9 = 0$ □ $x + y = 1$ □ $|y| - x = 0$

On the other hand, some equations involving x and y define x as a function of y (the other way round).

Select all of the following relations that make x a function of y. There are several correct answers.

□ $|y| - x = 0$ □ $5x + 8y + 9 = 0$ □ $y^2 + x^2 = 1$ □ $y - |x| = 0$ □ $y^4 + x^5 = 1$

48. Some equations involving x and y define y as a function of x, and others do not. For example, if $x + y = 1$, we can solve for y and obtain $y = 1 - x$. And we can then think of $y = f(x) = 1 - x$. On the other hand, if we have the equation $x = y^2$ then y is not a function of x, since for a given positive value of x, the value of y could equal $\sqrt{x}$ or it could equal $-\sqrt{x}$. Select all of the following relations that make y a function of x. There are several correct answers.

☐ $|y| - x = 0$ ☐ $y + x^2 = 1$ ☐ $x + y = 1$ ☐ $y^2 + x^2 = 1$ ☐ $6x + 5y + 4 = 0$
☐ $y^3 + x^4 = 1$ ☐ $y^6 + x = 1$ ☐ $y - |x| = 0$

On the other hand, some equations involving x and y define x as a function of y (the other way round).

Select all of the following relations that make x a function of y. There are several correct answers.

☐ $y^2 + x^2 = 1$ ☐ $|y| - x = 0$ ☐ $y - |x| = 0$ ☐ $y^4 + x^5 = 1$ ☐ $6x + 5y + 4 = 0$

Determine whether or not the following table could be the table of values of a function. If the table can not be the table of values of a function, give an input that has more than one possible output.

49.

Input	Output
2	7
4	−18
6	10
8	−4
−2	1

Could this be the table of values for a function?   (☐ yes ☐ no)
If not, which input has more than one possible output?   (☐ -2 ☐ 2 ☐ 4 ☐ 6 ☐ 8   ☐ None, the table represents a function.)

50.

Input	Output
2	12
4	9
6	−14
8	−15
−2	1

Could this be the table of values for a function?   (☐ yes ☐ no)
If not, which input has more than one possible output?   (☐ -2 ☐ 2 ☐ 4 ☐ 6 ☐ 8   ☐ None, the table represents a function.)

51.

Input	Output
−4	6
−3	2
−2	0
−3	13
−1	−3

Could this be the table of values for a function?   (☐ yes ☐ no)
If not, which input has more than one possible output?   (☐ -4 ☐ -3 ☐ -2 ☐ -1 ☐ None, the table represents a function.)

52.

Input	Output
−4	−14
−3	4
−2	17
−3	19
−1	15

Could this be the table of values for a function?   (☐ yes ☐ no)
If not, which input has more than one possible output?   (☐ -4 ☐ -3 ☐ -2 ☐ -1 ☐ None, the table represents a function.)

Chapter 12

Rational Functions and Equations

12.1 Introduction to Rational Functions

In this chapter we will learn about rational functions, which are ratios of two polynomial functions. Creating this ratio inherently requires division, and we'll explore the effect this has on the graphs of rational functions and their domain and range.

12.1.1 Graphs of Rational Functions

Example 12.1.2
When a drug is injected into a patient, the drug's concentration in the patient's bloodstream can be modeled by the function C, with formula

$$C(t) = \frac{3t}{t^2 + 8}$$

where $C(t)$ gives the drug's concentration, in milligrams per liter, t hours since the injection. A new injection is needed when the concentration falls to 0.35 milligrams per liter. Using graphing technology, we will graph $y = \frac{3t}{t^2+8}$ and $y = 0.35$ to examine the situation and answer some important questions.

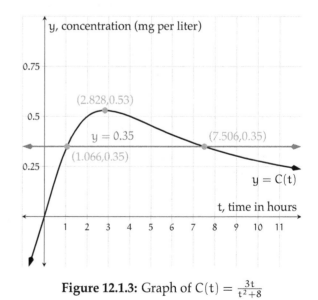

Figure 12.1.3: Graph of $C(t) = \frac{3t}{t^2+8}$

a. What is the concentration after 10 hours?

b. After how many hours since the first injection is the drug concentration greatest?

141

c. After how many hours since the first injection should the next injection be given?

d. What happens to the drug concentration if no further injections are given?

Explanation.

a. To determine the concentration after 10 hours, we will evaluate C at $t = 10$. After 10 hours, the concentration will be about $0.2777 \frac{mg}{L}$.

$$
\begin{aligned}
C(10) &= \frac{3(10)}{10^2 + 8} \\
&= \frac{30}{108} \\
&= \frac{5}{18} \\
&\approx 0.2777
\end{aligned}
$$

b. Using the graph, we can see that the maximum concentration of the drug will be $0.53 \frac{mg}{L}$ and will occur after about 2.828 hours.

c. The approximate points of intersection $(1.066, 0.35)$ and $(7.506, 0.35)$ tell us that the concentration of the drug will reach $0.35 \frac{mg}{L}$ after about 1.066 hours and again after about 7.506 hours. Given the rising, then falling shape of the graph, this means that another dose will need to be administered after about 7.506 hours.

d. From the initial graph, it appears that the concentration of the drug will diminish to zero with enough time passing. Exploring further, we can see both numerically and graphically that for larger and larger values of t, the function values get closer and closer to zero. This is shown in Figure 12.1.4 and Figure 12.1.5.

t	C(t)
24	0.123...
48	0.062...
72	0.041...
96	0.031...
120	0.020...

Figure 12.1.4: Numerical Values for $C(t) = \frac{3t}{t^2+8}$

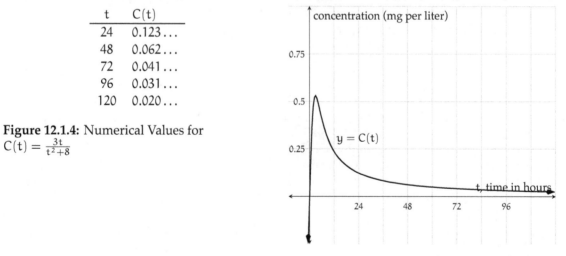

Figure 12.1.5: Graph of $C(t) = \frac{3t}{t^2+8}$

In Section 12.5, we'll explore how to algebraically solve $C(t) = 0.35$. For now, we will rely on technology to make the graph and determine intersection points.

The function C, where $C(t) = \frac{3t}{t^2+8}$, is a *rational function*, which is a type of function defined as follows.

Definition 12.1.6 Rational Function. A **rational function** f is a function in the form

$$f(x) = \frac{P(x)}{Q(x)}$$

where P and Q are polynomial functions, but Q is not the constant zero function. ◇

Checkpoint 12.1.7 Identify which of the following are rational functions and which are not.

a. f defined by $f(x) = \frac{25x^2+3}{25x^2+3}$ (☐ is   ☐ is not)   a rational function.

b. Q defined by $Q(x) = \frac{5x^2+3\sqrt{x}}{2x}$ (☐ is   ☐ is not)   a rational function.

c. g defined by $g(t) = \frac{t\sqrt{5}-t^3}{2t+1}$ (☐ is   ☐ is not)   a rational function.

d. P defined by $P(x) = \frac{5x+3}{|2x+1|}$ (☐ is   ☐ is not)   a rational function.

e. h defined by $h(x) = \frac{3^x+1}{x^2+1}$ (☐ is   ☐ is not)   a rational function.

Explanation.

a. f defined by $f(x) = \frac{25x^2+3}{25x^2+3}$ is a rational function as its formula is a polynomial divided by another polynomial.

b. Q defined by $Q(x) = \frac{5x^2+3\sqrt{x}}{2x}$ is not a rational function because the numerator contains $\sqrt{x}$ and is therefore not a polynomial.

c. g defined by $g(t) = \frac{t\sqrt{5}-t^3}{2t+1}$ is a rational function as its formula is a polynomial divided by another polynomial.

d. P defined by $P(x) = \frac{5x+3}{|2x+1|}$ is not a rational function because the denominator contains the absolute value of an expression with variables in it.

e. h defined by $h(x) = \frac{3^x+1}{x^2+1}$ is not a rational function because the numerator contains 3^x, which has a variable in the exponent.

A rational function's graph is not always smooth like the one shown in Example 12.1.3. It could have breaks, as we'll see now.

Example 12.1.8 Build a table and sketch the graph of the function f where $f(x) = \frac{1}{x-2}$. Find the function's domain and range.

Since $x = 2$ makes the denominator 0, the function will be undefined for $x = 2$. We'll start by choosing various x-values and plotting the associated points.

x	f(x)		Point
−6	$\frac{1}{-6-2}$	−0.125	$(-6, -0.125)$
−4	$\frac{1}{-4-2}$	≈ −0.167	$\left(-4, -\frac{1}{6}\right)$
−2	$\frac{1}{-2-2}$	−0.25	$(-2, -0.25)$
0	$\frac{1}{0-2}$	−0.5	$(0, -0.5)$
1	$\frac{1}{1-2}$	−1	$(1, -1)$
2	$\frac{1}{2-2}$	undefined	
3	$\frac{1}{3-2}$	1	$(3, 1)$
4	$\frac{1}{4-2}$	0.5	$(4, 0.5)$

Figure 12.1.9: Initial Values of $f(x) = \frac{1}{x-2}$

Figure 12.1.10: Initial Points for $f(x) = \frac{1}{x-2}$

Note that extra points were chosen near $x = 2$ in the Figure 12.1.9, but it's still not clear on the graph what happens really close to $x = 2$. It will be essential that we include at least one x-value between 1 and 2 and also between 2 and 3.

Further, we'll note that dividing one number by a number that is close to 0 yields a large number. For example, $\frac{1}{0.0005} = 2000$. In fact, the smaller the number is that we divide by, the larger our result becomes. So when x gets closer and closer to 2, then $x - 2$ gets closer and closer to 0. And then $\frac{1}{x-2}$ takes very large values.

When we plot additional points closer and closer to 2, we get larger and larger results. To the left of 2, the results are negative, so the connected curve has an arrow pointing downward there. The opposite happens to the right of $x = 2$, and an arrow points upward. We'll also draw the vertical line $x = 2$ as a dashed line to indicate that the graph never actually touches it.

x	f(x)		Point
−6	$\frac{1}{-6-2}$	−0.125	$(-6, -0.125)$
−4	$\frac{1}{-4-2}$	≈ −0.167	$\left(-4, -\frac{1}{6}\right)$
−2	$\frac{1}{-2-2}$	−0.25	$(-2, -0.25)$
0	$\frac{1}{0-2}$	−0.5	$(0, -0.5)$
1	$\frac{1}{1-2}$	−1	$(1, -1)$
1.5	$\frac{1}{1.5-2}$	−2	$(1.5, -2)$
1.8	$\frac{1}{1.8-2}$	−5	$(1.8, -5)$
2	$\frac{1}{2-2}$	undefined	
2.1	$\frac{1}{2.2-2}$	5	$(2.2, 5)$
2.5	$\frac{1}{2.5-2}$	2	$(2.5, 2)$
3	$\frac{1}{3-2}$	1	$(3, 1)$
4	$\frac{1}{4-2}$	0.5	$(4, 0.5)$

Figure 12.1.11: Values of $f(x) = \frac{1}{x-2}$

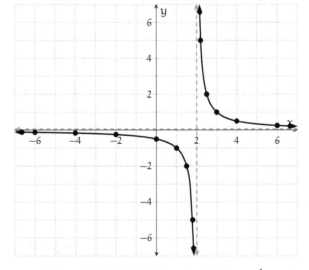

Figure 12.1.12: Full Graph of $f(x) = \frac{1}{x-2}$

Note that in Figure 12.1.12, the line $y = 0$ was also drawn as a dashed line. This is because the values of $y = f(x)$ will get closer and closer to zero as the inputs become more and more positive (or negative).

We know that the domain of this function is $(-\infty, 2) \cup (2, \infty)$ as the function is undefined at 2. We can determine this algebraically, and it is also evident in the graph.

We can see from the graph that the range of the function is $(-\infty, 0) \cup (0, \infty)$. See Checkpoint 11.2.26 for a discussion of how to see the range using a graph like this one.

Remark 12.1.13 The line $x = 2$ in Example 12.1.8 is referred to as a **vertical asymptote**. The line $y = 0$ is referred to as a **horizontal asymptote**. We'll use this vocabulary when referencing such lines, but the classification of vertical asymptotes and horizontal asymptotes is beyond the scope of this book.

Example 12.1.14 Algebraically find the domain of $g(x) = \frac{3x^2}{x^2-2x-24}$. Use technology to sketch a graph of this function.

Explanation. To find a rational function's domain, we set the denominator equal to 0 and solve:

$$x^2 - 2x - 24 = 0$$
$$(x - 6)(x + 4) = 0$$

$$x - 6 = 0 \qquad \text{or} \qquad x + 4 = 0$$
$$x = 6 \qquad \text{or} \qquad x = -4$$

Since $x = 6$ and $x = -4$ will cause the denominator to be 0, they are excluded from the domain. The function's domain is $\{x \mid x \neq 6, x \neq -4\}$. In interval notation, the domain is $(-\infty, -4) \cup (-4, 6) \cup (6, \infty)$.

To begin creating this graph, we'll use technology to create a table of function values, making sure to include values near both -4 and 6. We'll sketch an initial plot of these.

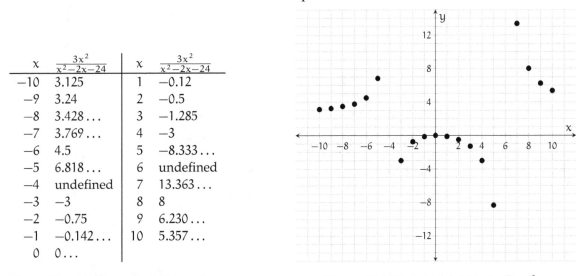

x	$\frac{3x^2}{x^2-2x-24}$	x	$\frac{3x^2}{x^2-2x-24}$
-10	3.125	1	-0.12
-9	3.24	2	-0.5
-8	3.428...	3	-1.285
-7	3.769...	4	-3
-6	4.5	5	$-8.333...$
-5	6.818...	6	undefined
-4	undefined	7	13.363...
-3	-3	8	8
-2	-0.75	9	6.230...
-1	$-0.142...$	10	5.357...
0	0...		

Figure 12.1.15: Numerical Values for g   **Figure 12.1.16:** Initial Set-Up to Graph g

We can now begin to see what happens near $x = -4$ and $x = 6$. These are referred to as vertical asymptotes and will be graphed as dashed vertical lines as they are features of the graph but do not include function values.

The last thing we need to consider is what happens for large positive values of x and large negative values of x. Choosing a few values, we find:

x	g(x)
1000	3.0060...
2000	3.0030...
3000	3.0020...
4000	3.0015...

Figure 12.1.17: Values for Large Positive x

x	g(x)
−1000	2.9940...
−2000	2.9970...
−3000	2.9980...
−4000	2.9985...

Figure 12.1.18: Values for Large Negative x

Thus for really large positive x and for really large negative x, we see that the function values get closer and closer to $y = 3$. This is referred to as the horizontal asymptote, and will be graphed as a dashed horizontal line on the graph.

Putting all of this together, we can sketch a graph of this function.

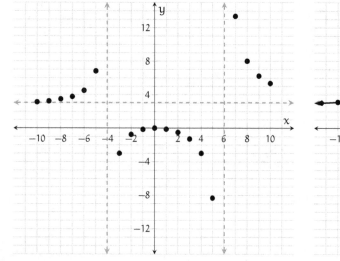

Figure 12.1.19: Asymptotes Added for Graphing $g(x) = \frac{3x^2}{x^2-2x-24}$

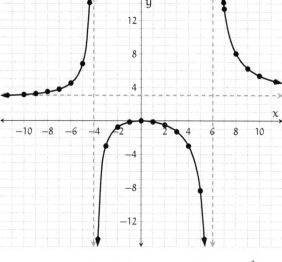

Figure 12.1.20: Full Graph of $g(x) = \frac{3x^2}{x^2-2x-24}$

Let's look at another example where a rational function is used to model real life data.

Example 12.1.21 The monthly operation cost of Saqui's shoe company is approximately $300,000.00. The cost of producing each pair of shoes is $30.00. As a result, the cost of producing x pairs of shoes is $30x + 300000$ dollars, and the average cost of producing each pair of shoes can be modeled by

$$\bar{C}(x) = \frac{30x + 300000}{x}.$$

Answer the following questions with technology.

a. What's the average cost of producing 100 pairs of shoes? Of producing 1000 pairs? Of producing 10,000 pairs? What's the pattern?

b. To make the average cost of producing each pair of shoes cheaper than $50.00, at least how many pairs of shoes must Saqui's company produce?

c. Assume that her company's shoes are very popular. What happens to the average cost of producing shoes if more and more people keep buying them?

Explanation. We will graph the function with technology. After adjusting window settings, we have:

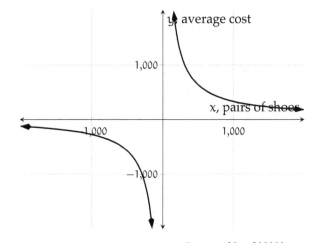

Figure 12.1.22: Graph of $\bar{C}(x) = \frac{30x+300000}{x}$

a. To answer this question, we locate the points where x values are 100, 1000 and 10,000. They are $(100, 3030), (1000, 330)$ and $(10000, 60)$. They imply:

- If the company produces 100 pairs of shoes, the average cost of producing one pair is $3030.00.
- If the company produces 1,000 pairs of shoes, the average cost of producing one pair is $330.00.
- If the company produces 10,000 pairs of shoes, the average cost of producing one pair is $60.00.

We can see the more shoes her company produces, the lower the average cost.

b. To answer this question, we locate the point where its y-value is 50. With technology, we graph both $y = \bar{C}(x)$ and $y = 50$, and locate their intersection.

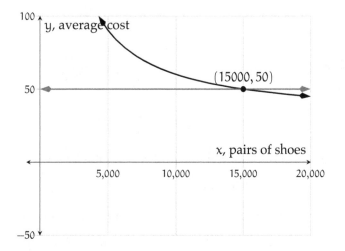

Figure 12.1.23: Intersection of $\bar{C}(x) = \frac{30x+300000}{x}$ and $y = 50$

The intersection $(15000, 50)$ implies the average cost of producing one pair is $50.00 if her company produces 15,000 pairs of shoes.

c. To answer this question, we substitute x with some large numbers, and use technology to create a table of values:

x	$g(x)$
100000	33
1000000	31
10000000	30.03
100000000	30.003

Figure 12.1.24: Values for Large Positive x

We can estimate that the average cost of producing one pair is getting closer and closer to $30.00 as her company produces more and more pairs of shoes.

Note that the cost of producing each pair is $30.00. This implies, for big companies whose products are very popular, the cost of operations can be ignored when calculating the average cost of producing each unit of product.

12.1.2 Reading Questions

1. What makes a function be a "rational" function?

2. Describe what an asymptote is.

3. If there is a rational function with a vertical asymptote at $x = 7$, what does that mean about the denominator of the rational function?

12.1.3 Exercises

Rational Functions in Context

1. The population of deer in a forest can be modeled by

$$P(x) = \frac{720x + 2310}{3x + 7}$$

where x is the number of years in the future. Answer the following questions.

a. How many deer live in this forest this year?

b. How many deer will live in this forest 27 years later? Round your answer to an integer.

c. After how many years, the deer population will be 247? Round your answer to an integer.

d. Use a calculator to answer this question: As time goes on, the population levels off at about how many deer?

2. The population of deer in a forest can be modeled by

$$P(x) = \frac{320x + 2200}{4x + 5}$$

where x is the number of years in the future. Answer the following questions.

a. How many deer live in this forest this year?

b. How many deer will live in this forest 14 years later? Round your answer to an integer.

c. After how many years, the deer population will be 100? Round your answer to an integer.

d. Use a calculator to answer this question: As time goes on, the population levels off at about how many deer?

3. In a certain store, cashiers can serve 50 customers per hour on average. If x customers arrive at the store in a given hour, then the average number of customers C waiting in line can be modeled by the function

$$C(x) = \frac{x^2}{2500 - 50x}$$

where x < 50.
Answer the following questions with a graphing calculator. Round your answers to integers.

a. If 38 customers arrived in the store in the past hour, there are approximately [   ] customers waiting in line.

b. If there are 8 customers waiting in line, approximately [   ] customers arrived in the past hour.

4. In a certain store, cashiers can serve 55 customers per hour on average. If x customers arrive at the store in a given hour, then the average number of customers C waiting in line can be modeled by the function

$$C(x) = \frac{x^2}{3025 - 55x}$$

where x < 55.
Answer the following questions with a graphing calculator. Round your answers to integers.

a. If 48 customers arrived in the store in the past hour, there are approximately [   ] customers waiting in line.

b. If there are 2 customers waiting in line, approximately [   ] customers arrived in the past hour.

Identify Rational Functions Select all rational functions. There are several correct answers.

5.

☐ $t(x) = \frac{5-7x^3}{6x^{0.7}+2x-3}$ ☐ $r(x) = \frac{6x^2+2x-3}{5-7x^{-6}}$ ☐ $c(x) = \frac{6x^2+2x-3}{5+|x|}$ ☐ $b(x) = \frac{6x^2+2x-3}{5}$

☐ $s(x) = \frac{\sqrt{6}x^2+2x-3}{5-7x^6}$ ☐ $n(x) = \frac{6x^2+2\sqrt{x}-3}{5-7x^6}$ ☐ $a(x) = \frac{6x^2+2x-3}{5-7x^6}$ ☐ $m(x) = \frac{6x+2}{6x+2}$

☐ $h(x) = \frac{5}{6x^2+2x-3}$

6.

☐ $n(x) = \frac{7x^2+6\sqrt{x}-6}{3-7x^7}$ ☐ $t(x) = \frac{3-7x^3}{7x^{0.7}+6x-6}$ ☐ $m(x) = \frac{7x+6}{7x+6}$ ☐ $r(x) = \frac{7x^2+6x-6}{3-7x^{-7}}$

☐ $c(x) = \frac{7x^2+6x-6}{3+|x|}$ ☐ $h(x) = \frac{3}{7x^2+6x-6}$ ☐ $b(x) = \frac{7x^2+6x-6}{3}$ ☐ $s(x) = \frac{\sqrt{7x^2+6x-6}}{3-7x^7}$

☐ $a(x) = \frac{7x^2+6x-6}{3-7x^7}$

Domain

7. Find the domain of K where $K(x) = \frac{x}{x+4}$.

8. Find the domain of K where $K(x) = \frac{5x}{x-10}$.

9. Find the domain of f where
$$f(x) = \frac{3x+9}{x^2+4x-12}.$$

10. Find the domain of g where
$$g(x) = -\frac{4x+3}{x^2-3x-40}.$$

11. Find the domain of h where $h(x) = \frac{9x+6}{x^2+7x}$.

12. Find the domain of F where $F(x) = \frac{2x-7}{x^2+2x}$.

13. Find the domain of F where $F(x) = \frac{2-5x}{x^2-49}$.

14. Find the domain of G where $G(x) = \frac{8x-10}{x^2-100}$.

15. Find the domain of the function c defined by
$$c(x) = \frac{x+6}{x^4}$$

16. Find the domain of the function n defined by
$$n(x) = \frac{x+8}{x^2}$$

17. Find the domain of the function t defined by
$$t(x) = \frac{x+10}{x^2+49}$$

18. Find the domain of the function p defined by
$$p(x) = \frac{x-8}{x^2+16}$$

19. Find the domain of the function r defined by
$$r(x) = \frac{x-6}{x-6}$$

20. Find the domain of the function n defined by
$$n(x) = \frac{x-4}{x-4}$$

A function is graphed. Find its domain.

21.

22.

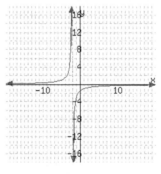

23.

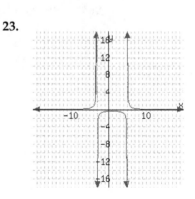

24. **25.** **26.**

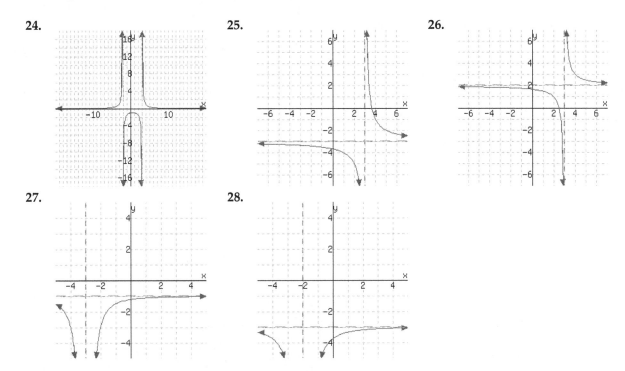

27. **28.**

Graphing Technology

29. In a forest, the number of deer can be modeled by the function $f(t) = \frac{200t+350}{0.8t+7}$, where t stands for the number of years from now. Answer the question with technology.

After 20 years, there would be approximately [ ] deer living in the forest.

30. In a forest, the number of deer can be modeled by the function $f(t) = \frac{240t+240}{0.6t+4}$, where t stands for the number of years from now. Answer the question with technology.

After [ ] years, there would be approximately 230 deer living in the forest.

31. In a forest, the number of deer can be modeled by the function $f(t) = \frac{60t+630}{0.3t+9}$, where t stands for the number of years from now. Answer the question with technology.

As time goes on, the population levels off at approximately [ ] deer living in the forest.

32. The concentration of a drug in a patient's blood stream, in milligrams per liter, can be modeled by the function $C(t) = \frac{7t}{t^2+6}$, where t is the number of hours since the drug is injected. Answer the following question with technology.

The drug's concentration after 1 hours is [ ] milligrams per liter.

33. The concentration of a drug in a patient's blood stream, in milligrams per liter, can be modeled by the function $C(t) = \frac{8t}{t^2+5}$, where t is the number of hours since the drug is injected. Answer the following question with technology.

[ ] hours since injection, the drug's concentration is 1.72 milligrams per liter.

34. The concentration of a drug in a patient's blood stream, in milligrams per liter, can be modeled by the function $C(t) = \frac{9t}{t^2+6}$, where t is the number of hours since the drug is injected. Answer the following question with technology.

[   ] hours since injection, the drug's concentration is at the maximum value of

[   ] milligrams per liter.

35. The concentration of a drug in a patient's blood stream, in milligrams per liter, can be modeled by the function $C(t) = \frac{9t}{t^2+7}$, where t is the number of hours since the drug is injected. Answer the following question with technology.

As time goes on, the drug's concentration in the patient's blood stream levels off at approximately [   ] milligrams per liter.

12.2 Multiplication and Division of Rational Expressions

In the last section, we learned some rational function applications. In this section, we will learn how to simplify rational expressions, and how to multiply and divide them.

12.2.1 Simplifying Rational Expressions

Consider the two rational functions below. At first glance, which function *looks* simpler?

$$f(x) = \frac{8x^3 - 12x^2 + 8x - 12}{2x^3 - 3x^2 + 10x - 15} \qquad g(x) = \frac{4(x^2 + 1)}{x^2 + 5}, \text{ for } x \neq \frac{3}{2}$$

It can be argued that the function g is simpler, at least with regard to the ease with which we can determine its domain, quickly evaluate it, and also determine where its function value is zero. All of these things are considerably more difficult with the function f.

These two functions are actually the *same* function. Using factoring and the same process of canceling that's used with numerical ratios, we will learn how to simplify the function f into the function g. (The full process for simplifying $f(x) = \frac{8x^3 - 12x^2 + 8x - 12}{2x^3 - 3x^2 + 10x - 15}$ will be shown in Example 12.2.8.)

To see a simple example of the process for simplifying a rational function or expression, let's look at simplifying $\frac{14}{21}$ and $\frac{(x+2)(x+7)}{(x+3)(x+7)}$ by canceling common factors:

$$\frac{14}{21} = \frac{2 \cdot 7}{3} \cdot 7 \qquad\qquad \frac{(x+2)(x+7)}{(x+3)(x+7)} = \frac{(x+2)\cancel{(x+7)}}{(x+3)\cancel{(x+7)}}$$

$$= \frac{2}{3} \qquad\qquad\qquad = \frac{x+2}{x+3}, \text{ for } x \neq -7$$

The statement "for $x \neq -7$" was added when the factors of $x+7$ were canceled. This is because $\frac{(x+2)(x+7)}{(x+3)(x+7)}$ was undefined for $x = -7$, so the simplified version must also be undefined for $x = -7$.

Warning 12.2.2 Cancel Factors, not Terms. It may be tempting to want to try to simplify $\frac{x+2}{x+3}$ into $\frac{2}{3}$ by canceling each x that appears. But these x's are *terms* (pieces that are added with other pieces), not *factors*. Canceling (an act of division) is only possible with *factors* (an act of multiplication).

The process of canceling factors is key to simplifying rational expressions. If the expression is not given in factored form, then this will be our first step. We'll now look at a few more examples.

Example 12.2.3 Simplify the rational function formula $Q(x) = \frac{3x-12}{x^2+x-20}$ and state the domain of Q.

Explanation.

To start, we'll factor the numerator and denominator. We'll then cancel any factors common to both the numerator and denominator.

$$Q(x) = \frac{3x - 12}{x^2 + x - 20}$$

$$Q(x) = \frac{3\cancel{(x-4)}}{(x+5)\cancel{(x-4)}}$$

$$Q(x) = \frac{3}{x+5}, \text{ for } x \neq 4$$

The domain of this function will incorporate the *explicit* domain restriction $x \neq 4$ that was stated when the factor of $x - 4$ was canceled from both the numerator and denominator. We will also exclude -5 from the domain as this value would make the denominator zero. Thus the domain of Q is $\{x \mid x \neq -5, 4\}$.

Warning 12.2.4 When simplifying the function Q in Example 12.2.3, we cannot simply write $Q(x) = \frac{3}{x+5}$. The reason is that this would result in our simplified version of the function Q having a different domain than the original Q. More specifically, for our original function Q it held that $Q(4)$ was undefined, and this still needs to be true for the simplified form of Q.

Example 12.2.5 Simplify the rational function formula $R(y) = \frac{-y-2y^2}{2y^3-y^2-y}$ and state the domain of R.

Explanation.

$$R(y) = \frac{-y - 2y^2}{2y^3 - y^2 - y}$$

$$R(y) = \frac{-2y^2 - y}{y(2y^2 - y - 1)}$$

$$R(y) = \frac{-\cancel{y}(2y+1)}{\cancel{y}(2y+1)(y - 1)}$$

$$R(y) = -\frac{1}{y - 1}, \text{ for } y \neq 0, y \neq -\frac{1}{2}$$

The domain of this function will incorporate the explicit restrictions $y \neq 0, y \neq -\frac{1}{2}$ that were stated when the factors of y and $2y + 1$ were canceled from both the numerator and denominator. Since the factor $y - 1$ is still in the denominator, we also need the restriction that $y \neq 1$. Therefore the domain of R is $\left\{y \mid y \neq -\frac{1}{2}, 0, 1\right\}$.

Example 12.2.6 Simplify the expression $\frac{9y+2y^2-5}{y^2-25}$.

Explanation.

To start, we need to recognize that $9y+2y^2-5$ is not written in standard form (where terms are written from highest degree to lowest degree). Before attempting to factor this expression, we'll re-write it as $2y^2 + 9y - 5$.

$$\frac{9y + 2y^2 - 5}{y^2 - 25} = \frac{2y^2 + 9y - 5}{y^2 - 25}$$

$$= \frac{(2y - 1)\cancel{(y+5)}}{\cancel{(y+5)}(y - 5)}$$

$$= \frac{2y - 1}{y - 5}, \text{ for } y \neq -5$$

Example 12.2.7 Simplify the expression $\frac{-48z+24z^2-3z^3}{4-z}$.

Explanation. To begin simplifying this expression, we will rewrite each polynomial in descending order. Then we'll factor out the GCF, including the constant -1 from both the numerator and denominator because their leading terms are negative.

$$\frac{-48z + 24z^2 - 3z^3}{4 - z} = \frac{-3z^3 + 24z^2 - 48z}{-z + 4}$$

$$= \frac{-3z(z^2 - 8z + 16)}{-(z - 4)}$$

$$= \frac{-3z(z - 4)^2}{-(z - 4)}$$

$$= \frac{-3z(z - 4)\cancel{(z-4)}}{-\cancel{(z-4)}}$$

$$= \frac{3z(z - 4)}{1}, \text{ for } z \neq 4$$

$$= 3z(z - 4), \text{ for } z \neq 4$$

Example 12.2.8 Simplify the rational function formula $f(x) = \frac{8x^3-12x^2+8x-12}{2x^3-3x^2+10x-15}$ and state the domain of f.

Explanation.

To simplify this rational function, we'll first note that both the numerator and denominator have four terms. To factor them we'll need to use factoring by grouping. (Note that if this technique didn't work, very few other approaches would be possible.) Once we've used factoring by grouping, we'll cancel any factors common to both the numerator and denominator and state the associated restrictions.

$$f(x) = \frac{8x^3 - 12x^2 + 8x - 12}{2x^3 - 3x^2 + 10x - 15}$$

$$f(x) = \frac{4(2x^3 - 3x^2 + 2x - 3)}{2x^3 - 3x^2 + 10x - 15}$$

$$f(x) = \frac{4(x^2(2x - 3) + (2x - 3))}{x^2(2x - 3) + 5(2x - 3)}$$

$$f(x) = \frac{4(x^2 + 1)\cancel{(2x - 3)}}{(x^2 + 5)\cancel{(2x - 3)}}$$

$$f(x) = \frac{4(x^2 + 1)}{x^2 + 5}, \text{ for } x \neq \frac{3}{2}$$

In determining the domain of this function, we'll need to account for any implicit and explicit restrictions. When the factor $2x - 3$ was canceled, the explicit statement of $x \neq \frac{3}{2}$ was given. The denominator in the final simplified form of this function has $x^2 + 5$. There is no value of x for which $x^2 + 5 = 0$, so the only restriction is that $x \neq \frac{3}{2}$. Therefore the domain is $\{x \mid x \neq \frac{3}{2}\}$.

Example 12.2.9 Simplify the expression $\frac{3y - x}{x^2 - xy - 6y^2}$. In this example, there are two variables. It is still possible that in examples like this, there can be domain restrictions when simplifying rational expressions. However since we are not studying *functions* of more than one variable, this textbook ignores domain restrictions with examples like this one.

Explanation.

$$\frac{3y - x}{x^2 - xy - 6y^2} = \frac{-\cancel{(x - 3y)}}{\cancel{(x - 3y)}(x + 2y)}$$

$$= \frac{-1}{x + 2y}$$

12.2.2 Multiplication of Rational Functions and Expressions

Recall the property for multiplying fractions A.2.16, which states that the product of two fractions is equal to the product of their numerators divided by the product of their denominators. We will use this same property for multiplying rational expressions.

When multiplying fractions, one approach is to multiply the numerator and denominator, and then simplify the fraction that results by determining the greatest common factor in both the numerator and denominator, like this:

$$\frac{14}{9} \cdot \frac{3}{10} = \frac{14 \cdot 3}{9 \cdot 10}$$

$$= \frac{42}{90}$$

$$= \frac{7 \cdot \cancel{6}}{15 \cdot \cancel{6}}$$

$$= \frac{7}{15}$$

This approach works great when we can easily identify that 6 is the greatest common factor in both 42 and 90. But in more complicated instances, it isn't always an easy approach. It also won't work particularly well when we have $(x + 2)$ instead of 2 as a factor, as we'll see shortly.

Another approach to multiplying and simplifying fractions involves utilizing the prime factorization of each the numerator and denominator, like this:

$$\frac{14}{9} \cdot \frac{3}{10} = \frac{2 \cdot 7}{3^2} \cdot \frac{3}{2 \cdot 5}$$

$$= \frac{2 \cdot 7 \cdot 3}{3 \cdot 3 \cdot 2 \cdot 5}$$

$$= \frac{7}{15}$$

The method for multiplying and simplifying rational expressions is nearly identical, as shown here:

$$\frac{x^2 + 9x + 14}{x^2 + 6x + 9} \cdot \frac{x+3}{x^2 + 7x + 10} = \frac{(x+2)(x+7)}{(x+3)^2} \cdot \frac{x+3}{(x+2)(x+5)}$$

$$= \frac{(x+2)(x+7)(x+3)}{(x+3)(x+3)(x+2)(x+5)}$$

$$= \frac{(x+7)}{(x+3)(x+5)}, \text{ for } x \neq -2$$

This process will be used for both multiplying and dividing rational expressions. The main distinctions in various examples will be in the factoring methods required.

Example 12.2.10 Multiply the rational expressions: $\dfrac{x^2 - 4x}{x^2 - 4} \cdot \dfrac{4 - 4x + x^2}{20 - x - x^2}$.

Explanation. Note that to factor the second rational expression, we'll want to re-write the terms in descending order for both the numerator and denominator. In the denominator, we'll first factor out -1 as the leading term is $-x^2$.

$$\frac{x^2 - 4x}{x^2 - 4} \cdot \frac{4 - 4x + x^2}{20 - x - x^2} = \frac{x^2 - 4x}{x^2 - 4} \cdot \frac{x^2 - 4x + 4}{-x^2 - x + 20}$$

$$= \frac{x^2 - 4x}{x^2 - 4} \cdot \frac{x^2 - 4x + 4}{-(x^2 + x - 20)}$$

$$= \frac{x(x-4)}{(x+2)(x-2)} \cdot \frac{(x-2)(x-2)}{-(x+5)(x-4)}$$

$$= -\frac{x(x-2)}{(x+2)(x+5)}, \text{ for } x \neq 2, x \neq 4$$

Example 12.2.11 Multiply the rational expressions: $\dfrac{p^2 q^4}{3r} \cdot \dfrac{9r^2}{pq^2}$. Note this book ignores domain restrictions on multivariable expressions.

Explanation. We won't need to factor anything in this example, and can simply multiply across and then simplify.

$$\frac{p^2 q^4}{3r} \cdot \frac{9r^2}{pq^2} = \frac{p^2 q^2 \cdot 9r^2}{3r \cdot pq^2}$$

$$= \frac{pq^2 \cdot 3r}{1}$$

$$= 3pq^2 r$$

12.2.3 Division of Rational Functions and Expressions

We can divide rational expressions using the property for dividing fractions A.2.18, which simply requires that we change dividing by an expression to multiplying by its reciprocal. Let's look at a few examples.

Example 12.2.12 Divide the rational expressions: $\dfrac{x+2}{x+5} \div \dfrac{x+2}{x-3}$.

Explanation.

$$\frac{x+2}{x+5} \div \frac{x+2}{x-3} = \frac{\cancel{x+2}}{x+5} \cdot \frac{x-3}{\cancel{x+2}}, \text{ for } x \neq 3$$
$$= \frac{x-3}{x+5}, \text{ for } x \neq -2, x \neq 3$$

Remark 12.2.13 In the first step of 12.2.12, the restriction $x \neq 3$ was used. We hadn't canceled anything yet, so why is there this restriction already? It's because the original expression $\frac{x+2}{x+5} \div \frac{x+2}{x-3}$ had $x - 3$ in a denominator, which means that 3 is not a valid input. In the first step of simplifying, the $x - 3$ denominator went to the numerator and we lost the information that 3 was not a valid input, so we stated it explicitly. Always be sure to compare the restrictions of the original expression with each step throughout the process.

Example 12.2.14 Simplify the rational expression using division: $\dfrac{\frac{3x-6}{2x+10}}{\frac{x^2-4}{3x+15}}$.

Explanation. To begin, we'll note that the larger fraction bar is denoting division, so we will use multiplication by the reciprocal. After that, we'll factor each expression and cancel any common factors.

$$\frac{\frac{3x-6}{2x+10}}{\frac{x^2-4}{3x+15}} = \frac{3x-6}{2x+10} \div \frac{x^2-4}{3x+15}$$
$$= \frac{3x-6}{2x+10} \cdot \frac{3x+15}{x^2-4}$$
$$= \frac{3\cancel{(x-2)}}{2\cancel{(x+5)}} \cdot \frac{3\cancel{(x+5)}}{(x+2)\cancel{(x-2)}}$$
$$= \frac{3 \cdot 3}{2(x+2)}, \text{ for } x \neq -5, x \neq 2$$
$$= \frac{9}{2x+4}, \text{ for } x \neq -5, x \neq 2$$

Example 12.2.15 Divide the rational expressions: $\dfrac{x^2-5x-14}{x^2+7x+10} \div \dfrac{x-7}{x+4}$.

Explanation.

$$\frac{x^2-5x-14}{x^2+7x+10} \div \frac{x-7}{x+4} = \frac{x^2-5x-14}{x^2+7x+10} \cdot \frac{x+4}{x-7}, \text{ for } x \neq -4$$
$$= \frac{\cancel{(x-7)}(x+2)}{(x+5)\cancel{(x+2)}} \cdot \frac{x+4}{\cancel{x-7}}, \text{ for } x \neq -4$$
$$= \frac{x+4}{x+5}, \text{ for } x \neq -4, x \neq -2, x \neq 7$$

Example 12.2.16 Divide the rational expressions: $(p^4 - 16) \div \dfrac{p^4 - 2p^3}{2p}$.

Explanation.

$$\begin{aligned}
(p^4 - 16) \div \frac{p^4 - 2p^3}{2p} &= \frac{p^4 - 16}{1} \cdot \frac{2p}{p^4 - 2p^3} \\
&= \frac{(p^2 + 4)(p + 2)\cancel{(p - 2)}}{1} \cdot \frac{2p}{p^3 \cancel{(p - 2)}} \\
&= \frac{2(p^2 + 4)(p + 2)}{p^2}, \text{ for } p \neq 2
\end{aligned}$$

Note here that we *didn't* have to include a restriction in the very first step. That restriction would have been $p \neq 0$, but since 0 *still* cannot be inputted into any of the subsequent expressions, we don't need to explicitly state $p \neq 0$ as a restriction because the expressions tell us that implicitly already.

Example 12.2.17 Divide the rational expressions: $\dfrac{3x^2}{x^2 - 9y^2} \div \dfrac{6x^3}{x^2 - 2xy - 15y^2}$. Note this book ignores domain restrictions on multivariable expressions.

Explanation.

$$\begin{aligned}
\frac{3x^2}{x^2 - 9y^2} \div \frac{6x^3}{x^2 - 2xy - 15y^2} &= \frac{3x^2}{x^2 - 9y^2} \cdot \frac{x^2 - 2xy - 15y^2}{6x^3} \\
&= \frac{3x^2}{\cancel{(x + 3y)}(x - 3y)} \cdot \frac{\cancel{(x + 3y)}(x - 5y)}{6x^3} \\
&= \frac{1}{x - 3y} \cdot \frac{x - 5y}{2x} \\
&= \frac{x - 5y}{2x(x - 3y)}
\end{aligned}$$

Example 12.2.18 Divide the rational expressions: $\dfrac{m^2 n^2 - 3mn - 4}{2mn} \div (m^2 n^2 - 16)$. Note this book ignores domain restrictions on multivariable expressions.

Explanation.

$$\begin{aligned}
\frac{m^2 n^2 - 3mn - 4}{2mn} \div (m^2 n^2 - 16) &= \frac{m^2 n^2 - 3mn - 4}{2mn} \cdot \frac{1}{m^2 n^2 - 16} \\
&= \frac{\cancel{(mn - 4)}(mn + 1)}{2mn} \cdot \frac{1}{(mn + 4)\cancel{(mn - 4)}} \\
&= \frac{mn + 1}{2mn} \cdot \frac{1}{mn + 4} \\
&= \frac{mn + 1}{2mn(mn + 4)}
\end{aligned}$$

12.2.4 Reading Questions

1. What is the difference between a factor and a term?

2. When canceling pieces of rational function expression to simplify it, what kinds of pieces are the only acceptable pieces to cancel?

3. When you simplify a rational funciton expression, you may need to make note of a ☐ ☐ .

12.2.5 Exercises

Review and Warmup

1. Multiply: $-\dfrac{3}{13} \cdot \dfrac{5}{9}$

2. Multiply: $-\dfrac{9}{11} \cdot \dfrac{13}{24}$

3. Multiply: $-\dfrac{8}{9} \cdot \left(-\dfrac{7}{18}\right)$

4. Multiply: $-\dfrac{10}{9} \cdot \left(-\dfrac{19}{4}\right)$

5. Divide: $\dfrac{3}{5} \div \dfrac{5}{2}$

6. Divide: $\dfrac{3}{8} \div \dfrac{8}{3}$

7. Divide: $\dfrac{3}{20} \div \left(-\dfrac{5}{8}\right)$

8. Divide: $\dfrac{4}{25} \div \left(-\dfrac{3}{10}\right)$

Factor the given polynomial.

9. $t^2 - 36$

10. $x^2 - 4$

11. $x^2 + 12x + 32$

12. $y^2 + 13y + 40$

13. $y^2 - 3y + 2$

14. $r^2 - 15r + 56$

15. $3r^2 - 15r + 18$

16. $10t^2 - 30t + 20$

17. $2t^{10} + 10t^9 + 12t^8$

18. $6t^5 + 18t^4 + 12t^3$

19. $144x^2 - 24x + 1$

20. $81x^2 - 18x + 1$

Simplifying Rational Expressions with One Variable

21. Simplify the following expressions, and if applicable, write the restricted domain on the simplified expression.

    a. $\dfrac{y+4}{y+4}$

    b. $\dfrac{y+4}{4+y}$

    c. $\dfrac{y-4}{y-4}$

    d. $\dfrac{y-4}{4-y}$

22. Simplify the following expressions, and if applicable, write the restricted domain on the simplified expression.

    a. $\dfrac{y+10}{y+10}$

    b. $\dfrac{y+10}{10+y}$

    c. $\dfrac{y-10}{y-10}$

    d. $\dfrac{y-10}{10-y}$

23. Select all correct simplifications, ignoring possible domain restrictions.

- [ ] $\frac{x+6}{x+7} = \frac{6}{7}$
- [ ] $\frac{7x+6}{x+6} = 7$
- [ ] $\frac{6}{x+6} = \frac{1}{x}$
- [ ] $\frac{x+6}{x} = 6$
- [ ] $\frac{7x+6}{7} = x + 6$
- [ ] $\frac{6}{x+6} = \frac{1}{x+1}$
- [ ] $\frac{x}{7x} = \frac{1}{7}$
- [ ] $\frac{6x}{x} = 6$
- [ ] $\frac{x+6}{x+6} = 1$
- [ ] $\frac{x+6}{6} = x$
- [ ] $\frac{7(x-6)}{x-6} = 7$

24. Select all correct simplifications, ignoring possible domain restrictions.

- [ ] $\frac{x+7}{7} = x$
- [ ] $\frac{7x}{x} = 7$
- [ ] $\frac{x+7}{x+4} = \frac{7}{4}$
- [ ] $\frac{4x+7}{4} = x + 7$
- [ ] $\frac{x+7}{x+7} = 1$
- [ ] $\frac{x+7}{x} = 7$
- [ ] $\frac{4x+7}{x+7} = 4$
- [ ] $\frac{4(x-7)}{x-7} = 4$
- [ ] $\frac{7}{x+7} = \frac{1}{x}$
- [ ] $\frac{x}{4x} = \frac{1}{4}$
- [ ] $\frac{7}{x+7} = \frac{1}{x+1}$

Simplify the following expression, and if applicable, write the restricted domain on the simplified expression.

25. $\dfrac{t-10}{(t-4)(t-10)}$

26. $\dfrac{t+7}{(t-10)(t+7)}$

27. $\dfrac{3(t-3)}{(t-8)(t-3)}$

28. $\dfrac{-8(x-9)}{(x-6)(x-9)}$

29. $\dfrac{(x+6)(x-2)}{2-x}$

30. $\dfrac{(y-3)(y-9)}{9-y}$

31. $\dfrac{9y-63}{y-7}$

32. $\dfrac{-6r+30}{r-5}$

33. $\dfrac{-2r}{r^2+3r}$

34. $\dfrac{9t}{t^2+8t}$

35. $\dfrac{3t-t^2}{t^2-9t+18}$

36. $\dfrac{t-t^2}{t^2-6t+5}$

37. $\dfrac{x^2+5x}{25-x^2}$

38. $\dfrac{x^2-3x}{9-x^2}$

39. $\dfrac{-y^2+y}{3-2y-y^2}$

40. $\dfrac{-y^2+5y}{5+4y-y^2}$

41. $\dfrac{3r^2+5r+2}{-r+4-5r^2}$

42. $\dfrac{5r^2+8r+3}{-r+5-6r^2}$

43. $\dfrac{r^2+6r+8}{-4r-r^2-4}$

44. $\dfrac{t^2-t-2}{-2t-t^2-1}$

45. $\dfrac{-t^2-11t-30}{t^2-25}$

46. $\dfrac{-x^2-7x-12}{x^2-9}$

47. $\dfrac{2x^2-x-3}{-11x-5-6x^2}$

48. $\dfrac{5y^2+11y+6}{-11y-5-6y^2}$

49. $\dfrac{4y^3-y^4}{y^2-2y-8}$

50. $\dfrac{-2r^2-r^3}{r^2-4}$

51. $\dfrac{r^6-3r^5-18r^4}{r^6-11r^5+30r^4}$

52. $\dfrac{r^5+3r^4-4r^3}{r^5+2r^4-3r^3}$

53. $\dfrac{t^3+8}{t^2-4}$

54. $\dfrac{t^3-125}{t^2-25}$

Simplifying Rational Expressions with More Than One Variable Simplify this expression.

55. $\dfrac{5xy-x^2y^2}{x^2y^2+xy-30}$

56. $\dfrac{5xr-x^2r^2}{x^2r^2-xr-20}$

57. $\dfrac{4y+16t}{y^2+5yt+4t^2}$

58. $\dfrac{2y+10t}{y^2+8yt+15t^2}$

59. $\dfrac{-r^2+rx+12x^2}{r^2-16x^2}$

60. $\dfrac{-r^2-rt+12t^2}{r^2-9t^2}$

61. $\dfrac{2r^2y^2+5ry+3}{-11ry-5-6r^2y^2}$

62. $\dfrac{3t^2x^2+5tx+2}{-7tx-2-5t^2x^2}$

Simplifying Rational Functions Simplify the function formula, and if applicable, write the restricted domain.

63. $G(t) = \dfrac{t+1}{t^2 - 6t - 7}$

Reduced $G(t) =$

64. $h(x) = \dfrac{x-5}{x^2 + x - 30}$

Reduced $h(x) =$

65. $K(x) = \dfrac{x^3 - 81x}{x^3 + 11x^2 + 18x}$

Reduced $K(x) =$

66. $G(y) = \dfrac{y^3 - 9y}{y^3 + 13y^2 + 30y}$

Reduced $G(y) =$

67. $h(y) = \dfrac{y^4 + 4y^3 + 4y^2}{3y^4 + 5y^3 - 2y^2}$

Reduced $h(y) =$

68. $K(r) = \dfrac{r^4 - 8r^3 + 16r^2}{3r^4 - 11r^3 - 4r^2}$

Reduced $K(r) =$

69. $G(r) = \dfrac{3r^3 + r^2}{3r^3 - 11r^2 - 4r}$

Reduced $G(r) =$

70. $g(r) = \dfrac{5r^3 + 3r^2}{5r^3 - 22r^2 - 15r}$

Reduced $g(r) =$

Multiplying and Dividing Rational Expressions with One Variable

71. Select all correct equations:

☐ $9 \cdot \dfrac{x}{y} = \dfrac{9x}{9y}$ 　　 ☐ $-\dfrac{x}{y} = \dfrac{-x}{-y}$

☐ $9 \cdot \dfrac{x}{y} = \dfrac{x}{9y}$ 　　 ☐ $-\dfrac{x}{y} = \dfrac{-x}{y}$

☐ $9 \cdot \dfrac{x}{y} = \dfrac{9x}{y}$ 　　 ☐ $-\dfrac{x}{y} = \dfrac{x}{-y}$

72. Select all correct equations:

☐ $10 \cdot \dfrac{x}{y} = \dfrac{10x}{10y}$ 　　 ☐ $-\dfrac{x}{y} = \dfrac{-x}{-y}$

☐ $-\dfrac{x}{y} = \dfrac{-x}{y}$ 　　 ☐ $10 \cdot \dfrac{x}{y} = \dfrac{10x}{y}$

☐ $10 \cdot \dfrac{x}{y} = \dfrac{x}{10y}$ 　　 ☐ $-\dfrac{x}{y} = \dfrac{x}{-y}$

73. Simplify the following expressions, and if applicable, write the restricted domain.

$-\dfrac{x^4}{x+4} \cdot x^3$

$-\dfrac{x^4}{x+4} \cdot \dfrac{1}{x^3}$

74. Simplify the following expressions, and if applicable, write the restricted domain.

$-\dfrac{y^4}{y+4} \cdot y^2$

$-\dfrac{y^4}{y+4} \cdot \dfrac{1}{y^2}$

Simplify this expression, and if applicable, write the restricted domain.

75. $\dfrac{y^2 - y - 2}{y+4} \cdot \dfrac{5y + 20}{y+1}$

76. $\dfrac{y^2 + 7y + 12}{y-6} \cdot \dfrac{5y - 30}{y+4}$

77. $\dfrac{r^2 - 9r}{r^2 - 9} \cdot \dfrac{r^2 - 3r}{r^2 - 11r + 18}$

78. $\dfrac{r^2 - 9r}{r^2 - 9} \cdot \dfrac{r^2 - 3r}{r^2 - 7r - 18}$

79. $\dfrac{12r - 12}{-20 - 25r - 5r^2} \cdot \dfrac{r^2 + 8r + 16}{4r^2 - 4r}$

80. $\dfrac{6t - 24}{28 - 21t - 7t^2} \cdot \dfrac{t^2 - 2t + 1}{2t^2 - 8t}$

81. $\dfrac{6t^2 - 11t + 5}{20t^3 - 50t^2} \cdot \dfrac{10t^2 - 4t^3}{36t^2 - 25}$

82. $\dfrac{5x^2 + (-1)x - 4}{126x^2 - 105x} \cdot \dfrac{15x - 18x^2}{25x^2 - 16}$

83. $\dfrac{x}{x-6} \div 3x^2$

84. $\dfrac{y}{y+10} \div 5y^2$

85. $8y \div \dfrac{2}{y^3}$

86. $12r \div \dfrac{3}{r^2}$

87. $(2r - 6) \div (4r - 12)$

88. $(4r - 12) \div (24r - 72)$

89. $\dfrac{25t^2 - 36}{5t^2 + (-9)t + (-18)} \div (6 - 5t)$

90. $\dfrac{4t^2 - 49}{2t^2 + 11t + 14} \div (7 - 2t)$

91. $\dfrac{x^4}{x^2 + 6x} \div \dfrac{1}{x^2 + x - 30}$

92. $\dfrac{x^3}{x^2 - 3x} \div \dfrac{1}{x^2 + x - 12}$

93. $\dfrac{\frac{5a+1}{a}}{\frac{a+1}{a}}$

94. $\dfrac{\frac{10a+10}{a}}{\frac{a+7}{a}}$

95. $\dfrac{\frac{u}{(u-6)^2}}{\frac{5u}{u^2-36}}$

96. $\dfrac{\frac{r}{(r-3)^2}}{\frac{9r}{r^2-9}}$

97. $\dfrac{x^2 + 3x}{x^2 - 16} \div \dfrac{x^2 - 9}{x^2 + 2x - 8}$

98. $\dfrac{x^2 + 4x}{x^2 - 1} \div \dfrac{x^2 - 16}{x^2 - 4x - 5}$

Multiplying and Dividing Rational Expressions with More Than One Variable Simplify this expression.

99. $\dfrac{8(t + x)}{t - x} \cdot \dfrac{t - x}{2(2t + x)}$

100. $\dfrac{12(x + t)}{x - t} \cdot \dfrac{x - t}{4(2x + t)}$

101. $\dfrac{4x^3y^2}{3x^4} \cdot \dfrac{9x^4y^2}{8y^5}$

102. $\dfrac{5yx}{3y} \cdot \dfrac{3y^2x^3}{25x^5}$

103. $\dfrac{y^2 + 9yt + 20t^2}{y + t} \cdot \dfrac{2y + 2t}{y + 5t}$

104. $\dfrac{r^2 + ry - 12y^2}{r + 6y} \cdot \dfrac{3r + 18y}{r - 3y}$

105. $\dfrac{rx^{10}}{4} \div \dfrac{rx^5}{8}$

106. $\dfrac{r^3t^2}{6} \div \dfrac{r^3t}{12}$

107. $(t^4 - 4t^3y + 4t^2y^2) \div (t^5 - 2t^4y)$

108. $(t^3 + 8t^2x + 16tx^2) \div (t^5 + 4t^4x)$

109. $\dfrac{1}{x^2 - 10xr + 24r^2} \div \dfrac{x^2}{x^2 - 4xr}$

110. $\dfrac{1}{x^2 + 5xy + 6y^2} \div \dfrac{x^5}{x^2 + 2xy}$

111. $\dfrac{y^5}{y^2x - 6y} \div \dfrac{1}{y^2x^2 - 7yx + 6}$

112. $\dfrac{y^3}{y^2r - 4y} \div \dfrac{1}{y^2r^2 + 2yr - 24}$

113. $\dfrac{36y^4t^2}{y + 10t} \div \dfrac{6y^5t}{y^2 - 100t^2}$

114. $\dfrac{15r^3t^4}{r + 9t} \div \dfrac{3r^8t}{r^2 - 81t^2}$

115. $\dfrac{\frac{p}{q}}{\frac{5p}{4q^2}}$

116. $\dfrac{\frac{m}{n}}{\frac{4m}{3n^2}}$

117. $\dfrac{\frac{mn^2}{10k}}{\frac{m}{6nk}}$

118. $\dfrac{\frac{xy^2}{7z}}{\frac{x}{10yz}}$

Challenge

119. Simplify the following: $\frac{1}{x+1} \div \frac{x+2}{x+1} \div \frac{x+3}{x+2} \div \frac{x+4}{x+3} \div \cdots \div \frac{x+35}{x+34}$. For this exercise, you do not have to write the restricted domain of the simplified expression.

12.3 Addition and Subtraction of Rational Expressions

In the last section, we learned how to multiply and divide rational expressions. In this section, we will learn how to add and subtract rational expressions.

12.3.1 Introduction

Example 12.3.2 Julia is taking her family on a boat trip 12 miles down the river and back. The river flows at a speed of 2 miles per hour and she wants to drive the boat at a constant speed, v miles per hour downstream and back upstream. Due to the current of the river, the actual speed of travel is $v + 2$ miles per hour going downstream, and $v - 2$ miles per hour going upstream. If Julia plans to spend 8 hours for the whole trip, how fast should she drive the boat?

We need to review three forms of the formula for movement at a constant rate:

$$d = vt \qquad\qquad v = \frac{d}{t} \qquad\qquad t = \frac{d}{v}$$

where d stands for distance, v represents speed, and t stands for time. According to the third form, the time it takes the boat to travel downstream is $\frac{12}{v+2}$, and the time it takes to get back upstream is $\frac{12}{v-2}$.

The function to model the time of the whole trip is

$$t(v) = \frac{12}{v - 2} + \frac{12}{v + 2}$$

where t stands for time in hours, and v is the boat's speed in miles per hour. Let's look at the graph of this function in Figure 12.3.3. Note that since the speed v and the time $t(v)$ should be positive in context, it's only the first quadrant of Figure 12.3.3 that matters.

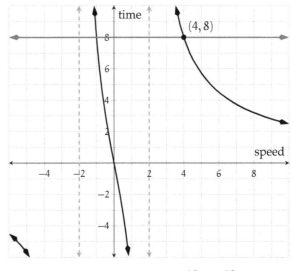

Figure 12.3.3: Graph of $t(v) = \frac{12}{v-2} + \frac{12}{v+2}$ and $t = 8$

To find the speed that Julia should drive the boat to make the round trip last 8 hours we can use graphing technology to solve the equation

$$\frac{12}{v - 2} + \frac{12}{v + 2} = 8$$

graphically and we see that $v = 4$. This tells us that a speed of 4 miles per hour will give a total time of 8 hours to complete the trip. To go downstream it would take $\frac{12}{v+2} = \frac{12}{4+2} = 2$ hours; and to go upstream it would take $\frac{12}{v-2} = \frac{12}{4-2} = 6$ hours.

The point of this section is to work with expressions like $\frac{12}{v-2} + \frac{12}{v+2}$, where two rational expressions are added (or subtracted). There are times when it is useful to combine them into a single fraction. We will learn that the expression $\frac{12}{v-2} + \frac{12}{v+2}$ is equal to the expression $\frac{24v}{v^2-4}$, and we will learn how to make that simplification.

12.3.2 Addition and Subtraction of Rational Expressions with the Same Denominator

The process of adding and subtracting rational expressions will be very similar to the process of adding and subtracting purely numerical fractions.

If the two expressions have the same denominator, then we can rely on the property of adding and subtracting fractions and simplify that result.

Let's review how to add fractions with the same denominator:

$$\begin{aligned} \frac{1}{10} + \frac{3}{10} &= \frac{1+3}{10} \\ &= \frac{4}{10} \\ &= \frac{2}{5} \end{aligned}$$

We can add and subtract rational expressions in the same way:

$$\begin{aligned} \frac{2}{3x} - \frac{5}{3x} &= \frac{2-5}{3x} \\ &= \frac{-3}{3x} \\ &= -\frac{1}{x} \end{aligned}$$

List 12.3.4: Steps to Adding/Subtracting Rational Expressions

> **Identify the LCD** Determine the least common denominator of all of the denominators.
>
> **Build** If necessary, build up each expression so that the denominators are the same.
>
> **Add/Subtract** Combine the numerators using the properties of adding and subtracting fractions.
>
> **Simplify** Simplify the resulting rational expression as much as possible. This may require factoring the numerator.

Example 12.3.5 Add the rational expressions: $\dfrac{2x}{x+y} + \dfrac{2y}{x+y}$.

Explanation.   These expressions already have a common denominator:

$$\begin{aligned} \frac{2x}{x+y} + \frac{2y}{x+y} &= \frac{2x+2y}{x+y} \\ &= \frac{2\cancel{(x+y)}}{\cancel{x+y}} \\ &= \frac{2}{1} \\ &= 2 \end{aligned}$$

Note that we didn't stop at $\frac{2x+2y}{x+y}$. If possible, we must simplify the numerator and denominator. Since this is a multivariable expression, this textbook ignores domain restrictions while canceling.

12.3.3 Addition and Subtraction of Rational Expressions with Different Denominators

To add rational expressions with different denominators, we'll need to build each fraction to the least common denominator, in the same way we do with numerical fractions. Let's briefly review this process by adding $\frac{3}{5}$ and $\frac{1}{6}$:

$$
\begin{aligned}
\frac{3}{5} + \frac{1}{6} &= \frac{3}{5} \cdot \frac{6}{6} + \frac{1}{6} \cdot \frac{5}{5} \\
&= \frac{18}{30} + \frac{5}{30} \\
&= \frac{18 + 5}{30} \\
&= \frac{23}{30}
\end{aligned}
$$

This exact method can be used when adding rational expressions containing variables. The key is that the expressions *must* have the same denominator before they can be added or subtracted. If they don't have this initially, then we'll identify the least common denominator and build each expression so that it has that denominator.

Let's apply this to adding the two expressions with denominators that are $v - 2$ and $v + 2$ from Example 12.3.2.

Example 12.3.6 Add the rational expressions and fully simplify the function given by $t(v) = \frac{12}{v-2} + \frac{12}{v+2}$.

Explanation.

$$
\begin{aligned}
t(v) &= \frac{12}{v-2} + \frac{12}{v+2} \\
t(v) &= \frac{12}{v-2} \cdot \frac{v+2}{v+2} + \frac{12}{v+2} \cdot \frac{v-2}{v-2} \\
t(v) &= \frac{12v + 24}{(v-2)(v+2)} + \frac{12v - 24}{(v+2)(v-2)} \\
t(v) &= \frac{(12v + 24) + (12v - 24)}{(v+2)(v-2)} \\
t(v) &= \frac{24v}{(v+2)(v-2)}
\end{aligned}
$$

Example 12.3.7 Add the rational expressions: $\dfrac{2}{5x^2y} + \dfrac{3}{20xy^2}$

Explanation. The least common denominator of $5x^2y$ and $20xy^2$ must include two x's and two y's, as well as 20. Thus it is $20x^2y^2$. We will build both denominators to $20x^2y^2$ before doing addition.

$$
\begin{aligned}
\frac{2}{5x^2y} + \frac{3}{20xy^2} &= \frac{2}{5x^2y} \cdot \frac{4y}{4y} + \frac{3}{20xy^2} \cdot \frac{x}{x} \\
&= \frac{8y}{20x^2y^2} + \frac{3x}{20x^2y^2} \\
&= \frac{8y + 3x}{20x^2y^2}
\end{aligned}
$$

Let's look at a few more complicated examples.

Example 12.3.8 Subtract the rational expressions: $\dfrac{y}{y-2} - \dfrac{8y-8}{y^2-4}$

Explanation. To start, we'll make sure each denominator is factored. Then we'll find the least common denominator and build each expression to that denominator. Then we will be able to combine the numerators and simplify the expression.

$$
\begin{aligned}
\frac{y}{y-2} - \frac{8y-8}{y^2-4} &= \frac{y}{y-2} - \frac{8y-8}{(y+2)(y-2)} \\
&= \frac{y}{y-2} \cdot \frac{y+2}{y+2} - \frac{8y-8}{(y+2)(y-2)} \\
&= \frac{y^2+2y}{(y+2)(y-2)} - \frac{8y-8}{(y+2)(y-2)} \\
&= \frac{y^2+2y - \overset{\downarrow}{(}8y - \overset{\downarrow}{8)}}{(y+2)(y-2)} \\
&= \frac{y^2+2y-8y+8}{(y+2)(y-2)} \\
&= \frac{y^2-6y+8}{(y+2)(y-2)} \\
&= \frac{\cancel{(y-2)}(y-4)}{(y+2)\cancel{(y-2)}} \\
&= \frac{y-4}{y+2}, \text{ for } y \neq 2
\end{aligned}
$$

Note that we must factor the numerator in $\frac{y^2-6y+8}{(y+2)(y-2)}$ and try to reduce the fraction (which we did).

Warning 12.3.9 In Example 12.3.8, be careful to subtract the entire numerator of $8y-8$. When this expression is in the numerator of $\frac{8y-8}{(y+2)(y-2)}$, it's implicitly grouped and doesn't need parentheses. But once $8y-8$ is subtracted from y^2+2y, we need to add parentheses so the entire expression is subtracted.

In the next example, we'll look at adding a rational expression to a polynomial. Much like adding a fraction and an integer, we'll rely on writing that expression as itself over one in order to build its denominator.

Example 12.3.10 Add the expressions: $-\dfrac{2}{r-1} + r$

Explanation.

$$
\begin{aligned}
-\frac{2}{r-1} + r &= -\frac{2}{r-1} + \frac{r}{1} \\
&= -\frac{2}{r-1} + \frac{r}{1} \cdot \frac{r-1}{r-1} \\
&= \frac{-2}{r-1} + \frac{r^2-r}{r-1} \\
&= \frac{-2+r^2-r}{r-1} \\
&= \frac{r^2-r-2}{r-1} \\
&= \frac{(r-2)(r+1)}{r-1}
\end{aligned}
$$

Note that we factored the numerator to reduce the fraction if possible. Even though it was not possible in this case, leaving it in factored form makes it easier to see that it is reduced.

Example 12.3.11 Subtract the expressions: $\dfrac{6}{x^2 - 2x - 8} - \dfrac{1}{x^2 + 3x + 2}$

Explanation. To start, we'll need to factor each of the denominators. After that, we'll identify the LCD and build each denominator accordingly. Then we can combine the numerators and simplify the resulting expression.

$$
\begin{aligned}
\frac{6}{x^2 - 2x - 8} - \frac{1}{x^2 + 3x + 2} &= \frac{6}{(x-4)(x+2)} - \frac{1}{(x+2)(x+1)} \\
&= \frac{6}{(x-4)(x+2)} \cdot \frac{x+1}{x+1} - \frac{1}{(x+2)(x+1)} \cdot \frac{x-4}{x-4} \\
&= \frac{6x+6}{(x-4)(x+2)(x+1)} - \frac{x-4}{(x+2)(x+1)(x-4)} \\
&= \frac{6x+6-(x-4)}{(x-4)(x+2)(x+1)} \\
&= \frac{6x+6-x+4}{(x-4)(x+2)(x+1)} \\
&= \frac{5x+10}{(x-4)(x+2)(x+1)} \\
&= \frac{5\cancel{(x+2)}}{(x-4)\cancel{(x+2)}(x+1)} \\
&= \frac{5}{(x-4)(x+1)}, \text{ for } x \neq -2
\end{aligned}
$$

12.3.4 Reading Questions

1. Describe how to add two rational expressions when they have the same denominator.

2. Suppose you are adding two rational expressions where one of them has a quadratic denominator, and the other has a linear denominator. What is the first thing you should try to do with respect to the quadratic denominator?

12.3.5 Exercises

Review and Warmup

1. Add: $\dfrac{31}{16} + \dfrac{5}{16}$

2. Add: $\dfrac{13}{16} + \dfrac{23}{16}$

3. Add: $\dfrac{5}{6} + \dfrac{9}{10}$

4. Add: $\dfrac{3}{5} + \dfrac{9}{10}$

5. Subtract: $\dfrac{25}{27} - \dfrac{10}{27}$

6. Subtract: $\dfrac{21}{40} - \dfrac{17}{40}$

7. Subtract: $\dfrac{5}{9} - \dfrac{8}{27}$

8. Subtract: $\dfrac{4}{9} - \dfrac{1}{27}$

Factor the given polynomial.

9. $x^2 - 4$

10. $y^2 - 81$

11. $y^2 + 14y + 40$

12. $y^2 + 5y + 4$ **13.** $r^2 - 17r + 72$ **14.** $r^2 - 7r + 12$

15. $3t^2 - 18t + 15$ **16.** $7t^2 - 28t + 21$

Addition and Subtraction of Rational Expressions with One Variable Add or subtract the rational expressions to a single rational expression and then simplify. If applicable, state the restricted domain.

17. $\dfrac{4x}{x+4} + \dfrac{16}{x+4}$

18. $\dfrac{6x}{x+2} + \dfrac{12}{x+2}$

19. $\dfrac{3y}{y+6} + \dfrac{18}{y+6}$

20. $\dfrac{5y}{y+4} + \dfrac{20}{y+4}$

21. $\dfrac{3}{y^2 - 4y - 5} - \dfrac{y-2}{y^2 - 4y - 5}$

22. $\dfrac{6}{r^2 - 13r + 40} - \dfrac{r-2}{r^2 - 13r + 40}$

23. $\dfrac{6}{r^2 - 9r - 10} - \dfrac{r-4}{r^2 - 9r - 10}$

24. $\dfrac{4}{t^2 - 3t - 40} - \dfrac{t-4}{t^2 - 3t - 40}$

25. $\dfrac{6t}{5} + \dfrac{t}{20}$

26. $\dfrac{3x}{2} + \dfrac{x}{10}$

27. $\dfrac{1}{x+1} + \dfrac{2}{x-1}$

28. $\dfrac{5}{y+5} - \dfrac{1}{y+2}$

29. $\dfrac{5}{y-4} - \dfrac{4}{y-2}$

30. $\dfrac{1}{y+6} + \dfrac{4}{y-3}$

31. $\dfrac{1}{r-2} - \dfrac{4}{r^2 - 4}$

32. $\dfrac{1}{r+1} + \dfrac{2}{r^2 - 1}$

33. $\dfrac{1}{t-1} - \dfrac{2}{t^2 - 1}$

34. $\dfrac{1}{t-2} - \dfrac{4}{t^2 - 4}$

35. $\dfrac{3}{x-4} - \dfrac{6x}{x^2 - 16}$

36. $\dfrac{3}{x-3} - \dfrac{6x}{x^2 - 9}$

37. $\dfrac{3}{y-6} - \dfrac{6y}{y^2 - 36}$

38. $\dfrac{3}{y+2} - \dfrac{6y}{y^2 - 4}$

39. $\dfrac{y}{y-6} - \dfrac{10y - 24}{y^2 - 6y}$

40. $\dfrac{r}{r+6} - \dfrac{r+42}{r^2 + 6r}$

41. $\dfrac{r}{r-8} - \dfrac{4r + 32}{r^2 - 8r}$

42. $\dfrac{t}{t-7} - \dfrac{t+42}{t^2 - 7t}$

43. $\dfrac{2}{t^2 - 1} + \dfrac{1}{t+1} + \dfrac{3}{t-1}$

44. $-\dfrac{4}{x^2 - 4} - \dfrac{4}{x+2} + \dfrac{1}{x-2}$

45. $-\dfrac{9x}{x^2 - 7x + 10} - \dfrac{3x}{x-2}$

46. $-\dfrac{12y}{y^2 - y - 2} + \dfrac{4y}{y-2}$

47. $\dfrac{12y}{y^2 + 8y + 12} - \dfrac{3y}{y+2}$

48. $-\dfrac{18y}{y^2 + 4y - 5} - \dfrac{3y}{y+5}$

49. $\dfrac{r^2 + 8}{r^2 + 4r} - \dfrac{r+2}{r}$

50. $\dfrac{r^2 + 8}{r^2 - 4r} - \dfrac{r-2}{r}$

51. $\dfrac{2}{t-5} - 3$

52. $\dfrac{4}{t+1} + 5$

53. $\dfrac{4x}{x+4} + \dfrac{x}{x-4} - 5$

54. $\dfrac{6x}{x+2} + \dfrac{x}{x-2} - 7$

Addition and Subtraction of Rational Expressions with More Than Variable Add or subtract the rational expressions to a single rational expression and then simplify.

55. $\dfrac{16y^2}{4y - 3x} - \dfrac{9x^2}{4y - 3x}$

56. $\dfrac{64y^2}{8y + 3t} - \dfrac{9t^2}{8y + 3t}$

57. $\dfrac{y}{6x} - \dfrac{5y}{3x}$

58. $\dfrac{r}{20x} - \dfrac{4r}{5x}$

59. $\dfrac{6r}{5t^4} + \dfrac{4}{3rt}$

60. $-\dfrac{5t}{4y^2} + \dfrac{5}{3ty}$

61. $\dfrac{2}{tx - 5} - \dfrac{4tx}{t^2x^2 - 25}$

62. $\dfrac{2}{xr - 2} - \dfrac{4xr}{x^2r^2 - 4}$

63. $-\dfrac{24xy}{x^2 + 8xy + 12y^2} - \dfrac{6x}{x + 6y}$

64. $\dfrac{2xt}{x^2 + 9xt + 20t^2} - \dfrac{2x}{x + 4t}$

12.4 Complex Fractions

In this section, we will learn how to simplify complex fractions, which have fractions in the numerator and/or denominator of another fraction.

12.4.1 Simplifying Complex Fractions

Consider the rational expression

$$\frac{\frac{6}{x-4}}{\frac{6}{x-4}+3}.$$

It's difficult to quickly evaluate this expression, or determine the important information such as its domain. This type of rational expression, which contains a "fraction within a fraction," is referred to as a **complex fraction**. Our goal is to simplify such a fraction so that it has a *single* numerator and a *single* denominator, neither of which contain any fractions themselves.

A complex fraction may have fractions in its numerator and/or denominator. Here is an example to show how we use division to simplify a complex fraction.

$$\begin{aligned}
\frac{\frac{1}{2}}{3} &= \frac{1}{2} \div 3 \\
&= \frac{1}{2} \div \frac{3}{1} \\
&= \frac{1}{2} \cdot \frac{1}{3} \\
&= \frac{1}{6}
\end{aligned}$$

What if the expression had something more complicated in the denominator, like $\frac{\frac{1}{2}}{\frac{1}{3}+\frac{1}{4}}$? We would no longer be able to simply multiply by the reciprocal of the denominator, since we don't immediately know the reciprocal of that denominator. Instead, we could multiply the "main" numerator and denominator by something that eliminates all of the "internal" denominators. (We'll use the LCD to determine this). For example, with $\frac{\frac{1}{2}}{3}$, we can multiply by $\frac{2}{2}$:

$$\begin{aligned}
\frac{\frac{1}{2}}{3} &= \frac{\frac{1}{2}}{3} \cdot \frac{2}{2} \\
&= \frac{1}{6}
\end{aligned}$$

Remark 12.4.2 In the last example, it's important to identify which fraction bar is the "main" fraction bar, and which fractions are "internal." Comparing the two expressions below, both of which are "one over two over three", we see that they are not equivalent.

$$\frac{\frac{1}{2}}{3} = \frac{\frac{1}{2}}{3} \cdot \frac{2}{2} \qquad\qquad \text{versus} \qquad\qquad \frac{1}{\frac{2}{3}} = \frac{1}{2} \cdot \frac{3}{3}$$

$$= \frac{1}{6} \qquad\qquad\qquad\qquad\qquad\qquad\qquad = \frac{3}{2}$$

For the first of these, the "main" fraction bar is above the 3, but for the second of these, the "main" fraction bar is above the $\frac{2}{3}$.

To attack multiple fractions in a complex fraction, we need to multiply the numerator and denominator by the LCD of all the internal fractions, as we will show in the next example.

Example 12.4.3 Simplify the complex fraction $\dfrac{\frac{1}{2}}{\frac{1}{3}+\frac{1}{4}}$.

Explanation.

The internal denominators are 2, 3, and 4, so the LCD is 12. We will thus multiply the main numerator and denominator by 12 and simplify the result:

$$\frac{\frac{1}{2}}{\frac{1}{3}+\frac{1}{4}} = \frac{\frac{1}{2}}{\frac{1}{3}+\frac{1}{4}} \cdot \frac{12}{12}$$

$$= \frac{\frac{1}{2} \cdot 12}{\left(\frac{1}{3}+\frac{1}{4}\right) \cdot 12}$$

$$= \frac{\frac{1}{2} \cdot 12}{\frac{1}{3} \cdot 12 + \frac{1}{4} \cdot 12}$$

$$= \frac{6}{4+3}$$

$$= \frac{6}{7}$$

Next we will evaluate a function whose formula is a complex fraction and then simplify the result.

Example 12.4.4 Find each function value for $f(x) = \dfrac{\frac{x+2}{x+3}}{\frac{2}{x+3}-\frac{3}{x-1}}$.
   a. $f(4)$ b. $f(0)$ c. $f(-3)$ d. $f(-11)$

Explanation. We will determine each function value by replacing x with the specified number and then simplify the complex fraction:

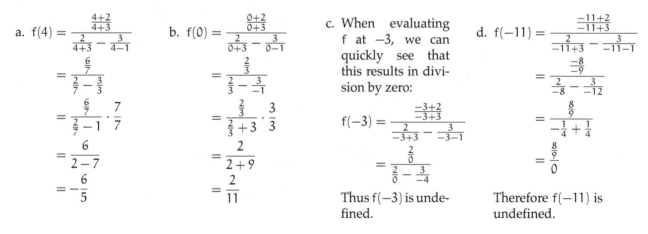

a. $f(4) = \dfrac{\frac{4+2}{4+3}}{\frac{2}{4+3}-\frac{3}{4-1}}$

$= \dfrac{\frac{6}{7}}{\frac{2}{7}-\frac{3}{3}}$

$= \dfrac{\frac{6}{7}}{\frac{2}{7}-1} \cdot \dfrac{7}{7}$

$= \dfrac{6}{2-7}$

$= -\dfrac{6}{5}$

b. $f(0) = \dfrac{\frac{0+2}{0+3}}{\frac{2}{0+3}-\frac{3}{0-1}}$

$= \dfrac{\frac{2}{3}}{\frac{2}{3}-\frac{3}{-1}}$

$= \dfrac{\frac{2}{3}}{\frac{2}{3}+3} \cdot \dfrac{3}{3}$

$= \dfrac{2}{2+9}$

$= \dfrac{2}{11}$

c. When evaluating f at -3, we can quickly see that this results in division by zero:

$f(-3) = \dfrac{\frac{-3+2}{-3+3}}{\frac{2}{-3+3}-\frac{3}{-3-1}}$

$= \dfrac{\frac{2}{0}}{\frac{2}{0}-\frac{3}{-4}}$

Thus $f(-3)$ is undefined.

d. $f(-11) = \dfrac{\frac{-11+2}{-11+3}}{\frac{2}{-11+3}-\frac{3}{-11-1}}$

$= \dfrac{\frac{-8}{-9}}{\frac{2}{-8}-\frac{3}{-12}}$

$= \dfrac{\frac{8}{9}}{-\frac{1}{4}+\frac{1}{4}}$

$= \dfrac{\frac{8}{9}}{0}$

Therefore $f(-11)$ is undefined.

We have simplified complex fractions involving numbers and now we will apply the same concept to complex fractions with variables.

Example 12.4.5 Simplify the complex fraction $\dfrac{3}{\frac{1}{y}+\frac{5}{y^2}}$.

Explanation.

To start, we look at the internal denominators and identify the LCD as y^2. We'll multiply the main numerator and denominator by the LCD, and then simplify. Since we are multiplying by $\frac{y^2}{y^2}$, it is important to note that y cannot be 0, since $\frac{0}{0}$ is undefined.

$$\frac{3}{\frac{1}{y}+\frac{5}{y^2}} = \frac{3}{\frac{1}{y}+\frac{5}{y^2}} \cdot \frac{y^2}{y^2}$$

$$= \frac{3 \cdot y^2}{\frac{1}{y} \cdot y^2 + \frac{5}{y^2} \cdot y^2}$$

$$= \frac{3y^2}{y+5}, \text{ for } y \neq 0$$

Example 12.4.6 Simplify the complex fraction $\dfrac{\frac{5x-6}{2x+1}}{\frac{3x+2}{2x+1}}$.

Explanation.

The internal denominators are both $2x+1$, so this is the LCD and we will multiply the main numerator and denominator by this expression. Since we are multiplying by $\frac{2x+1}{2x+1}$, what x-value would cause $2x+1$ to equal 0? Solving $2x+1=0$ leads to $x=-\frac{1}{2}$. So x cannot be $-\frac{1}{2}$, since $\frac{0}{0}$ is undefined.

$$\frac{\frac{5x-6}{2x+1}}{\frac{3x+2}{2x+1}} = \frac{\frac{5x-6}{2x+1}}{\frac{3x+2}{2x+1}} \cdot \frac{2x+1}{2x+1}$$

$$= \frac{5x-6}{3x+2}, \text{ for } x \neq -\frac{1}{2}$$

Example 12.4.7 Completely simplify the function defined by $f(x) = \dfrac{\frac{x+2}{x+3}}{\frac{2}{x+3}-\frac{3}{x-1}}$. Then determine the domain of this function.

Explanation. The LCD of the internal denominators is $(x+3)(x-1)$. We will thus multiply the main numerator and denominator by the expression $(x+3)(x-1)$ and then simplify the resulting expression.

$$f(x) = \frac{\frac{x+2}{x+3}}{\frac{2}{x+3}-\frac{3}{x-1}}$$

$$= \frac{\frac{x+2}{x+3}}{\frac{2}{x+3}-\frac{3}{x-1}} \cdot \frac{(x+3)(x-1)}{(x+3)(x-1)}$$

$$= \frac{\frac{x+2}{x+3} \cdot (x+3)(x-1)}{\left(\frac{2}{x+3}-\frac{3}{x-1}\right) \cdot (x+3)(x-1)}$$

$$= \frac{\frac{x+2}{x+3}(x+3)(x-1)}{\frac{2}{x+3}(x+3)(x-1)-\frac{3}{x-1}(x+3)(x-1)}$$

$$= \frac{(x+2)(x-1)}{2(x-1)-3(x+3)}, \text{ for } x \neq -3, x \neq 1$$

$$= \frac{(x+2)(x-1)}{2x-2-3x-9}, \text{ for } x \neq -3, x \neq 1$$

$$= \frac{(x+2)(x-1)}{-x-11}, \text{ for } x \neq -3, x \neq 1$$

$$= \frac{(x+2)(x-1)}{-(x+11)}, \text{ for } x \neq -3, x \neq 1$$

In the original (unsimplified) function, we could see that $x \neq -3$ and $x \neq 1$. In the simplified function, we need $x+11 \neq 0$, so we can also see that $x \neq -11$. Therefore the domain of the function f is $\{x \mid x \neq -11, -3, 1\}$.

Example 12.4.8 Simplify the complex fraction $\dfrac{2\left(\frac{-4x+3}{x-2}\right)+3}{\frac{-4x+3}{x-2}+4}$.

Explanation. The only internal denominator is $x-2$, so we will begin by multiplying the main numerator and denominator by this. Then we'll simplify the resulting expression.

$$
\begin{aligned}
\frac{2\left(\frac{-4x+3}{x-2}\right)+3}{\frac{-4x+3}{x-2}+4} &= \frac{2\left(\frac{-4x+3}{x-2}\right)+3}{\frac{-4x+3}{x-2}+4}\cdot\frac{x-2}{x-2}\\[2mm]
&= \frac{2\left(\frac{-4x+3}{x-2}\right)(x-2)+3(x-2)}{\left(\frac{-4x+3}{x-2}\right)(x-2)+4(x-2)}\\[2mm]
&= \frac{2(-4x+3)+3(x-2)}{(-4x+3)+4(x-2)},\ \text{for } x\neq 2\\[2mm]
&= \frac{-8x+6+3x-6}{-4x+3+4x-8},\ \text{for } x\neq 2\\[2mm]
&= \frac{-5x}{-5},\ \text{for } x\neq 2\\[2mm]
&= x,\ \text{for } x\neq 2
\end{aligned}
$$

Example 12.4.9 Simplify the complex fraction $\dfrac{\frac{5}{x}+\frac{4}{y}}{\frac{3}{x}-\frac{2}{y}}$. Recall that with a multivariable expression, this textbook ignores domain restrictions.

Explanation.

We multiply the numerator and denominator by the common denominator of x and y, which is xy:

$$
\begin{aligned}
\frac{\frac{5}{x}+\frac{4}{y}}{\frac{3}{x}-\frac{2}{y}} &= \frac{\frac{5}{x}+\frac{4}{y}}{\frac{3}{x}-\frac{2}{y}}\cdot\frac{xy}{xy}\\[2mm]
&= \frac{\left(\frac{5}{x}+\frac{4}{y}\right)xy}{\left(\frac{3}{x}-\frac{2}{y}\right)xy}\\[2mm]
&= \frac{\frac{5}{x}xy+\frac{4}{y}xy}{\frac{3}{x}xy-\frac{2}{y}xy}\\[2mm]
&= \frac{5y+4x}{3y-2x}
\end{aligned}
$$

Example 12.4.10 Simplify the complex fraction $\dfrac{\frac{t}{t+3}+\frac{2}{t-3}}{1-\frac{t}{t^2-9}}$.

Explanation. First, we check all quadratic polynomials to see if they can be factored and factor them:

$$
\frac{\frac{t}{t+3}+\frac{2}{t-3}}{1-\frac{t}{t^2-9}} = \frac{\frac{t}{t+3}+\frac{2}{t-3}}{1-\frac{t}{(t-3)(t+3)}}
$$

Next, we identify the common denominator of the three fractions, which is $(t+3)(t-3)$. We then multiply the main numerator and denominator by that expression:

$$
\frac{\frac{t}{t+3}+\frac{2}{t-3}}{1-\frac{t}{t^2-9}} = \frac{\frac{t}{t+3}+\frac{2}{t-3}}{1-\frac{t}{(t-3)(t+3)}}\cdot\frac{(t+3)(t-3)}{(t+3)(t-3)}
$$

$$= \frac{\frac{t}{t+3}(t+3)(t-3) + \frac{2}{t-3}(t+3)(t-3)}{1(t+3)(t-3) - \frac{t}{(t-3)(t+3)}(t+3)(t-3)}$$

$$= \frac{t(t-3) + 2(t+3)}{(t+3)(t-3) - t} \text{ for } t \neq -3, t \neq 3$$

$$= \frac{t^2 - 3t + 2t + 6}{t^2 - 9 - t} \text{ for } t \neq -3, t \neq 3$$

$$= \frac{t^2 - t + 6}{t^2 - t - 9} \text{ for } t \neq -3, t \neq 3$$

Note that since both the numerator and denominator are prime trinomials, this expression can neither factor nor simplify any further.

12.4.2 Reading Questions

1. What does it mean for a fraction to be a "complex" fraction?

2. When simplifying a complex fraction, why is it necessary to keep track of domain restrictions?

12.4.3 Exercises

Review and Warmup Calculate the following. Use an improper fraction in your answer.

1. a. $\frac{\frac{5}{2}}{\frac{5}{7}}$

    b. $\frac{\frac{y}{r}}{\frac{x}{t}}$

2. a. $\frac{\frac{25}{3}}{\frac{5}{4}}$

    b. $\frac{\frac{y}{t}}{\frac{x}{r}}$

3. a. $\frac{4}{\frac{9}{4}}$

    b. $\frac{\frac{4}{9}}{4}$

4. a. $\frac{5}{\frac{6}{7}}$

    b. $\frac{\frac{5}{6}}{7}$

5. $\frac{\frac{1}{6} - \frac{2}{3}}{\frac{3}{2}}$

6. $\frac{\frac{1}{6} - \frac{3}{4}}{\frac{3}{5}}$

7. $\frac{1}{\frac{4}{3} - \frac{3}{4}}$

8. $\frac{1}{\frac{2}{3} - \frac{3}{5}}$

Simplifying Complex Fractions with One Variable Simplify this expression, and if applicable, write the restricted domain.

9. $\frac{\frac{9a+7}{a}}{\frac{a+10}{a}}$

10. $\frac{\frac{6a-6}{a}}{\frac{a-5}{a}}$

11. $\frac{\frac{u}{(u-2)^2}}{\frac{7u}{u^2-4}}$

12. $\frac{\frac{u}{(u-9)^2}}{\frac{2u}{u^2-81}}$

13. $\frac{6 + \frac{1}{p}}{p + 6}$

14. $\frac{2 + \frac{1}{p}}{p + 10}$

15. $\frac{3}{\frac{2}{t} - \frac{4}{t+5}}$

16. $\frac{4}{\frac{6}{x} + \frac{3}{x-6}}$

17. $\frac{2 + \frac{1}{y-2}}{\frac{1}{y-2} - \frac{1}{8}}$

18. $\frac{8 + \frac{1}{b-6}}{\frac{1}{b-6} - \frac{1}{6}}$

19. $\frac{\frac{1}{c+4} + \frac{10}{c-4}}{3 - \frac{1}{c-4}}$

20. $\frac{\frac{1}{u+1} + \frac{5}{u-1}}{10 - \frac{1}{u-1}}$

21. $\frac{\frac{1}{s-7} + \frac{9}{s-7}}{8 - \frac{1}{s+7}}$

22. $\frac{\frac{1}{p-4} + \frac{4}{p-4}}{5 - \frac{1}{p+4}}$

23. $\frac{\frac{10}{q-1} - 7}{\frac{1}{q-1} + \frac{1}{q-3}}$

24. $\dfrac{\frac{7}{n-1}-2}{\frac{1}{n-1}+\frac{1}{n-9}}$

25. $\dfrac{\frac{4x}{x^2-25}+1}{\frac{2}{x+5}-\frac{5}{x-5}}$

26. $\dfrac{\frac{6x}{x^2-25}-5}{\frac{2}{x+5}+\frac{1}{x-5}}$

27. $\dfrac{\frac{c}{c^2-36}-\frac{1}{c^2-36}}{\frac{1}{c+36}}$

28. $\dfrac{\frac{c}{c^2-9}-\frac{1}{c^2-9}}{\frac{1}{c+9}}$

Simplifying Complex Fractions with More Than One Variable Simplify this expression.

29. $\dfrac{\frac{s}{t}}{\frac{6s}{5t^2}}$

30. $\dfrac{\frac{s}{t}}{\frac{5s}{4t^2}}$

31. $\dfrac{\frac{pq^2}{4r}}{\frac{p}{10qr}}$

32. $\dfrac{\frac{pq^2}{9r}}{\frac{p}{5qr}}$

33. a. $\dfrac{\frac{t}{r}}{y}$

b. $\dfrac{t}{\frac{r}{y}}$

34. a. $\dfrac{\frac{x}{r}}{t}$

b. $\dfrac{x}{\frac{r}{t}}$

35. $\dfrac{\frac{4}{x}}{20+4t}$

36. $\dfrac{\frac{2}{x}}{8+2y}$

37. $\dfrac{\frac{2}{y}+\frac{2}{x}}{\frac{2}{y}-\frac{12}{x}}$

38. $\dfrac{\frac{2}{y}+\frac{10}{t}}{\frac{12}{y}+\frac{2}{t}}$

12.5 Solving Rational Equations

12.5.1 Solving Rational Equations

We open this section looking back on Example 12.3.2. Julia is taking her family on a boat trip 12 miles down the river and back. The river flows at a speed of 2 miles per hour and she wants to drive the boat at a constant speed, v miles per hour downstream and back upstream. Due to the current of the river, the actual speed of travel is $v + 2$ miles per hour going downstream, and $v - 2$ miles per hour going upstream. If Julia plans to spend 8 hours for the whole trip, how fast should she drive the boat?

The time it takes Julia to drive the boat downstream is $\frac{12}{v+2}$ hours, and upstream is $\frac{12}{v-2}$ hours. The function to model the whole trip's time is

$$t(v) = \frac{12}{v-2} + \frac{12}{v+2}$$

where t stands for time in hours. The trip will take 8 hours, so we want $t(v)$ to equal 8, and we have:

$$\frac{12}{v-2} + \frac{12}{v+2} = 8.$$

Instead of using the function's graph, we will solve this equation algebraically. You may wish to review the technique of eliminating denominators discussed in Subsection 2.3.2. We can use the same technique with variable expressions in the denominators. To remove the fractions in this equation, we will multiply both sides of the equation by the least common denominator $(v - 2)(v + 2)$, and we have:

$$\frac{12}{v-2} + \frac{12}{v+2} = 8$$

$$(v+2)(v-2) \cdot \left(\frac{12}{v-2} + \frac{12}{v+2} \right) = (v+2)(v-2) \cdot 8$$

$$(v+2)\cancel{(v-2)} \cdot \frac{12}{\cancel{v-2}} + \cancel{(v+2)}(v-2) \cdot \frac{12}{\cancel{v+2}} = (v+2)(v-2) \cdot 8$$

$$12(v+2) + 12(v-2) = 8(v^2 - 4)$$

$$12v + 24 + 12v - 24 = 8v^2 - 32$$

$$24v = 8v^2 - 32$$

$$0 = 8v^2 - 24v - 32$$

$$0 = 8(v^2 - 3v - 4)$$

$$0 = 8(v-4)(v+1)$$

$$v - 4 = 0 \qquad \text{or} \qquad v + 1 = 0$$
$$v = 4 \qquad \text{or} \qquad v = -1$$

Remark 12.5.2 At this point, logically all that we know is that the only *possible* solutions are -1 and 4. Because of the step where factors were canceled, it's possible that these might not actually be solutions to the original equation. They each might be what is called an **extraneous solution**. An extraneous solution is a number that would appear to be a solution based on the solving process, but actually does not make the original equation true. Because of this, it is important that these proposed solutions be checked. Note that we're not checking to see if we made a calculation error, but are instead checking to see if the proposed solutions actually solve the original equation.

We check these values.

$$\frac{12}{-1-2} + \frac{12}{-1+2} \stackrel{?}{=} 8 \qquad\qquad \frac{12}{4-2} + \frac{12}{4+2} \stackrel{?}{=} 8$$

$$\frac{12}{-3} + \frac{12}{1} \stackrel{?}{=} 8 \qquad\qquad \frac{12}{2} + \frac{12}{6} \stackrel{?}{=} 8$$

$$-4 + 12 \stackrel{\checkmark}{=} 8 \qquad\qquad 6 + 2 \stackrel{\checkmark}{=} 8$$

Algebraically, both values do check out to be solutions. In the context of this scenario, the boat's speed can't be negative, so we only take the solution 4. If Julia drives at 4 miles per hour, the whole trip would take 8 hours. This result matches the solution in Example 12.3.2.

Definition 12.5.3 Rational Equation. A rational equation is an equation involving one or more rational expressions. Usually, we consider these to be equations that have the variable in the denominator of at least one term. ◇

Let's look at another application problem.

Example 12.5.4 It takes Ku 3 hours to paint a room and it takes Jacob 6 hours to paint the same room. If they work together, how long would it take them to paint the room?

Explanation. Since it takes Ku 3 hours to paint the room, he paints $\frac{1}{3}$ of the room each hour. Similarly, Jacob paints $\frac{1}{6}$ of the room each hour. If they work together, they paint $\frac{1}{3} + \frac{1}{6}$ of the room each hour.

Assume it takes x hours to paint the room if Ku and Jacob work together. This implies they paint $\frac{1}{x}$ of the room together each hour. Now we can write this equation:

$$\frac{1}{3} + \frac{1}{6} = \frac{1}{x}.$$

To clear away denominators, we multiply both sides of the equation by the common denominator of 3, 6 and x, which is 6x:

$$\frac{1}{3} + \frac{1}{6} = \frac{1}{x}$$

$$6x \cdot \left(\frac{1}{3} + \frac{1}{6} \right) = 6\cancel{x} \cdot \frac{1}{\cancel{x}}$$

$$6x \cdot \frac{1}{3} + 6x \cdot \frac{1}{6} = 6$$

$$2x + x = 6$$

$$3x = 6$$

$$x = 2$$

Does the possible solution $x = 2$ check as an actual solution?

$$\frac{1}{3} + \frac{1}{6} \stackrel{?}{=} \frac{1}{2}$$

$$\frac{2}{6} + \frac{1}{6} \stackrel{?}{=} \frac{1}{2}$$

$$\frac{3}{6} \stackrel{\checkmark}{=} \frac{1}{2}$$

It does, so it is a solution. If Ku and Jacob work together, it would take them 2 hours to paint the room.

We are ready to outline a general process for solving a rational equation.

Process 12.5.5 Solving Rational Equations. *To solve a rational equation,*

1. *Find the least common denominator for all terms in the equation.*

2. *Multiply every term in the equation by the least common denominator*

3. *Every denominator should cancel leaving a simpler kind of equation to solve. Use previous method to solve that equation.*

Let's look at a few more examples of solving rational equations.

Example 12.5.6 Solve for y in $\frac{2}{y+1} = \frac{3}{y}$.

Explanation.   The common denominator is $y(y+1)$. We will multiply both sides of the equation by $y(y+1)$:

$$\frac{2}{y+1} = \frac{3}{y}$$

$$y(y+1) \cdot \frac{2}{y+1} = y(y+1) \cdot \frac{3}{y}$$

$$2y = 3(y+1)$$

$$2y = 3y+3$$

$$-y = 3$$

$$y = -3$$

Does the possible solution $y = -3$ check as an actual solution?

$$\frac{2}{-3+1} \overset{?}{=} \frac{3}{-3}$$

$$\frac{2}{-2} \overset{\checkmark}{=} -1$$

It checks, so -3 is a solution. We write the solution set as $\{-3\}$.

Example 12.5.7 Solve for z in $z + \frac{1}{z-4} = \frac{z-3}{z-4}$.

Explanation.   The common denominator is $z - 4$. We will multiply both sides of the equation by $z - 4$:

$$z + \frac{1}{z-4} = \frac{z-3}{z-4}$$

$$(z-4) \cdot \left(z + \frac{1}{z-4}\right) = (z-4) \cdot \frac{z-3}{z-4}$$

$$(z-4) \cdot z + (z-4) \cdot \frac{1}{z-4} = z-3$$

$$(z-4) \cdot z + 1 = z-3$$

$$z^2 - 4z + 1 = z-3$$

$$z^2 - 5z + 4 = 0$$

$$(z-1)(z-4) = 0$$

$$z - 1 = 0 \qquad\qquad \text{or} \qquad\qquad z - 4 = 0$$

$$z = 1 \qquad \text{or} \qquad z = 4$$

Do the possible solutions $z = 1$ and $z = 4$ check as actual solutions?

$$1 + \frac{1}{1-4} \stackrel{?}{=} \frac{1-3}{1-4} \qquad\qquad 4 + \frac{1}{4-4} \stackrel{?}{=} \frac{4-3}{4-4}$$
$$1 - \frac{1}{3} \stackrel{\checkmark}{=} \frac{-2}{-3} \qquad\qquad 4 + \frac{1}{0} \stackrel{\text{no}}{=} \frac{1}{0}$$

The possible solution $z = 4$ does not actually work, since it leads to division by 0 in the equation. It is an extraneous solution. However, $z = 1$ is a valid solution. The only solution to the equation is 1, and thus we can write the solution set as $\{1\}$.

Example 12.5.8 Solve for p in $\frac{3}{p-2} + \frac{5}{p+2} = \frac{12}{p^2-4}$.

Explanation. To find the common denominator, we need to factor all denominators if possible:

$$\frac{3}{p-2} + \frac{5}{p+2} = \frac{12}{(p+2)(p-2)}$$

Now we can see the common denominator is $(p+2)(p-2)$. We will multiply both sides of the equation by $(p+2)(p-2)$:

$$\frac{3}{p-2} + \frac{5}{p+2} = \frac{12}{p^2-4}$$
$$\frac{3}{p-2} + \frac{5}{p+2} = \frac{12}{(p+2)(p-2)}$$
$$(p+2)(p-2) \cdot \left(\frac{3}{p-2} + \frac{5}{p+2} \right) = (p+2)(p-2) \cdot \frac{12}{(p+2)(p-2)}$$
$$(p+2)\cancel{(p-2)} \cdot \frac{3}{\cancel{p-2}} + \cancel{(p+2)}(p-2) \cdot \frac{5}{\cancel{p+2}} = \cancel{(p+2)}\cancel{(p-2)} \cdot \frac{12}{\cancel{(p+2)}\cancel{(p-2)}}$$
$$3(p+2) + 5(p-2) = 12$$
$$3p + 6 + 5p - 10 = 12$$
$$8p - 4 = 12$$
$$8p = 16$$
$$p = 2$$

Does the possible solution $p = 2$ check as an actual solution?

$$\frac{3}{2-2} + \frac{5}{2+2} \stackrel{?}{=} \frac{12}{2^2-4}$$
$$\frac{3}{0} + \frac{5}{4} \stackrel{\text{no}}{=} \frac{12}{0}$$

The possible solution $p = 2$ does not actually work, since it leads to division by 0 in the equation. So this is an extraneous solution, and the equation actually has no solution. We could say that its solution set is the empty set, $\emptyset$.

Example 12.5.9 Solve $C(t) = 0.35$, where $C(t) = \frac{3t}{t^2+8}$ gives a drug's concentration in milligrams per liter t hours since an injection. (This function was explored in the introduction of Section 12.1.)

Explanation.   To solve $C(t) = 0.35$, we'll begin by setting up $\frac{3t}{t^2+8} = 0.35$. We'll begin by identifying that the LCD is $t^2 + 8$, and multiply each side of the equation by this:

$$\frac{3t}{t^2+8} = 0.35$$

$$\frac{3t}{t^2+8} \cdot (t^2+8) = 0.35 \cdot (t^2+8)$$

$$3t = 0.35 (t^2+8)$$

$$3t = 0.35t^2 + 2.8$$

This results in a quadratic equation so we will put it in standard form and use the quadratic formula:

$$0 = 0.35t^2 - 3t + 2.8$$

$$t = \frac{-(-3) \pm \sqrt{(-3)^2 - 4(0.35)(2.8)}}{2(0.35)}$$

$$t = \frac{3 \pm \sqrt{5.08}}{0.7}$$

$$t \approx 1.066 \text{ or } t \approx 7.506$$

Each of these answers should be checked in the original equation; they both work. In context, this means that the drug concentration will reach 0.35 milligrams per liter about 1.066 hours after the injection was given, and again 7.506 hours after the injection was given.

12.5.2 Solving Rational Equations for a Specific Variable

Rational equations can contain many variables and constants and we can solve for any one of them. The process for solving still involves multiplying each side of the equation by the LCD. Instead of having a numerical answer though, our final result will contain other variables and constants.

Example 12.5.10 In physics, when two resistances, R_1 and R_2, are connected in a parallel circuit, the combined resistance, R, can be calculated by the formula

$$\frac{1}{R} = \frac{1}{R_1} + \frac{1}{R_2}.$$

Solve for R in this formula.

Explanation.   The common denominator is RR_1R_2. We will multiply both sides of the equation by RR_1R_2:

$$\frac{1}{R} = \frac{1}{R_1} + \frac{1}{R_2}$$

$$RR_1R_2 \cdot \frac{1}{R} = RR_1R_2 \cdot \left(\frac{1}{R_1} + \frac{1}{R_2} \right)$$

$$R_1R_2 = RR_1R_2 \cdot \frac{1}{R_1} + RR_1R_2 \cdot \frac{1}{R_2}$$

$$R_1R_2 = RR_2 + RR_1$$

$$R_1 R_2 = R(R_2 + R_1)$$
$$\frac{R_1 R_2}{R_2 + R_1} = R$$
$$R = \frac{R_1 R_2}{R_1 + R_2}$$

Example 12.5.11 Here is the slope formula

$$m = \frac{y_2 - y_1}{x_2 - x_1}.$$

Solve for x_1 in this formula.

Explanation. The common denominator is $x_2 - x_1$. We will multiply both sides of the equation by $x_2 - x_1$:

$$m = \frac{y_2 - y_1}{x_2 - x_1}$$
$$(x_2 - x_1) \cdot m = (x_2 - x_1) \cdot \frac{y_2 - y_1}{x_2 - x_1}$$
$$mx_2 - mx_1 = y_2 - y_1$$
$$-mx_1 = y_2 - y_1 - mx_2$$
$$\frac{-mx_1}{-m} = \frac{y_2 - y_1 - mx_2}{-m}$$
$$x_1 = -\frac{y_2 - y_1 - mx_2}{m}$$

Example 12.5.12 Solve the rational equation $x = \frac{4y-1}{2y-3}$ for y.

Explanation. Our first step will be to multiply each side by the LCD, which is simply $2y - 3$. After that, we'll isolate all terms containing y, factor out y, and then finish solving for that variable.

$$x = \frac{4y - 1}{2y - 3}$$
$$x \cdot (2y - 3) = \frac{4y - 1}{2y - 3} \cdot (2y - 3)$$
$$2xy - 3x = 4y - 1$$
$$2xy = 4y - 1 + 3x$$
$$2xy - 4y = -1 + 3x$$
$$y(2x - 4) = 3x - 1$$
$$\frac{y(2x - 4)}{2x - 4} = \frac{3x - 1}{2x - 4}$$
$$y = \frac{3x - 1}{2x - 4}$$

12.5.3 Solving Rational Equations Using Technology

In some instances, it may be difficult to solve rational equations algebraically. We can instead use graphing technology to obtain approximate solutions. Let's look at one such example.

Example 12.5.13 Solve the equation $\frac{2}{x-3} = \frac{x^3}{8}$ using graphing technology.

Explanation.

We will define $f(x) = \frac{2}{x-3}$ and $g(x) = \frac{x^3}{8}$, and then look for the points of intersection.

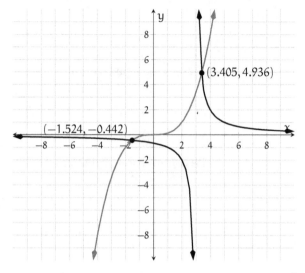

Figure 12.5.14: Graph of $f(x) = \frac{2}{x-3}$ and $g(x) = \frac{x^3}{8}$

Since the two functions intersect at approximately $(-1.524, -0.442)$ and $(3.405, 4.936)$, the solutions to $\frac{2}{x-3} = \frac{x^3}{8}$ are approximately -1.524 and 3.405. We can write the solution set as $\{-1.524\ldots, 3.405\ldots\}$ or in several other forms. It may be important to do *something* to communicate that these solutions are approximations. Here we used "...", but you could also just say in words that the solutions are approximate.

12.5.4 Reading Questions

1. Describe what an "extraneous solution" to a rational equation is.

2. In general, when solving a rational equation, multiplying through by the ⬚ will leave you with a simpler equation to solve.

3. When you believe you have the solutions to a rational equation, what is more important than usual (compared to other kinds of equations) for you to do?

12.5.5 Exercises

Review and Warmup Solve the equation.

1. $8A + 4 = A + 60$

2. $6C + 8 = C + 33$

3. $50 = 8 - 3(n - 6)$

4. $-3 = 4 - 7(p - 6)$

5. $2(x + 10) - 8(x - 2) = 36$

6. $4(y + 5) - 7(y - 7) = 72$

7. $(x - 6)^2 = 25$

8. $(x - 3)^2 = 144$

9. $x^2 + 2x - 3 = 0$

10. $x^2 - 3x - 10 = 0$

11. $x^2 + 15x + 61 = 17$

12. $x^2 + 9x + 31 = 17$

13. Recall the time that Filip traveled with his kids to kick a soccer ball on Mars? We should examine one more angle to our soccer kick question. The formula $H(t) = -6.07t^2 + 27.1t$ finds the height of the

soccer ball in feet above the ground at a time t seconds after being kicked.

(a) Using technology, find out what the maximum height of the ball was and when it reached that height.

(b) Using technology, solve for when $H(t) = 20$ and interpret the meaning of this in a complete sentence.

(c) Using technology, solve for when $H(t) = 0$ and interpret the meaning of this in a complete sentence.

Solving Rational Equations Solve the equation.

14. $\dfrac{20}{t} = -5$

15. $\dfrac{40}{x} = 8$

16. $\dfrac{x}{x+3} = 4$

17. $\dfrac{x}{x+4} = -3$

18. $\dfrac{y+10}{3y-8} = \dfrac{9}{8}$

19. $\dfrac{y-4}{3y-2} = \dfrac{3}{4}$

20. $\dfrac{-7r+4}{r-4} = -\dfrac{7r}{r-8}$

21. $\dfrac{2r+9}{r+8} = \dfrac{2r}{r+7}$

22. $\dfrac{3}{t} = 4 + \dfrac{23}{t}$

23. $\dfrac{3}{t} = -2 + \dfrac{13}{t}$

24. $\dfrac{5}{4x} + \dfrac{1}{3x} = -5$

25. $\dfrac{3}{5y} + \dfrac{4}{3y} = -5$

26. $\dfrac{x}{5x-30} - \dfrac{2}{x-6} = 1$

27. $\dfrac{y}{2y+12} + \dfrac{6}{y+6} = 2$

28. $\dfrac{y-2}{y^2+2} = 0$

29. $\dfrac{r-9}{r^2+6} = 0$

30. $\dfrac{3}{r} = 0$

31. $-\dfrac{3}{t} = 0$

32. $\dfrac{t+9}{t^2+15t+54} = 0$

33. $\dfrac{t+3}{t^2-2t-15} = 0$

34. $-\dfrac{2}{x} + \dfrac{8}{x+7} = -1$

35. $-\dfrac{8}{x} - \dfrac{5}{x+9} = 1$

36. $\dfrac{1}{y+2} + \dfrac{2}{y^2+2y} = \dfrac{1}{5}$

37. $\dfrac{1}{y-5} - \dfrac{5}{y^2-5y} = -\dfrac{1}{9}$

38. $\dfrac{1}{r+9} - \dfrac{5}{r^2+9r} = \dfrac{1}{2}$

39. $\dfrac{1}{r-7} - \dfrac{4}{r^2-7r} = \dfrac{1}{2}$

40. $\dfrac{t-4}{t+8} + \dfrac{2}{t+3} = -4$

41. $\dfrac{t+9}{t-3} + \dfrac{4}{t-8} = 3$

Solve the equation.

42. $\dfrac{2}{t+1} = \dfrac{3}{t-1} - \dfrac{2}{t^2-1}$

43. $-\dfrac{4}{x+3} = -\left(\dfrac{2}{x-3} + \dfrac{6}{x^2-9}\right)$

44. $\dfrac{8}{x+6} - \dfrac{9}{x+9} = -\dfrac{9}{x^2+15x+54}$

45. $\dfrac{2}{y+5} - \dfrac{5}{y+1} = -\dfrac{2}{y^2+6y+5}$

46. $-\dfrac{8}{y-6} + \dfrac{4y}{y-5} = -\dfrac{8}{y^2-11y+30}$

47. $\dfrac{4}{r-7} + \dfrac{2r}{r-5} = \dfrac{8}{r^2-12r+35}$

48. $-\dfrac{6}{r-3} + \dfrac{8r}{r+9} = -\dfrac{4}{r^2+6r-27}$

49. $\dfrac{6}{t-7} + \dfrac{2t}{t-3} = -\dfrac{8}{t^2-10t+21}$

Solving Rational Equations for a Specific Variable

50. Solve this equation for a:
$$p = \frac{m}{a}$$

51. Solve this equation for m:
$$q = \frac{b}{m}$$

52. Solve this equation for x:
$$y = \frac{x}{r}$$

53. Solve this equation for C:
$$r = \frac{C}{B}$$

54. Solve this equation for a:
$$\frac{1}{2a} = \frac{1}{x}$$

55. Solve this equation for c:
$$\frac{1}{8c} = \frac{1}{q}$$

56. Solve this equation for B:
$$\frac{1}{A} = \frac{8}{B+2}$$

57. Solve this equation for a:
$$\frac{1}{C} = \frac{8}{a+6}$$

Solving Rational Equations Using Technology Use technology to solve the equation.

58.
$$\frac{10}{x^2+3} = \frac{x+1}{x+5}.$$

59.
$$\frac{x-9}{x^5+1} = -3x - 7.$$

60.
$$\frac{1}{x} + \frac{1}{x^2} = \frac{1}{x^3}.$$

61.
$$\frac{12x}{x-5} + \frac{3}{x+1} = \frac{x-5}{x^2}.$$

62.
$$2x - \frac{1}{x+4} = \frac{3}{x+6}.$$

63.
$$\frac{1}{x^2-1} - \frac{2}{x-4} = \frac{3}{x-2}.$$

Application Problems

64. Scot and Jay are working together to paint a room. If Scot paints the room alone, it would take him 18 hours to complete the job. If Jay paints the room alone, it would take him 12 hours to complete the job. Answer the following question:

    If they work together, it would take them ⬚ hours to complete the job. Use a decimal in your answer if needed.

65. There are three pipes at a tank. To fill the tank, it would take Pipe A 3 hours, Pipe B 12 hours, and Pipe C 4 hours. Answer the following question:

    If all three pipes are turned on, it would take ⬚ hours to fill the tank.

66. Casandra and Tien are working together to paint a room. Casandra works 1.5 times as fast as Tien does. If they work together, it took them 9 hours to complete the job. Answer the following questions:

    If Casandra paints the room alone, it would take her ⬚ hours to complete the job.

    If Tien paints the room alone, it would take him ⬚ hours to complete the job.

67. Two pipes are being used to fill a tank. Pipe A can fill the tank 4.5 times as fast as Pipe B does. When both pipes are turned on, it takes 18 hours to fill the tank. Answer the following questions:

    If only Pipe A is turned on, it would take ⬚ hours to fill the tank.

    If only Pipe B is turned on, it would take ⬚ hours to fill the tank.

68. Kandace and Jenny worked together to paint a room, and it took them 2 hours to complete the job. If they work alone, it would take Jenny 3 more hours than Kandace to complete the job. Answer the following questions:

    If Kandace paints the room alone, it would take her ⬚ hours to complete the job.

If Jenny paints the room alone, it would take her ⬚ hours to complete the job.

69. If both Pipe A and Pipe B are turned on, it would take 2 hours to fill a tank. If each pipe is turned on alone, it takes Pipe B 3 fewer hours than Pipe A to fill the tank. Answer the following questions:

If only Pipe A is turned on, it would take ⬚ hours to fill the tank.

If only Pipe B is turned on, it would take ⬚ hours to fill the tank.

70. Town A and Town B are 570 miles apart. A boat traveled from Town A to Town B, and then back to Town A. Since the river flows from Town B to Town A, the boat's speed was 25 miles per hour faster when it traveled from Town B to Town A. The whole trip took 19 hours. Answer the following questions:

The boat traveled from Town A to Town B at the speed of ⬚ miles per hour.

The boat traveled from Town B back to Town A at the speed of ⬚ miles per hour.

71. A river flows at 7 miles per hour. A boat traveled with the current from Town A to Town B, which are 260 miles apart. Then, the boat turned around, and traveled against the current to reach Town C, which is 160 miles away from Town B. The second leg of the trip (Town B to Town C) took the same time as the first leg (Town A to Town B). During this whole trip, the boat was driving at a constant still-water speed. Answer the following question:

During this trip, the boat's speed on still water was ⬚ miles.

72. A river flows at 5 miles per hour. A boat traveled with the current from Town A to Town B, which are 100 miles apart. The boat stayed overnight at Town B. The next day, the water's current stopped, and boat traveled on still water to reach Town C, which is 190 miles away from Town B. The second leg of the trip (Town B to Town C) took 9 hours longer than the first leg (Town A to Town B). During this whole trip, the boat was driving at a constant still-water speed. Find this speed.

Note that you should not consider the unreasonable answer.

During this trip, the boat's speed on still water was ⬚ miles per hour.

73. Town A and Town B are 600 miles apart. With a constant still-water speed, a boat traveled from Town A to Town B, and then back to Town A. During this whole trip, the river flew from Town A to Town B at 20 miles per hour. The whole trip took 16 hours. Answer the following question:

During this trip, the boat's speed on still water was ⬚ miles per hour.

74. Town A and Town B are 350 miles apart. With a constant still-water speed of 24 miles per hour, a boat traveled from Town A to Town B, and then back to Town A. During this whole trip, the river flew from Town B to Town A at a constant speed. The whole trip took 30 hours. Answer the following question:

During this trip, the river's speed was ⬚ miles per hour.

75. Suppose that a large pump can empty a swimming pool in 43 hr and that a small pump can empty the same pool in 53 hr. If both pumps are used at the same time, how long will it take to empty the pool?

If both pumps are used at the same time, it will take ⬚ to empty the pool.

76. The winner of a 9 mi race finishes 14.73 min ahead of the second-place runner. On average, the winner ran 0.6 $\frac{mi}{hr}$ faster than the second place runner. Find the average running speed for each runner.

The winner's average speed was ⬚ and the second-place runner's average speed was ⬚.

77. In still water a tugboat can travel 15 $\frac{mi}{hr}$. It travels 42 mi upstream and then 42 mi downstream in a total time of 5.96 hr. Find the speed of the current.

The current's speed is ⬚.

78. Without any wind an airplane flies at 300 $\frac{mi}{hr}$. The plane travels 600 mi into the wind and then returns with the wind in a total time of 4.04 hr. Find the average speed of the wind.

The wind's speed is ⬚.

79. When there is a 11.8 $\frac{mi}{hr}$ wind, an airplane can fly 770 mi with the wind in the same time that it can fly 702 mi against the wind. Find the speed of the plane when there is no wind.

The plane's airspeed is ⬚.

80. It takes one employee 2.5 hr longer to mow a football field than it does a more experienced employee. Together they can mow the grass in 1.9 hr. How long does it take each person to mow the football field working alone?

The more experienced worker takes ⬚ to mow the field alone, and the less experienced worker takes ⬚.

81. It takes one painter 13 hr longer to paint a house than it does a more experienced painter. Together they can paint the house in 30 hr. How long does it take for each painter to paint the house working alone?

The more experienced painter takes ⬚ to paint the house alone, and the less experienced painter takes ⬚.

12.6 Rational Functions and Equations Chapter Review

12.6.1 Introduction to Rational Functions

In Section 12.1 we learned about rational functions and explored them with tables and graphs.

Example 12.6.1 Graphs of Rational Functions. In an apocalypse, a zombie infestation begins with 1 zombie and spreads rapidly. The population of zombies can be modeled by $Z(x) = \frac{200000x+100}{5x+100}$, where x is the number of days after the apocalypse began. Use technology to graph the function and answer these questions:

    a. How many zombies are there 2 days after the apocalypse began?

    b. After how many days will the zombie population be 20,000?

    c. As time goes on, the population will level off at about how many zombies?

Explanation. We will graph the function with technology. After adjusting window settings, we have:

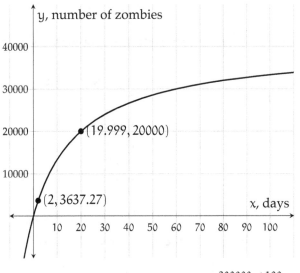

Figure 12.6.2: Graph of $y = Z(x) = \frac{200000x+100}{5x+100}$

    a. To find the number of zombies after 2 days, we locate the point $(2, 3637.27)$. Since we can only have a whole number of zombies, we round to 3,637 zombies.

    b. To find the number of days it will take for the zombie population reach 20,000, we locate the point $(19.999, 20000)$ so it will take about 20 days.

    c. When we look far to the right on the graph using technology we can see that the population will level off at about 40,000 zombies.

12.6.2 Multiplication and Division of Rational Expressions

In Section 12.2 we covered how to simplify rational expressions. It is very important to list any domain restrictions from factors that are canceled. We also multiplied and divided rational expressions.

Example 12.6.3 Simplifying Rational Expressions. Simplify the expression $\frac{8t+4t^2-12t^3}{1-t}$.

Explanation. To begin simplifying this expression, we will rewrite each polynomial in descending order. Then we'll factor out the GCF, including the constant -1 from both the numerator and denominator because their leading terms are negative.

$$
\begin{aligned}
\frac{8t+4t^2-12t^3}{1-t} &= \frac{-12t^3+4t^2+8t}{-t+1} \\
&= \frac{-4t(3t^2-t-2)}{-(t-1)} \\
&= \frac{-4t(3t+2)(t-1)}{-(t-1)} \\
&= \frac{-4t(3t+2)\cancel{(t-1)}}{-\cancel{(t-1)}} \\
&= \frac{-4t(3t+2)}{-1}, \text{ for } t \neq 1 \\
&= 4t(3t+2), \text{ for } t \neq 1
\end{aligned}
$$

Example 12.6.4 Multiplication of Rational Functions and Expressions. Multiply the rational expressions: $\frac{r^3s}{4t} \cdot \frac{2t^2}{r^2s^3}$.

Explanation. Note that we won't need to factor anything in this problem, and can simply multiply across and then simplify. With multivariable expressions, this textbook ignores domain restrictions.

$$
\begin{aligned}
\frac{r^3s}{4t} \cdot \frac{2t^2}{r^2s^3} &= \frac{r^3s \cdot 2t^2}{4t \cdot r^2s^3} \\
&= \frac{2r^3st^2}{4r^2s^3t} \\
&= \frac{rt}{2s^2}
\end{aligned}
$$

Example 12.6.5 Division of Rational Functions and Expressions. Divide the rational expressions: $\frac{2x^2+8xy}{x^2-4x+3} \div \frac{x^3+4x^2y}{x^2+4x-5}$.

Explanation. To divide rational expressions, we multiply by the reciprocal of the second fraction. Then we will factor and cancel any common factors. With multivariable expressions, this textbook ignores domain restrictions.

$$
\begin{aligned}
\frac{2x^2+8xy}{x^2-4x+3} \div \frac{x^3+4x^2y}{x^2+4x-5} &= \frac{2x^2+8xy}{x^2-4x+3} \cdot \frac{x^2+4x-5}{x^3+4x^2y} \\
&= \frac{2x\cancel{(x+4y)}}{\cancel{(x-1)}(x-3)} \cdot \frac{\cancel{(x-1)}(x+5)}{x^2\cancel{(x+4y)}} \\
&= \frac{2x}{x-3} \cdot \frac{x+5}{x^2}
\end{aligned}
$$

$$= \frac{2(x+5)}{x(x-3)}$$

12.6.3 Addition and Subtraction of Rational Expressions

In Section 12.3 we covered how to add and subtract rational expressions.

Example 12.6.6 Addition and Subtraction of Rational Expressions with the Same Denominator. Add the rational expressions: $\frac{5x}{x+5} + \frac{25}{x+5}$.

Explanation. These expressions already have a common denominator:

$$\frac{5x}{x+5} + \frac{25}{x+5} = \frac{5x+25}{x+5}$$
$$= \frac{5\cancel{(x+5)}}{\cancel{x+5}}$$
$$= \frac{5}{1}, \text{ for } x \neq -5$$
$$= 5, \text{ for } x \neq -5$$

Note that we didn't stop at $\frac{5x+25}{x+5}$. If possible, we must simplify the numerator and denominator.

Example 12.6.7 Addition and Subtraction of Rational Expressions with Different Denominators. Add and subtract the rational expressions: $\frac{6y}{y+2} + \frac{y}{y-2} - 7$

Explanation. The denominators can't be factored, so we'll find the least common denominator and build each expression to that denominator. Then we will be able to combine the numerators and simplify the expression.

$$\frac{6y}{y+2} + \frac{y}{y-2} - 7 = \frac{6y}{y+2} \cdot \frac{y-2}{y-2} + \frac{y}{y-2} \cdot \frac{y+2}{y+2} - 7 \cdot \frac{(y-2)(y+2)}{(y-2)(y+2)}$$
$$= \frac{6y(y-2)}{(y-2)(y+2)} + \frac{y(y+2)}{(y-2)(y+2)} - \frac{7(y-2)(y+2)}{(y-2)(y+2)}$$
$$= \frac{6y^2 - 12y + y^2 + 2y - \overset{\downarrow}{(7(y^2-4))}\overset{\downarrow}{}}{(y-2)(y+2)}$$
$$= \frac{6y^2 - 12y + y^2 + 2y - 7y^2 + 28}{(y-2)(y+2)}$$
$$= \frac{-10y + 28}{(y-2)(y+2)}$$
$$= \frac{-2(5y-14)}{(y-2)(y+2)}$$

12.6.4 Complex Fractions

In Section 12.4 we covered how to simplify a rational expression that has fractions in the numerator and/or denominator.

Example 12.6.8 Simplifying Complex Fractions. Simplify the complex fraction $\dfrac{\frac{2t}{t^2-9}+3}{\frac{6}{t+3}+\frac{1}{t-3}}$.

Explanation.   First, we check all quadratic polynomials to see if they can be factored and factor them:

$$\frac{\frac{2t}{t^2-9}+3}{\frac{6}{t+3}+\frac{1}{t-3}} = \frac{\frac{2t}{(t-3)(t+3)}+3}{\frac{6}{t+3}+\frac{1}{t-3}}$$

Next, we identify the common denominator of the three fractions, which is $(t+3)(t-3)$. We then multiply the main numerator and denominator by that expression:

$$\frac{\frac{2t}{(t-3)(t+3)}+3}{\frac{6}{t+3}+\frac{1}{t-3}} = \frac{\frac{2t}{(t-3)(t+3)}+3}{\frac{6}{t+3}+\frac{1}{t-3}} \cdot \frac{(t-3)(t+3)}{(t-3)(t+3)}$$

$$= \frac{\frac{2t}{(t-3)(t+3)}(t-3)(t+3)+3(t-3)(t+3)}{\frac{6}{t+3}(t-3)(t+3)+\frac{1}{t-3}(t-3)(t+3)}$$

$$= \frac{2t+3(t-3)(t+3)}{6(t-3)+1(t+3)} \text{ for } t \neq -3, t \neq 3$$

$$= \frac{2t+3(t^2-9)}{6t-18+t+3} \text{ for } t \neq -3, t \neq 3$$

$$= \frac{2t+3t^2-27}{7t-15} \text{ for } t \neq -3, t \neq 3$$

$$= \frac{3t^2+2t-27}{7t-15} \text{ for } t \neq -3, t \neq 3$$

Both the numerator and denominator are prime polynomials so this expression can neither factor nor simplify any further.

12.6.5 Solving Rational Equations

In Section 12.5 we covered how to solve rational equations. We looked at rate problems, solved for a specified variable and used technology to solve rational equations.

Example 12.6.9 Solving Rational Equations. Two pipes are being used to fill a large tank. Pipe B can fill the tank twice as fast as Pipe A can. When both pipes are turned on, it takes 12 hours to fill the tank. Write and solve a rational equation to answer the following questions:

   a. If only Pipe A is turned on, how many hours would it take to fill the tank?

   b. If only Pipe B is turned on, how many hours would it take to fill the tank?

Explanation.   Since both pipes can fill the tank in 12 hours, they fill $\frac{1}{12}$ of the tank together each hour. We will let a represent the number of hours it takes pipe A to fill the tank alone, so pipe A will fill $\frac{1}{a}$ of the tank each hour. Pipe B can fill the tank twice as fast so it fills $2 \cdot \frac{1}{a}$ of the tank each hour or $\frac{2}{a}$. When they are both turned on, they fill $\frac{1}{a} + \frac{2}{a}$ of the tank each hour.

Now we can write this equation:

$$\frac{1}{a} + \frac{2}{a} = \frac{1}{12}$$

To clear away denominators, we multiply both sides of the equation by the common denominator of 12 and a, which is $12a$:

$$\frac{1}{a} + \frac{2}{a} = \frac{1}{12}$$
$$12a \cdot \left(\frac{1}{a} + \frac{2}{a}\right) = 12a \cdot \frac{1}{12}$$
$$12a \cdot \frac{1}{a} + 12a \cdot \frac{2}{a} = 12a \cdot \frac{1}{12}$$
$$12 + 24 = a$$
$$36 = a$$
$$a = 36$$

The possible solution $a = 36$ should be checked

$$\frac{1}{36} + \frac{2}{36} \overset{?}{=} \frac{1}{12}$$
$$\frac{3}{36} \overset{\checkmark}{=} \frac{1}{12}$$

So it is a solution.

a. If only Pipe A is turned on, it would take 36 hours to fill the tank.

b. Since Pipe B can fill the tank twice as fast, it would take half the time, or 18 hours to fill the tank.

Example 12.6.10 Solving Rational Equations for a Specific Variable. Solve the rational equation $y = \frac{2x+5}{3x-1}$ for x.

Explanation. To get the x out of the denominator, our first step will be to multiply each side by the LCD, which is $3x-1$. Then we'll isolate all terms containing x, factor out x, and then finish solving for that variable.

$$y = \frac{2x+5}{3x-1}$$
$$y \cdot (3x-1) = \frac{2x+5}{3x-1} \cdot (3x-1)$$
$$3xy - y = 2x + 5$$
$$3xy = 2x + 5 + y$$
$$3xy - 2x = y + 5$$
$$x(3y-2) = y + 5$$
$$\frac{x(3y-2)}{3y-2} = \frac{y+5}{3y-2}$$
$$x = \frac{y+5}{3y-2}$$

Example 12.6.11 Solving Rational Equations Using Technology. Solve the equation $\frac{1}{x+2} + 1 = \frac{10x}{x^2+5}$ using graphing technology.

Explanation.

We will define $f(x) = \frac{1}{x+2} + 1$ and $g(x) = \frac{10x}{x^2+5}$, and then find a window where we can see all of the points of intersection.

Since the two functions intersect at approximately $(-2.309, -2.235)$, $(0.76, 1.362)$ and $(8.549, 1.095)$, the solutions to $\frac{1}{x+2} + 1 = \frac{10x}{x^2+5}$ are approximately -2.309, 0.76 and 8.549. The solution set is approximately $\{-2.309\ldots, 0.76\ldots, 8.549\ldots\}$.

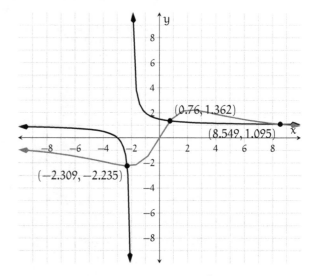

Figure 12.6.12: Graph of $f(x) = \frac{1}{x+2} + 1$ and $g(x) = \frac{10x}{x^2+5}$

12.6.6 Exercises

Introduction to Rational Functions

1. A function is graphed.

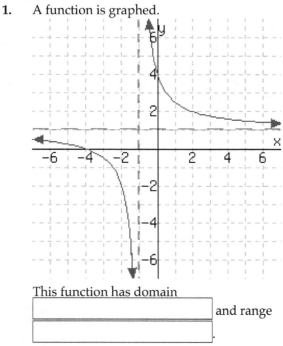

This function has domain _____ and range _____ .

2. A function is graphed.

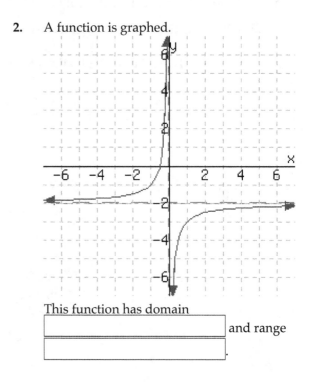

This function has domain _____ and range _____ .

3. The population of deer in a forest can be modeled by

$$P(x) = \frac{3220x + 2940}{7x + 6}$$

where x is the number of years in the future. Answer the following questions.

   a. How many deer live in this forest this year?

   b. How many deer will live in this forest 17 years later? Round your answer to an integer.

   c. After how many years, the deer population will be 461? Round your answer to an integer.

   d. Use a calculator to answer this question: As time goes on, the population levels off at about how many deer?

4. The population of deer in a forest can be modeled by

$$P(x) = \frac{2400x + 1850}{8x + 5}$$

where x is the number of years in the future. Answer the following questions.

   a. How many deer live in this forest this year?

   b. How many deer will live in this forest 5 years later? Round your answer to an integer.

   c. After how many years, the deer population will be 302? Round your answer to an integer.

   d. Use a calculator to answer this question: As time goes on, the population levels off at about how many deer?

5. In a certain store, cashiers can serve 55 customers per hour on average. If x customers arrive at the store in a given hour, then the average number of customers C waiting in line can be modeled by the function

$$C(x) = \frac{x^2}{3025 - 55x}$$

where $x < 55$.
Answer the following questions with a graphing calculator. Round your answers to integers.

   a. If 41 customers arrived in the store in the past hour, there are approximately [ ] customers waiting in line.

   b. If there are 7 customers waiting in line, approximately [ ] customers arrived in the past hour.

6. In a certain store, cashiers can serve 60 customers per hour on average. If x customers arrive at the store in a given hour, then the average number of customers C waiting in line can be modeled by the function

$$C(x) = \frac{x^2}{3600 - 60x}$$

where $x < 60$.
Answer the following questions with a graphing calculator. Round your answers to integers.

   a. If 48 customers arrived in the store in the past hour, there are approximately [ ] customers waiting in line.

   b. If there are 8 customers waiting in line, approximately [ ] customers arrived in the past hour.

7. The concentration of a drug in a patient's blood stream, in milligrams per liter, can be modeled by the function $C(t) = \frac{2t}{t^2+7}$, where t is the number of hours since the drug is injected. Answer the following question with technology. Round your answer to two decimal places if needed.

[   ] hours since injection, the drug's concentration is at the maximum value of [   ] milligrams per liter.

8. The concentration of a drug in a patient's blood stream, in milligrams per liter, can be modeled by the function $C(t) = \frac{3t}{t^2+5}$, where t is the number of hours since the drug is injected. Answer the following question with technology. Round your answer to two decimal places if needed.

[   ] hours since injection, the drug's concentration is at the maximum value of [   ] milligrams per liter.

Multiplication and Division of Rational Expressions

9. Simplify this expression.
$$\frac{-y^2 - 2yt + 3t^2}{y^2 - 9t^2}$$

10. Simplify this expression.
$$\frac{-y^2 + 5yx - 6x^2}{y^2 - 4x^2}$$

11. Simplify the function formula, and if applicable, write the restricted domain.
$$f(r) = \frac{r^4 + 8r^3 + 16r^2}{5r^4 + 19r^3 - 4r^2}$$
Reduced $f(r) =$ [   ]

12. Simplify the function formula, and if applicable, write the restricted domain.
$$H(r) = \frac{r^4 - 6r^3 + 9r^2}{3r^4 - 10r^3 + 3r^2}$$
Reduced $H(r) =$
[   ]

13. Simplify this expression, and if applicable, write the restricted domain.
$$\frac{t^2 - 16t}{t^2 - 16} \cdot \frac{t^2 - 4t}{t^2 - 13t - 48}$$

14. Simplify this expression, and if applicable, write the restricted domain.
$$\frac{t^2 - 4t}{t^2 - 4} \cdot \frac{t^2 - 2t}{t^2 + 5t - 36}$$

15. Simplify this expression, and if applicable, write the restricted domain.
$$\frac{9t^2 - 49}{3t^2 + t + (-14)} \div (7 - 3t)$$

16. Simplify this expression, and if applicable, write the restricted domain.
$$\frac{25x^2 - 16}{5x^2 + (-1)x + (-4)} \div (4 - 5x)$$

17. Simplify this expression.
$$\frac{x^5}{x^2y - 5x} \div \frac{1}{x^2y^2 - 8xy + 15}$$

18. Simplify this expression.
$$\frac{y^3}{y^2r + 3y} \div \frac{1}{y^2r^2 + 7yr + 12}$$

Addition and Subtraction of Rational Expressions Add or subtract the rational expressions to a single rational expression and then simplify. If applicable, state the restricted domain.

19. $\dfrac{1}{y+1} + \dfrac{2}{y^2-1}$

20. $\dfrac{1}{r+2} + \dfrac{4}{r^2-4}$

21. $-\dfrac{15r}{r^2 + 9r + 18} + \dfrac{5r}{r+3}$

22. $-\dfrac{12t}{t^2 + t - 2} - \dfrac{4t}{t+2}$

23. $\dfrac{t^2 - 20}{t^2 - 4t} - \dfrac{t+5}{t}$

24. $\dfrac{t^2 + 15}{t^2 - 3t} - \dfrac{t-5}{t}$

Add or subtract the rational expressions to a single rational expression and then simplify.

25. $-\dfrac{4x}{3y^4} + \dfrac{2}{5xy}$

26. $-\dfrac{2x}{3t^5} - \dfrac{6}{5xt}$

27. $-\dfrac{20yr}{y^2 - 8yr + 12r^2} + \dfrac{5y}{y - 6r}$

28. $\dfrac{10yx}{y^2 + 7yx + 6x^2} - \dfrac{2y}{y + x}$

Complex Fractions

29. Calculate the following. Use an improper fraction in your answer.

    a. $\dfrac{\frac{10}{9}}{\frac{5}{4}}$

    b. $\dfrac{\frac{r}{t}}{\frac{y}{x}}$

30. Calculate the following. Use an improper fraction in your answer.

    a. $\dfrac{\frac{25}{7}}{\frac{5}{4}}$

    b. $\dfrac{\frac{r}{t}}{\frac{y}{x}}$

31. Simplify this expression, and if applicable, write the restricted domain.
$$\dfrac{\frac{2}{q-1} - 3}{\frac{1}{q-1} + \frac{1}{q-3}}$$

32. Simplify this expression, and if applicable, write the restricted domain.
$$\dfrac{\frac{9}{n-1} - 7}{\frac{1}{n-1} + \frac{1}{n-10}}$$

33. Simplify this expression, and if applicable, write the restricted domain.
$$\dfrac{\frac{2t}{t^2-36} - 5}{\frac{3}{t+6} + \frac{4}{t-6}}$$

34. Simplify this expression, and if applicable, write the restricted domain.
$$\dfrac{\frac{3x}{x^2-9} - 2}{\frac{2}{x+3} - \frac{3}{x-3}}$$

35. Simplify this expression.
$$\dfrac{\frac{x}{y}}{\frac{6x}{5y^2}}$$

36. Simplify this expression.
$$\dfrac{\frac{a}{b}}{\frac{4a}{3b^2}}$$

37. Simplify this expression.
$$\dfrac{\frac{5}{y}}{20 - 5x}$$

38. Simplify this expression.
$$\dfrac{\frac{3}{r}}{3 - \frac{3x}{2}}$$

Solving Rational Equations Solve the equation.

39. $\dfrac{3}{r+3} - \dfrac{5}{r+9} = \dfrac{4}{r^2 + 12r + 27}$

40. $\dfrac{5}{r+2} - \dfrac{7}{r+9} = -\dfrac{1}{r^2 + 11r + 18}$

41. $\dfrac{1}{t+4} + \dfrac{4}{t^2 + 4t} = \dfrac{1}{4}$

42. $\dfrac{1}{t-3} - \dfrac{3}{t^2 - 3t} = \dfrac{1}{8}$

43. $-\dfrac{2}{x-2} + \dfrac{2x}{x+7} = \dfrac{6}{x^2 + 5x - 14}$

44. $\dfrac{6}{x-8} + \dfrac{9x}{x+4} = \dfrac{3}{x^2 - 4x - 32}$

45. $\dfrac{y-6}{y-9} - \dfrac{7}{y+3} = 2$

46. $\dfrac{y-3}{y+9} + \dfrac{5}{y+7} = 2$

47. Solve this equation for B:
$$\dfrac{1}{A} = \dfrac{9}{B+8}$$

48. Solve this equation for t:
$$\dfrac{1}{B} = \dfrac{4}{t+7}$$

49. Use technology to solve the equation

$$2x - \frac{1}{x+4} = \frac{3}{x+6}.$$

50. Use technology to solve the equation

$$\frac{1}{x^2-1} - \frac{2}{x-4} = \frac{3}{x-2}.$$

51. Two pipes are being used to fill a tank. Pipe A can fill the tank 4.5 times as fast as Pipe B does. When both pipes are turned on, it takes 18 hours to fill the tank. Answer the following questions:

If only Pipe A is turned on, it would take ⬚ hours to fill the tank.

If only Pipe B is turned on, it would take ⬚ hours to fill the tank.

52. Two pipes are being used to fill a tank. Pipe A can fill the tank 5.5 times as fast as Pipe B does. When both pipes are turned on, it takes 11 hours to fill the tank. Answer the following questions:

If only Pipe A is turned on, it would take ⬚ hours to fill the tank.

If only Pipe B is turned on, it would take ⬚ hours to fill the tank.

53. Town A and Town B are 580 miles apart. A boat traveled from Town A to Town B, and then back to Town A. Since the river flows from Town B to Town A, the boat's speed was 30 miles per hour faster when it traveled from Town B to Town A. The whole trip took 29 hours. Answer the following questions:

The boat traveled from Town A to Town B at the speed of ⬚ miles per hour.

The boat traveled from Town B back to Town A at the speed of ⬚ miles per hour.

54. Town A and Town B are 390 miles apart. A boat traveled from Town A to Town B, and then back to Town A. Since the river flows from Town B to Town A, the boat's speed was 25 miles per hour faster when it traveled from Town B to Town A. The whole trip took 13 hours. Answer the following questions:

The boat traveled from Town A to Town B at the speed of ⬚ miles per hour.

The boat traveled from Town B back to Town A at the speed of ⬚ miles per hour.

Chapter 13

Graphs and Equations

13.1 Overview of Graphing

In this section, we will review how to graph lines and general functions which will be useful when we graph parabolas in the next section.

13.1.1 Graphing Lines by Plotting Points

Sometimes, the easiest way to make a graph of an equation is by making a table and plotting points. (This was the approach in Section 3.2.) Let's refresh ourselves on how this works.

Example 13.1.2 A bathtub is holding 12 gallons of water. The drain starts to leak water at a constant rate of 0.6 gallons per second. A linear function with formula $W(x) = -0.6x + 12$ can be used to model the amount of water, in gallons, in the tub x seconds after it started draining. Let's make a graph of this function. The most straightforward method to graph any function is to build a table of x- and y-values, and then plot the points.

x	$W(x) = -0.6x + 12$	Point	Interpretation
0	$-0.6(0) + 12$ $= 12$	$(0, 12)$	There were 12 gallons of water in the tub when the tub started to drain.
1	$-0.6(1) + 12$ $= 11.4$	$(1, 11.4)$	There were 11.4 gallons in the tub 1 second after the tub started to drain.
2	$-0.6(2) + 12$ $= 10.8$	$(2, 10.8)$	There were 10.8 gallons in the tub 2 seconds after the tub started to drain.
3	$-0.6(3) + 12$ $= 10.2$	$(3, 10.2)$	There were 10.2 gallons in the tub 3 seconds after the tub started to drain.
4	$-0.6(4) + 12$ $= 9.6$	$(4, 9.6)$	There were 9.6 gallons in the tub 4 seconds after the tub started to drain.

Figure 13.1.3: A table of values for $W(x) = -0.6x + 12$

197

Could we have made a more helpful table? Maybe. The y-values are close together and for the most part they are decimals which can be difficult to plot accurately. No matter, for now we use these points and make a plot.

The advantage of plotting points is that it is a universal method to graph any function. It is easy to forget about this method after learning faster ways to graph functions, so to keep this method in your mathematical tool box in case you come across something that you don't know or remember how to graph.

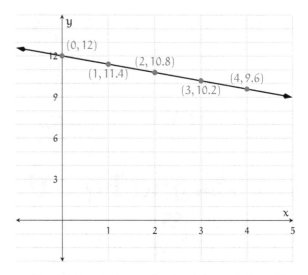

Figure 13.1.4: A graph of $W(x) = -0.6x + 12$

Checkpoint 13.1.5 Make a table for the equation.

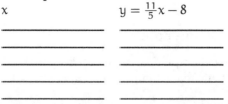

$$x \qquad\qquad y = \tfrac{11}{5}x - 8$$

Explanation. Since this equation has a fractional coefficient for x with denominator 5, it would be wise to choose our own x-values that are multiples of 5. Then when we use them to solve for y, the denominator will be cleared, and we will not need to continue with fraction arithmetic.

This solution will use the x-values −5, 0, 5, 10 and 15. The choice to use these x-values is arbitrary, but they are small multiples of 5, which will make computation easier.

One at a time, we substitute these x-values into the equation $y = \tfrac{11}{5}x - 8$, and solve for y:

$$y = \frac{11}{5}(-5) - 8 \implies y = -19$$

$$y = \frac{11}{5}(0) - 8 \implies y = -8$$

$$y = \frac{11}{5}(5) - 8 \implies y = 3$$

$$y = \frac{11}{5}(10) - 8 \implies y = 14$$

$$y = \frac{11}{5}(15) - 8 \implies y = 25$$

So the table may be completed as:

x	y
−5	−19
0	−8
5	3
10	14
15	25

13.1.2 Graphing Lines in Slope-Intercept Form

Recall that the slope-intercept form (3.5.1) of a line equation is $y = mx + b$ where m is the slope and $(0, b)$ is the vertical intercept.

Example 13.1.6 An efficient method to graph $y = -0.6x + 12$ is to use the fact that it is in slope-intercept form. To quickly make a graph, examine the equation and pick out the slope (in this case -0.6) and vertical intercept (in this case $(0, 12)$), and then plot slope-triangles from the intercept to locate more points on the line. One key point here is that it helps to have the slope written as a fraction. In this case,

$$-0.6 = -\frac{6}{10} = -\frac{3}{5}.$$

So start our graph at $(0, 12)$ and go forward 5 units and then down 3 units to reach more points.

Since we know that we will go forward 5 units and then down 3 units, and that we will start our graph at $(0, 12)$, we can choose to orient and scale our axes to see a more complete picture of W than we achieved by plotting convenient points in Example 13.1.2.

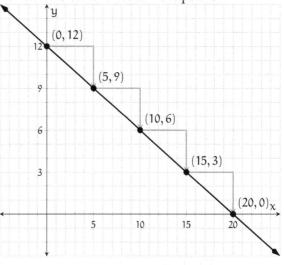

Figure 13.1.7: A graph of $W(x) = -0.6x + 12$

Example 13.1.8 Find the slope and vertical intercept of $y = h(x)$, where $h(x) = \frac{5}{3}x - 4$. Then use slope triangles to find two more points on the line and sketch it.

Explanation.

The slope is $\frac{5}{3}$ and the vertical intercept is $(0, -4)$. Starting at $(0, -4)$, we go forward 3 units and up 5 units to reach more points: $(3, 1)$ and $(6, 6)$.

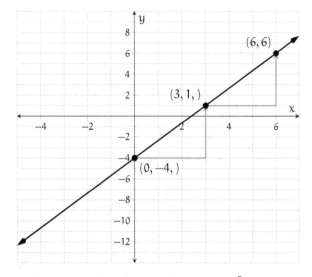

Figure 13.1.9: A graph of $h(x) = \frac{5}{3}x - 4$

13.1.3 Graphing Lines in Point-Slope Form

Recall that the point-slope form (3.6.1) of a line equation is $y = m(x - x_0) + y_0$ where m is the slope and (x_0, y_0) is a point on the line. The reason that (x_0, y_0) is a point on the line is because you can substitute in x_0 for x and then y_0 is the result for y.

$$y = m(\overset{\overset{x_0}{\downarrow}}{x} - x_0) + \underset{\underset{y_0}{\downarrow}}{y_0}$$

Example 13.1.10 The population of Monarch butterflies has been on an overall downward trajectory since the 1980s, as have populations of many migratory animals. Efforts to restore the population haven't had great success yet. There are several distinct populations of Monarchs that probably never meet each other: the Hawaii population, the Florida Keys population, the Western population, and the Eastern population. Of these, the Eastern population is by far the largest and we can model this population of Monarch butterflies with a simple linear function.

$$M(x) = -(x - 2006) + 15$$

approximates the total number of acres of Mexican forest that the Eastern population of Monarchs hibernates in during winter in year x. This formula is only valid from 1995 to 2018, the years that the population has been well studied.

Let's make graph of this equation given the information provided, but only between 1995 and 2018.

Since this formula is linear and given in point-slope form, we can easily read that the slope of the line is -1, and the point given by the equation is $(2006, 15)$. This means that we should scale our graph appropriately to be able to see these details. We can interpret the point $(2006, 15)$ to mean that in the year 2006, the Monarchs overwintered in 15 acres of Mexican forest. The slope means that for every one year that goes by, the overwintering population takes up about one less acre of forest.

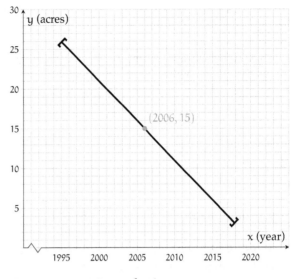

Figure 13.1.11: A graph of
$M(x) = -(x - 2006) + 15$

Example 13.1.12 Find the slope and a point on the graph of $y = m(x)$, where $m(x) = -\frac{9}{5}(x + 1) - 3$. Then use slope triangles to find two more points on the line and sketch it.

Explanation.

The slope of the line is $-\frac{9}{5}$, and the point given by the equation is $(-1, -3)$. So to graph h, start at $(-1, -3)$, and the go forward 5 units and down 9 units to reach more points: $(4, -12)$ and $(9, -21)$.

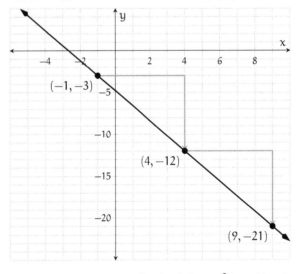

Figure 13.1.13: A graph of $m(x) = -\frac{9}{5}(x + 1) - 3$

13.1.4 Graphing Lines Using Intercepts

Recall that the standard form (3.7.1) of a line equation is $Ax + By = C$ where where A, B, and C are three numbers (each of which might be 0, although at least one of A and B must be nonzero).

Example 13.1.14 Recall our bathtub draining problem from Example 13.1.2, where $W(x) = -0.6x + 12$ modeled the amount of water, in gallons, in the tub x seconds after it started draining. Let's write the line equation $y = -0.6x + 12$ in standard form.

To find the standard form of the equation, we do as in Subsection 3.7.3. First, we will replace the variable $W(x)$ with y because standard form relates x and y and does not use function notation. So $W(x) = -0.6x + 12$ becomes $y = -0.6x + 12$. Now to convert to standard form, move both x and y to the left-hand side.

$$y = -0.6x + 12$$
$$0.6x + y = 12$$

The equation is in standard form written as $0.6x + y = 12$.

If a linear function is given in standard form, we can relative easily find the equation's x- and y-intercepts by substituting in $y = 0$ and $x = 0$, respectively.

Example 13.1.15 Let's find the intercepts of $0.6x + y = 12$, still relating back to Example 13.1.2. Then we may graph the equation using those intercepts.

To find the x-intercept, set $y = 0$ and solve for x.

$$0.6x + (0) = 12$$
$$0.6x = 12$$
$$x = 20$$

So the x-intercept is the point $(20, 0)$. In context, this means that 20 minutes after the tub started to drain, 0 gallons of water remained. This is telling us that the tub is empty!

Now with the x- and y-intercepts known, we may plot these points and draw the line that runs through them.

To find the y-intercept, set $x = 0$ and solve for y.

$$0.6(0) + y = 12$$
$$y = 12$$

So, the y-intercept is the point $(0, 12)$. In context, this means that 0 minutes after the tub started to drain, 12 gallons of water remained. This is telling us how much water was initially in the tub.

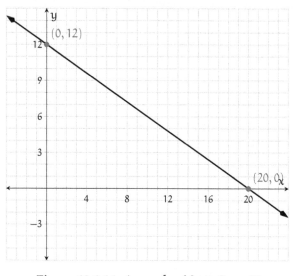

Figure 13.1.16: A graph of $3x + 5y = 60$

Checkpoint 13.1.17 Find the y-intercept and x-intercept of the line given by the equation. If a particular intercept does not exist, enter none into all the answer blanks for that row.

$$2x + 5y = -20$$

	x-value	y-value	Location (as an ordered pair)
y-intercept	_____	_____	_____
x-intercept	_____	_____	_____

Explanation. A line's y-intercept is on the y-axis, implying that its x-value must be 0. To find a line's y-intercept, we substitute in $x = 0$. In this problem we have:

$$2x + 5y = -20$$
$$2(0) + 5y = -20$$
$$5y = -20$$
$$\frac{5y}{5} = \frac{-20}{5}$$
$$y = -4$$

This line's y-intercept is $(0, -4)$.

Next, a line's x-intercept is on the x-axis, implying that its y-value must be 0. To find a line's x-intercept, we substitute in $y = 0$. In this problem we have:

$$2x + 5y = -20$$
$$2x + 5(0) = -20$$
$$2x = -20$$
$$\frac{2x}{2} = \frac{-20}{2}$$
$$x = -10$$

The line's x-intercept is $(-10, 0)$.
The entries for the table are:

	x-value	y-value	Location
y-intercept	0	−4	$(0, -4)$
x-intercept	−10	0	$(-10, 0)$

13.1.5 Graphing Functions by Plotting Points

Any function, linear or not, can be graphed by building a table of x- and y-values and plotting points. Let's look at a few more examples.

Example 13.1.18 Imagine a company called Corduroy's-Я-Us that makes pants. Their profit from their Royal Blue Corduroys, in thousands of dollars, can be modeled by the function $P(x) = -0.5x^2 + 33x - 200$ where x is the price of each pair of Royal Blue pants that they sell. Let's build a table of values and plot the function's graph.

In this context, the value of x must be positive. Furthermore, we shouldn't really consider x-values like 1, 2, etc., because it is not realistic that the price of a pair of new pants would be so low. Instead we try multiples of 10: 10, 20, etc.

x	$P(x) = -0.5x^2 + 33x - 200$	Point	Interpretation
0	$-0.5(0)^2 + 33(0) - 200$ $= -200$	$(0, -200)$	If each pair costs \$0, there is a loss of \$200,000.
10	$-0.5(10)^2 + 33(10) - 200$ $= 80$	$(10, 80)$	If each pair costs \$10, the profit is \$80,000.
20	$-0.5(20)^2 + 33(20) - 200$ $= 260$	$(20, 260)$	If each pair costs \$20, the profit is \$260,000.
30	$-0.5(30)^2 + 33(30) - 200$ $= 340$	$(30, 340)$	If each pair costs \$30, the profit is \$340,000.
40	$-0.5(40)^2 + 33(40) - 200$ $= 320$	$(40, 320)$	If each pair costs \$40, the profit is \$320,000.
50	$-0.5(50)^2 + 33(50) - 200$ $= 200$	$(50, 200)$	If each pair costs \$50, the profit is \$200,000.
60	$-0.5(60)^2 + 33(60) - 200$ $= -20$	$(60, -20)$	If each pair costs \$60, there is a loss of \$20,000.

Figure 13.1.19: A table of values for $P(x) = -0.5x^2 + 33x - 200$

With the values in Table 13.1.19, we can sketch the graph. Note that we have to estimate the how the graph curves which is a limitation of graphing a function by plotting points compared with using algebraic techniques.

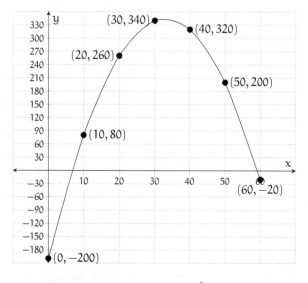

Figure 13.1.20: $P(x) = -0.5x^2 + 33x - 200$

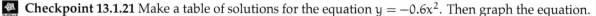

Checkpoint 13.1.21 Make a table of solutions for the equation $y = -0.6x^2$. Then graph the equation.

x	y

Explanation. This solution will use the x values $-2, -1, 0, 1$ and 2. The choice to use these x-values is arbitrary. Since they are small numbers, they might make calculations easier. It's important to include negative numbers.

One at a time, we substitute these x-values into the equation $y = -0.6x^2$, and solve for y

$$y = -0.6(-2)^2 \implies y = -2.4$$
$$y = -0.6(-1)^2 \implies y = -0.6$$
$$y = -0.6 \cdot 0^2 \implies y = 0$$
$$y = -0.6 \cdot 1^2 \implies y = -0.6$$
$$y = -0.6 \cdot 2^2 \implies y = -2.4$$

So the table may be completed as:

x	y
-2	-2.4
-1	-0.6
0	0
1	-0.6
2	-2.4

Using the values in the table, we can plot the following graph.

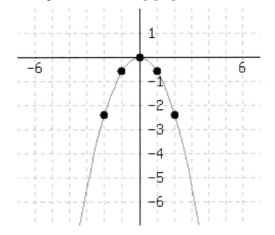

Example 13.1.22 Human-initiated global warming has been the subject of some debate. However, one aspect of the debate is undeniable fact: the amount of atmospheric carbon dioxide (CO_2: a greenhouse gas [1]) is being regularly and carefully measured [2] and is increasing faster and faster. The measured yearly average atmospheric carbon dioxide levels in parts per million (ppm) since 1958 can be very closely approximated by the function $C(x) = 244 + 29 \cdot 1.0148^x$ where x represents the number of years since the year 1900. Before 1958, the greenhouse gases weren't regularly measured. Create a table of values rounded to the nearest whole number for the carbon dioxide levels since 1958.

Explanation. Since 1958 is 58 years since 1900, we will start our table at $x = 58$ and go by 10s up through $x = 118$, which would stand for the year 2018.

x	C(x)	Point	Interpretation
58	$w(58) \approx 312$	(5, 312)	In 1958, the atmosphere was about 312 ppm CO_2.
68	$w(68) \approx 323$	(68, 323)	In 1968, the atmosphere was about 323 ppm CO_2.
78	$w(78) \approx 335$	(78, 335)	In 1978, the atmosphere was about 335 ppm CO_2.
88	$w(88) \approx 350$	(88, 350)	In 1988, the atmosphere was about 350 ppm CO_2.
98	$w(98) \approx 366$	(98, 366)	In 1998, the atmosphere was about 366 ppm CO_2.
108	$w(108) \approx 386$	(108, 386)	In 2008, the atmosphere was about 386 ppm CO_2.
118	$w(118) \approx 408$	(118, 408)	In 2018, the atmosphere was about 408 ppm CO_2.

Figure 13.1.23: A table of values for $C(x) = 244 + 29 \cdot 1.0148^x$

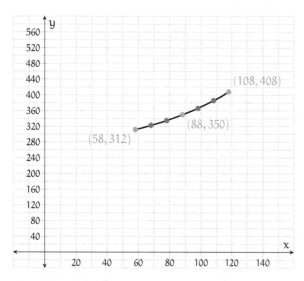

Figure 13.1.24: A graph of
$C(x) = 244 + 29 \cdot 1.0148^x$

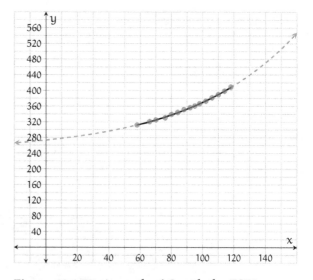

Figure 13.1.25: A graph of C with the ESRL overlaid and the function extrapolated beyond known dates.

13.1.6 Reading Questions

1. What are the four methods we recalled to graph lines in this section?

2. Why might it be better to represent a line in point-slope form than slope intercept form?

3. Explain how an equation for a line given in slope-intercept or point-slope form can be graphed without creating a table of values.

4. Describe one or more possible issues you might encounter after creating a table of points for a function and trying to use those points to make a graph.

---

[1]epa.gov/ghgemissions/overview-greenhouse-gases
[2]esrl.noaa.gov/gmd/ccgg/trends/graph.html

13.1.7 Exercises

Graphing Lines by Plotting Points Create a table of ordered pairs and then make a plot of the equation.

1. $y = 2x + 3$

2. $y = 3x + 5$

3. $y = -\frac{2}{5}x - 3$

4. $y = -\frac{3}{4}x + 2$

Graphing Lines in Slope-Intercept Form

5. Graph the equation $y = \frac{2}{3}x + 4$.

6. Graph the equation $y = \frac{3}{2}x - 5$.

7. Graph the equation $y = -\frac{3}{5}x - 1$.

8. Graph the equation $y = -\frac{1}{5}x + 1$.

Graphing Lines in Point-Slope Form

9. Graph the linear equation $y = -\frac{8}{3}(x - 4) - 5$ by identifying the slope and one point on this line.

10. Graph the linear equation $y = \frac{5}{7}(x + 3) + 2$ by identifying the slope and one point on this line.

11. Graph the linear equation $y = \frac{3}{4}(x + 2) + 1$ by identifying the slope and one point on this line.

12. Graph the linear equation $y = -\frac{5}{2}(x - 1) - 5$ by identifying the slope and one point on this line.

13. Graph the linear equation $y = -3(x - 9) + 4$ by identifying the slope and one point on this line.

14. Graph the linear equation $y = 7(x + 3) - 10$ by identifying the slope and one point on this line.

Graphing Lines Using Intercepts

15. Find the x- and y-intercepts of the line with equation $5x - 2y = 10$. Then find one other point on the line. Use your results to graph the line.

16. Find the x- and y-intercepts of the line with equation $5x - 6y = -90$. Then find one other point on the line. Use your results to graph the line.

17. Find the x- and y-intercepts of the line with equation $x + 5y = -15$. Then find one other point on the line. Use your results to graph the line.

18. Find the x- and y-intercepts of the line with equation $6x + y = -18$. Then find one other point on the line. Use your results to graph the line.

19. Make a graph of the line $-5x - y = -3$.

20. Make a graph of the line $x + 5y = 5$.

21. Make a graph of the line $20x - 4y = 8$.

22. Make a graph of the line $3x + 5y = 10$.

Graphing Functions by Plotting Points Create a table of ordered pairs and then make a plot of the equation.

23. $y = -3x^2$

24. $y = -x^2 - 2x - 3$

25. $y = \frac{1}{2}x^3 - x$

26. $y = \frac{1}{4}x^3 + x + 2$

27. $y = \sqrt{x + 5}$

28. $y = 3 - \sqrt{x + 2}$

13.2 Quadratic Graphs and Vertex Form

In this section, we will explore quadratic functions using graphing technology and learn the vertex and factored forms of a quadratic function's formula. We will also see how parabola graphs can be shifted.

13.2.1 Exploring Quadratic Functions with Graphing Technology

Graphing technology is very important and useful for applications and for finding points quickly. Let's explore some quadratic functions with graphing technology.

Example 13.2.2 Use technology to graph and make a table of the quadratic function f defined by $f(x) = 2x^2 + 4x - 3$ and find each of the key points or features.

   a. Find the vertex.

   b. Find the vertical intercept (i.e. y-intercept).

   c. Find the horizontal or (i.e. x-intercept(s)).

   d. Find $f(-2)$.

   e. Solve $f(x) = 3$ using the graph.

   f. Solve $f(x) \leq 3$ using the graph.

   g. State the domain and range of the function.

Explanation.

The specifics of how to use any one particular technology tool vary. Whether you use an app, a physical calculator, or something else, a table and graph should look like:

x	f(x)
-2	-3
-1	-5
0	-3
1	3
2	13

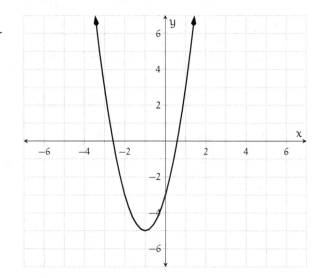

Additional features of your technology tool can enhance the graph to help answer these questions.
You may be able to make the graph appear like:

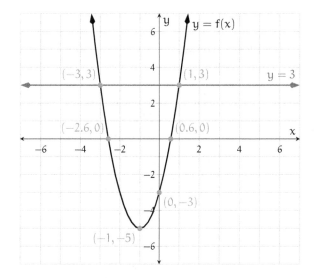

a. The vertex is $(-1, -5)$.

b. The vertical intercept is $(0, -3)$.

c. The horizontal intercepts are approximately $(-2.6, 0)$ and $(0.6, 0)$.

d. When $x = -2$, $y = -3$, so $f(-2) = -3$.

e. The solutions to $f(x) = 3$ are the x-values where $y = 3$. We graph the horizontal line $y = 3$ and find
the x-values where the graphs intersect. The solution set is $\{-3, 1\}$.

f. The solutions are all of the x-values where the function's graph is below (or touching) the line $y = 3$.
The interval is $[-3, 1]$.

g. The domain is $(-\infty, \infty)$ and the range is $[-5, \infty)$.

Now we will look at an application with graphing technology and put the points of interest in context.

Example 13.2.3 A reduced-gravity aircraft[1] is a fixed-wing airplane that astronauts use for training. The
airplane flies up and then down in a parabolic path to simulate the feeling of weightlessness. In one training
flight, the pilot will fly 40 to 60 parabolic maneuvers.

For the first parabolic maneuver, the altitude of the plane, in feet, at time t, in seconds since the maneuver
began, is given by $H(t) = -16t^2 + 400t + 30500$.

a. Determine the starting altitude of the plane for the first maneuver.

b. What is the altitude of the plane 10 seconds into the maneuver?

c. Determine the maximum altitude of the plane and how long it takes to reach that altitude.

d. The zero-gravity effect is experienced when the plane begins the parabolic path until it gets back down
to 30,500 feet. Write an inequality to express this and solve it using the graph. Write the times of the
zero-gravity effect as an interval and determine how long the astronauts experience weightlessness
during each cycle.

e. Use technology to make a table for H with t-values from 0 to 25 seconds. Use an increment of 5 seconds
and then use the table to solve $H(t) = 32100$.

f. State the domain and range for this context.

Explanation.   We can answer the questions based on the information in the graph.

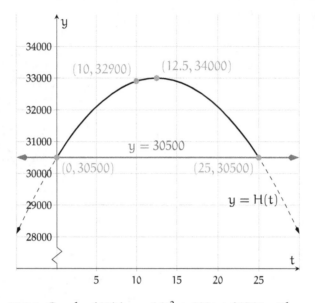

Figure 13.2.4: Graph of $H(t) = -16t^2 + 400t + 30500$ with $y = 30500$

a. The starting altitude can be read from the vertical intercept, which is $(0, 30500)$. The feeling of weightlessness begins at 30,500 feet.

b. After 10 seconds, the altitude of the plane is 32,900 feet.

c. For the maximum altitude of the plane we look at the vertex, which is approximately $(12.5, 33000)$. This tells us that after 12.5 seconds the plane will be at its maximum altitude of 33,000 feet.

d. We can write an inequality to describe when the plane is at or above 30,500 feet and solve it graphically.

$$H(t) \geq 30500$$
$$-16t^2 + 400t + 30500 \geq 30500.$$

We graph the line $y = 30500$ and find the points of intersection with the parabola. The astronauts experience weightlessness from 0 seconds to 25 seconds into the maneuver, or $[0, 25]$ seconds. They experience weightlessness for 25 seconds in each cycle.

e. To solve $H(t) = 32100$ using the table, we look for where the H-values are equal to 32100.

t	0	5	10	15	20	25
$H(t)$	30500	32100	32900	32900	32100	30500

There are two solutions, 5 seconds and 20 seconds. The solution set is $\{5, 20\}$.

f. When we use technology we see the entire function but in this context the plane is only on a parabolic path from $t = 0$ to $t = 25$ seconds. So the domain is $[0, 25]$, and the range is the set of corresponding y-values which is $[30500, 33000]$ feet.

Let's look at the remote-controlled airplane dive from Example 9.3.18. This time we will use technology to answer the questions.

Example 13.2.5 Maia has a remote-controlled airplane and she is going to do a stunt dive where the plane dives toward the ground and back up along a parabolic path. The altitude or height of the plane is given by the function H where $H(t) = 0.7t^2 - 23t + 200$, for $0 \leq t \leq 30$. The height is measured in feet and the time, t, is measured in seconds since the stunt began.

 a. Determine the starting height of the plane as the dive begins.

 b. Determine the height of the plane after 5 seconds.

 c. Will the plane hit the ground, and if so, at what time?

 d. If the plane does not hit the ground, what is the closest it gets to the ground, and at what time?

 e. At what time(s) will the plane have an altitude of 50 feet?

 f. State the domain and the range of the function (in context).

Explanation.   We have graphed the function and we will find the key information and put it in context.

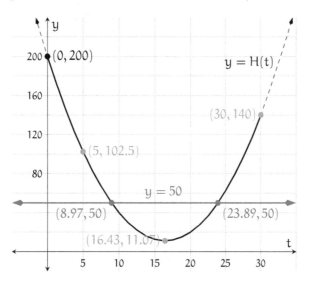

Figure 13.2.6: Graph of $H(t) = 0.7t^2 - 23t + 200$

 a. The starting altitude can be read from the vertical intercept, which is $(0, 200)$. When the stunt begins, the plane has a altitude of 200 feet.

 b. When $x = 5$, the y-value is 102.5. So $H(5) = 102.5$. This means that after 5 seconds, the plane is 102.5 feet above the ground.

 c. From the graph we can see that the parabola does not touch or cross the x-axis, which represents the ground. This means the plane does not hit the ground and there are no real solutions to the equation $H(t) = 0$.

---
[1]en.wikipedia.org/wiki/Reduced-gravity_aircraft

d. The lowest point is the vertex, which is approximately $(16.43, 11.07)$. The minimum altitude of the plane is about 11 feet, which occurs after about 16.4 seconds.

e. We graph the horizontal line $y = 50$ and look for the points of intersection. The plane will be 50 feet above the ground about 9 seconds after the plane begins the stunt, and again at about 24 seconds.

f. The domain for this function is given in the problem statement because only part of the parabola represents the path of the plane. The domain is $[0, 30]$. For the range we look at the possible altitudes of the plane and see that it is $[11.07\ldots, 200]$. The plane is doing this stunt from 0 to 30 seconds and its height ranges from about 11 to 200 feet above the ground.

13.2.2 The Vertex Form of a Parabola

We have learned the standard form of a quadratic function's formula, which is $f(x) = ax^2 + bx + c$. In this subsection, we will learn another form called the "vertex form".

Using graphing technology, consider the graphs of $f(x) = x^2 - 6x + 7$ and $g(x) = (x-3)^2 - 2$ on the same axes.

We see only one parabola because these are two different forms of the same function. Indeed, if we convert $g(x)$ into standard form:

$$g(x) = (x-3)^2 - 2$$
$$g(x) = x^2 - 6x + 9 - 2$$
$$g(x) = x^2 - 6x + 7$$

it is clear that f and g are the same function.

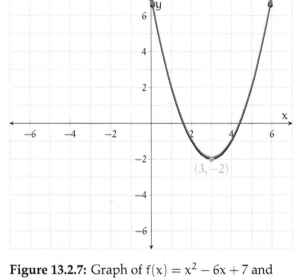

Figure 13.2.7: Graph of $f(x) = x^2 - 6x + 7$ and $g(x) = (x-3)^2 - 2$

The formula given for g is said to be in "vertex form" because it allows us to read the vertex without doing any calculations. The vertex of the parabola is $(3, -2)$. We can see those numbers in $g(x) = (x-3)^2 - 2$. The x-value is the solution to $(x-3) = 0$, and the y-value is the constant *added* at the end.

Here are the graphs of three more functions with formulas in vertex form. Compare each function with the vertex of its graph.

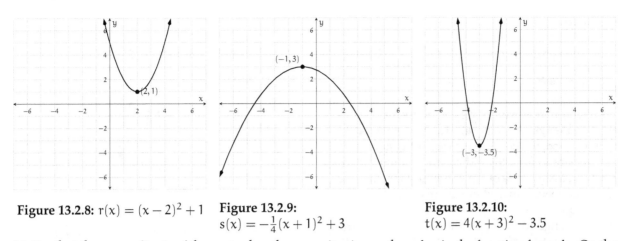

Figure 13.2.8: $r(x) = (x-2)^2 + 1$ **Figure 13.2.9:**
$s(x) = -\frac{1}{4}(x+1)^2 + 3$

Figure 13.2.10:
$t(x) = 4(x+3)^2 - 3.5$

Notice that the x-coordinate of the vertex has the opposite sign as the value in the function formula. On the other hand, the y-coordinate of the vertex has the same sign as the value in the function formula. Let's look at an example to understand why. We will evaluate $r(2)$.

$$r(2) = (2-2)^2 + 1$$
$$= 1$$

The x-value is the solution to $(x-2) = 0$, which is positive 2. When we substitute 2 for x we get the value $y = 1$. Note that these coordinates create the vertex at $(2, 1)$. Now we can define the vertex form of a quadratic function.

Fact 13.2.11 Vertex Form of a Quadratic Function. *A quadratic function with the vertex at the point* (h, k) *is given by* $f(x) = a(x-h)^2 + k$.

Checkpoint 13.2.12 Find the vertex of each quadratic function.

a. $r(x) = -2(x+4)^2 + 10$

b. $s(x) = 5(x-1)^2 + 2$

c. $t(x) = (x-10)^2 - 5$

d. $u(x) = 3(x+7)^2 - 13$

Explanation.

a. The vertex of $r(x) = -2(x+4)^2 + 10$ is $(-4, 10)$.

b. The vertex of $s(x) = 5(x-1)^2 + 2$ is $(1, 2)$.

c. The vertex of $t(x) = (x-10)^2 - 5$ is $(10, -5)$.

d. The vertex of $u(x) = 3(x+7)^2 - 13$ is $(-7, -13)$.

Now let's do the reverse. When given the vertex and the value of a, we can write the function in vertex form.

Example 13.2.13 Write a formula for the quadratic function f with the given vertex and value of a.

a. Vertex $(-2, 8)$, $a = 1$

b. Vertex $(4, -9)$, $a = -4$

c. Vertex $(-3, -1)$, $a = 2$

d. Vertex $(5, 12)$, $a = -3$

Explanation.

a. The vertex form is $f(x) = (x+2)^2 + 8$.

b. The vertex form is $f(x) = -4(x-4)^2 - 9$.

c. The vertex form is $f(x) = 2(x+3)^2 - 1$.

d. The vertex form is $f(x) = -3(x-5)^2 + 12$.

Once we read the vertex we can also state the domain and range. All quadratic functions have a domain of $(-\infty, \infty)$ because we can put in any value to a quadratic function. The range, however, depends on the y-value of the vertex and whether the parabola opens upward or downward. When we have a quadratic function in vertex form we can read the range from the formula. Let's look at the graph of f, where $f(x) = 2(x-3)^2 - 5$, as an example.

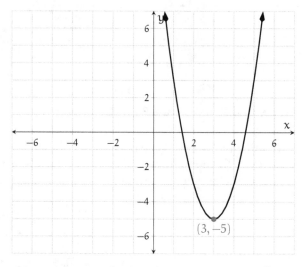

Figure 13.2.14: The graph of $f(x) = 2(x-3)^2 - 5$

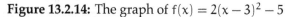

The domain is $(-\infty, \infty)$. The graph of f opens upward (which we know because $a = 2$ is positive) so the vertex is the minimum point. The y-value of -5 is the minimum. The range is $[-5, \infty)$.

Example 13.2.15 Identify the domain and range of g, where $g(x) = -3(x+1)^2 + 6$.

Explanation.

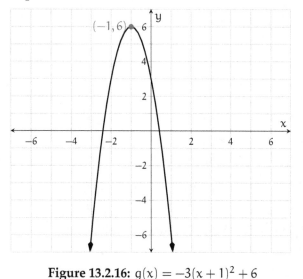

Figure 13.2.16: $g(x) = -3(x+1)^2 + 6$

The domain is $(-\infty, \infty)$. The graph of g opens downward (which we know because $a = -3$ is negative) so the vertex is the maximum point. The y-value of 6 is the maximum. The range is $(-\infty, 6]$.

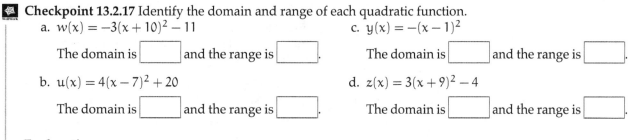

Checkpoint 13.2.17 Identify the domain and range of each quadratic function.

a. $w(x) = -3(x + 10)^2 - 11$

    The domain is [   ] and the range is [   ].

b. $u(x) = 4(x - 7)^2 + 20$

    The domain is [   ] and the range is [   ].

c. $y(x) = -(x - 1)^2$

    The domain is [   ] and the range is [   ].

d. $z(x) = 3(x + 9)^2 - 4$

    The domain is [   ] and the range is [   ].

Explanation.

a. The domain of w is $(-\infty, \infty)$. The parabola opens downward so the range is $(-\infty, -11]$.

b. The domain of u is $(-\infty, \infty)$. The parabola opens upward so the range is $[20, \infty)$.

c. The domain of y is $(-\infty, \infty)$. The parabola opens downward so the range is $(-\infty, 0]$.

d. The domain of z is $(-\infty, \infty)$. The parabola opens upward so the range is $[-4, \infty)$.

13.2.3 Horizontal and Vertical Shifts

Let $f(x) = x^2$ and $g(x) = (x - 4)^2 + 1$. The graph of $y = f(x)$ has its vertex at the point $(0, 0)$. Now we will compare this with the graph of $y = g(x)$ on the same axes.

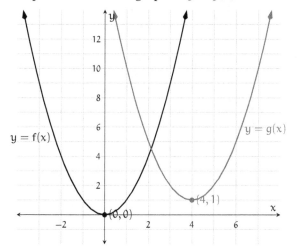

Both graphs open upward and have the same shape. Notice that the graph of g is the same as the graph of f but is shifted to the right by 4 units and up by 1 units because its vertex is $(4, 1)$.

Figure 13.2.18: The graph of f and g

Let's look at another graph. Let $h(x) = -x^2$ and let $j(x) = -(x + 3)^2 + 4$.

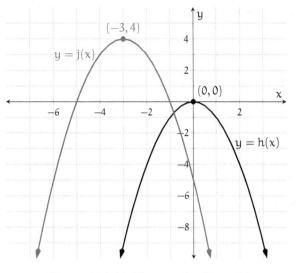

Both parabolas open downward and have the same shape. The graph of j is the same as the graph of h but it has been shifted to the left by 3 units and up by 4 units making its vertex $(-3, 4)$.

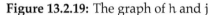

Figure 13.2.19: The graph of h and j

To summarize, when a quadratic function is written in vertex form, the h-value is the horizontal shift of its graph from the graph of $y = ax^2$ and the k-value is the vertical shift of its graph from the graph of $y = ax^2$.

Example 13.2.20 Identify the horizontal and vertical shifts compared with $y = x^2$.

   a. $m(x) = (x + 7)^2 + 3$ c. $o(x) = (x - 5)^2 - 1$

   b. $n(x) = (x - 1)^2 + 6$ d. $p(x) = (x + 3)^2 - 11$

Explanation.

   a. The graph of $y = m(x)$ has vertex at $(-7, 3)$. Therefore the graph is the same as $y = x^2$ shifted to the left 7 units and up 3 units.

   b. The graph of $y = n(x)$ has vertex at $(1, 6)$. Therefore the graph is the same as $y = x^2$ shifted to the right 1 unit and up 6 units.

   c. The graph of $y = o(x)$ has vertex at $(5, -1)$. Therefore the graph is the same as $y = x^2$ shifted to the right 5 units and down 1 unit.

   d. The graph of $y = p(x)$ has vertex at $(-3, -11)$. Therefore the graph is the same as $y = x^2$ shifted to the left 3 units and down 11 units.

13.2.4 The Factored Form of a Parabola

There is another form of a quadratic function's formula, called "factored form", which we will explore next. Let's consider the two functions $q(x) = -x^2 + 3x + 4$ and $s(x) = -(x - 4)(x + 1)$. Using graphing technology, we will graph $y = q(x)$ and $y = s(x)$ on the same axes.

These graphs coincide because the functions are actually the same. We can tell by multiplying out the formula for g to get back to the formula for f.

$$g(x) = -(x-4)(x+1)$$
$$g(x) = -(x^2 - 3x - 4)$$
$$g(x) = -x^2 + 3x + 4$$

Now we can see that f and g are really the same function.

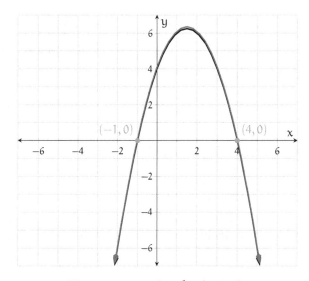

Figure 13.2.21: Graph of q and s

Factored form is very useful because we can read the x-intercepts directly from the function, which in this case are $(4,0)$ and $(-1,0)$. We find these by looking for the values that make the factors equal to 0, so the x-values have the opposite signs as are shown in the formula. To demonstrate this, we will find the roots by solving $g(x) = 0$.

$$g(x) = -(x-4)(x+1)$$
$$0 = -(x-4)(x+1)$$

$$x - 4 = 0 \qquad \text{or} \qquad x + 1 = 0$$
$$x = 4 \qquad \text{or} \qquad x = -1$$

This shows us that the x-intercepts are $(4,0)$ and $(-1,0)$.

The x-values of the x-intercepts are also called **zeros** or **roots**. The zeros or roots of the function g are -1 and 4.

Fact 13.2.22 Factored Form of a Quadratic Function. *A quadratic function with horizontal intercepts at $(r,0)$ and $(s,0)$ has the formula $f(x) = a(x-r)(x-s)$.*

Checkpoint 13.2.23 Write the horizontal intercepts of each function.

a. $t(x) = -(x+2)(x-4)$

b. $u(x) = 6(x-7)(x-5)$

c. $v(x) = -2(x+1)(x+4)$

d. $w(x) = 10(x-8)(x+3)$

Explanation.

a. The horizontal intercepts of t are $(-2,0)$ and $(4,0)$.

b. The horizontal intercepts of u are $(7,0)$ and $(5,0)$.

c. The horizontal intercepts of v are $(-1,0)$ and $(-4,0)$.

d. The horizontal intercepts of w are $(8,0)$ and $(-3,0)$.

Let's summarize the three forms of a quadratic function's formula:

Standard Form $f(x) = ax^2 + bx + c$, with y-intercept $(0, c)$.

Vertex Form $f(x) = a(x - h)^2 + k$, with vertex (h, k).

Factored Form $f(x) = a(x - r)(x - s)$, with x-intercepts $(r, 0)$ and $(s, 0)$.

13.2.5 Reading Questions

1. With the vertex form of a quadratic function, the formula shows you a point on the graph (without having to do any calculation). What is the name of that point?

2. With the standard form of a quadratic function, the formula shows you a point on the graph (without having to do any calculation). What is the name of that point?

3. What makes the vertex form of a quadratic function nicer for graphing compared to standard form?

4. If a fellow student attempted to graph the equation $y = (x - 4)^2 + 6$ and put the vertex at (-4,6), how would you explain to them that they have made an error?

13.2.6 Exercises

Review and Warmup

1. Multiply the polynomials.
    $(t + 7)(t - 4)$

2. Multiply the polynomials.
    $(t + 4)(t - 10)$

3. Multiply the polynomials.
    $(10t - 5)(t + 7)$

4. Multiply the polynomials.
    $(7x - 1)(x + 5)$

5. Factor the given polynomial.
    $x^2 + 7x + 12$

6. Factor the given polynomial.
    $y^2 + 18y + 80$

7. Factor the given polynomial.
    $8y^2 + 24y + 16$

8. Factor the given polynomial.
    $2r^2 + 12r + 10$

9. For the interval expressed in the number line, write it using set-builder notation and interval notation.

10. For the interval expressed in the number line, write it using set-builder notation and interval notation.

11. For the interval expressed in the number line, write it using set-builder notation and interval notation.

12. For the interval expressed in the number line, write it using set-builder notation and interval notation.

Technology and Tables

13. Let $f(x) = x^2 + x - 1$. Use technology to make a table of values f.

x	f(x)

14. Let $g(x) = x^2 - 3x - 3$. Use technology to make a table of values g.

x	g(x)

15. Let $h(x) = -x^2 + 3x - 1$. Use technology to make a table of values h.

x	h(x)

16. Let $F(x) = -x^2 + 4x - 3$. Use technology to make a table of values F.

x	F(x)

17. Let $F(x) = -2x^2 + 5x + 1$. Use technology to make a table of values F.

x	F(x)

18. Let $G(x) = 3x^2 - 5x - 4$. Use technology to make a table of values G.

x	G(x)

19. Let $H(x) = -2x^2 - 4x + 30$. Use technology to make a table of values H.

x	H(x)

20. Let $K(x) = 3x^2 - 8x + 53$. Use technology to make a table of values K.

x	K(x)

Technology and Graphs

21. Use technology to make a graph of f where $f(x) = x^2 + 3x - 2$.

22. Use technology to make a graph of f where $f(x) = x^2 - 2x - 1$.

23. Use technology to make a graph of f where $f(x) = -x^2 + 3x + 2$.

24. Use technology to make a graph of f where $f(x) = -x^2 + x + 2$.

25. Use technology to make a graph of f where $f(x) = 3x^2 - 6x - 5$.

26. Use technology to make a graph of f where $f(x) = -3x^2 - 8x + 3$.

27. Use technology to make a graph of f where $f(x) = -3x^2 + 4x + 49$.

28. Use technology to make a graph of f where $f(x) = 2x^2 - 2x + 41$.

Technology and Features of Quadratic Function Graphs Use technology to find features of a quadratic function and its graph.

29. Let $K(x) = x^2 - 4x + 2$. Use technology to find the following.

   a. The vertex is [____].

   b. The y-intercept is [____].

   c. The x-intercept(s) is/are
   [_____].

   d. The domain of K is [____].

   e. The range of K is [____].

   f. Calculate K(1). [____].

   g. Solve $K(x) = 2$. [____]

   h. Solve $K(x) \geq 2$. [_____]

30. Let $f(x) = -x^2 - x - 1$. Use technology to find the following.

   a. The vertex is [____].

   b. The y-intercept is [____].

   c. The x-intercept(s) is/are
   [_____].

   d. The domain of f is [____].

   e. The range of f is [____].

   f. Calculate f(1). [____].

   g. Solve $f(x) = -3$. [____]

   h. Solve $f(x) \geq -3$. [_____]

31. Let $g(x) = 1.1x^2 - 2.1x + 4.2$. Use technology to find the following.

   a. The vertex is [____].

   b. The y-intercept is [____].

   c. The x-intercept(s) is/are
   [_____].

   d. The domain of g is [____].

   e. The range of g is [____].

   f. Calculate g(2). [____].

   g. Solve $g(x) = 5$. [____]

   h. Solve $g(x) > 5$. [_____]

32. Let $h(x) = 1.1x^2 - 2.8x + 3.7$. Use technology to find the following.

   a. The vertex is [____].

   b. The y-intercept is [____].

   c. The x-intercept(s) is/are
   [_____].

   d. The domain of h is [____].

   e. The range of h is [____].

   f. Calculate h(5). [____].

   g. Solve $h(x) = 3$. [____]

   h. Solve $h(x) \leq 3$. [_____]

33. Let $F(x) = \frac{x^2}{3} + 2.3x + 0.9$. Use technology to find the following.

    a. The vertex is $\boxed{}$.

    b. The y-intercept is $\boxed{}$.

    c. The x-intercept(s) is/are
$\boxed{}$.

    d. The domain of F is $\boxed{}$.

    e. The range of F is $\boxed{}$.

    f. Calculate $F(-3)$. $\boxed{}$.

    g. Solve $F(x) = -1$. $\boxed{}$

    h. Solve $F(x) < -1$. $\boxed{}$

34. Let $F(x) = \frac{x^2}{4} + 2.2x + 3.2$. Use technology to find the following.

    a. The vertex is $\boxed{}$.

    b. The y-intercept is $\boxed{}$.

    c. The x-intercept(s) is/are
$\boxed{}$.

    d. The domain of F is $\boxed{}$.

    e. The range of F is $\boxed{}$.

    f. Calculate $F(1)$. $\boxed{}$.

    g. Solve $F(x) = 7$. $\boxed{}$

    h. Solve $F(x) \leq 7$. $\boxed{}$

Applications

35. An object was launched from the top of a hill with an upward vertical velocity of 150 feet per second. The height of the object can be modeled by the function $h(t) = -16t^2 + 150t + 250$, where t represents the number of seconds after the launch. Assume the object landed on the ground at sea level. Find the answer using graphing technology.

    The object's height was $\boxed{}$ when it was launched.

36. An object was launched from the top of a hill with an upward vertical velocity of 170 feet per second. The height of the object can be modeled by the function $h(t) = -16t^2 + 170t + 150$, where t represents the number of seconds after the launch. Assume the object landed on the ground at sea level. Find the answer using graphing technology.

    Use a table to list the object's height within the first second after it was launched, at an increment of 0.1 second. Fill in the blanks. Round your answers to two decimal places when needed.

Time in Seconds	Height in Feet
0.1	_____
0.2	_____
0.3	_____

37. An object was launched from the top of a hill with an upward vertical velocity of 190 feet per second. The height of the object can be modeled by the function $h(t) = -16t^2 + 190t + 300$, where t represents the number of seconds after the launch. Assume the object landed on the ground at sea level. Use technology to find the answer.

    The object was $\boxed{}$ feet in the air 5 seconds after it was launched.

38. An object was launched from the top of a hill with an upward vertical velocity of 200 feet per second. The height of the object can be modeled by the function $h(t) = -16t^2 + 200t + 200$, where t represents the number of seconds after the launch. Assume the object landed on the ground at sea level. Find the answer using technology.

$\boxed{}$ seconds after its launch, the object reached its maximum height of $\boxed{}$ feet.

39. An object was launched from the top of a hill with an upward vertical velocity of 60 feet per second. The height of the object can be modeled by the function $h(t) = -16t^2 + 60t + 150$, where t represents the number of seconds after the launch. Assume the object landed on the ground at sea level. Find the answer using technology.

$\boxed{}$ seconds after its launch, the object fell to the ground at sea level.

40. An object was launched from the top of a hill with an upward vertical velocity of 80 feet per second. The height of the object can be modeled by the function $h(t) = -16t^2 + 80t + 300$, where t represents the number of seconds after the launch. Assume the object landed on the ground at sea level. Find the answer using technology. Round your answers to two decimal places. If there is more than one answer, use a comma to separate them.

The object was 359 feet high at the following number of seconds after it was launched: $\boxed{}$.

41. In a race, a car drove through the starting line at the speed of 7 meters per second. It was accelerating at 2.3 meters per second squared. Its distance from the starting position can be modeled by the function $d(t) = 1.15t^2 + 7t$. Find the answer using technology.

After $\boxed{}$ seconds, the car was 63.75 meters away from the starting position.

42. In a race, a car drove through the starting line at the speed of 4 meters per second. It was accelerating at 2.7 meters per second squared. Its distance from the starting position can be modeled by the function $d(t) = 1.35t^2 + 4t$. Find the answer using technology.

After $\boxed{}$ seconds, the car was 242.4 meters away from the starting position.

43. A farmer purchased 520 meters of fencing, and will build a rectangular pen with it. To enclose the largest possible area, what should the pen's length and width be? Model the pen's area with a function, and then find its maximum value.

Use a comma to separate your answers.

To enclose the largest possible area, the pen's length and width should be $\boxed{}$ meters.

44. A farmer purchased 310 meters of fencing, and will build a rectangular pen along a river. This implies the pen has only 3 fenced sides. To enclose the largest possible area, what should the pen's length and width be? Model the pen's area with a function, and then find its maximum value.

To enclose the largest possible area, the pen's length and width should be $\boxed{}$ meters.

Quadratic Functions in Vertex Form

45. Find the vertex of the graph of
$y = 5(x + 7)^2 + 4$.

46. Find the vertex of the graph of
$y = 8(x - 7)^2 - 8$.

47. Find the vertex of the graph of
$y = 10(x + 1)^2 + 4$.

48. Find the vertex of the graph of
$y = -9(x + 8)^2 + 9$.

49. Find the vertex of the graph of
$y = -5.9(x - 5.4)^2 - 2.9$.

50. Find the vertex of the graph of
$y = -3.7(x + 1.5)^2 + 5.5$.

A graph of a function f is given. Use the graph to write a formula for f in vertex form. You will need to identify the vertex and also one more point on the graph to find the leading coefficient a.

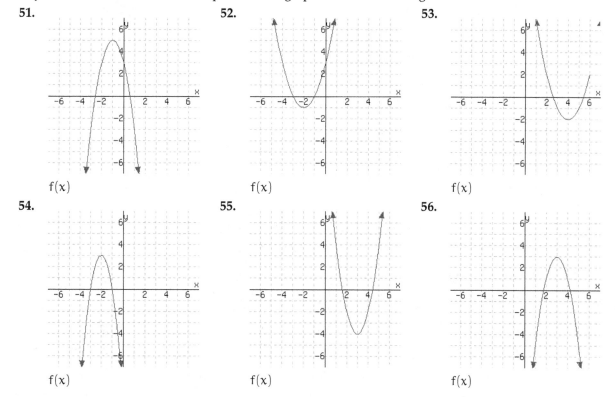

51.

f(x)

52.

f(x)

53.

f(x)

54.

f(x)

55.

f(x)

56.

f(x)

57. Write the vertex form for the quadratic function f, whose vertex is $(9, 4)$ and has leading coefficient $a = -8$.

58. Write the vertex form for the quadratic function f, whose vertex is $(3, -7)$ and has leading coefficient $a = -6$.

59. Write the vertex form for the quadratic function f, whose vertex is $(-4, -2)$ and has leading coefficient $a = -4$.

60. Write the vertex form for the quadratic function f, whose vertex is $(8, -7)$ and has leading coefficient $a = -1$.

61. Let F be defined by $F(x) = (x - 2)^2 - 3$.

    a. What is the domain of F?

    b. What is the range of F?

62. Let G be defined by $G(x) = (x + 5)^2 + 5$.

    a. What is the domain of G?

    b. What is the range of G?

63. Let H be defined by $H(x) = 9.1(x + 6)^2 - 4$.

    a. What is the domain of H?

    b. What is the range of H?

64. Let K be defined by $K(x) = 5.5(x - 2)^2 + 9$.

    a. What is the domain of K?

    b. What is the range of K?

65. Let K be defined by $K(x) = -6(x+9)^2 + 4$.

    a. What is the domain of K?

    b. What is the range of K?

67. Let g be defined by $g(x) = 6\left(x - \frac{3}{4}\right)^2 + 1$.

    a. What is the domain of g?

    b. What is the range of g?

69. Let h be defined by $h(x) = 8\left(x + \frac{2}{9}\right)^2 + 2$.

    a. What is the domain of h?

    b. What is the range of h?

66. Let f be defined by $f(x) = 7(x+1)^2 - 1$.

    a. What is the domain of f?

    b. What is the range of f?

68. Let h be defined by $h(x) = -3\left(x + \frac{7}{9}\right)^2 - \frac{4}{5}$.

    a. What is the domain of h?

    b. What is the range of h?

70. Let F be defined by
$$F(x) = -5\left(x - \frac{1}{3}\right)^2 + (-4).$$

    a. What is the domain of F?

    b. What is the range of F?

71. Consider the graph of the equation $y = (x-3)^2 - 7$. Compared to the graph of $y = x^2$, the vertex has been shifted _____ units (☐ left ☐ right) and _____ units (☐ down ☐ up) .

72. Consider the graph of the equation $y = (x-8)^2 + 5$. Compared to the graph of $y = x^2$, the vertex has been shifted _____ units (☐ left ☐ right) and _____ units (☐ down ☐ up) .

73. Consider the graph of the equation $y = (x-71.6)^2 - 14.5$. Compared to the graph of $y = x^2$, the vertex has been shifted _____ units (☐ left ☐ right) and _____ units (☐ down ☐ up) .

74. Consider the graph of the equation $y = (x-93.5)^2 - 83.4$. Compared to the graph of $y = x^2$, the vertex has been shifted _____ units (☐ left ☐ right) and _____ units (☐ down ☐ up) .

75. Consider the graph of the equation $y = \left(x - \frac{9}{5}\right)^2 + \frac{3}{2}$. Compared to the graph of $y = x^2$, the vertex has been shifted _____ units (☐ left ☐ right) and _____ units (☐ down ☐ up) .

76. Consider the graph of the equation $y = \left(x - \frac{2}{3}\right)^2 + \frac{9}{8}$. Compared to the graph of $y = x^2$, the vertex has been shifted _____ units (☐ left ☐ right) and _____ units (☐ down ☐ up) .

Three Forms of Quadratic Functions

77. The quadratic expression $(x-2)^2 - 1$ is written in vertex form.

    a. Write the expression in standard form.

    b. Write the expression in factored form.

79. The quadratic expression $(x-4)^2 - 81$ is written in vertex form.

    a. Write the expression in standard form.

    b. Write the expression in factored form.

78. The quadratic expression $(x-3)^2 - 25$ is written in vertex form.

    a. Write the expression in standard form.

    b. Write the expression in factored form.

80. The quadratic expression $(x-1)^2 - 36$ is written in vertex form.

    a. Write the expression in standard form.

    b. Write the expression in factored form.

Factored Form and Intercepts

81. The formula for a quadratic function G is
    $G(x) = (x - 5)(x - 3)$.

    a. The y-intercept is [   ].

    b. The x-intercept(s) is/are [   ].

82. The formula for a quadratic function f is
    $f(x) = (x - 7)(x + 4)$.

    a. The y-intercept is [   ].

    b. The x-intercept(s) is/are [   ].

83. The formula for a quadratic function H is
    $H(x) = 9(x - 9)(x - 1)$.

    a. The y-intercept is [   ].

    b. The x-intercept(s) is/are [   ].

84. The formula for a quadratic function F is
    $F(x) = -8(x - 2)(x - 9)$.

    a. The y-intercept is [   ].

    b. The x-intercept(s) is/are [   ].

85. The formula for a quadratic function h is
    $h(x) = -6x(x + 5)$.

    a. The y-intercept is [   ].

    b. The x-intercept(s) is/are [   ].

86. The formula for a quadratic function H is
    $H(x) = -4(x - 8)x$.

    a. The y-intercept is [   ].

    b. The x-intercept(s) is/are [   ].

87. The formula for a quadratic function g is
    $g(x) = -2(x - 1)(x - 1)$.

    a. The y-intercept is [   ].

    b. The x-intercept(s) is/are .

88. The formula for a quadratic function h is
    $h(x) = -5(x - 2)(x - 2)$.

    a. The y-intercept is [   ].

    b. The x-intercept(s) is/are [   ].

89. The formula for a quadratic function g is
    $g(x) = 3(8x + 9)(2x - 5)$.

    a. The y-intercept is [   ].

    b. The x-intercept(s) is/are [   ].

90. The formula for a quadratic function G is
    $G(x) = 5(6x + 1)(8x - 5)$.

    a. The y-intercept is [   ].

    b. The x-intercept(s) is/are [   ].

13.3 Completing the Square

In this section, we will learn how to "complete the square" with a quadratic expression. This topic is useful for solving quadratic equations and putting quadratic functions in vertex form.

13.3.1 Solving Quadratic Equations by Completing the Square

When we have an equation like $(x + 5)^2 = 4$, we can solve it quickly using the square root property:

$$(x + 5)^2 = 4$$

$$x + 5 = -2 \qquad \text{or} \qquad x + 5 = 2$$
$$x = -7 \qquad \text{or} \qquad x = -3$$

The method of **completing the square** allows us to solve *any* quadratic equation using the square root property.

Suppose you have a small quadratic expression in the form $x^2 + bx$. It can be visualized as an "L"-shape as in Figure 13.3.2.

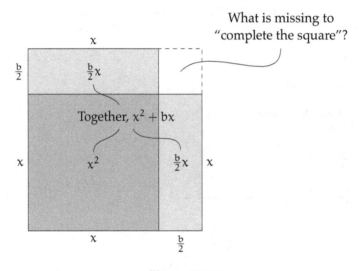

Figure 13.3.2

The "missing" square in the upper right corner of Figure 13.3.2 is $\frac{b}{2}$ on each side, so its area is $\left(\frac{b}{2}\right)^2$. This means that if we have $x^2 + bx$ and add $\left(\frac{b}{2}\right)^2$, we are "completing" the larger square.

Fact 13.3.3 The Term that Completes the Square. *For a polynomial $x^2 + bx$, the constant term needed to make a perfect square trinomial is $\left(\frac{b}{2}\right)^2$.*

Process 13.3.4 Completing the Square. *For a quadratic equation simplified to the form $x^2 + bx = c$, to solve for x by completing the square,*

1. *Use Fact 13.3.3 to find the number to add to both sides of the equation to make the left hand side a perfect square.*

This number is always $\left(\frac{b}{2}\right)^2$.

2. *Add that number to both sides of $x^2 + bx = c$ to get*

$$x^2 + bx + \left(\frac{b}{2}\right)^2 = c + \left(\frac{b}{2}\right)^2$$

3. *The left hand side is now a perfect square that factors as $x^2 + bx + \left(\frac{b}{2}\right)^2 = \left(x + \frac{b}{2}\right)^2$, so the equation becomes*

$$\left(x + \frac{b}{2}\right)^2 = c + \left(\frac{b}{2}\right)^2$$

4. *Solve remaining equation using the Square Root Property.*

Example 13.3.5 Solve the quadratic equation $x^2 + 6x = 16$ by completing the square.

Explanation. To solve the quadratic equation $x^2 + 6x = 16$, on the left side we can complete the square by adding $\left(\frac{b}{2}\right)^2$; note that $b = 6$ in this case, which makes $\left(\frac{b}{2}\right)^2 = \left(\frac{6}{2}\right)^2 = 3^2 = 9$. We add it to both sides to maintain equality.

$$x^2 + 6x + 9 = 16 + 9$$
$$x^2 + 6x + 9 = 25$$
$$(x + 3)^2 = 25$$

Now that we have completed the square, we can solve the equation using the square root property.

$$\begin{array}{ccc} x + 3 = -5 & \text{or} & x + 3 = 5 \\ x = -8 & \text{or} & x = 2 \end{array}$$

The solution set is $\{-8, 2\}$.

Now let's see the process for completing the square when the quadratic equation is given in standard form.

Example 13.3.6 Solve $x^2 - 14x + 11 = 0$ by completing the square.

Explanation. We see that the polynomial on the left side is not a perfect square trinomial, so we need to complete the square. We subtract 11 from both sides so we can add the missing term on the left.

$$x^2 - 14x + 11 = 0$$
$$x^2 - 14x = -11$$

Next comes the completing-the-square step. We need to add the correct number to both sides of the equation to make the left side a perfect square. Remember that Fact 13.3.3 states that we need to use $\left(\frac{b}{2}\right)^2$ for this. In our case, $b = -14$, so $\left(\frac{b}{2}\right)^2 = \left(\frac{-14}{2}\right)^2 = 49$

$$x^2 - 14x + 49 = -11 + 49$$
$$(x - 7)^2 = 38$$

$$\begin{array}{ccc} x - 7 = -\sqrt{38} & \text{or} & x - 7 = \sqrt{38} \end{array}$$

$$x = 7 - \sqrt{38} \qquad \text{or} \qquad x = 7 + \sqrt{38}$$

The solution set is $\{7 - \sqrt{38}, 7 + \sqrt{38}\}$.

Checkpoint 13.3.7 Complete the square to solve for y in $y^2 - 20y - 21 = 0$.

Explanation. To complete the square, first move the constant term to the right side of the equation. Then use Fact 13.3.3 to find $\left(\frac{b}{2}\right)^2$ to add to both sides.

$$y^2 - 20y - 21 = 0$$
$$y^2 - 20y = 21$$

In our case, $b = -20$, so $\left(\frac{b}{2}\right)^2 = \left(\frac{-20}{2}\right)^2 = 100$

$$y^2 - 20y + 100 = 21 + 100$$
$$(y - 10)^2 = 121$$

$$y - 10 = -11 \quad \text{or} \quad y - 10 = 11$$
$$y = -1 \quad \text{or} \quad y = 21$$

The solution set is $\{-1, 21\}$.

So far, the value of b has been even each time, which makes $\frac{b}{2}$ a whole number. When b is odd, we end up adding a fraction to both sides. Here is an example.

Example 13.3.8 Complete the square to solve for z in $z^2 - 3z - 10 = 0$.

Explanation. First move the constant term to the right side of the equation:

$$z^2 - 3z - 10 = 0$$
$$z^2 - 3z = 10$$

Next, to complete the square, we need to find the right number to add to both sides. According to Fact 13.3.3, we need to divide the value of b by 2 and then square the result to find the right number. First, divide by 2:

$$\frac{b}{2} = \frac{-3}{2} = -\frac{3}{2} \tag{13.3.1}$$

and then we square that result:

$$\left(-\frac{3}{2}\right)^2 = \frac{9}{4} \tag{13.3.2}$$

Now we can add the $\frac{9}{4}$ from Equation (13.3.2) to both sides of the equation to complete the square.

$$z^2 - 3z + \frac{9}{4} = 10 + \frac{9}{4}$$

Now, to factor the seemingly complicated expression on the left, just know that it should always factor using the number from the first step in the completing the square process, Equation (13.3.1).

$$\left(z - \frac{3}{2}\right)^2 = \frac{49}{4}$$

$$z - \frac{3}{2} = -\frac{7}{2} \quad \text{or} \quad z - \frac{3}{2} = \frac{7}{2}$$

$$z = \frac{3}{2} - \frac{7}{2} \quad \text{or} \quad z = \frac{3}{2} + \frac{7}{2}$$

$$z = -\frac{4}{2} \quad \text{or} \quad z = \frac{10}{2}$$

$$z = -2 \quad \text{or} \quad z = 5$$

The solution set is $\{-2, 5\}$.

In each of the previous examples, the value of a was equal to 1. This is necessary for our missing term formula to work. When a is not equal to 1 we will divide both sides by a. Let's look at an example of that.

Example 13.3.9 Solve for r in $2r^2 + 2r = 3$ by completing the square.

Explanation. Because there is a leading coefficient of 2, we divide both sides by 2.

$$2r^2 + 2r = 3$$

$$\frac{2r^2}{2} + \frac{2r}{2} = \frac{3}{2}$$

$$r^2 + r = \frac{3}{2}$$

Next, we complete the square. Since $b = 1$, first,

$$\frac{b}{2} = \frac{1}{2} \tag{13.3.3}$$

and next, squaring that, we have

$$\left(\frac{1}{2}\right)^2 = \frac{1}{4}. \tag{13.3.4}$$

So we add $\frac{1}{4}$ from Equation (13.3.4) to both sides of the equation:

$$r^2 + r + \frac{1}{4} = \frac{3}{2} + \frac{1}{4}$$

$$r^2 + r + \frac{1}{4} = \frac{6}{4} + \frac{1}{4}$$

Here, remember that we always factor with the number found in the first step of completing the square, Equation (13.3.3).

$$\left(r + \frac{1}{2}\right)^2 = \frac{7}{4}$$

$$r + \frac{1}{2} = -\frac{\sqrt{7}}{2} \quad \text{or} \quad r + \frac{1}{2} = \frac{\sqrt{7}}{2}$$

$$r = -\frac{1}{2} - \frac{\sqrt{7}}{2} \quad \text{or} \quad r = -\frac{1}{2} + \frac{\sqrt{7}}{2}$$

$$r = \frac{-1 - \sqrt{7}}{2} \quad \text{or} \quad r = \frac{-1 + \sqrt{7}}{2}$$

The solution set is $\left\{\frac{-1-\sqrt{7}}{2}, \frac{-1+\sqrt{7}}{2}\right\}$.

13.3.2 Deriving the Quadratic Formula by Completing the Square

In Section 7.2, we learned the Quadratic Formula. You may have wondered where the formula comes from, and now that we know how to complete the square, we can derive it. We will solve the standard form equation $ax^2 + bx + c = 0$ for x.

First, we subtract c from both sides and divide both sides by a.

$$ax^2 + bx + c = 0$$
$$ax^2 + bx = -c$$
$$\frac{ax^2}{a} + \frac{bx}{a} = -\frac{c}{a}$$
$$x^2 + \frac{b}{a}x = -\frac{c}{a}$$

Next, we complete the square by taking half of the middle coefficient and squaring it. First,

$$\frac{\frac{b}{a}}{2} = \frac{b}{2a} \tag{13.3.5}$$

and then squaring that we have

$$\left(\frac{b}{2a}\right)^2 = \frac{b^2}{4a^2} \tag{13.3.6}$$

We add the $\frac{b^2}{4a^2}$ from Equation (13.3.6) to both sides of the equation:

$$x^2 + \frac{b}{a}x + \frac{b^2}{4a^2} = +\frac{b^2}{4a^2} - \frac{c}{a}$$

Remember that the left side always factors with the value we found in Equation (13.3.5). So we have:

$$\left(x + \frac{b}{2a}\right)^2 = \frac{b^2}{4a^2} - \frac{c}{a}$$

To find a common denominator on the right, we multiply by 4a in the numerator and denominator on the second term.

$$\left(x + \frac{b}{2a}\right)^2 = \frac{b^2}{4a^2} - \frac{c}{a} \cdot \frac{4a}{4a}$$
$$\left(x + \frac{b}{2a}\right)^2 = \frac{b^2}{4a^2} - \frac{4ac}{4a^2}$$
$$\left(x + \frac{b}{2a}\right)^2 = \frac{b^2 - 4ac}{4a^2}$$

Now that we have completed the square, we can see that the x-value of the vertex is $-\frac{b}{2a}$. That is the vertex formula. Next, we solve the equation using the square root property to find the Quadratic Formula.

$$x + \frac{b}{2a} = \pm\sqrt{\frac{b^2 - 4ac}{4a^2}}$$

$$x + \frac{b}{2a} = \pm\frac{\sqrt{b^2 - 4ac}}{2a}$$

$$x = -\frac{b}{2a} \pm \frac{\sqrt{b^2 - 4ac}}{2a}$$

$$x = \frac{-b \pm \sqrt{b^2 - 4ac}}{2a}$$

This shows us that the solutions to the equation $ax^2 + bx + c = 0$ are $\frac{-b \pm \sqrt{b^2 - 4ac}}{2a}$.

13.3.3 Putting Quadratic Functions in Vertex Form

In Section 13.2, we learned about the vertex form of a parabola, which allows us to quickly read the coordinates of the vertex. We can now use the method of completing the square to put a quadratic function in vertex form. Completing the square with a function is a little different than with an equation so we will start with an example.

Example 13.3.10 Write a formula in vertex form for the function q defined by $q(x) = x^2 + 8x$

Explanation.   The formula is in the form $x^2 + bx$, so we need to add $\left(\frac{b}{2}\right)^2$ to complete the square by Fact 13.3.3. When we had an equation, we could add the same quantity to both sides. But now we do not wish to change the left side, since we are trying to end up with a formula that still says $q(x) = \ldots$. Instead, we add *and subtract* the term from the right side in order to maintain equality. In this case,

$$\left(\frac{b}{2}\right)^2 = \left(\frac{8}{2}\right)^2$$
$$= 4^2$$
$$= 16$$

To maintain equality, we both add *and* subtract 16 on the same side of the equation. It is functionally the same as adding 0 on the right, but the 16 makes it possible to factor the expression in a particular way:

$$q(x) = x^2 + 8x + 16 - 16$$
$$= \left(x^2 + 8x + 16\right) - 16$$
$$= (x + 4)^2 - 16$$

Now that we have completed the square, our function is in vertex form. The vertex is $(-4, -16)$. One way to verify that our work is correct is to graph the original version of the function and check that the vertex is where it should be.

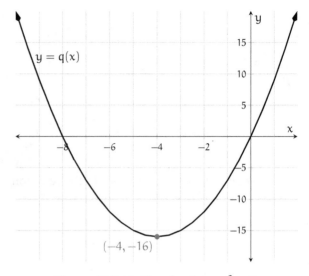

Figure 13.3.11: Graph of $y = x^2 + 8x$

Let's look at a function that has a constant term and see how to complete the square.

Example 13.3.12 Write a formula in vertex form for the function f defined by $f(x) = x^2 - 12x + 3$

Explanation.   To complete the square, we need to add and subtract $\left(-\frac{12}{2}\right)^2 = (-6)^2 = 36$ on the right side.

$$f(x) = x^2 - 12x + 36 - 36 + 3$$
$$= \left(x^2 - 12x + 36\right) - 36 + 3$$
$$= (x - 6)^2 - 33$$

The vertex is $(6, -33)$.

In the first two examples, a was equal to 1. When a is not equal to one, we have an additional step. Since we are working with an expression where we intend to preserve the left side as $f(x) = \ldots$, we cannot divide both sides by a. Instead we factor a out of the first two terms. Let's look at an example of that.

Example 13.3.13 Write a formula in vertex form for the function g defined by $g(x) = 5x^2 + 20x + 25$

Explanation.   Before we can complete the square, we factor the 5 out of the first two terms.

$$g(x) = 5\left(x^2 + 4x\right) + 25$$

Now we complete the square inside the parentheses by adding and subtracting $\left(\frac{4}{2}\right)^2 = 2^2 = 4$.

$$g(x) = 5\left(x^2 + 4x + 4 - 4\right) + 25$$

Notice that the constant that we subtracted is inside the parentheses, but it will not be part of our perfect square trinomial. In order to bring it outside, we need to multiply it by 5. We are distributing the 5 to that term so we can combine it with the outside term.

$$g(x) = 5\left(\left(x^2 + 4x + 4\right) - 4\right) + 25$$
$$= 5(x^2 + 4x + 4) - 5 \cdot 4 + 25$$

$$= 5(x+2)^2 - 20 + 25$$
$$= 5(x+2)^2 + 5$$

The vertex is $(-2, 5)$.

Here is an example that includes fractions.

Example 13.3.14 Write a formula in vertex form for the function h defined by $h(x) = -3x^2 - 4x - \frac{7}{4}$.

Explanation. First, we factor the leading coefficient out of the first two terms.

$$h(x) = -3x^2 - 4x - \frac{7}{4}$$
$$= -3\left(x^2 + \frac{4}{3}x\right) - \frac{7}{4}$$

Next, we complete the square for $x^2 + \frac{4}{3}x$ inside the grouping symbols by adding and subtracting the right number. To find that number, we divide the value of b by two and square the result. That looks like:

$$\frac{b}{2} = \frac{\frac{4}{3}}{2} = \frac{4}{3} \cdot \frac{1}{2} = \frac{2}{3} \tag{13.3.7}$$

and then,

$$\left(\frac{2}{3}\right)^2 = \frac{2^2}{3^2} = \frac{4}{9} \tag{13.3.8}$$

Adding and subtracting the value from Equation (13.3.8), we have:

$$h(x) = -3\left(x^2 + \frac{4}{3}x + \frac{4}{9} - \frac{4}{9}\right) - \frac{7}{4}$$
$$= -3\left(\left(x^2 + \frac{4}{3}x + \frac{4}{9}\right) - \frac{4}{9}\right) - \frac{7}{4}$$
$$= -3\left(x^2 + \frac{4}{3}x + \frac{4}{9}\right) - \left(3 \cdot -\frac{4}{9}\right) - \frac{7}{4}$$

Remember that when completing the square, the expression should always factor with the number found in the first step of the completing-the-square process, Equation (13.3.7).

$$= -3\left(x + \frac{2}{3}\right)^2 + \frac{4}{3} - \frac{7}{4}$$
$$= -3\left(x + \frac{2}{3}\right)^2 + \frac{16}{12} - \frac{21}{12}$$
$$= -3\left(x + \frac{2}{3}\right)^2 - \frac{5}{12}$$

The vertex is $\left(-\frac{2}{3}, -\frac{5}{12}\right)$.

Completing the square can also be used to find a minimum or maximum in an application.

Example 13.3.15 In Example 5.4.16, we learned that artist Tyrone's annual income from paintings can be modeled by $I(x) = -100x^2 + 1000x + 20000$, where x is the number of times he will raise the price per painting by \$20.00. To maximize his income, how should Tyrone set his price per painting? Find the maximum by completing the square.

Explanation. To find the maximum is essentially the same as finding the vertex, which we can find by completing the square. To complete the square for $I(x) = -100x^2 + 1000x + 20000$, we start by factoring out the -100 from the first two terms:

$$\begin{aligned} I(x) &= -100x^2 + 1000x + 20000 \\ &= -100\left(x^2 - 10x\right) + 20000 \end{aligned}$$

Next, we complete the square for $x^2 - 10x$ by adding and subtracting $\left(-\frac{10}{2}\right)^2 = (-5)^2 = 25$.

$$\begin{aligned} I(x) &= -100\left(x^2 - 10x + 25 - 25\right) + 20000 \\ &= -100\left(\left(x^2 - 10x + 25\right) - 25\right) + 20000 \\ &= -100\left(x^2 - 10x + 25\right) - (100 \cdot -25) + 20000 \\ &= -100(x-5)^2 + 2500 + 20000 \\ &= -100(x-5)^2 + 22500 \end{aligned}$$

The vertex is the point $(5, 22500)$. This implies Tyrone should raise the price per painting 5 times, which is $5 \cdot 20 = 100$ dollars. He would sell $100 - 5(5) = 75$ paintings. This would make the price per painting $200 + 100 = 300$ dollars, and his annual income from paintings would become \$22,500 by this model.

13.3.4 Graphing Quadratic Functions by Hand

Now that we know how to put a quadratic function in vertex form, let's review how to graph a parabola by hand.

Example 13.3.16 Graph the function h defined by $h(x) = 2x^2 + 4x - 6$ by determining its key features algebraically.

Explanation. To start, we'll note that this function opens upward because the leading coefficient, 2, is positive.

Now we may complete the square to find the vertex. We factor the 2 out of the first two terms, and then add and subtract $\left(\frac{2}{2}\right)^2 = 1^2 = 1$ on the right side.

$$\begin{aligned} h(x) &= 2\left(x^2 + 2x\right) - 6 \\ &= 2\left[x^2 + 2x + 1 - 1\right] - 6 \\ &= 2\left[\left(x^2 + 2x + 1\right) - 1\right] - 6 \\ &= 2\left(x^2 + 2x + 1\right) - (2 \cdot 1) - 6 \\ &= 2\left(x + 1\right)^2 - 2 - 6 \\ &= 2\left(x + 1\right)^2 - 8 \end{aligned}$$

The vertex is $(-1, -8)$ so the axis of symmetry is the line $x = -1$.

To find the y-intercept, we'll replace x with 0 or read the value of c from the function in standard form:

$$h(0) = 2(0)^2 + 2(0) - 6$$
$$= -6$$

The y-intercept is $(0, -6)$ and we can find its symmetric point on the graph, which is $(-2, -6)$.

Next, we'll find the horizontal intercepts. We see this function factors so we write the factored form to get the horizontal intercepts.

$$h(x) = 2x^2 + 4x - 6$$
$$= 2\left(x^2 + 2x - 3\right)$$
$$= 2(x - 1)(x + 3)$$

The x-intercepts are $(1, 0)$ and $(-3, 0)$.

Now we plot all of the key points and draw the parabola.

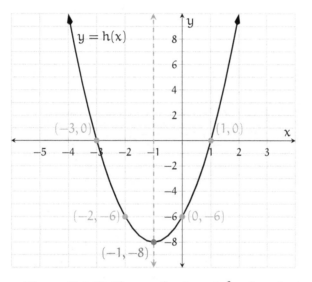

Figure 13.3.17: The graph of $y = 2x^2 + 4x - 6$.

Example 13.3.18 Write a formula in vertex form for the function p defined by $p(x) = -x^2 - 4x - 1$, and find the graph's key features algebraically. Then sketch the graph.

Explanation.   In this function, the leading coefficient is negative so it will open downward. To complete the square we first factor -1 out of the first two terms.

$$p(x) = -x^2 - 4x - 1$$
$$= -\left(x^2 + 4x\right) - 1$$

Now, we add and subtract the correct number on the right side of the function: $\left(\frac{b}{2}\right)^2 = \left(\frac{4}{2}\right)^2 = 2^2 = 4$.

$$p(x) = -\left(x^2 + 4x + 4 - 4\right) - 1$$
$$= -\left(\left(x^2 + 4x + 4\right) - 4\right) - 1$$

$$= -(x^2 + 4x + 4) - (-4) - 1$$
$$= -(x + 2)^2 + 4 - 1$$
$$= -(x + 2)^2 + 3$$

The vertex is $(-2, 3)$ so the axis of symmetry is the line $x = -2$.

We find the y-intercept by looking at the value of c, which is -1. So, the y-intercept is $(0, -1)$ and we can find its symmetric point on the graph, $(-4, -1)$.

The original expression, $-x^2 - 4x - 1$, does not factor so to find the x-intercepts we need to set $p(x) = 0$ and complete the square or use the quadratic formula. Since we just went through the process of completing the square above, we can use that result to save several repetitive steps.

$$p(x) = 0$$
$$-(x + 2)^2 + 3 = 0$$
$$-(x + 2)^2 = -3$$
$$(x + 2)^2 = 3$$

$x + 2 = -\sqrt{3}$	or	$x + 2 = \sqrt{3}$
$x = -2 - \sqrt{3}$	or	$x = -2 + \sqrt{3}$
$x \approx -3.73$	or	$x \approx -0.268$

The x-intercepts are approximately $(-3.7, 0)$ and $(-0.3, 0)$. Now we can plot all of the points and draw the parabola.

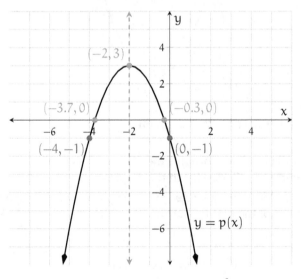

Figure 13.3.19: The graph of $y = -x^2 - 4x - 1$.

13.3.5 Reading Questions

1. For the expression $y = x^2 + 10x - 9$, explain in words what is the next step to complete the square.

2. Why is completing the square called completing the square?

3. How can you check that they completed the square correctly?

13.3.6 Exercises

Review and Warmup

1. Use a square root to solve $(t + 6)^2 = 16$.

2. Use a square root to solve $(x - 1)^2 = 49$.

3. Use a square root to solve $(3x - 7)^2 = 49$.

4. Use a square root to solve $(8y + 1)^2 = 25$.

5. Use a square root to solve $(y - 1)^2 = 19$.

6. Use a square root to solve $(r - 8)^2 = 7$.

7. Use a square root to solve $r^2 + 8r + 16 = 64$.

8. Use a square root to solve $r^2 - 4r + 4 = 9$.

9. Use a square root to solve $4t^2 + 8t + 4 = 4$.

10. Use a square root to solve $49t^2 - 126t + 81 = 49$.

11. Use a square root to solve $16x^2 - 8x + 1 = 10$.

12. Use a square root to solve $81x^2 + 126x + 49 = 5$.

Completing the Square to Solve Equations Solve the equation by completing the square.

13. $y^2 - 6y = 16$

14. $y^2 - 4y = -3$

15. $r^2 - 5r = -6$

16. $r^2 - 3r = -2$

17. $r^2 + 6r = -2$

18. $t^2 + 10t = 3$

19. $t^2 - 6t + 5 = 0$

20. $x^2 - 10x + 9 = 0$

21. $x^2 - 9x + 14 = 0$

22. $y^2 + 9y + 8 = 0$

23. $y^2 - 8y - 1 = 0$

24. $r^2 + 8r + 8 = 0$

25. $12r^2 - 44r + 35 = 0$

26. $3r^2 - 2r - 1 = 0$

27. $2t^2 + 5t - 4 = 0$

28. $2t^2 - 2t - 5 = 0$

Converting to Vertex Form

29. Consider $f(x) = x^2 + 8x - 1$.

    a. Give the formula for f in vertex form.

    b. What is the vertex of the parabola graph of f?

30. Consider $g(r) = r^2 - 2r - 3$.

    a. Give the formula for g in vertex form.

    b. What is the vertex of the parabola graph of g?

31. Consider $h(y) = y^2 + 5y + 5$.

    a. Give the formula for h in vertex form.

    b. What is the vertex of the parabola graph of h?

32. Consider $h(x) = x^2 - 5x + 2$.

    a. Give the formula for h in vertex form.

    b. What is the vertex of the parabola graph of h?

33. Consider $F(r) = 6r^2 - 12r - 2$.

    a. Give the formula for F in vertex form.

    b. What is the vertex of the parabola graph of F?

34. Consider $G(y) = 2y^2 - 16y - 2$.

    a. Give the formula for G in vertex form.

    b. What is the vertex of the parabola graph of G?

Domain and Range Complete the square to convert the quadratic function from standard form to vertex form, and use the result to find the function's domain and range.

35. $f(x) = x^2 - 10x + 15$

36. $f(x) = x^2 - 14x + 52$

37. $f(x) = -x^2 + 18x - 85$

38. $f(x) = -x^2 - 18x - 71$

39. $f(x) = 2x^2 + 28x + 100$

40. $f(x) = 4x^2 + 40x + 95$

41. $f(x) = -5x^2 - 20x - 11$

42. $f(x) = -5x^2 + 10x - 8$

Sketching Graphs of Quadratic Functions Graph each function by algebraically determining its key features. Then state the domain and range of the function.

43. $f(x) = x^2 - 7x + 12$

44. $f(x) = x^2 + 5x - 14$

45. $f(x) = -x^2 - x + 20$

46. $f(x) = -x^2 + 4x + 21$

47. $f(x) = x^2 - 8x + 16$

48. $f(x) = x^2 + 6x + 9$

49. $f(x) = x^2 - 4$

50. $f(x) = x^2 - 9$

51. $f(x) = x^2 + 6x$

52. $f(x) = x^2 - 8x$

53. $f(x) = -x^2 + 5x$

54. $f(x) = -x^2 + 16$

55. $f(x) = x^2 + 4x + 7$

56. $f(x) = x^2 - 2x + 6$

57. $f(x) = x^2 + 2x - 5$

58. $f(x) = x^2 - 6x + 2$

59. $f(x) = -x^2 + 4x - 1$

60. $f(x) = -x^2 - x + 3$

61. $f(x) = 2x^2 - 4x - 30$

62. $f(x) = 3x^2 + 21x + 36$

Information from Vertex Form

63. Find the minimum value of the function

$$f(x) = 7x^2 - 6x + 6$$

64. Find the minimum value of the function

$$f(x) = 8x^2 + 8x - 6$$

65. Find the maximum value of the function

$$f(x) = x - 9x^2 + 3$$

66. Find the maximum value of the function

$$f(x) = -\left(10x^2 + 7x + 10\right)$$

67. Find the range of the function

$$f(x) = 7x - x^2 - 1$$

68. Find the range of the function

$$f(x) = 8 - 2x^2$$

69. Find the range of the function

$$f(x) = 3x^2 - 8x - 4$$

70. Find the range of the function

$$f(x) = 4x^2 + 6x + 4$$

71. If a ball is throw straight up with a speed of $60 \frac{\text{ft}}{\text{s}}$, its height at time t (in seconds) is given by

$$h(t) = -8t^2 + 60t + 2$$

Find the maximum height the ball reaches.

72. If a ball is throw straight up with a speed of $62 \frac{\text{ft}}{\text{s}}$, its height at time t (in seconds) is given by

$$h(t) = -8t^2 + 62t + 2$$

Find the maximum height the ball reaches.

Challenge

73. Let $f(x) = x^2 + bx + c$. Let b and c be real numbers. Complete the square to find the vertex of $f(x) = x^2 + bx + c$. Write $f(x)$ in vertex form and then state the vertex.

13.4 Absolute Value Equations

Whether it's a washer, nut, bolt, or gear, when a machine part is made, it must be made to fit with all of the other parts of the system. Since no manufacturing process is perfect, there are small deviations from the norm when each piece is made. In fact, manufacturers have a *range* of acceptable values for each measurement of every screw, bolt, etc.

Let's say we were examining some new bolts just out of the factory. The manufacturer specifies that each bolt should be within a *tolerance* of 0.04 mm to 10 mm in diameter. So the lowest diameter that the bolt could be to make it through quality assurance is 0.04 mm smaller than 10 mm, which is 9.96 mm. Similarly, the largest diameter that the bolt could be is 0.04 mm larger than 10 mm, which is 10.04 mm.

To write an equation that describes the minimum and maximum deviation from average, we want the difference between the actual diameter and the specification to be equal to 0.04 mm. Since absolute values are used to describe distances, we can summarize our thoughts mathematically as $|x - 10| = 0.04$, where x represents the diameter of an acceptably sized bolt, in millimeters. This equation says the same thing as the lowest diameter that the bolt could be to make it through quality assurance is 9.96 mm and the largest diameter that the bolt could be is 10.04 mm.

In this section we will examine a variety of problems that relate to this sort of math with absolute values.

13.4.1 Graphs of Absolute Value Functions

Absolute value functions have generally the same shape. They are usually described as "V"-shaped graphs and the tip of the "V" is called the **vertex**. A few graphs of various absolute value functions are shown in Figure 13.4.2. In general, the domain of an absolute value function (where there is a polynomial inside the absolute value) is $(-\infty, \infty)$.

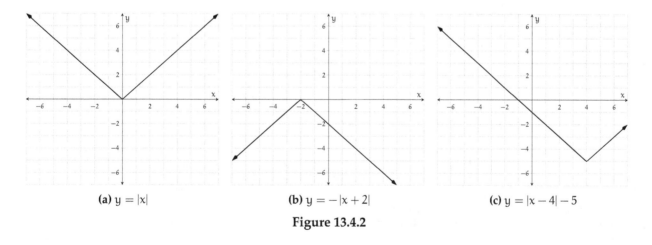

(a) $y = |x|$ **(b)** $y = -|x + 2|$ **(c)** $y = |x - 4| - 5$

Figure 13.4.2

Example 13.4.3 Let $h(x) = -2|x - 3| + 5$. Using technology, create table of values with x-values from -3 to 3, using an increment of 1. Then sketch a graph of $y = h(x)$. State the domain and range of h.

Explanation.

x	y
−3	−7
−2	−5
−1	−3
0	−1
1	1
2	3
3	5

Figure 13.4.4: Table for $y = h(x)$.

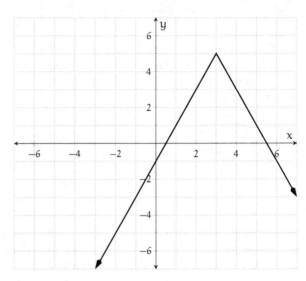

Figure 13.4.5: Graph of $y = h(x)$

The graph indicates that the domain is (∞, ∞) as it goes to the right and left indefinitely. The range is $(-\infty, 5]$.

Example 13.4.6 Let $j(x) = \left| |x + 1| - 2 \right| - 1$. Using technology, create table of values with x-values from −5 to 5, using an increment of 1 and sketch a graph of $y = j(x)$. State the domain and range of j.

Explanation.   This is a strange one because it has an absolute value within an absolute value.

x	y
−5	1
−4	0
−3	−1
−2	0
−1	1
0	0
1	−1
2	0
3	1
4	2
5	3

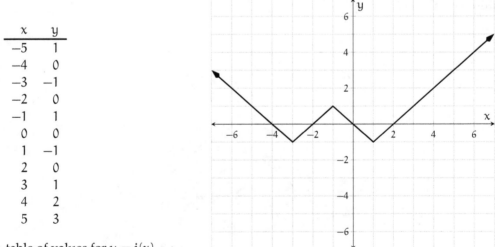

Figure 13.4.7: A table of values for $y = j(x)$.

Figure 13.4.8: $y = \left| |x + 1| - 2 \right| - 1$

The graph indicates that the domain is (∞, ∞) as it goes to the right and left indefinitely. The range is $[-1, \infty)$.

13.4.2 Solving Absolute Value Equations with One Absolute Value

We can solve absolute value equations graphically.

Example 13.4.9 Solve the equations graphically using the graphs provided.

a. $|x| = 3$ b. $|2x + 3| = 5$

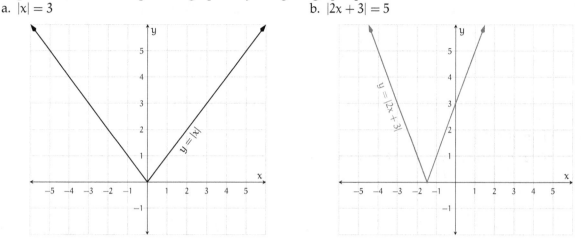

Explanation. To solve the equations graphically, first we need to graph the right sides of the equations also.

a. $|x| = 3$ b. $|2x + 3| = 5$

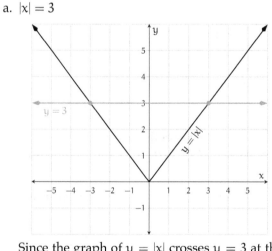

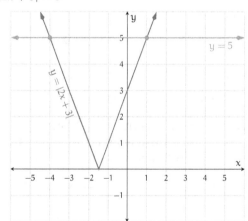

Since the graph of $y = |x|$ crosses $y = 3$ at the x-values -3 and 3, the solution set to the equation $|x| = 3$ must be $\{-3, 3\}$.

Since the graph of $y = |2x + 3|$ crosses $y = 5$ at the x-values -4 and 1, the solution set to the equation $|2x + 3| = 5$ must be $\{-4, 1\}$.

Remark 13.4.10 Please note that there is a big difference between the expression $|3|$ and the equation $|x| = 3$.

1. The expression $|3|$ is describing the distance from 0 to the number 3. The distance is just 3. So $|3| = 3$.

2. The equation $|x| = 3$ is asking you to find the numbers that are a distance of 3 from 0. These two numbers are 3 and -3.

Let's solve some absolute value equations algebraically. To motivate this, we will think about what an absolute value equation means in terms of the "distance from zero" definition of absolute value. If

$$|X| = n,$$

where $n \geq 0$, then this means that we want all of the numbers, X, that are a distance n from 0. Since we can only go left or right along the number line, this is describing both $X = n$ as well as $X = -n$.

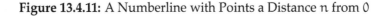

Figure 13.4.11: A Numberline with Points a Distance n from 0

Let's summarize this.

Fact 13.4.12 Equations with an Absolute Value Expression. *Let n be a non-negative number and X be an algebraic expression. Then the equation*

$$|X| = n$$

has the same solutions as

$$X = n \text{ or } X = -n.$$

Example 13.4.13 Solve the absolute value equations using Fact 13.4.12. Write solutions in a solution set.

   a. $|x| = 6$ c. $|5x - 7| = 23$ e. $|3 - 4x| = 0$

   b. $|x| = -4$ d. $|14 - 3x| = 8$

Explanation.

   a. Fact 13.4.12 says that the equation $|x| = 6$ is the same as

$$x = 6 \text{ or } x = -6.$$

Thus the solution set is $\{6, -6\}$.

   b. Fact 13.4.12 doesn't actually apply to the equation $|x| = -4$ because the value on the right side is *negative*. How often is an absolute value of a number negative? Never! Thus, there are no solutions and the solution set is the empty set, denoted $\emptyset$.

   c. The equation $|5x - 7| = 23$ breaks into two pieces, each of which needs to be solved independently.

$$
\begin{aligned}
5x - 7 &= 23 &\quad \text{or} \quad& & 5x - 7 &= -23 \\
5x &= 30 &\quad \text{or} \quad& & 5x &= -16 \\
x &= 6 &\quad \text{or} \quad& & x &= -\frac{16}{5}
\end{aligned}
$$

Thus the solution set is $\left\{6, -\frac{16}{5}\right\}$.

   d. The equation $|14 - 3x| = 8$ breaks into two pieces, each of which needs to be solved independently.

$$
\begin{aligned}
14 - 3x &= 8 &\quad \text{or} \quad& & 14 - 3x &= -8 \\
-3x &= -6 &\quad \text{or} \quad& & -3x &= -22
\end{aligned}
$$

$$x = 2 \qquad \text{or} \qquad x = \frac{22}{3}$$

Thus the solution set is $\left\{2, \frac{22}{3}\right\}$.

e. The equation $|3 - 4x| = 0$ breaks into two pieces, each of which needs to be solved independently.

$$3 - 4x = 0 \qquad \text{or} \qquad 3 - 4x = -0$$

Since these are identical equations, all we have to do is solve one equation.

$$3 - 4x = 0$$
$$-4x = -3$$
$$x = \frac{3}{4}$$

Thus, the equation $|3 - 4x| = 0$ only has one solution, and the solution set is $\left\{\frac{3}{4}\right\}$.

13.4.3 Solving Absolute Value Equations with Two Absolute Values

Example 13.4.14 Let's graphically solve an equation with an absolute value expression on each side: $|x| = |2x + 6|$. Since $|x| = 3$ had two solutions as we saw in Example 13.4.9, you might be wondering how many solutions $|x| = |2x + 6|$ will have. Make a graph to find out what the solutions of the equation are.

Explanation.

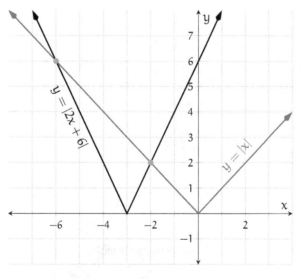

Figure 13.4.15: $y = |x|$ and $y = |2x + 6|$

Figure 13.4.15 shows that there are also two points of intersection between the graphs of $y = |x|$ and $y = |2x + 6|$. The solutions to the equation $|x| = |2x + 6|$ are the x-values where the graphs cross. So, the solution set is $\{-6, -2\}$.

Example 13.4.16 Solve the equation $|x + 1| = |2x - 4|$ graphically.

Explanation.

First break up the equation into the left side and the right side and graph each separately, as in $y = |x + 1|$ and $y = |2x - 4|$. We can see in the graph that the graphs intersect twice. The x-values of those intersections are 1 and 5 so the solution set to the equation $|x + 1| = |2x - 4|$ is $\{1, 5\}$.

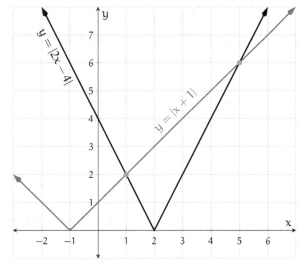

Figure 13.4.17: $y = |x + 1|$ and $y = |2x - 4|$

Fortunately, this kind of equation also has a rule to solve these types of equations algebraically that is similar to the rule for equations with one absolute value.

Fact 13.4.18 Equations with Two Absolute Value Expressions. *Let X and Y be linear algebraic expressions. Then, the equation*

$$|X| = |Y|$$

has the same solutions as

$$X = Y \text{ or } X = -Y.$$

Remark 13.4.19 You might wonder why the negative sign "has" to go on the right side of the equation in $X = -Y$. It doesn't; it can go on either side of the equation. The equations $X = -Y$ and $-X = Y$ are equivalent. Similarly, $-X = -Y$ is equivalent to $X = Y$. That's why we only need to solve two of the four possible equations.

Example 13.4.20 Solve the equations using Fact 13.4.18.
  a. $|x - 4| = |3x - 2|$ c. $|x - 2| = |x + 1|$

  b. $\left|\frac{1}{2}x + 1\right| = \left|\frac{1}{3}x + 2\right|$ d. $|x - 1| = |1 - x|$

Explanation.

  a. The equation $|x - 4| = |3x - 2|$ breaks down into two pieces:

$$
\begin{array}{ccc}
x - 4 = 3x - 2 & \text{or} & x - 4 = -(3x - 2) \\
x - 4 = 3x - 2 & \text{or} & x - 4 = -3x + 2 \\
-2 = 2x & \text{or} & 4x = 6 \\
\dfrac{-2}{2} = \dfrac{2x}{2} & \text{or} & \dfrac{4x}{4} = \dfrac{6}{4}
\end{array}
$$

$$-1 = x \qquad \text{or} \qquad x = \frac{3}{2}$$

So, the solution set is $\left\{-1, \frac{3}{2}\right\}$.

b. The equation $\left|\frac{1}{2}x + 1\right| = \left|\frac{1}{3}x + 2\right|$ breaks down into two pieces:

$$\frac{1}{2}x + 1 = \frac{1}{3}x + 2 \qquad \text{or} \qquad \frac{1}{2}x + 1 = -\left(\frac{1}{3}x + 2\right)$$

$$\frac{1}{2}x + 1 = \frac{1}{3}x + 2 \qquad \text{or} \qquad \frac{1}{2}x + 1 = -\frac{1}{3}x - 2$$

$$6 \cdot \left(\frac{1}{2}x + 1\right) = 6 \cdot \left(\frac{1}{3}x + 2\right) \qquad \text{or} \qquad 6 \cdot \left(\frac{1}{2}x + 1\right) = 6 \cdot \left(-\frac{1}{3}x - 2\right)$$

$$3x + 6 = 2x + 12 \qquad \text{or} \qquad 3x + 6 = -2x - 12$$

$$x = 6 \qquad \text{or} \qquad 5x = -18$$

$$x = 6 \qquad \text{or} \qquad x = -\frac{18}{5}$$

So, the solution set is $\left\{6, -\frac{18}{5}\right\}$.

c. The equation $|x - 2| = |x + 1|$ breaks down into two pieces:

$$x - 2 = x + 1 \qquad \text{or} \qquad x - 2 = -(x + 1)$$

$$x - 2 = x + 1 \qquad \text{or} \qquad x - 2 = -x - 1$$

$$x = x + 3 \qquad \text{or} \qquad 2x = 1$$

$$0 = 3 \qquad \text{or} \qquad x = \frac{1}{2}$$

Note that one of the two pieces gives us an equation with no solutions. Since $0 \neq 3$, we can safely ignore this piece. Thus the only solution is $\frac{1}{2}$.

We should visualize this equation graphically because our previous assumption was that two absolute value graphs would cross twice. The graph shows why there is only one crossing: the left and right sides of each "V" are parallel.

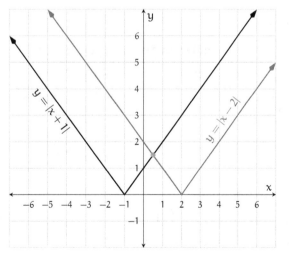

d. The equation $|x - 1| = |1 - x|$ breaks down into two pieces:

$x - 1 = 1 - x$	or	$x - 1 = -(1 - x)$
$x - 1 = 1 - x$	or	$x - 1 = -1 + x$
$2x = 2$	or	$x = 0 + x$
$x = 1$	or	$0 = 0$

Note that our second equation is an identity so recall from Section 2.4 that the solution set is "all real numbers."

So, our two pieces have solutions 1 and "all real numbers." Since 1 *is* a real number and we have an *or* statement, our overall solution set is $(-\infty, \infty)$. The graph confirms our answer since the two "V" graphs are coinciding.

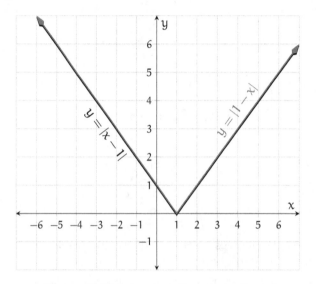

Figure 13.4.21: $y = |x - 1|$ and $y = |1 - x|$

13.4.4 Reading Questions

1. How many solutions does an absolute value equation typically have?

2. The graph of an absolute value function is typically shaped like which letter?

3. Solving an absolute value equation like $|2x + 1| = 3$ is "easy" because we can turn it into two equations of what simpler type?

13.4.5 Exercises

Review and Warmup Solve the equation.

1. $\dfrac{n}{5} - 6 = \dfrac{n}{8}$

2. $\dfrac{q}{3} - 2 = \dfrac{q}{9}$

3. $56 = -8(x + 3)$

4. $-60 = -5(r + 7)$

5. $2t + 7 = 9t + 6$

6. $2b + 3 = 8b + 2$

Solving Absolute Value Equations Algebraically

7. a. Write the equation $5 = |7x| - 4$ as two separate equations. Neither of your equations should use absolute value.

   [ ]
   [ ]

   b. Solve both equations above.

8. a. Write the equation $6 = |4x| - 7$ as two separate equations. Neither of your equations should use absolute value.

   [ ]
   [ ]

   b. Solve both equations above.

9. a. Write the equation $\left|6 - \dfrac{r}{5}\right| = 7$ as two separate equations. Neither of your equations should use absolute value.

   [ ]
   [ ]

   b. Solve both equations above.

10. a. Write the equation $\left|8 - \dfrac{r}{3}\right| = 7$ as two separate equations. Neither of your equations should use absolute value.

    [ ]
    [ ]

    b. Solve both equations above.

11.
   (a) Verify that the value -1 is a solution to the absolute value equation $\left|\frac{x-3}{2}\right| = 2$.

   (b) Verify that the value $\frac{2}{3}$ is a solution to the absolute value inequality $|6x - 5| < 4$.

12.
   (a) Verify that the value 8 is a solution to the absolute value equation $\left|\frac{1}{2}x - 2\right| = 2$.

   (b)

13. Solve the following equation.
    $|10x + 9| = 6$

14. Solve the following equation.
    $|x + 1| = 10$

15. Solve the equation $|2x - 2| = 14$.

16. Solve the equation $|3x + 3| = 18$.

17. Solve: $|b| = 7$

18. Solve: $|t| = 3$

19. Solve: $|x - 7| = 9$

20. Solve: $|x - 3| = 13$

21. Solve: $|2y + 1| = 17$

22. Solve: $|2y + 7| = 11$

23. Solve: $\left|\dfrac{2a - 3}{7}\right| = 1$

24. Solve: $\left|\dfrac{2a - 1}{3}\right| = 3$

25. Solve: $|b| = -6$

26. Solve: $|b| = -8$

27. Solve: $|t + 2| = 0$

28. Solve: $|x + 4| = 0$

29. Solve: $|2 - 3x| = 7$

30. Solve: $|2 - 3y| = 11$

31. Solve: $\left|\frac{1}{4}y + 1\right| = 5$

32. Solve: $\left|\frac{1}{2}a + 5\right| = 3$

33. Solve: $|0.9 - 0.8a| = 2$

34. Solve: $|0.6 - 0.2b| = 5$

35. Solve: $|b + 3| - 6 = 6$

36. Solve: $|t + 9| - 2 = 4$

37. Solve: $|4t - 12| + 2 = 2$

38. Solve: $|2x - 10| + 7 = 7$

39. Solve: $|y + 9| + 7 = 4$

40. Solve: $|y + 5| + 8 = 6$

41. Solve: $|6a + 1| + 3 = 2$

42. Solve: $|6a + 9| + 8 = 4$

43. Solve the equation *by inspection* (meaning in your head).
    $|5x + 15| = 0$

44. Solve the equation *by inspection* (meaning in your head).
    $|5x + 10| = 0$

45. The equation $|x| = |y|$ is satisfied if $x = y$ or $x = -y$. Use this fact to solve the following equation.
$|3x + 4| = |4x + 3|$

46. The equation $|x| = |y|$ is satisfied if $x = y$ or $x = -y$. Use this fact to solve the following equation.
$|4x - 4| = |-x + 4|$

47. The equation $|x| = |y|$ is satisfied if $x = y$ or $x = -y$. Use this fact to solve the following equation.
$|x + 6| = |x - 5|$

48. The equation $|x| = |y|$ is satisfied if $x = y$ or $x = -y$. Use this fact to solve the following equation.
$|x + 6| = |x - 1|$

49. Solve the equation: $|8x - 5| = |7x + 8|$

50. Solve the equation: $|2x - 2| = |9x + 6|$

51. Solve the following equation.
$|x + 4| = |7x - 5|$

52. Solve the following equation.
$|2x - 3| = |10x + 10|$

Challenge

53. Algebraically, solve for x in the equation:

$$5 = |x - 5| + |x - 10|$$

13.5 Solving Mixed Equations

In this section, we will learn to differentiate between different types of equations and recall the various methods used to solve them. Real life doesn't come with instructions, so it is important to develop the skills in this section. One day, you might be faced with a geometry problem in your home or a rational equation in a lab, and it will be your challenge to solve the equation with some strategy.

We have solved a variety of equations throughout this book, and we covered some general equation-solving strategies in Solving Equations in General. Since then, we have covered even more topics, and it seems time to refresh ourselves on everything that we have done so far. Here is a reference guide to all of the sections that cover solving equations. We hope that this section will help pinpoint those that you need help with.

Section 2.1 Solving linear equations.

Section 2.5 Solving linear equations with more than one variable.

Sections 4.2, 4.3 Algebraically solving systems of linear equations.

Section 6.4 Solving equations with roots in them.

Sections 7.1, 7.2, 10.7, 13.3 Solving quadratic equations.

Section 12.5 Solving rational equations.

13.5.1 Types of Equations

The point of this section isn't to compartmentalize your knowledge to help learn small pieces, it's to put all the pieces that we've learned previously together and how to differentiate those pieces from one another. To do that, we need to recall the different types of equations that we have had before.

Linear Equation This is a type of equation where the variable that we are solving for only appears with addition, subtraction, multiplication and division by constant numbers. Examples are $7(x-2) = \frac{3}{5}x+1$ and $rt = 4t+3r-1$ where r is the variable and t is considered a constant. Use the Steps to Solve Linear Equations.

System of Linear Equations This is a grouping of two linear equations. An example is

$$\begin{cases} y = 3x + 1 \\ y = 2x - 5 \end{cases}$$

One can use either substitution or elimination to solve these systems.

Quadratic Equation This is a type of equation where at least one side of the equation is a quadratic function, and the other side is either constant, linear, or quadratic with a different leading coefficient. Examples are $3x^2 + 2x - 4 = 0$ and $6(y-2)^2 - 1 = 7$. There are several methods to solve quadratic equations including using the square root method, the quadratic formula, factoring, and completing the square.

Radical Equation This is a type of equation where the variable is inside a root of some kind. We usually solve radical equations by isolating the radical and raising both sides to a power to cancel the radical.

Rational Equation This is a type of equation where both sides of the equation are rational functions, although it's possible one side is a very simple rational function like a constant function. Solving these equations involves clearing the denominators and solving the equation that remains.

Absolute Value Equation This is a type of equation where the variable is inside absolute value bars. Solving these equations involves using a rule to convert an equation from absolute value into two separate equations without absolute values.

For all of these equation types, in this section we only concern ourselves with equations in one variable, i.e. the solution will be a number or expression rather than points. For example, the equation $3 = 2x + 5$ has a single solution, -1, whereas the equation $y = 2x + 5$ has infinitely many solutions, all points, that make up the line with slope 2 and vertical intercept $(0, 5)$. The only exceptions that we will be covering are systems of linear equations, which have a point or points as solutions.

Example 13.5.2 Identify the type of equation as linear, a system of linear equations, quadratic, radical, rational, absolute value, or something else.

a. $3 - \sqrt{2x - 3} = x$

b. $2x^2 + 3x = 7$

c. $7 - 2(3x - 5) = x + \sqrt{2}$

d. $\frac{1}{x-2} + \frac{x}{x^2-4} = \frac{3}{x+2}$

e. $|5x - 9| + 2 = 7$

f. $(4x - 1)^2 + 9 = 16$

g. $\sqrt[3]{6x - 5} = 2$

h. $6x^2 - 7x = 20$

i. $\begin{cases} 4x + 2y = 8 \\ 3x - y = 11 \end{cases}$

j. $3^x + 2^x = 1$

Explanation.

a. The equation $3 - \sqrt{2x - 3} = x$ is a radical equation since the variable appears inside the radical.

b. The equation $2x^2 + 3x = 7$ is a quadratic equation since the variable is being squared (but doesn't have any higher power).

c. The equation $7 - 2(3x - 5) = x + \sqrt{2}$ is a linear equation since the variable is only to the first power. The square root in the equation is only on the number 2 and not x, so it doesn't make it a radical equation.

d. The equation $\frac{1}{x-2} + \frac{x}{x^2-4} = \frac{3}{x+2}$ is a rational equation since the variable is present in a denominator.

e. The equation $|5x - 9| + 2 = 7$ is an absolute value equation since the variable is inside an absolute value.

f. The equation $(4x - 1)^2 + 9 = 16$ is a quadratic equation since if we were to distribute everything out, we would have a term with x^2.

g. The equation $\sqrt[3]{6x - 5} = 2$ is a radical equation since the variable is inside the radical.

h. The equation $6x^2 - 7x = 20$ is a quadratic equation since there is a degree-two term.

i. This is a system of linear equations.

j. The equation $3^x + 2^x = 1$ is an equation type that we have not covered and is not listed above.

13.5.2 Solving Mixed Equations

After you have identified which type of equation confronts you, the next step is to consider the methods for solving that type of equation.

Example 13.5.3 Solve the equations using appropriate techniques.

a. $3 - \sqrt{2x - 3} = x$

b. $2x^2 + 3x = 7$

c. $7 - 2(3x - 5) = x + \sqrt{2}$

d. $\frac{1}{x-2} + \frac{x}{x^2-4} = \frac{3}{x+2}$

e. $|5x - 9| + 2 = 7$

f. $(4x - 1)^2 + 9 = 16$

g. $\sqrt[3]{6x - 5} = 2$

h. $6x^2 - 7x = 20$

i. $\begin{cases} 4x + 2y = 8 \\ 3x - y = 11 \end{cases}$

j. $2x^2 - 12x = 7$ (using completing the square)

Explanation.

a. Since the equation $3 - \sqrt{2x - 3} = x$ is a radical equation, we can isolate the radical and then square both sides to cancel the square root. After that, we will solve whatever remains.

$$3 - \sqrt{2x - 3} = x$$
$$-\sqrt{2x - 3} = x - 3$$
$$\sqrt{2x - 3} = -x + 3$$
$$\left(\sqrt{2x - 3}\right)^2 = (-x + 3)^2$$
$$2x - 3 = x^2 - 6x + 9$$
$$0 = x^2 - 8x + 12$$

We now have a quadratic equation. We will solve by factoring.

$$0 = (x - 2)(x - 6)$$

$$\begin{array}{ccc} x - 2 = 0 & \text{or} & x - 6 = 0 \\ x = 2 & \text{or} & x = 6 \end{array}$$

Every potential solution to a radical equation should be verified to check for any "extraneous solutions".

$$\begin{array}{ccc} 3 - \sqrt{2(2) - 3} \overset{?}{=} 2 & \text{or} & 3 - \sqrt{2(6) - 3} \overset{?}{=} 6 \\ 3 - \sqrt{1} \overset{?}{=} 2 & \text{or} & 3 - \sqrt{9} \overset{?}{=} 6 \\ 3 - 1 \overset{\checkmark}{=} 2 & \text{or} & 3 - 3 \overset{\text{no}}{=} 6 \end{array}$$

So the solution set is $\{2\}$.

b. Since the equation $2x^2 + 3x = 7$ is quadratic we should consider the square root method, the quadratic formula, factoring, and completing the square. In this case, we will start with the quadratic formula. First, note that we should rearrange the terms in equation into standard form.

$$2x^2 + 3x = 7$$
$$2x^2 + 3x - 7 = 0$$

Note that $a = 2$, $b = 3$, and $c = -7$.

$$x = \frac{-b \pm \sqrt{b^2 - 4ac}}{2a}$$
$$x = \frac{-(3) \pm \sqrt{(3)^2 - 4(2)(-7)}}{2(2)}$$
$$x = \frac{-3 \pm \sqrt{9 + 56}}{4}$$
$$x = \frac{-3 \pm \sqrt{65}}{4}$$

The solution set is $\left\{ \frac{-3+\sqrt{65}}{4}, \frac{-3-\sqrt{65}}{4} \right\}$.

c. Since the equation $7 - 2(3x - 5) = x + \sqrt{2}$ is a linear equation, we isolate the variable step-by-step.

$$7 - 2(3x - 5) = x + \sqrt{2}$$
$$7 - 6x + 10 = x + \sqrt{2}$$
$$17 - 6x = x + \sqrt{2}$$
$$17 = 7x + \sqrt{2}$$
$$17 - \sqrt{2} = 7x$$
$$\frac{17 - \sqrt{2}}{7} = x$$

The solution set is $\left\{ \frac{17-\sqrt{2}}{7} \right\}$.

d. Since the equation $\frac{1}{x-2} + \frac{x}{x^2-4} = \frac{3}{x+2}$ is a rational equation, we first need to cancel the denominators after factoring and finding the least common denominator.

$$\frac{1}{x - 2} + \frac{x}{x^2 - 4} = \frac{3}{x + 2}$$
$$\frac{1}{x - 2} + \frac{x}{(x - 2)(x + 2)} = \frac{3}{x + 2}$$

At this point, we note that the least common denominator is $(x - 2)(x + 2)$. We need to multiply every term by this least common denominator.

$$\frac{1}{x - 2} \cdot (x - 2)(x + 2) + \frac{x}{(x - 2)(x + 2)} \cdot (x - 2)(x + 2) = \frac{3}{x + 2} \cdot (x - 2)(x + 2)$$

$$\frac{1}{x-2} \cdot (x-2)(x+2) + \frac{x}{(x-2)(x+2)} \cdot (x-2)(x+2) = \frac{3}{x+2} \cdot (x-2)(x+2)$$

$$1(x+2) + x = 3(x-2)$$
$$x + 2 + x = 3x - 6$$
$$2x + 2 = 3x - 6$$
$$8 = x$$

We always check solutions to rational equations to ensure we don't have any "extraneous solutions".

$$\frac{1}{8-2} + \frac{8}{8^2 - 4} \stackrel{?}{=} \frac{3}{8+2}$$
$$\frac{1}{6} + \frac{8}{60} \stackrel{?}{=} \frac{3}{10}$$
$$\frac{10}{60} + \frac{8}{60} \stackrel{?}{=} \frac{3}{10}$$
$$\frac{18}{60} \stackrel{\checkmark}{=} \frac{3}{10}$$

So, the solution set is $\{8\}$.

e. Since the equation $|5x - 9| + 2 = 7$ is an absolute value equation, we will first isolate the absolute value and then use Equations with an Absolute Value Expression to solve the remaining equation.

$$|5x - 9| + 2 = 7$$
$$|5x - 9| = 5$$

$5x - 9 = 5$	or	$5x - 9 = -5$
$5x = 14$	or	$5x = 4$
$x = \dfrac{14}{5}$	or	$x = \dfrac{4}{5}$

The solution set is $\left\{ \frac{14}{5}, \frac{4}{5} \right\}$.

f. Since the equation $(4x - 1)^2 + 9 = 16$ is a quadratic equation, we again have several options. Since the variable only appears once in this equation we will use the the square root method to solve.

$$(4x - 1)^2 + 9 = 16$$
$$(4x - 1)^2 = 7$$

$4x - 1 = \sqrt{7}$	or	$4x - 1 = -\sqrt{7}$
$4x = 1 + \sqrt{7}$	or	$4x = 1 - \sqrt{7}$
$x = \dfrac{1 + \sqrt{7}}{4}$	or	$x = \dfrac{1 - \sqrt{7}}{4}$

The solution set is $\left\{ \frac{1+\sqrt{7}}{4}, \frac{1-\sqrt{7}}{4} \right\}$.

g. Since the equation $\sqrt[3]{6x-5} = 2$ is a radical equation, we will isolate the radical (which is already done) and then raise both sides to the third power to cancel the cube root.

$$\sqrt[3]{6x-5} = 2$$
$$\left(\sqrt[3]{6x-5}\right)^3 = 2^3$$
$$6x - 5 = 8$$
$$6x = 13$$
$$x = \frac{13}{6}$$

The solution set is $\left\{\frac{13}{6}\right\}$.

h. Since the equation $6x^2 - 7x = 20$ is a quadratic equation, we again have several options to consider. We will try factoring on this one after first converting it to standard form.

$$6x^2 - 7x = 20$$
$$6x^2 - 7x - 20 = 0$$

Here, $ac = -120$ and two numbers that multiply to be -120 but add to be -7 are 8 and -15.

$$6x^2 + 8x - 15x - 20 = 0$$
$$\left(6x^2 + 8x\right) + (-15x - 20) = 0$$
$$2x(3x + 4) - 5(3x + 4) = 0$$
$$(2x - 5)(3x + 4) = 0$$

$2x - 5 = 0$	or	$3x + 4 = 0$
$x = \dfrac{5}{2}$	or	$x = -\dfrac{4}{3}$

The solution set is $\left\{\frac{5}{2}, -\frac{4}{3}\right\}$.

i. Since

$$\begin{cases} 4x + 2y = 8 \\ 3x - y = 11 \end{cases}$$

is a system of linear equations, we can either use substitution or elimination to solve. Here we will use elimination. To use elimination, we need to make one variable have equal but opposite sign in the two equations. We will accomplish this by multiplying the second equation by 2.

$$3x - y = 11$$
$$2 \cdot (3x - y) = 2 \cdot 11$$
$$6x - 2y = 22$$

So our original system becomes:

$$\begin{cases} 4x + 2y = 8 \\ 6x - 2y = 22 \end{cases}$$

Adding the sides of the equations, we get:

$$10x = 30$$
$$x = 3$$

Now that we have found x, we can substitute that back into one of the equations to find y. We will substitute into the first equation.

$$4(3) + 2y = 8$$
$$12 + 2y = 8$$
$$2y = -4$$
$$y = -2$$

So, the solution must be the point $(3, -2)$.

j. Since the equation $2x^2 - 10x = 7$ is quadratic and we are instructed to solve by using completing the square, we should recall how to complete the square, after we have sufficiently simplified. Let's start by dividing all of the terms by 2.

$$2x^2 - 12x = 7$$
$$x^2 - 6x = \frac{7}{2}$$

Next, we need to add $\left(\frac{b}{2}\right)^2 = \left(\frac{6}{2}\right)^2 = 9$ to both sides of the equation.

$$x^2 - 6x + 9 = \frac{7}{2} + 9$$
$$(x - 3)^2 = \frac{7}{2} + \frac{18}{2}$$
$$(x - 3)^2 = \frac{25}{2}$$
$$x - 3 = \pm\sqrt{\frac{25}{2}}$$
$$x - 3 = \pm\frac{\sqrt{25}}{\sqrt{2}}$$
$$x - 3 = \pm\frac{5}{\sqrt{2}}$$
$$x - 3 = \pm\frac{5}{\sqrt{2}} \cdot \frac{\sqrt{2}}{\sqrt{2}}$$
$$x - 3 = \pm\frac{5\sqrt{2}}{2}$$
$$x = 3 \pm \frac{5\sqrt{2}}{2}$$

So, our solution set is $\left\{3 + \frac{5\sqrt{2}}{2}, 3 - \frac{5\sqrt{2}}{2}\right\}$

13.5.3 Reading Questions

1. What are all the types of equation that *you* know how to solve? (Don't worry about which types you think you *should* know how to solve. Just try to list all the kinds of equations that you know you know.)

2. There are two types of equation that have been covered in this book where it is especially important to verify solutions. What are those two types of equation?

3. What are all the ways that you know of for solving a quadratic equation? (This book has covered five general methods, but answer with as many mehtods as you know you know).

13.5.4 Exercises

Solving Mixed Equations Solve the equation.

1. $\sqrt{y} + 72 = y$

2. $\sqrt{r} + 30 = r$

3. $5 + 8(C - 9) = -72 - (4 - 5C)$

4. $4 + 10(n - 7) = -72 - (9 - 5n)$

5. $x^2 + 6x = 27$

6. $x^2 - 2x = 80$

7. $-8 - 5r + 7 = -r + 6 - 4r$

8. $-6 - 8t + 3 = -t + 4 - 7t$

Solve the equation by completing the square.

9. $2y^2 - 6y - 3 = 0$

10. $2y^2 + 8y - 3 = 0$

Solve the equation.

11. $x^2 + 2x - 7 = 0$

12. $x^2 + 7x + 1 = 0$

13. Solve: $\left| \dfrac{2y - 3}{7} \right| = 1$

14. Solve: $\left| \dfrac{2y - 1}{3} \right| = 3$

Solve the equation.

15. $\dfrac{x + 6}{x - 4} + \dfrac{9}{x - 6} = 2$

16. $\dfrac{x + 8}{x + 2} + \dfrac{9}{x + 8} = 2$

17. $12 - 2(y - 7)^2 = 10$

18. $49 - 5(y - 7)^2 = 4$

19. $14 = \dfrac{c}{5} + \dfrac{c}{2}$

20. $3 = \dfrac{B}{3} + \dfrac{B}{6}$

21. $r = \sqrt{r + 4} + 86$

22. $t = \sqrt{t + 2} + 40$

23. $x^2 + 8x - 9 = 0$

24. $x^2 - 3x - 70 = 0$

25. Solve the equation: $|2x - 4| = |7x + 8|$

26. Solve the equation: $|2x - 9| = |3x + 5|$

Solve the equation.

27. $x^2 + 11x = -28$

28. $x^2 + 8x = -15$

29. $\dfrac{1}{r+8} + \dfrac{8}{r^2+8r} = -\dfrac{1}{4}$

30. $\dfrac{1}{r+2} + \dfrac{2}{r^2+2r} = \dfrac{1}{7}$

31. $x^2 = -6x$

32. $x^2 = -9x$

33. Solve: $|8a+5| + 9 = 6$

34. Solve: $|8a+1| + 6 = 4$

Solve the equation.

35. $59x^2 + 11 = 0$

36. $29x^2 + 17 = 0$

37. Solve: $|t-1| = 15$

38. Solve: $|t-7| = 9$

Solve the equation.

39. $5x^2 = -31x - 44$

40. $5x^2 = -52x - 20$

41. $t = \sqrt{t+7} + 5$

42. $x = \sqrt{x+5} + 7$

43. $\dfrac{1}{x-7} + \dfrac{5}{x+6} = -\dfrac{5}{x^2-x-42}$

44. $\dfrac{1}{x-5} + \dfrac{4}{x+3} = -\dfrac{7}{x^2-2x-15}$

Solve the equation by completing the square.

45. $y^2 - 6y = 27$

46. $y^2 - 14y = -45$

13.6 Compound Inequalities

On the newest version of the SAT (an exam that often qualifies students for colleges) the minimum score that you can earn is 400 and the maximum score that you can earn is 1600. This means that only numbers between 400 and 1600, including these endpoints, are possible scores. To plot all of these values on a number line would look something like:

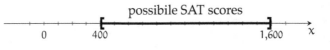

Figure 13.6.1: Possible SAT Scores

Going back to the original statement, "the minimum score that you can earn is 400 and the maximum score that you can earn is 1600," this really says two things. First, it says that (a SAT score) $\geq$ 400, and second, that (a SAT score) $\leq$ 1600. When we combine two inequalities like this into a single problem, it becomes a **compound inequality**.

Our lives are often constrained by the compound inequalities of reality: you need to buy enough materials to complete your project, but you can only fit so much into your vehicle; you would like to finish your degree early, but only have so much money and time to put toward your courses; you would like a vegetable garden big enough to supply you with veggies all summer long, but your yard or balcony only gets so much sun. In the rest of the section we hope to illuminate how to think mathematically about problems like these.

Before continuing, a review on how notation for intervals works may be useful, and you may benefit from revisiting Section 1.3. Then a refresher on solving linear inequalities may also benefit you, which you can revisit in Section 2.2 and Section 2.3.

13.6.1 Unions of Intervals

Definition 13.6.3 The **union** of two sets, A and B, is the set of all elements contained in either A or B (or both). We write $A \cup B$ to indicate the union of the two sets.

In other words, the union of two sets is what you get if you toss every number in both sets into a bigger set.   ◇

Example 13.6.4 The union of sets $\{1, 2, 3, 4\}$ and $\{3, 4, 5, 6\}$ is the set of all elements from either set. So $\{1, 2, 3, 4\} \cup \{3, 4, 5, 6\} = \{1, 2, 3, 4, 5, 6\}$. Note that we don't write duplicates.

Example 13.6.5 Visualize the union of the sets $(-\infty, 4)$ and $[7, \infty)$.

Explanation.   First we make a number line with both intervals drawn to understand what both sets mean.

Figure 13.6.6: A number line sketch of $(-\infty, 4)$ as well as $[7, \infty)$

The two intervals should be viewed as a single object when stating the union, so here is the picture of the union. It looks the same, but now it is a graph of a single set.

Figure 13.6.7: A number line sketch of $(-\infty, 4) \cup [7, \infty)$

Definition 13.6.8 The **intersection** of two sets, A and B, is the set of all elements that are in A **and** B. We write A ∩ B to indicate the intersection of the two sets.

In other words, the intersection of two sets is where the two sets overlap. ◇

Example 13.6.9 The intersection of sets $\{1, 2, 3, 4\}$ and $\{3, 4, 5, 6\}$ is the set of all elements that are in common to both sets. So $\{1, 2, 3, 4\} \cap \{3, 4, 5, 6\} = \{3, 4\}$.

Example 13.6.10 Find the intersection of the sets $(-\infty, 5)$ and $[3, \infty)$.

Explanation. To find the intersection of the sets $(-\infty, 5)$ and $[3, \infty)$, first we draw a number line with both intervals drawn to visualize where the sets overlap.

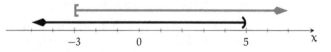

Figure 13.6.11: A number line sketch of $(-\infty, 5)$ and $[-3, \infty)$

Recall that the intersection of two sets is the set of the numbers in common to both sets. In English, we might say that the lines overlap at every number between -3 and 5. This description is the same as the interval $[-3, 5)$.

Figure 13.6.12: A number line sketch of $[-3, 5)$

In conclusion,
$$[-3, \infty) \cap (-\infty, 5) = [-3, 5).$$

Remark 13.6.13 Note that every intersection of two intervals can and should be simplified in some way. On the other hand, there *are* unions which cannot be algebraically simplified. For example, if the two sets have nothing in common, as in $(-\infty, 4)$ and $[7, \infty)$ again, then the union is simply $(-\infty, 4) \cup [7, \infty)$ which is our final simplification.

Example 13.6.14 Simplify the intersections and unions.
  a. $(-\infty, 12) \cup [-3, \infty)$ c. $(-\infty, -2] \cup [4, \infty)$

  b. $(-\infty, 12) \cap [-3, \infty)$ d. $(-\infty, -2] \cap [4, \infty)$

Explanation.

  a. $(-\infty, 12) \cup [-3, \infty) = \mathbb{R}$

  b. $(-\infty, 12) \cap [-3, \infty) = [-3, 12)$

c. $(-\infty, -2] \cup [4, \infty) = (-\infty, -2] \cup [4, \infty)$

This union cannot be simplified because the two sets have nothing in common.

d. $(-\infty, -2] \cap [4, \infty) = \emptyset$

Since the two sets have nothing in common, their intersection is empty.

Remark 13.6.15 In this section, we mostly use interval notation to answer questions. Recall that we can also use set builder notation. For example, the set $[3, \infty)$ can also be written as $\{x \mid x \geq 3\}$.

13.6.2 "Or" Compound Inequalities

Definition 13.6.16 A **compound inequality** is a grouping of two or more inequalities into a larger inequality statement. These usually come in two flavors: "or" and "and" inequalities. For an example of an "or" compound inequality, you might get a discount at the movie theater if your age is less than 13 *or* greater than 64. For an example of an "and" compound inequality, to purchase a drink at a bar in Oregon, you need to be over 21 years old *and* be have money for your drink. You need to fulfill *both* requirements.   ◊

In math, the technical term **or** means "either or both." So, mathematically, if we asked if you would like "chocolate cake *or* apple pie" for dessert, your choices are either "chocolate cake," "apple pie," or "both chocolate cake and apple pie." This is slightly different than the English "or" which usually means "one or the other but not both."

"Or" shows up in math between equations (as in when solving a quadratic equation, you might end up with "$x = 2$ or $x = -3$") or between inequalities (which is what we're about to discuss).

Remark 13.6.17 The definition of "or" is very close to the definition of a union where you combine elements from either or both sets together. In fact, when you have an "or" between inequalities in a compound inequality, to find the solution set of the compound inequality, you find the union of the the solutions sets of each of the pieces.

Example 13.6.18 Solve the compound inequality.

$$x \leq 1 \quad \text{or} \quad x > 4$$

Explanation.

Writing the solution set to this compound inequality doesn't require any algebra beforehand because each of the inequalities is already solved for x. The first thing we should do is understand what each inequality is saying using a graph.

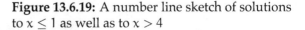

Figure 13.6.19: A number line sketch of solutions to $x \leq 1$ as well as to $x > 4$

An "or" statement becomes a union of solution sets, so the solution set to the compound inequality must be:

$$(-\infty, 1] \cup (4, \infty).$$

Example 13.6.20 Solve the compound inequality.

$$3 - 5x > -7 \quad \text{or} \quad 2 - x \leq -3$$

Explanation. First we need to do some algebra to isolate x in each piece. Note that we are going to do algebra on both pieces simultaneously. Also note that the mathematical symbol "or" should be written on each line.

$$3 - 5x > -7 \qquad \text{or} \qquad 2 - x \le -3$$
$$-5x > -10 \qquad \text{or} \qquad -x \le -5$$
$$\frac{-5x}{-5} < \frac{-10}{-5} \qquad \text{or} \qquad \frac{-x}{-1} \ge \frac{-5}{-1}$$
$$x < 2 \qquad \text{or} \qquad x \ge 5$$

The solution set for the compound inequality $x < 2$ is $(-\infty, 2)$ and the solution set to $x \ge 5$ is $[5, \infty)$. To do the "or" portion of the problem, we need to take the union of these two sets. Let's first make a graph of the solution sets to visualize the problem.

Figure 13.6.21: A number line sketch of $(-\infty, 2)$ as well as $[5, \infty)$

The union combines both solution sets into one, and so

$$(-\infty, 2) \cup [5, \infty)$$

We have finished the problem, but for the sake of completeness, let's try to verify that our answer is reasonable.

- First, let's choose a number that is *not* in our proposed solution set. We will arbitrarily choose 3.

$$3 - 5x > -7 \qquad \text{or} \qquad 2 - x \le -3$$
$$3 - 5(3) \overset{?}{>} -7 \qquad \text{or} \qquad 2 - (3) \overset{?}{\le} -3$$
$$-9 \overset{no}{>} -7 \qquad \text{or} \qquad -1 \overset{no}{\le} -3$$

This value made *both* inequalities false which is why 3 isn't in our solution set.

- Next, let's choose a number that *is* in our solution region. We will arbitrarily choose 1.

$$3 - 5x > -7 \qquad \text{or} \qquad 2 - x \le -3$$
$$3 - 5(1) \overset{?}{>} -7 \qquad \text{or} \qquad 2 - (1) \overset{?}{\le} -3$$
$$-12 \overset{\checkmark}{<} -7 \qquad \text{or} \qquad -1 \overset{no}{\le} -3$$

This value made *one* of the inequalities true. Since this is an "or" statement, only one *or* the other piece has to be true to make the compound inequality true.

- Last, what will happen if we choose a value that was in the other solution region in Figure 13.6.21, like the number 6?

$$3 - 5x > -7 \qquad \text{or} \qquad 2 - x \le -3$$

$$3 - 5(6) \overset{?}{>} -7 \qquad\qquad \text{or} \qquad\qquad 2 - (6) \overset{?}{\leq} -3$$

$$-27 \overset{no}{>} -7 \qquad\qquad \text{or} \qquad\qquad -4 \overset{\checkmark}{\leq} -3$$

This solution made the *other* inequality piece true.

This completes the check. Numbers from within the solution region make the compound inequality true and numbers outside the solution region make the compound inequality false.

Example 13.6.22 Solve the compound inequality.

$$\frac{3}{4}t + 2 \leq \frac{5}{2} \quad \text{or} \quad -\frac{1}{2}(t-3) < -2$$

Explanation. First we will solve each inequality for t. Recall that we usually try to clear denominators by multiplying both sides by the least common denominator.

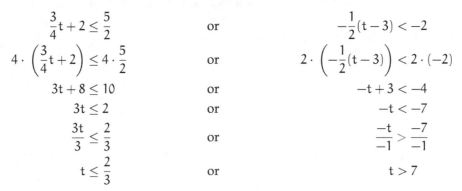

The solution set to $t \leq \frac{2}{3}$ is $\left(-\infty, \frac{2}{3}\right]$ and the solution set to $t > 7$ is $(7, \infty)$. Figure 13.6.23 shows these two sets.

Figure 13.6.23: A number line sketch of $\left(-\infty, \frac{2}{3}\right]$ and also $(7, \infty)$

Note that the two sets do not overlap so there will be no way to simplify the union. Thus the solution set to the compound inequality is:

$$\left(-\infty, \frac{2}{3}\right] \cup (7, \infty)$$

Example 13.6.24 Solve the compound inequality.

$$3y - 15 > 6 \quad \text{or} \quad 7 - 4y \geq y - 3$$

Explanation. First we solve each inequality for y.

$$3y - 15 > 6 \qquad\qquad \text{or} \qquad\qquad 7 - 4y \geq y - 3$$

$$
\begin{array}{ccc}
3y > 21 & \text{or} & -5y \geq -10 \\
\dfrac{3y}{3} > \dfrac{21}{3} & \text{or} & \dfrac{-5y}{-5} \leq \dfrac{-10}{-5} \\
y > 7 & \text{or} & y \leq 2
\end{array}
$$

The solution set to $y > 7$ is $(7, \infty)$ and the solution set to $y \leq 2$ is $(-\infty, 2]$. Figure 13.6.25 shows these two sets.

Figure 13.6.25: A number line sketch of $(7, \infty)$ as well as $(-\infty, 2]$

So the solution set to the compound inequality is:

$$(-\infty, 2] \cup (7, \infty)$$

13.6.3 Three-Part Inequalities

There are two different kinds of "and" compound inequalities. One type has an expression that is "between" two values, like $A < B \leq C$, that we will call "three-part inequalities". The other type has two inequalities joined by the word "and," as in $A < B$ and $C \geq D$. We will start with the three-part inequalities.

The inequality $1 \leq 2 < 3$ says a lot more than you might think. It actually says four different single inequalities which are highlighted for you to see.

$$1 \leq 2 < 3 \quad 1 \leq 2 < 3 \quad 1 \leq 2 < 3 \quad 1 \leq 2 < 3$$

This might seem trivial at first, but if you are presented with an inequality like $-1 < 3 \geq 2$, at first it might look sensible; however, in reality, you need to check that *all four* linear inequalities make sense. Those are highlighted here.

$$-1 < 3 \geq 2 \quad -1 < 3 \geq 2 \quad -1 < 3 \geq 2 \quad -1 < 3 \geq 2$$

One of these inequalities is false: $-1 \not\geq 2$. This implies that the entire original inequality, $-1 < 3 \geq 2$, is nonsense.

Example 13.6.26 Decide whether or not the following inequalities are true or false.

a. True or False: $-5 < 7 \leq 12$?

b. True or False: $-7 \leq -10 < 4$?

c. True or False: $-2 \leq 0 \geq 1$?

d. True or False: $5 > -3 \geq -9$?

e. True or False: $3 < 3 \leq 5$?

f. True or False: $9 > 1 < 5$?

g. True or False: $3 < 8 \leq -2$?

h. True or False: $-9 < -4 \leq -2$?

Explanation. We need to go through all four single inequalities for each. If the inequality is false, for simplicity's sake, we will only highlight the one single inequality that makes the inequality false.

a. True: $-5 < 7 \leq 12$.

b. False: $-7 \overset{no}{\leq} -10 < 4$.

c. False: $-2 < 0 \overset{no}{\geq} 1$.

d. True: $5 > -3 \geq -9$.

e. False: $3 \overset{no}{<} 3 \leq 5$.

f. False: $9 > 1 \overset{no}{<} 5$.

g. False: $3 < 8 \overset{no}{\leq} -2$.

h. True: $-9 < -4 \leq -2$.

As a general hint, no (nontrivial) three-part inequality can ever be true if the inequality signs are not pointing in the same direction. So no matter what numbers a, b, and c are, both $a < b \geq c$ and $a \geq b < c$ cannot be true! Soon you will be writing inequalities like $2 < x \leq 4$ and you need to be sure to check that your answer is feasible. You will know that if you get $2 > x \leq 4$ or $2 < x \geq 4$ that something went wrong in the solving process. The only exception is that something like $1 \leq 1 \geq 1$ is true because $1 = 1 = 1$, although this shouldn't come up very often!

Example 13.6.27 Write the solution set to the compound inequality.

$$-7 < x \leq 5$$

Explanation.   The solutions to the three-part inequality $-7 < x \leq 5$ are those numbers that are trapped between -7 and 5, including 5 but not -7. Keep in mind that there are infinitely many decimal numbers and irrational numbers that satisfy this inequality like -2.781828 and π. We will write these numbers in interval notation as $(-7, 5]$ or in set builder notation as $\{x \mid -7 < x \leq 5\}$.

Example 13.6.28 Solve the compound inequality.

$$4 \leq 9x + 13 < 20$$

Explanation.

This is a three-part inequality which we can treat just as a regular inequality with three "sides." The goal is to isolate x in the middle and whatever you do to one "side," you have to do to the other two "sides."

The solutions to the three-part inequality $-1 \leq x < \frac{7}{9}$ are those numbers that are trapped between -1 and $\frac{7}{9}$, including -1 but not $\frac{7}{9}$. The solution set in interval notation is $\left[-1, \frac{7}{9}\right)$.

$$4 \leq 9x + 13 < 20$$
$$4 - 13 \leq 9x + 13 - 13 < 20 - 13$$
$$-9 \leq 9x < 7$$
$$\frac{-9}{9} \leq \frac{9x}{9} < \frac{7}{9}$$
$$-1 \leq x < \frac{7}{9}$$

Example 13.6.29 Solve the compound inequality.

$$-13 < 7 - \frac{4}{3}x \leq 15$$

Explanation.

This is a three-part inequality which we can treat just as a regular inequality with three "sides." The goal is to isolate x in the middle and whatever you do to one "side," you have to do to the other two "sides." We will begin by canceling the fraction by multiplying each part by the least common denominator.

At the end we reverse the entire statement to go from smallest to largest. The solution set is $[-6, 15)$.

$$-13 < 7 - \frac{4}{3}x \le 15$$

$$-13 \cdot 3 < \left(7 - \frac{4}{3}x\right) \cdot 3 \le 15 \cdot 3$$

$$-39 < 21 - 4x \le 45$$

$$-60 < -4x \le 24$$

$$\frac{-60}{-4} > \frac{-4x}{-4} \ge \frac{24}{-4}$$

$$15 > x \ge -6$$

$$-6 \le x < 15$$

13.6.4 Solving "And" Inequalities

Here we will deal with the other kind of compound inequality: the "and" variety.

Remark 13.6.30 An "and" statement means that you need both inequalities to be true simultaneously. In English, if you say, "I need Khaleem *and* Freja to paint the fence," then the only way you will be happy is if *both* people are working simultaneously on the fence. This statement that both things happen at the same time should be very reminiscent of our discussion of intersections earlier in this section. In fact, every "and" statement will result in the intersection of the solution sets of the pieces.

Example 13.6.31 Solve the compound inequality.

$$4 - 2t > -2 \quad \text{and} \quad 3t + 1 \ge -2$$

Explanation.

$4 - 2t > -2$	and	$3t + 1 \ge -2$
$4 - 2t - 4 > -2 - 4$	and	$3t + 1 - 1 \ge -2 - 1$
$-2t > -6$	and	$3t \ge -3$
$\dfrac{-2t}{-2} < \dfrac{-6}{-2}$	and	$\dfrac{3t}{3} \ge \dfrac{-3}{3}$
$t < 3$	and	$t \ge -1$

The solution set to $t < 3$ is $(-\infty, 3)$ and the solution set to $t \ge -1$ is $[-1, \infty)$. Shown is a graph of these solution sets.

Figure 13.6.32: A number line sketch of $(-\infty, 3)$ and also $[-1, \infty)$

Recall that an "and" problem finds the intersection of the solution sets. Intersection finds the t-values where the two lines overlap, so the solution to the compound inequality must be

$$(-\infty, 3) \cap [-1, \infty) = [-1, 3).$$

We have finished the problem, but for the sake of completeness, let's try to "verify" that our answer is reasonable.

- First, choose a number within our solution region and test that it makes both original inequalities true. We will arbitrarily choose 1.

$$4 - 2t > -2 \qquad\qquad \text{and} \qquad\qquad 3t + 1 \geq -2$$
$$4 - 2(1) \overset{?}{>} -2 \qquad\qquad \text{and} \qquad\qquad 3(1) + 1 \overset{?}{\geq} -2$$
$$2 \overset{\checkmark}{>} -2 \qquad\qquad \text{and} \qquad\qquad 4 \overset{\checkmark}{\geq} -2$$

- Next, choose a value outside the solution set and test that it makes *at least* one of the inequalities false. We will arbitrarily choose 4.

$$4 - 2t > -2 \qquad\qquad \text{and} \qquad\qquad 3t + 1 \geq -2$$
$$4 - 2(4) \overset{?}{>} -2 \qquad\qquad \text{and} \qquad\qquad 3(4) + 1 \overset{?}{\geq} -2$$
$$-4 \overset{no}{>} -2 \qquad\qquad \text{and} \qquad\qquad 13 \overset{\checkmark}{\geq} -2$$

Since one of the inequalities is false and this is an "and" question, the compound inequality is false for this value which is what expected by picking a number outside the solution set.

- Last, we should choose a number that is not a solution that is on the "other side" of the solution set. We will arbitrarily choose -2.

$$4 - 2t > -2 \qquad\qquad \text{and} \qquad\qquad 3t + 1 \geq -2$$
$$4 - 2(-2) \overset{?}{>} -2 \qquad\qquad \text{and} \qquad\qquad 3(-2) + 1 \overset{?}{\geq} -2$$
$$8 \overset{\checkmark}{>} -2 \qquad\qquad \text{and} \qquad\qquad -5 \overset{no}{\geq} -2$$

Again, since one of the inequalities is false and this is an "and" question, the compound inequality is false for -2.

So, numbers outside the proposed solution region make the compound inequality false, and numbers inside the region make the compound inequality true. We have verified our solution set.

Checkpoint 13.6.33 Solve the compound inequality.

$$-6 \geq 3x + 3 \quad \text{and} \quad 3x + 9 > -6$$

Explanation.

$$-6 \geq 3x + 3 \qquad\qquad \text{and} \qquad\qquad 3x + 9 > -6$$
$$-9 \geq 3x \qquad\qquad \text{and} \qquad\qquad 3x > -15$$
$$-3 \geq x \qquad\qquad \text{and} \qquad\qquad x > -5$$
$$x \leq -3 \qquad\qquad \text{and} \qquad\qquad x > -5$$

The solution set to $x \leq -3$ is $(-\infty, -3]$ and the solution set to $x > -5$ is $(-5, \infty)$. Shown is a graph of these solution sets on a number line.

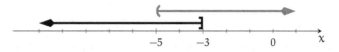

Figure 13.6.34: A number line sketch of $(-\infty, -3]$ and $(-5, \infty)$

Recall that "and" statements of inequalities become intersections of the solution sets. Since intersections refer to where the sets overlap, and these sets overlap between -5 (exclusive) and -3 (inclusive), we would say

$$(-\infty, -3] \cap (-5, \infty) = (-5, -3].$$

13.6.5 Applications of Compound inequalities

Example 13.6.35 Raphael's friend is getting married and he's decided to give them some dishes from their registry. Raphael doesn't want to seem cheap but isn't a wealthy man either, so he wants to buy "enough" but not "too many." He's decided that he definitely wants to spend at least $150 on his friend, but less than $250. Each dish is $21.70 and shipping on an order of any size is going to be $19.99. Given his budget, set up and algebraically solve a compound inequality to find out what his different options are for the number of dishes that he can buy.

Explanation. First, we should define our variable. Let x represent the number of dishes that Raphael can afford. Next we should write a compound inequality that describes this situation. In this case, Raphael wants to spend between $150 and $250 and, since he's buying x dishes, the price that he will pay is $21.70x + 19.99$. All of this translates to a triple inequality

$$150 < 21.70x + 19.99 < 250$$

Now we have to solve this inequality in the usual way.

$$150 < 21.70x + 19.99 < 250$$
$$150 - 19.99 < 21.70x + 19.99 - 19.99 < 250 - 19.99$$
$$130.01 < 21.70x < 230.01$$
$$\frac{130.01}{21.70} < \frac{21.70x}{21.70} < \frac{230.01}{21.70}$$
$$5.991 < x < 10.6 \qquad \text{(note: these values are approximate)}$$

The interpretation of this inequality is a little tricky. Remember that x represents the number of dishes Raphael can afford. Since you cannot buy 5.991 dishes (manufacturers will typically only ship whole number amounts of tableware) his minimum purchase must be 6 dishes. We have a similar problem with his maximum purchase: clearly he cannot buy 10.6 dishes. So, should we round up or down? If we rounded up, that would be 11 dishes and that would cost $21.70 \cdot 11 + \$19.99 = \$258.69$, which is outside his price range. Therefore, we should actually round *down* in this case.

In conclusion, Raphael should buy somewhere between 6 and 10 dishes for his friend to stay within his budget.

Example 13.6.36 Oak Ridge National Laboratory, a renowned scientific research facility, compiled some data[1] on fuel efficiency of a mid-size hybrid car versus the speed that the car was driven. A model for the fuel efficiency $e(x)$ (in miles per gallon, mpg) at a speed x (in miles per hour, mph) is $e(x) = 88 - 0.7x$.

    a. Evaluate and interpret $e(60)$ in the context of the problem.

    b. Note that this model only applies between certain speeds. The maximum fuel efficiency for which this formula applies is 55 mpg and the minimum fuel efficiency for which it applies is 33 mpg. Set up and algebraically solve a compound inequality to find the range of speeds for which this model applies.

Explanation.

    a. Let's evaluate $e(60)$ first.

$$e(x) = 88 - 0.7x$$
$$e(60) = 88 - 0.7(60)$$
$$= 46$$

    So, when the hybrid car travels at a speed of 60 mph, it has a fuel efficiency of 46 mpg.

    b. In this case, the minimum efficiency is 33 mpg and the maximum efficiency is 55 mpg. We need to trap our formula between these two values to solve for the respective speeds.

$$33 < 88 - 0.7x < 55$$
$$33 - 88 < 88 - 0.7x - 88 < 55 - 88$$
$$-55 < -0.7x < -33$$
$$\frac{-55}{-0.7} > \frac{-0.7x}{-0.7} > \frac{-33}{-0.7}$$
$$78.57 > x > 47.14 \qquad \text{(note: these values are approximate)}$$

    This inequality says that our model is applicable when the car's speed is between about 47 mph and about 79 mph.

13.6.6 Reading Questions

1.   What is the difference between an "inequality" and a "compound inequality"?

2.   What is the difference between a union and an intersection?

3.   Explain why $-3 < 5 \geq 2$ doesn't make mathematical sense.

4.   If you solve a compound inequality and your final simplification is "$x > 7$ and $x < 12$", how many solutions are in your solution set? How would you write those solutions?

---

[1]tedb.ornl.gov/data/

13.6.7 Exercises

Review and Warmup

1. For the interval expressed in the number line, write it using set-builder notation and interval notation.

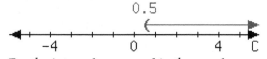

2. For the interval expressed in the number line, write it using set-builder notation and interval notation.

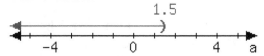

3. For the interval expressed in the number line, write it using set-builder notation and interval notation.

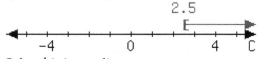

4. For the interval expressed in the number line, write it using set-builder notation and interval notation.

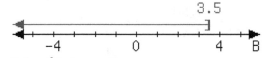

5. Solve this inequality.
$1 > x + 7$

6. Solve this inequality.
$1 > x + 10$

7. Solve this inequality.
$-2x \geq 6$

8. Solve this inequality.
$-3x \geq 6$

9. Solve this inequality.
$5 \geq -6x + 5$

10. Solve this inequality.
$4 \geq -7x + 4$

11. Solve this inequality.
$9t + 3 < 5t + 43$

12. Solve this inequality.
$9t + 9 < 3t + 51$

Check Solutions Decide whether the given value for the variable is a solution.

13.
 a. $x > 9$ and $x \leq 5$ $x = 8$ The given value ($\square$ is $\square$ is not) a solution.

 b. $x < 4$ or $x \geq 6$ $x = 1$ The given value ($\square$ is $\square$ is not) a solution.

 c. $x \geq -2$ and $x \leq 8$ $x = -2$ The given value ($\square$ is $\square$ is not) a solution.

 d. $-3 \leq x \leq 3$ $x = 2$ The given value ($\square$ is $\square$ is not) a solution.

14.
 a. $x > 1$ and $x \leq 2$ $x = 2$ The given value ($\square$ is $\square$ is not) a solution.

 b. $x < 1$ or $x \geq 6$ $x = 6$ The given value ($\square$ is $\square$ is not) a solution.

 c. $x \geq -2$ and $x \leq 3$ $x = 4$ The given value ($\square$ is $\square$ is not) a solution.

 d. $-1 \leq x \leq 1$ $x = 1$ The given value ($\square$ is $\square$ is not) a solution.

Compound Inequalities and Interval Notation

15. Solve the compound inequality. Write the solution set in interval notation.
$-9 < x \leq 9$

16. Solve the compound inequality. Write the solution set in interval notation.
$-8 < x \leq 5$

17. Solve the compound inequality. Write the solution set in interval notation.
$-7 > x$ or $x \geq 2$

18. Solve the compound inequality. Write the solution set in interval notation.
$-6 > x$ or $x \geq 8$

19. Express the following inequality using interval notation.
$x < -5$ or $x \leq 5$

20. Express the following inequality using interval notation.
$x < -4$ or $x \leq 1$

21. Express the following inequality using interval notation.

$-3 < x$ and $x \geq 8$

22. Express the following inequality using interval notation.

$-2 < x$ and $x \geq 4$

23. Express the following inequality using interval notation.

$-10 \leq x$ and $x < 1$

24. Express the following inequality using interval notation.

$-9 \leq x$ and $x < 7$

Solving a Compound Inequality Algebraically Solve the compound inequality algebraically.

25. $-5 < 7 - x \leq 0$

26. $-7 < 20 - x \leq -2$

27. $10 \leq x + 13 < 15$

28. $12 \leq x + 6 < 17$

29. $21 \leq \frac{5}{9}(F - 32) \leq 49$

F is in [   ]

30. $24 \leq \frac{5}{9}(F - 32) \leq 42$

F is in [   ]

31. $-16x + 11 \leq 1$ or $-14x - 13 \geq -13$

32. $16x + 10 \leq -17$ and $5x - 1 < 3$

33. $2x - 14 \leq 13$ and $-16x + 3 \leq 20$

34. $-12x + 3 \leq 1$ and $5x + 7 \geq -5$

35. $-8x - 5 \geq -17$ and $19x + 20 \geq -14$

36. $-4x + 20 > -7$ and $14x - 13 \geq -5$

37. $10x + 11 \leq -18$ or $-11x + 10 \leq -10$

38. $5x - 20 \geq -4$ or $-4x - 15 \geq 15$

39. $8 < \frac{4}{3}x < 36$

40. $5 < \frac{5}{2}x < 50$

41. $11 > 1 - \frac{2}{7}x \geq -3$

42. $12 > -3 - \frac{5}{4}x \geq -23$

Applications

43. As dry air moves upward, it expands. In so doing, it cools at a rate of about 1°C for every 100 m rise, up to about 12 km.

    a. If the ground temperature is 17°C, write a formula for the temperature at height x km. $T(x) =$

[   ]

    b. What range of temperature will a plane be exposed to if it takes off and reaches a maximum height of 5 km? Write answer in interval notation.

    The range is [   ].

Challenge

44. Algebraically, solve for x in the equation:

$$5 = |x - 5| + |x - 10|$$

13.7 Solving Inequalities Graphically

In this text, we have mostly focused on solving inequalities algebraically. While we have had some practice solving inequalities graphically 11.3.3 with technology, we want to solidify those skills. Solving using graphing is special because the graphing utility we use can do much of the heavy lifting and all that is left is to analyze the graph that is shown to us. So let's let our favorite graphing program make some graphs for us and then we can interpret the results.

13.7.1 Solving Inequalities Graphically

Example 13.7.1
Business leaders and professionals around the world concern themselves with money and how to grow their wealth. While a vast majority of people who live in the United States own few or no stocks, the stock market is important to learn about for anyone interested in earning a retirement. Stock owners need to know when to buy or sell their stocks to make a profit and the most essential tool to do so is the ability to read a graph. Let's examine a graph of the actual closing value of Apple (AAPL) stock from June 3, 2019 to August 6, 2019.

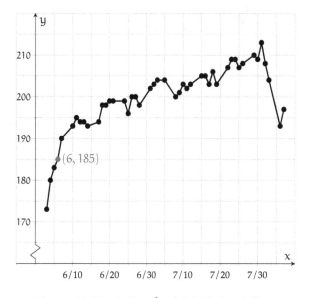

Figure 13.7.2: A Graph of AAPL Stock Data

If a person bought the stock on June 6, when the stock was valued at $185 per share, and they wanted at least a $20 per share profit, during what days could they have sold that stock?

If we want a $20 per share profit, then we should be interested in stock prices of $205 or more. Let's draw a line at $y = 205$, representing the price of $205, and find any days when the stock was on or above that line. According to the graph, there are several dates in question in starting in late July. Let's zoom in on those dates to read our solutions better.

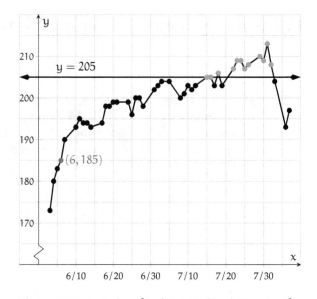

Figure 13.7.3: A Graph of AAPL Stock Data with $y = 205$

With a zoomed-in and rescaled graph, we can clearly see the dates that would have resulted in a $20 per share profit. Those dates were July 15, 16, 18, 22, 23, 24, 25, 26, 29, 30, 31, and August 1. Keep in mind that the stock market is closed on weekends and holidays, so we are only counting the solid dots as our solutions.

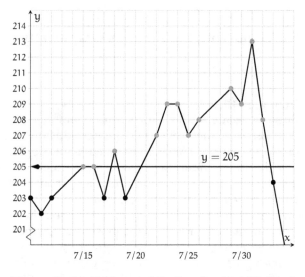

Figure 13.7.4: A Zoomed-In Graph of AAPL Stock Data with $y = 205$

Let's turn to an example involving a linear equation.

Example 13.7.5 Solve the inequality $3x - 2 < 7$ graphically.

Explanation.

To solve any inequality (or equation) graphically, we first take each side of the equation and graph $y = $ "left hand side" and $y = $ "right hand side". In this case, that would be $y = 3x - 2$ and $y = 7$. Now we can see that the graphs of $y = 3x - 2$ and $y = 7$ intersect at the point $(3, 7)$.

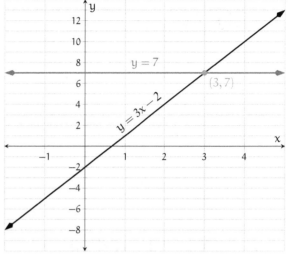

Figure 13.7.6: A Graph of Both $y = 3x - 2$ and $y = 7$

Since we are trying to solve the inequality $3x - 2 < 7$, we need to examine the graph for where (what x-values) the graph of $y = 3x - 2$ is below the graph of $y = 7$. This happens for x-values less than 3. So we would say that the solution set to $3x - 2 < 7$ is $(-\infty, 3)$. It is review to solve the inequality algebraically to verify our result.

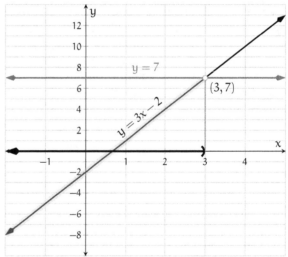

Figure 13.7.7: A Graph of Both $y = 3x - 2$ and $y = 7$

13.7.2 Solving Absolute Value and Quadratic Inequalities Graphically

Recall in Section 13.4 that we learned that graphs of absolute value function are in general shaped like "V"s. We can now solve some absolute value inequalities graphically.

Example 13.7.8
Graphically solving the inequality $|2x - 1| \leq 5$ means looking for the x-values where the graph of $y = |2x - 1|$ is below (or touching) the line $y = 5$. On the graph the highlighted region of $y = |2x - 1|$ is the portion that is below the line $y = 5$, and the x-values in that region are $[-2, 5]$.

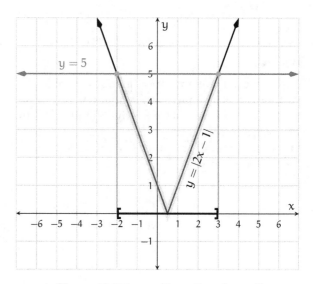

Figure 13.7.9: $y = |2x - 1|$ and $y = 5$

Example 13.7.10 Solve the inequality $\left|\frac{2}{3}x + 1\right| < 3$ graphically.

Explanation. To solve the inequality $\left|\frac{2}{3}x + 1\right| < 3$, we will start by making a graph with both $y = \left|\frac{2}{3}x + 1\right|$ and $y = 3$.

The portion of the graph of $y = \left|\frac{2}{3}x + 1\right|$ that is below $y = 3$ is highlighted and the x-values of that highlighted region are trapped between -6 and 3: $-6 < x < 3$. That means that the solution set is $(-6, 3)$. Note that we shouldn't include the endpoints of the interval because at those values, the two graphs are *equal* whereas the original inequality was only *less than* and not equal.

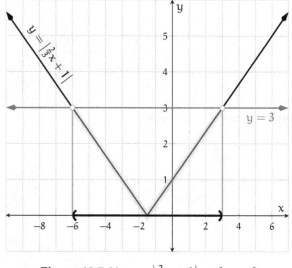

Figure 13.7.11: $y = \left|\frac{2}{3}x + 1\right|$ and $y = 3$

The last examples had absolute value expressions being *less than* some value. We now need to investigate what happens when we have an absolute value expression that is *greater than* a value.

Example 13.7.12 To graphically solve the inequality $|x - 1| > 3$ would mean looking for the x-values where the graph of $y = |x - 1|$ is *above* the line $y = 3$.

On the graph the highlighted region of $y = |x - 1|$ is the portion that is above the line $y = 3$ and the x-values in that region can be represented by $(-\infty, -2) \cup (4, \infty)$.

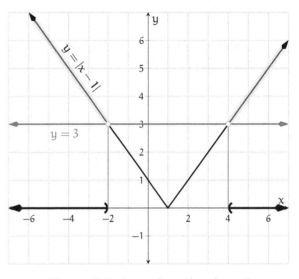

Figure 13.7.13: $y = |x - 1|$ and $y = 3$

Example 13.7.14 Solve the inequality $\left|\frac{1}{3}x + 2\right| \geq 6$ graphically.

Explanation. To solve the inequality $\left|\frac{1}{3}x + 2\right| \geq 6$, we will start by making a graph with both $y = \left|\frac{1}{3}x + 2\right|$ and $y = 6$.

The portion of the graph of $y = \left|\frac{1}{3}x + 2\right|$ that is above $y = 6$ is highlighted and the x-values of that highlighted region are those below (or equal to) -24 and those above (or equal to) 12: $x \leq -24$ or $x \geq 12$. That means that the solution set is $(-\infty, -24) \cup (12, \infty)$.

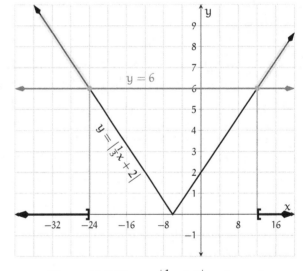

Figure 13.7.15: $y = \left|\frac{1}{3}x + 2\right|$ and $y = 3$

Solving inequalities with quadratic expressions graphically is very similar to solving absolute value inequalities graphically.

Example 13.7.16 Graphically solve the following quadratic inequalities.

    a. $42(x - 2)^2 - 60 \geq 21x - 39$ b. $42(x - 2)^2 - 60 < 21x - 39$

Explanation.

For both parts of this example, we start by graphing the equations $y = 42(x - 2)^2 - 60$ and $y = 21x - 39$ using graphing technology, and determining the points of intersection.

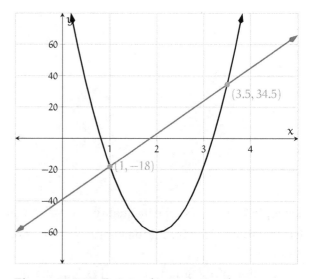

Figure 13.7.17: Points of intersection for $y = 42(x - 2)^2 - 60$ and $y = 21x - 39$

    a. To solve $42(x - 2)^2 - 60 \geq 21x - 39$, we need to determine where the y-values of the parabola are higher than (or equal to) those of the line. This region is highlighted in Figure 13.7.18.

We can see that $42(x - 2)^2 - 60 \geq 21x - 39$ for all values of x where $x \leq 1$ or $x \geq 3.5$. We can write this solution set in interval notation as $(-\infty, 1] \cup [3.5, \infty)$ or in set-builder notation as $\{x \mid x \leq 1 \text{ or } x \geq 3.5\}$.

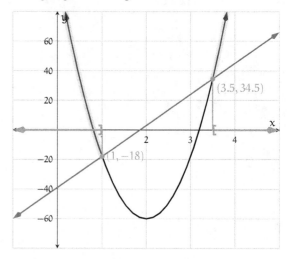

Figure 13.7.18: Where $42(x - 2)^2 - 60 \geq 21x - 39$

b. To now solve $42(x-2)^2 - 60 < 21x - 39$, we will need to determine where the y-values of the parabola are *less* than those of the line. This region is highlighted in Figure 13.7.19.

So the solutions to this inequality include all values of x for which $1 < x < 3.5$. We can write this solution set in interval notation as $(1, 3.5)$ or in set-builder notation as $\{x \mid 1 < x < 3.5\}$.

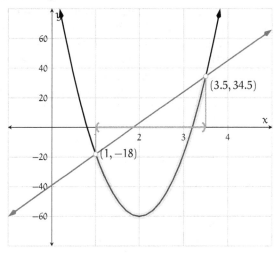

Figure 13.7.19: Where
$42(x-2)^2 - 60 < 21x - 39$

13.7.3 Solving Compound Inequalities Graphically

Example 13.7.20
Figure 13.7.21 shows a graph of $y = f(x)$. Use the graph to solve the inequality $2 \le f(x) < 6$.

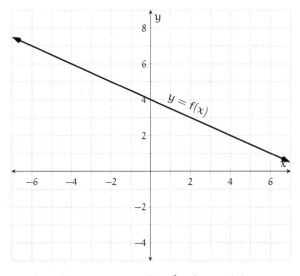

Figure 13.7.21: Graph of $y = f(x)$

Explanation.

To solve the inequality $2 \le f(x) < 6$ means to find the x-values that give function values between 2 and 6, not including 6. We draw the horizontal lines $y = 2$ and $y = 6$. Then we look for the points of intersection and find their x-values. We see that when x is between -4 and 4, not including -4, the inequality will be true. We have drawn the interval $(-4, 4]$ along the x-axis, which is the solution set.

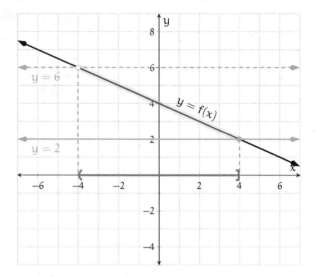

Figure 13.7.22: Graph of $y = f(x)$ and the solution set to $2 \le f(x) < 6$

Example 13.7.23 Figure 13.7.24 shows a graph of $y = g(x)$. Use the graph to solve the inequality $-4 < g(x) \le 3$.

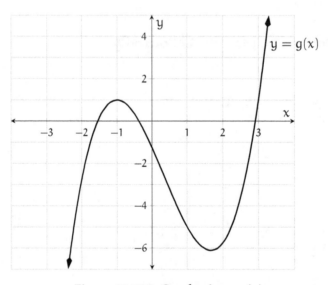

Figure 13.7.24: Graph of $y = g(x)$

Explanation. To solve $-4 < g(x) \le 3$, we first draw the horizontal lines $y = -4$ and $y = 3$. To solve this inequality we notice that there are two pieces of the function g that are trapped between the y-values -4 and 3.

The solution set is the compound inequality $(-2.1, 0.7) \cup (2.4, 3.2]$.

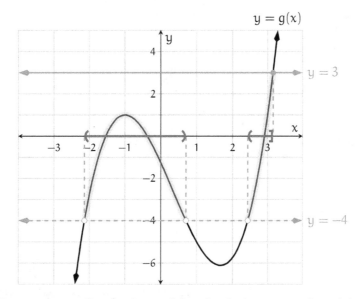

Figure 13.7.25: Graph of $y = g(x)$ and solution set to $-4 < g(x) \leq 3$

Example 13.7.26 Phuong is taking the standard climbing route on Mount Hood from Timberline Lodge up the Southside Hogsback to the summit and back down the same way. Her altitude can be very closely modeled by an absolute value function since the angle of ascent is nearly constant. Let x represent the number of miles walked from Timberline Lodge, and let $f(x)$ represent the altitude, in miles, after walking for a distance x. The altitude can be modeled by $f(x) = 2.1 - 0.3077 \cdot |x - 3.25|$. Note that below Timberline Lodge this model fails to be accurate.

a. Solve the equation $f(x) = 1.1$ graphically and interpret the results in the context of the problem.

b. Altitude sickness can occur at or above altitudes 1.5 miles. Set up and solve an inequality graphically to find out how far Phuong can walk the trail and still be under 1.5 miles of elevation.

Explanation.

a. First, we substitute the formula for $f(x)$ and simplify the equation.

$$f(x) = 1.1$$
$$2.1 - 0.3077 \cdot |x - 3.25| = 1.1$$

At this point, we should make a graph of both $y = 2.1 - 0.3077 \cdot |x - 3.25|$ and $y = 1.1$ and find their intersections.

Next, we should note that we are looking for the x-values of the intersections. These solutions are 0 and 6.5. According to the model, Phuong will be at 1.1 miles of elevation after walking about 0 miles as well as about 6.5 miles along the trail. This implies that Timberline Lodge is at 1.1 miles of elevation. In addition, it implies that the entire hike is 6.5 miles round trip, ending at Timberline Lodge again.

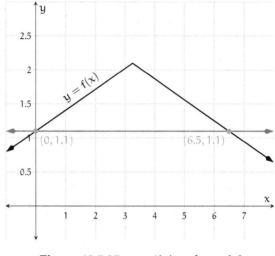

Figure 13.7.27: $y = f(x)$ and $y = 1.1$

b. The inequality we are looking for will describe when the altitude is below 1.5 miles, but also above 1.1 miles based on the reality of the situation (since the model only works above Timberline lodge at 1.1 miles of altitude). Since $f(x)$ is the altitude, the inequality we need is $1.1 \le f(x) < 1.5$, which becomes $1.1 \le 2.1 - 0.3077 \cdot |x - 3.25| < 1.5$.

Let's examine the graph again to solve this inequality: We are looking for places on the graph where the y-value is above 1.1, but also where the graph is below 1.5. To find this, we will draw in lines at both of those y-values and find intersections with f.

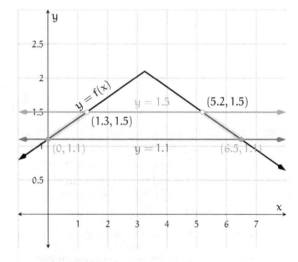

Figure 13.7.28: $y = f(x)$, the Graph of the Mt Hood Ascent and Descent

The highlighted portions of the graph have x-values that satisfy the inequalities $0 \le x < 1.3$ or $5.2 < x \le 6.5$.

In conclusion, based both on our math and the reality of the situation, regions of the trail that are below 1.5 miles are those that are from Timberline Lodge (at 0 miles on the trail), to 1.3 miles along the trail and then also from 5.2 miles along the trail (and by now we are on our way back down) to 6.5 miles along the trail (back at Timberline Lodge). If we wanted to write this in interval notation, we might write $[0, 1.3) \cup (5.2, 6.5]$. There is a big portion along the trail (from 1.3 miles to 5.2 miles) that Phuong will be above the 1.5 mile altitude and should watch for signs of altitude sickness.

13.7.4 Reading Questions

1. The graph of the function f is above the graph of the function g between $x = 6$ and $x = 9$. How many solutions does the inequality $f(x) > g(x)$ have?

2. Can the solution set to the inequality $h(x) > k(x)$ be the set of all real numbers? Why or why not?

3. Can the solution set to the inequality $h(x) > k(x)$ be the empty set (i.e., the inequality has no solutions)? Why or why not?

13.7.5 Exercises

Review and Warmup For the interval expressed in the number line, write it using set-builder notation and interval notation.

1.

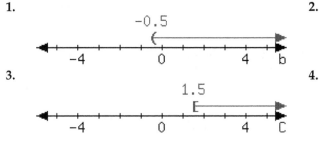

2.

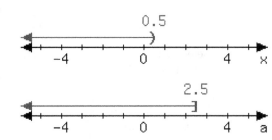

3.

4.

5. For the function L defined by
$$L(x) = 3000x^2 + 10x + 4,$$
use technology to determine the following. Round answers as necessary.

   a. Any intercepts.

   b. The vertex.

   c. The domain.

   d. The range.

6. For the function M defined by
$$M(x) = -(300x - 2950)^2,$$
use technology to determine the following. Round answers as necessary.

   a. Any intercepts.

   b. The vertex.

   c. The domain.

   d. The range.

7. For the function N defined by
$$N(x) = (300x - 1.05)^2,$$
use technology to determine the following. Round answers as necessary.

   a. Any intercepts.

   b. The vertex.

   c. The domain.

   d. The range.

8. For the function B defined by
$$B(x) = x^2 - 0.05x + 0.0006,$$
use technology to determine the following. Round answers as necessary.

   a. Any intercepts.

   b. The vertex.

   c. The domain.

   d. The range.

Solving Inequalities Graphically

9. Solve the equations and inequalities graphically. Use interval notation when applicable.

    a. $\left|\frac{2}{3}x + 2\right| = 4$ b. $\left|\frac{2}{3}x + 2\right| > 4$ c. $\left|\frac{2}{3}x + 2\right| \leq 4$

10. Solve the equations and inequalities graphically. Use interval notation when applicable.

    a. $\left|\frac{11-2x}{5}\right| = 4$ b. $\left|\frac{11-2x}{5}\right| > 4$ c. $\left|\frac{11-2x}{5}\right| \leq 4$

11. Solve the equations and inequalities graphically. Use interval notation when applicable.

    a. $x^2 - 3 = 1$ b. $x^2 - 3 > 1$ c. $x^2 - 3 \leq 1$

12. Solve the equations and inequalities graphically. Use interval notation when applicable.

    a. $x^2 - x - 3 = x$ b. $x^2 - x - 3 > x$ c. $x^2 - x - 3 \leq x$

13. The equations $y = \frac{1}{2}x^2 + 2x - 1$ and $y = 5$ are plotted.

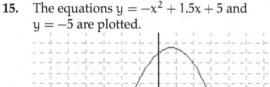

    a. What are the points of intersection?

    b. Solve $\frac{1}{2}x^2 + 2x - 1 = 5$.

    c. Solve $\frac{1}{2}x^2 + 2x - 1 > 5$.

14. The equations $y = \frac{1}{3}x^2 - 3x + 3$ and $y = -3$ are plotted.

    a. What are the points of intersection?

    b. Solve $\frac{1}{3}x^2 - 3x + 3 = -3$.

    c. Solve $\frac{1}{3}x^2 - 3x + 3 > -3$.

15. The equations $y = -x^2 + 1.5x + 5$ and $y = -5$ are plotted.

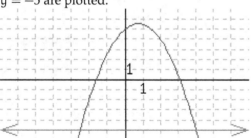

    a. What are the points of intersection?

    b. Solve $-x^2 + 1.5x + 5 = -5$.

    c. Solve $-x^2 + 1.5x + 5 > -5$.

16. The equations $y = -x^2 - 3.5x + 2$ and $y = 2$ are plotted.

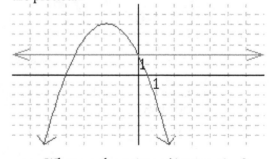

    a. What are the points of intersection?

    b. Solve $-x^2 - 3.5x + 2 = 2$.

    c. Solve $-x^2 - 3.5x + 2 > 2$.

17. The equations $y = \frac{1}{2}x^2 - x - 1$ and $y = -x + 1$ are plotted.

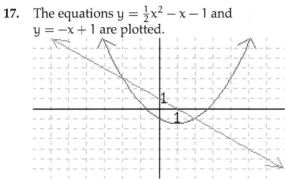

    a. What are the points of intersection?

    b. Solve $\frac{1}{2}x^2 - x - 1 = -x + 1$.

    c. Solve $\frac{1}{2}x^2 - x - 1 > -x + 1$.

18. The equations $y = \frac{-1}{3}x^2 + 2x + 3$ and $y = x - 3$ are plotted.

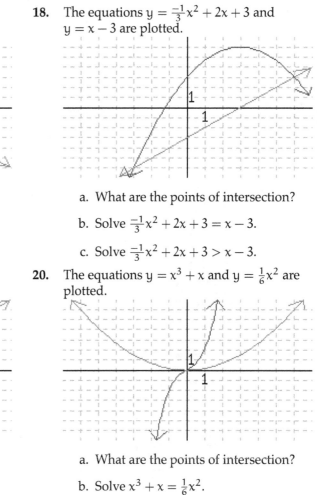

    a. What are the points of intersection?

    b. Solve $\frac{-1}{3}x^2 + 2x + 3 = x - 3$.

    c. Solve $\frac{-1}{3}x^2 + 2x + 3 > x - 3$.

19. The equations $y = \frac{1}{4}x^3$ and $y = x$ are plotted.

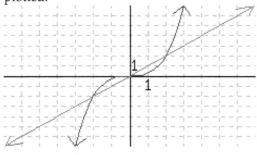

    a. What are the points of intersection?

    b. Solve $\frac{1}{4}x^3 = x$.

    c. Solve $\frac{1}{4}x^3 > x$.

20. The equations $y = x^3 + x$ and $y = \frac{1}{6}x^2$ are plotted.

    a. What are the points of intersection?

    b. Solve $x^3 + x = \frac{1}{6}x^2$.

    c. Solve $x^3 + x > \frac{1}{6}x^2$.

21. The equations $y = \sqrt{x+4}$ and $y = \frac{4x^2+x+3}{36}$ are plotted.

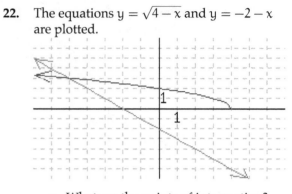

    a. What are the points of intersection?

    b. Solve $\sqrt{x+4} = \frac{4x^2+x+3}{36}$.

    c. Solve $\sqrt{x+4} > \frac{4x^2+x+3}{36}$.

22. The equations $y = \sqrt{4-x}$ and $y = -2-x$ are plotted.

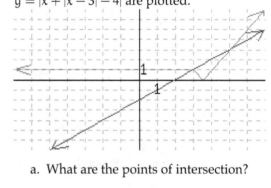

    a. What are the points of intersection?

    b. Solve $\sqrt{4-x} = -2-x$.

    c. Solve $\sqrt{4-x} > -2-x$.

23. The equations $y = \frac{1}{2}x^2 + 2x$ and $y = \sqrt[3]{9 - 2x^2} + \frac{23}{50}x - \frac{52}{25}$ are plotted.

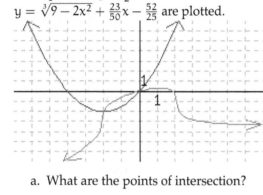

    a. What are the points of intersection?

    b. Solve
$$\frac{1}{2}x^2 + 2x = \sqrt[3]{9 - 2x^2} + \frac{23}{50}x - \frac{52}{25}.$$

    c. Solve
$$\frac{1}{2}x^2 + 2x > \sqrt[3]{9 - 2x^2} + \frac{23}{50}x - \frac{52}{25}.$$

24. The equations $y = x - 2$ and $y = |x + |x - 3| - 4|$ are plotted.

    a. What are the points of intersection?

    b. Solve $x - 2 = |x + |x - 3| - 4|$.

    c. Solve $x - 2 > |x + |x - 3| - 4|$.

Solving Equations and Inequalities Graphically Using Technology

25. Let $s(x) = \frac{1}{5}x^2 - 2x + 10$ and $t(x) = -x + 40$. Use graphing technology to determine the following.

    a. What are the points of intersection for these two functions?

    b. Solve $s(x) = t(x)$.

    c. Solve $s(x) > t(x)$.

    d. Solve $s(x) \le t(x)$.

26. Let $w(x) = \frac{1}{4}x^2 - 3x - 8$ and $m(x) = x + 12$. Use graphing technology to determine the following.

    a. What are the points of intersection for these two functions?

    b. Solve $w(x) = m(x)$.

    c. Solve $w(x) > m(x)$.

    d. Solve $w(x) \le m(x)$.

27. Let $f(x) = 4x^2 + 5x - 1$ and $g(x) = 5$. Use graphing technology to determine the following.

    a. What are the points of intersection for these two functions?

    b. Solve $f(x) = g(x)$.

    c. Solve $f(x) < g(x)$.

    d. Solve $f(x) \geq g(x)$.

28. Let $p(x) = 6x^2 - 3x + 4$ and $k(x) = 7$. Use graphing technology to determine the following.

    a. What are the points of intersection for these two functions?

    b. Solve $p(x) = k(x)$.

    c. Solve $p(x) < k(x)$.

    d. Solve $p(x) \geq k(x)$.

29. Let $q(x) = -4x^2 - 24x + 10$ and $r(x) = 2x + 22$. Use graphing technology to determine the following.

    a. What are the points of intersection for these two functions?

    b. Solve $q(x) = r(x)$.

    c. Solve $q(x) > r(x)$.

    d. Solve $q(x) \leq r(x)$.

30. Let $h(x) = -10x^2 - 5x + 3$ and $j(x) = -3x - 9$. Use graphing technology to determine the following.

    a. What are the points of intersection for these two functions?

    b. Solve $h(x) = j(x)$.

    c. Solve $h(x) > j(x)$.

    d. Solve $h(x) \leq j(x)$.

31. Use graphing technology to solve the equation $(200 + 5x)(100 - 2x) = 15000$. Approximate the solution(s) if necessary.

32. Use graphing technology to solve the inequality $2x^2 + 5x - 3 > -5$. State the solution set using interval notation, and approximate if necessary.

33. Use graphing technology to solve the inequality $-x^2 + 4x - 7 > -12$. State the solution set using interval notation, and approximate if necessary.

34. Use graphing technology to solve the inequality $10x^2 - 11x + 7 \leq 7$. State the solution set using interval notation, and approximate if necessary.

35. Use graphing technology to solve the inequality $-10x^2 - 15x + 4 \leq 9$. State the solution set using interval notation, and approximate if necessary.

36. Use graphing technology to solve the inequality $-x^2 - 6x + 1 > x + 5$. State the solution set using interval notation, and approximate if necessary.

37. Use graphing technology to solve the inequality $3x^2 + 5x - 4 > -2x + 1$. State the solution set using interval notation, and approximate if necessary.

38. Use graphing technology to solve the inequality $-10x + 4 \leq 20x^2 - 34x + 6$. State the solution set using interval notation, and approximate if necessary.

39. Use graphing technology to solve the inequality $-15x^2 - 6 \leq 10x - 4$. State the solution set using interval notation, and approximate if necessary.

40. Use graphing technology to solve the inequality $\frac{1}{2}x^2 + \frac{3}{2}x \geq \frac{1}{2}x - \frac{3}{2}$. State the solution set using interval notation, and approximate if necessary.

41. Use graphing technology to solve the inequality $\frac{3}{4}x \geq \frac{1}{4}x^2 - 3x$. State the solution set using interval notation, and approximate if necessary.

13.8 Graphs and Equations Chapter Review

13.8.1 Overview of Graphing

In Section 13.1 we reviewed several ways of making graphs of both lines (by hand) and general functions (using technology).

Example 13.8.1 Graphing Lines by Plotting Points. Graph the equation $y = \frac{5}{3}x - 3$ by creating a table of values and plotting those points.

Explanation.   To make a good table for this line, we should have x-values that are multiples of 3 to make sure that the fraction cancels nicely for the outputs.

x	$y = \frac{5}{3}x - 3$	Point
-3	$\frac{5}{3}(-3) - 3 = -8$	$(1, -8)$
0	$\frac{5}{3}(0) - 3 = -3$	$(2, -3)$
3	$\frac{5}{3}(3) - 3 = 2$	$(3, 2)$
6	$\frac{5}{3}(6) - 3 = 7$	$(4, 7)$

Figure 13.8.2: A table of values for $y = \frac{5}{3}x - 3$

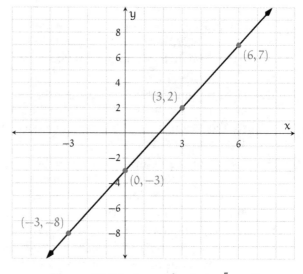

Figure 13.8.3: A graph of $y = \frac{5}{3}x - 3$

Example 13.8.4 Graphing Lines in Slope-Intercept Form. Find the slope and vertical intercept of $j(x) = -\frac{7}{2}x + 5$, and then use slope triangles to find the next two points on the line. Draw the line.

Explanation.   The slope of $j(x) = -\frac{7}{2}x + 5$ is $-\frac{7}{2}$, and the vertical intercept is $(0, 5)$. Starting at $(0, 5)$, we go down 7 units and right 2 units to reach more points.

From the graph, we can read that two more points that $j(x) = -\frac{7}{2}x + 5$ passes through are $(2, -2)$ and $(4, 9)$.

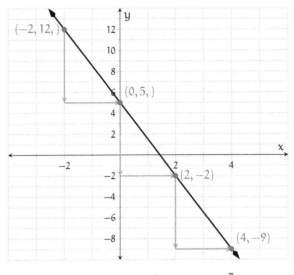

Figure 13.8.5: A graph of $j(x) = -\frac{7}{2}x + 5$

Example 13.8.6 Graphing Lines in Point-Slope Form. From the equation, find the slope and a point on the graph of $k(x) = \frac{3}{4}(x - 2) - 5$, and then use slope triangles to find the next two points on the line. Draw the line.

Explanation. The slope of $k(x) = \frac{3}{4}(x - 2) - 5$ is $\frac{3}{4}$ and the point on the graph given in the equation is $(2, -5)$. So to graph k, start at $(2, -5)$, and the go up 3 units and right 4 units (or down 3 left 4) to reach more points.

From the graph, we can read that two more points that $k(x) = \frac{3}{4}(x - 2) - 5$ passes through are $(6, -2)$ and $(10, 1)$.

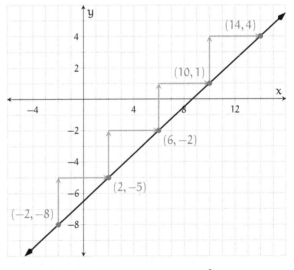

Figure 13.8.7: A graph of $k(x) = \frac{3}{4}(x - 2) - 5$

Example 13.8.8 Graphing Lines Using Intercepts. Use the intercepts of $4x - 2y = 16$ to graph the equation.
Explanation.

To find the x-intercept, set $y = 0$ and solve for x.

$$4x - 2(0) = 16$$
$$4x = 16$$
$$x = 4$$

The x-intercept is the point $(4, 0)$.

To find the y-intercept, set $x = 0$ and solve for y.

$$4(0) - 2y = 16$$
$$-2y = 16$$
$$y = -8$$

The y-intercept is the point $(0, -8)$.

Next, we just plot these points and draw the line that runs through them.

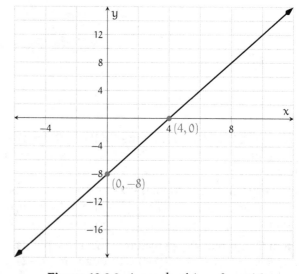

Figure 13.8.9: A graph of $4x - 2y = 16$

Example 13.8.10 Graphing Functions by Plotting Points. The wind chill[1] is how cold it *feels* outside due to the wind. Imagine a chilly 32 °F day with a breeze blowing over the snowy ground. The wind chill, $w(v)$, at this temperature can be approximated by the formula $w(v) = 54.5 - 21 \sqrt[6]{v}$ where v is the speed of the wind in miles per hour. This formula only approximates the wind chill for reasonable wind values of about 5 mph to 60 mph. Create a table of values rounded to the nearest tenth for the wind chill at realistic wind speeds and make a graph of w.

Explanation. Typical wind speeds vary between 5 and 20 mph, with gusty conditions up to 60 mph, depending on location. A good way to enter the sixth root into a calculator is to recall that $\sqrt[6]{x} = x^{\frac{1}{6}}$.

v	$w(v) = 54.5 - 21\sqrt[6]{v}$	Point	Interpretation
5	$w(5) \approx 27.0$	$(5, 27.0)$	A 5 mph wind causes a wind chill of 27.0 °F.
10	$w(10) \approx 23.7$	$(10, 23.7)$	A 10 mph wind causes a wind chill of 23.7 °F.
20	$w(20) \approx 19.9$	$(20, 19.9)$	A 20 mph wind causes a wind chill of 19.9 °F.
30	$w(30) \approx 17.5$	$(30, 17.5)$	A 30 mph wind causes a wind chill of 17.5 °F.
40	$w(40) \approx 15.7$	$(40, 15.7)$	A 40 mph wind causes a wind chill of 15.7 °F.
50	$w(50) \approx 14.2$	$(50, 14.2)$	A 50 mph wind causes a wind chill of 14.2 °F.
60	$w(60) \approx 12.9$	$(60, 12.9)$	A 60 mph wind causes a wind chill of 12.9 °F.

Figure 13.8.11: A table of values for $w(v) = 54.5 - 21\sqrt[6]{v}$

With the values in Table 13.8.11, we can sketch the graph.

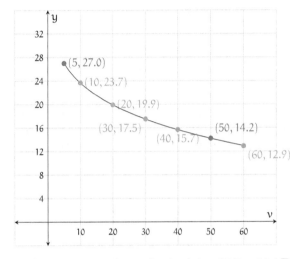

Figure 13.8.12: A graph of $w(v) = 54.5 - 21\sqrt[6]{v}$

13.8.2 Quadratic Graphs and Vertex Form

In Section 13.2 we covered the use of technology in analyzing quadratic functions, the vertex form of a quadratic function and how it affects horizontal and vertical shifts of the graph of a parabola, and the factored form of a quadratic function.

Example 13.8.13 Exploring Quadratic Functions with Graphing Technology. Use technology to graph and make a table of the quadratic function g defined by $g(x) = -x^2 + 5x - 6$ and find each of the key points or features.

a. Find the vertex.

b. Find the vertical intercept.

c. Find the horizontal intercept(s).

d. Find $g(-1)$.

e. Solve $g(x) = -6$ using the graph.

f. Solve $g(x) \leq -6$ using the graph.

g. State the domain and range of the function.

---

[1]en.wikipedia.org/wiki/Wind_chill

Explanation.

The specifics of how to use any one particular technology tool vary. Whether you use an app, a physical calculator, or something else, a table and graph should look like:

x	g(x)
−1	−12
0	−6
1	−2
2	0
2	0
3	0
4	−2

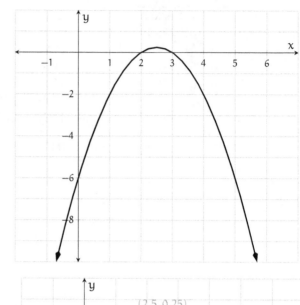

Additional features of your technology tool can enhance the graph to help answer these questions. You may be able to make the graph appear like:

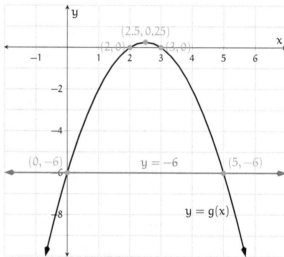

a. The vertex is $(2.5, 0.25)$.

b. The vertical intercept is $(0, −6)$.

c. The horizontal intercepts are $(2, 0)$ and $(3, 0)$.

d. $g(−1) = −2$.

e. The solutions to $g(x) = −6$ are the x-values where $y = 6$. We graph the horizontal line $y = −6$ and find the x-values where the graphs intersect. The solution set is $\{0, 5\}$.

f.

The solutions are all x-values where the function below (or touching) the line $y = -6$. The solution set is $(-\infty, 0] \cup [5, \infty)$.

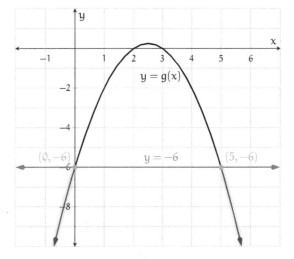

g. The domain is $(-\infty, \infty)$ and the range is $(-\infty, 0.25]$.

Example 13.8.14 The Vertex Form of a Parabola. Recall that the vertex form of a quadratic function tells us the location of the vertex of a parabola.

a. State the vertex of the quadratic function $r(x) = -8(x+1)^2 + 7$.

b. State the vertex of the quadratic function $u(x) = 5(x-7)^2 - 3$.

c. Write the formula for a parabola with vertex $(-5, 3)$ and $a = 2$.

d. Write the formula for a parabola with vertex $(1, -17)$ and $a = -4$.

Explanation.

a. The vertex of the quadratic function $r(x) = -8(x+1)^2 + 7$ is $(-1, 7)$.

b. The vertex of the quadratic function $u(x) = 5(x-7)^2 - 3$ is $(7, -3)$.

c. The formula for a parabola with vertex $(-5, 3)$ and $a = 2$ is $y = 2(x+5)^2 + 3$.

d. The formula for a parabola with vertex $(1, -17)$ and $a = -4$ is $y = 4(x-1)^2 - 17$.

Example 13.8.15 Horizontal and Vertical Shifts. Identify the horizontal and vertical shifts compared with $f(x) = x^2$.

a. $s(x) = (x+1)^2 + 7$.

b. $v(x) = (x-7)^2 - 3$.

Explanation.

a. The graph of the quadratic function $s(x) = -8(x+1)^2 + 7$ is the same as the graph of $f(x) = x^2$ shifted to the left 1 unit and up 7 units.

b. The graph of the quadratic function $v(x) = 5(x-7)^2 - 3$ is the same as the graph of $f(x) = x^2$ shifted to the right 7 units and down 3 units.

Example 13.8.16 The Factored Form of a Parabola. Recall that the factored form of a quadratic function tells us the horizontal intercepts very quickly.

a. $n(x) = 13(x-1)(x+6)$.

b. $p(x) = -6(x - \frac{2}{3})(x + \frac{1}{2})$.

Explanation.

a. The horizontal intercepts of n are $(1,0)$ and $(-6,0)$.

b. The horizontal intercepts of p are $(\frac{2}{3},0)$ and $(-\frac{1}{2},0)$.

13.8.3 Completing the Square

In Section 13.3 we covered how to complete the square to both solve quadratic equations in one variable and to put quadratic functions into vertex form.

Example 13.8.17 Solving Quadratic Equations by Completing the Square. Solve the equations by completing the square.

a. $k^2 - 18k + 1 = 0$ b. $4p^2 - 3p = 2$

Explanation.

a. To complete the square in the equation $k^2 - 18k + 1 = 0$, we first we will first move the constant term to the right side of the equation. Then we will use Fact 13.3.3 to find $\left(\frac{b}{2}\right)^2$ to add to both sides.

$$k^2 - 18k + 1 = 0$$
$$k^2 - 18k = -1$$

In our case, $b = -18$, so $\left(\frac{b}{2}\right)^2 = \left(\frac{-18}{2}\right)^2 = 81$

$$k^2 - 18k + 81 = -1 + 81$$
$$(k-9)^2 = 80$$

$$
\begin{array}{ccc}
k - 9 = -\sqrt{80} & \text{or} & k - 9 = \sqrt{80} \\
k - 9 = -4\sqrt{5} & \text{or} & k - 9 = 4\sqrt{5} \\
k = 9 - 4\sqrt{5} & \text{or} & k = 9 + 4\sqrt{5}
\end{array}
$$

The solution set is $\{9 + 4\sqrt{5}, 9 - 4\sqrt{5}\}$.

b. To complete the square in the equation $4p^2 - 3p = 2$, we first divide both sides by 4 since the leading coefficient is 4.

$$\frac{4p^2}{4} - \frac{3p}{4} = \frac{2}{4}$$
$$p^2 - \frac{3}{4}p = \frac{1}{2}$$
$$p^2 - \frac{3}{4}p = \frac{1}{2}$$

Next, we will complete the square. Since $b = -\frac{3}{4}$, first,

$$\frac{b}{2} = \frac{-\frac{3}{4}}{2} = -\frac{3}{8} \tag{13.8.1}$$

and next, squaring that, we have

$$\left(-\frac{3}{8}\right)^2 = \frac{9}{64}. \tag{13.8.2}$$

So we will add $\frac{9}{64}$ from Equation (13.8.2) to both sides of the equation:

$$p^2 - \frac{3}{4}p + \frac{9}{64} = \frac{1}{2} + \frac{9}{64}$$
$$p^2 - \frac{3}{4}p + \frac{9}{64} = \frac{32}{64} + \frac{9}{64}$$
$$p^2 - \frac{3}{4}p + \frac{9}{64} = \frac{41}{64}$$

Here, remember that we always factor with the number found in the first step of completing the square, Equation (13.8.1).

$$\left(p - \frac{3}{8}\right)^2 = \frac{41}{64}$$

$$p - \frac{3}{8} = -\frac{\sqrt{41}}{8} \qquad \text{or} \qquad p - \frac{3}{8} = \frac{\sqrt{41}}{8}$$

$$p = \frac{3}{8} - \frac{\sqrt{41}}{8} \qquad \text{or} \qquad p = \frac{3}{8} + \frac{\sqrt{41}}{8}$$

$$p = \frac{3 - \sqrt{41}}{8} \qquad \text{or} \qquad p = \frac{3 + \sqrt{41}}{8}$$

The solution set is $\left\{\frac{3-\sqrt{41}}{8}, \frac{3+\sqrt{41}}{8}\right\}$.

Example 13.8.18 Putting Quadratic Functions in Vertex Form. Write a formula in vertex form for the function T defined by $T(x) = 4x^2 + 20x + 24$.

Explanation. Before we can complete the square, we will factor the 4 out of the first two terms. Don't be tempted to factor the 4 out of the constant term.

$$T(x) = 4\left(x^2 + 5x\right) + 24$$

Now we will complete the square inside the parentheses by adding and subtracting $\left(\frac{5}{2}\right)^2 = \frac{25}{4}$.

$$T(x) = 4\left(x^2 + 5x + \frac{25}{4} - \frac{25}{4}\right) + 24$$

Notice that the constant that we subtracted is inside the parentheses, but it will not be part of our perfect square trinomial. In order to bring it outside, we need to multiply it by 4. We are distributing the 4 to that term so we can combine it with the outside term.

$$T(x) = 4\left(\left(x^2 + 5x + \frac{25}{4}\right) - \frac{25}{4}\right) + 24$$
$$= 4\left(x^2 + 5x + \frac{25}{4}\right) - 4 \cdot \frac{25}{4} + 24$$

$$= 4\left(x + \frac{5}{2}\right)^2 - 25 + 24$$

$$= 4\left(x + \frac{5}{2}\right)^2 - 1$$

Note that The vertex is $\left(-\frac{5}{2}, -1\right)$.

Example 13.8.19 Graphing Quadratic Functions by Hand. Graph the function H defined by $H(x) = -x^2 - 8x - 15$ by determining its key features algebraically.

Explanation.   To start, we'll note that this function opens downward because the leading coefficient, -1, is negative.

Now we will complete the square to find the vertex. We will factor the -1 out of the first two terms, and then add and subtract $\left(\frac{8}{2}\right)^2 = 4^2 = 16$ on the right side.

$$\begin{aligned}
H(x) &= -\left[x^2 + 8x\right] - 15 \\
&= -\left[x^2 + 8x + 16 - 16\right] - 15 \\
&= -\left[(x^2 + 8x + 16) - 16\right] - 15 \\
&= -(x^2 + 8x + 16) - (-1 \cdot 16) - 15 \\
&= -(x + 4)^2 + 16 - 15 \\
&= -(x + 4)^2 + 1
\end{aligned}$$

The vertex is $(-4, 1)$ so the axis of symmetry is the line $x = -4$.

To find the y-intercept, we'll replace x with 0 or read the value of c from the function in standard form:

$$\begin{aligned}
H(0) &= -(0)^2 - 8(0) - 15 \\
&= -15
\end{aligned}$$

The y-intercept is $(0, -15)$ and we will find its symmetric point on the graph, which is $(-8, -15)$.

Next, we'll find the horizontal intercepts. We see this function factors so we will write the factored form to get the horizontal intercepts.

$$\begin{aligned}
H(x) &= -x^2 - 8x - 15 \\
&= -\left(x^2 + 8x + 15\right) \\
&= -(x + 3)(x + 5)
\end{aligned}$$

The x-intercepts are $(-3, 0)$ and $(-5, 0)$.

Now we will plot all of the key points and draw the parabola.

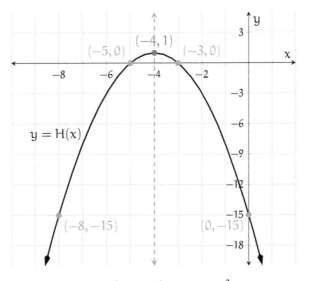

Figure 13.8.20: The graph of $y = -x^2 - 8x - 15$.

13.8.4 Absolute Value Equations

In Section 13.4 we covered how to solve equations when an absolute value is equal to a number and when an absolute value is equal to an absolute value.

Example 13.8.21 Solving an Equation with an Absolute Value. Solve the absolute value equation $|9 - 4x| = 17$ using Fact 13.4.12.

Explanation. The equation $|9 - 4x| = 17$ breaks into two pieces, each of which needs to be solved independently.

$$
\begin{array}{ccc}
9 - 4x = 17 & \text{or} & 9 - 4x = -17 \\
-4x = 8 & \text{or} & -4x = -26 \\
\dfrac{-4x}{-4} = \dfrac{8}{-4} & \text{or} & \dfrac{-4x}{-4} = \dfrac{-26}{-4} \\
x = -2 & \text{or} & x = \dfrac{13}{2}
\end{array}
$$

The solution set is $\left\{-2, \frac{13}{2}\right\}$.

Example 13.8.22 Solving an Equation with Two Absolute Values. Solve the absolute value equation $|7 - 3x| = |6x - 5|$ using Fact 13.4.18.

Explanation. The equation $|7 - 3x| = |6x - 5|$ breaks into two pieces, each of which needs to be solved independently.

$$
\begin{array}{ccc}
7 - 3x = 6x - 5 & \text{or} & 7 - 3x = -(6x - 5) \\
7 - 3x = 6x - 5 & \text{or} & 7 - 3x = -6x + 5 \\
12 - 3x = 6x & \text{or} & 2 - 3x = -6x \\
12 = 9x & \text{or} & 2 = -3x
\end{array}
$$

$$\frac{12}{9} = \frac{9x}{9} \qquad \text{or} \qquad \frac{2}{-3} = \frac{-3x}{-3}$$

$$\frac{4}{3} = x \qquad \text{or} \qquad -\frac{2}{3} = x$$

The solution set is $\left\{ \frac{4}{3}, -\frac{2}{3} \right\}$.

13.8.5 Solving Mixed Equations

In Section 13.5 we reviewed all of the various solving methods covered so far including solving linear equations with one variable and for a specified variable; solving systems of linear equations using substitution and elimination; solving equations with radicals; solving quadratic equations using the square root method, the quadratic formula, factoring, completing the square; and solving rational equations.

Example 13.8.23 Types of equations. Identify the type of equation as linear, a system of linear equations, quadratic, radical, rational, absolute value, or something else.

a. $5x^2 - 2x = 9$

b. $\pi x - 3 = 4(x + 1)$

c. $8x^2 = x + 9$

d. $\frac{2}{x+2} + \frac{3}{2x+4} = \frac{7}{x+8}$

e. $|2x - 7| + 2 = 3$

f. $\sqrt{x + 2} = x - 4$

g. $(3 - 2x)^2 - 9 = 9$

h. $3 = \sqrt[3]{5 - 2x}$

i.
$$\begin{cases} 5x - y = -6 \\ 2x - 3y = 8 \end{cases}$$

j. $x^x = x - \left| x - x^2 - 3 \right|$

Explanation.

a. The equation $5x^2 - 2x = 9$ is a quadratic equation since the variable is being squared (but doesn't have any higher power).

b. The equation $\pi x - 3 = 4(x + 1)$ is a linear equation since the variable is only to the first power.

c. The equation $8x^2 = x + 9$ is a quadratic equation since there is a degree-two term.

d. The equation $\frac{2}{x+2} + \frac{3}{2x+4} = \frac{7}{x+8}$ is a rational equation since the variable exists in the denominator.

e. The equation $|2x - 7| + 2 = 3$ is an absolute value equation since the variable is inside an absolute value.

f. The equation $\sqrt{x + 2} = x - 4$ is a radical equation since the variable appears inside the radical.

g. The equation $(3 - 2x)^2 - 9 = 9$ is a quadratic equation since if we were to distribute everything out, we would have a term with x^2.

h. The equation $3 = \sqrt[3]{5 - 2x}$ is a radical equation since the variable is inside the radical.

i. The system

$$\begin{cases} 5x - y = -6 \\ 2x - 3y = 8 \end{cases}$$

is a system of linear equations.

j. The equation $x^x = x - |x - x^2 - 3|$ is an equation type that we have not covered and is not listed above.

Example 13.8.24 Solving Mixed Equations. Solve the equations using appropriate techniques.

a. $5x^2 - 2x = 9$

b. $\pi x - 3 = 4(x + 1)$

c. $8x^2 = x + 9$

d. $\frac{2}{x+2} + \frac{3}{2x+4} = \frac{7}{x+8}$

e. $|2x - 7| + 2 = 3$

f. $\sqrt{x + 2} = x - 4$

g. $(3 - 2x)^2 - 9 = 9$

h. $3 = \sqrt[3]{5 - 2x}$

i.
$$\begin{cases} 5x - y = -6 \\ 2x - 3y = 8 \end{cases}$$

j. $x^2 + 10x = 12$ (using completing the square)

Explanation.

a. Since the equation $5x^2 - 2x = 9$ is a quadratic we should consider the square root method, the quadratic formula, factoring, and completing the square. In this case, we will start with the quadratic formula. First, note that we should rearrange the terms in equation into standard form.

$$5x^2 - 2x = 9$$
$$5x^2 - 2x - 9 = 0$$

Note that $a = 5$, $b = -2$, and $c = -9$.

$$x = \frac{-b \pm \sqrt{b^2 - 4ac}}{2a}$$
$$x = \frac{-(-2) \pm \sqrt{(-2)^2 - 4(5)(-9)}}{2(5)}$$
$$x = \frac{2 \pm \sqrt{4 + 180}}{10}$$
$$x = \frac{2 \pm \sqrt{184}}{10}$$
$$x = \frac{2 \pm \sqrt{4 \cdot 46}}{10}$$
$$x = \frac{2 \pm 2\sqrt{46}}{10}$$
$$x = \frac{1 \pm \sqrt{46}}{5}$$

The solution set is $\left\{ \frac{1+\sqrt{46}}{5}, \frac{1-\sqrt{46}}{5} \right\}$.

b. Since the equation $\pi x - 3 = 4(x + 1)$ is a linear equation, we isolate the variable step-by-step.

$$\pi x - 3 = 4(x + 1)$$
$$\pi x - 3 = 4x + 4$$

$$\pi x - 4x = 7$$
$$x(\pi - 4) = 7$$
$$x = \frac{7}{\pi - 4}$$

The solution set is $\left\{ \frac{7}{\pi-4} \right\}$.

c. Since the equation $8x^2 = x + 9$ is a quadratic equation, we again have several options to consider. We will try factoring on this one first after converting it to standard form.

$$8x^2 = x + 9$$
$$8x^2 - x - 9 = 0$$

Here, $ac = -72$ and two numbers that multiply to be -72 but add to be -1 are 8 and -9.

$$8x^2 + 8x - 9x - 9 = 0$$
$$\left(8x^2 + 8x\right) + (-9x - 9) = 0$$
$$8x(x + 1) - 9(x + 1) = 0$$
$$(8x - 9)(x + 1) = 0$$

$8x - 9 = 0$	or	$x + 1 = 0$
$x = \dfrac{9}{8}$	or	$x = -1$

The solution set is $\left\{ \frac{9}{8}, -1 \right\}$

d. Since the equation $\frac{2}{x+2} + \frac{3}{2x+4} = \frac{7}{x+8}$ is a rational we first need to cancel the denominators after factoring and finding the least common denominator.

$$\frac{2}{x+2} + \frac{3}{2x+4} = \frac{7}{x+8}$$
$$\frac{2}{x+2} + \frac{3}{2(x+2)} = \frac{7}{x+8}$$

At this point, we note that the least common denominator is $2(x+2)(x+8)$. We need to multiply every term by this least common denominator.

$$\frac{2}{x+2} \cdot 2(x+2)(x+8) + \frac{3}{2(x+2)} \cdot 2(x+2)(x+8) = \frac{7}{x+8} \cdot 2(x+2)(x+8)$$
$$\frac{2}{\cancel{x+2}} \cdot 2\cancel{(x+2)}(x+8) + \frac{3}{\cancel{2(x+2)}} \cdot \cancel{2(x+2)}(x+8) = \frac{7}{\cancel{x+8}} \cdot 2(x+2)\cancel{(x+8)}$$
$$2 \cdot 2(x+8) + 3(x+8) = 7 \cdot 2(x+2)$$
$$4(x+8) + 3(x+8) = 14(x+2)$$
$$4x + 32 + 3x + 24 = 14x + 28$$
$$7x + 56 = 14x + 28$$

$$28 = 7x$$
$$4 = x$$

We always check solutions to rational equations to ensure we don't have any "extraneous solutions".

$$\frac{2}{(4)+2} + \frac{3}{2(4)+4} \overset{?}{=} \frac{7}{(4)+8}$$
$$\frac{2}{6} + \frac{3}{12} \overset{?}{=} \frac{7}{12}$$
$$\frac{4}{12} + \frac{3}{12} \overset{?}{=} \frac{7}{12}$$
$$\frac{7}{12} \overset{\checkmark}{=} \frac{7}{12}$$

So, the solution set is $\{4\}$.

e. Since the equation $|2x - 7| + 2 = 3$ is an absolute value equation, we will first isolate the absolute value and then use Equations with an Absolute Value Expression to solve the remaining equation.

$$|2x - 7| + 2 = 3$$
$$|2x - 7| = 1$$

$2x - 7 = 5$	or	$2x - 7 = -5$
$2x = 12$	or	$2x = 2$
$x = 6$	or	$x = 1$

The solution set is $\{6, 1\}$.

f. Since the equation $\sqrt{x+2} = x - 4$ is a radical equation, we will have to isolate the radical (which is already done), then square both sides to cancel the square root. After that, we will solve whatever remains.

$$\sqrt{x+2} = x - 4$$
$$\sqrt{x+2} = x - 4$$
$$(\sqrt{x+2})^2 = (x-4)^2$$
$$x + 2 = (x-4)(x-4)$$
$$x + 2 = x^2 - 8x + 16$$
$$0 = x^2 - 9x + 14$$

We now have a quadratic equation. We will solve by factoring.

$$0 = (x-2)(x-7)$$

$x - 2 = 0$	or	$x - 7 = 0$
$x = 2$	or	$x = 7$

Every potential solution to a radical equation should be verified to check for any "extraneous solutions".

$$\sqrt{2+2} \overset{?}{=} 2-4 \qquad \text{or} \qquad \sqrt{7+2} \overset{?}{=} 7-4$$

$$\sqrt{4} \overset{?}{=} -2 \qquad \text{or} \qquad \sqrt{9} \overset{?}{=} 3$$

$$2 \overset{no}{=} -2 \qquad \text{or} \qquad 3 \overset{\checkmark}{=} 3$$

So the solution set is $\{7\}$

g. Since the equation $(3-2x)^2 - 9 = 9$ is a quadratic equation, we again have several options. Since the variable only appears once in this equation we will use the the square root method to solve.

$$(3-2x)^2 - 9 = 9$$
$$(3-2x)^2 = 18$$

$$3 - 2x = \sqrt{18} \qquad \text{or} \qquad 3 - 2x = -\sqrt{18}$$

$$3 - 2x = 3\sqrt{2} \qquad \text{or} \qquad 3 - 2x = -3\sqrt{2}$$

$$-2x = -3 + 3\sqrt{2} \qquad \text{or} \qquad -2x = -3 - 3\sqrt{2}$$

$$x = \frac{-3 + 3\sqrt{2}}{-2} \qquad \text{or} \qquad x = \frac{-3 - 3\sqrt{2}}{-2}$$

$$x = \frac{3 - 3\sqrt{2}}{2} \qquad \text{or} \qquad x = \frac{3 + 3\sqrt{2}}{2}$$

The solution set is $\left\{ \frac{3-3\sqrt{2}}{2}, \frac{3+3\sqrt{2}}{2} \right\}$.

h. Since the equation $3 = \sqrt[3]{5 - 2x}$ is a radical equation, we will isolate the radical (which is already done) and then raise both sides to the third power to cancel the cube root.

$$3 = \sqrt[3]{5 - 2x}$$
$$(3)^3 = \left(\sqrt[3]{6x - 5} \right)^3$$
$$27 = 6x - 5$$
$$32 = 6x$$
$$x = \frac{32}{6}$$
$$x = \frac{16}{3}$$

The solution set is $\left\{ \frac{16}{3} \right\}$.

i. Since

$$\begin{cases} 5x - y = -6 \\ 2x - 3y = 8 \end{cases}$$

is a system of linear equations, we can either use substitution or elimination to solve. Here we will use substitution. To use substitution, we need to solve one of the equations for one of the variables. We will solve the top equation for y.

$$5x - y = -6$$
$$-y = -5x - 6$$
$$y = 5x + 6$$

Now, we substitute $5x + 6$ where ever we see y in the other equation.

$$2x - 3y = 8$$
$$2x - 3(5x + 6) = 8$$
$$2x - 15x - 18 = 8$$
$$-13x - 18 = 8$$
$$-13x = 26$$
$$x = -2$$

Now that we have found x, we can substitute that back into one of the equations to find y. We will substitute into the first equation.

$$5(-2) - y = -6$$
$$-10 - y = -6$$
$$-y = 4$$
$$y = -4$$

So, the solution must be the point $(-2, -4)$.

j. Since the equation $x^2 + 10x = 12$ is quadratic and we are instructed to solve by using completing the square, we should recall that Fact 13.3.3 tells us how to complete the square, after we have sufficiently simplified. Since our equation is already in a simplified state, we need to add $\left(\frac{b}{2}\right)^2 = \left(\frac{10}{2}\right)^2 = 25$ to both sides of the equation.

$$x^2 + 10x = 12$$
$$x^2 + 10x + 25 = 12 + 25$$
$$(x + 5)^2 = 37$$
$$x + 5 = \pm\sqrt{37}$$
$$x = -5 \pm \sqrt{37}$$

So, our solution set is $\left\{-5 + \sqrt{37}, -5 - \sqrt{37}\right\}$.

13.8.6 Compound Inequalities

In Section 13.6 we defined the union of intervals, what compound inequalities are, and how to solve both "or" inequalities and triple inequalities.

Example 13.8.25 Unions of Intervals. Draw a representation of the union of the sets $(-\infty, -1]$ and $(2, \infty)$.

Explanation. First we make a number line with both intervals drawn to understand what both sets mean.

Figure 13.8.26: A number line sketch of $(-\infty, -1]$ as well as $(2, \infty)$

The two intervals should be viewed as a single object when stating the union, so here is the picture of the union. It looks the same, but now it is a graph of a single set.

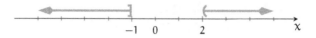

Figure 13.8.27: A number line sketch of $(-\infty, -1] \cup (2, \infty)$

Example 13.8.28 "Or" Compound Inequalities. Solve the compound inequality.

$$5z + 12 \leq 7 \text{ or } 3 - 9z < -2$$

Explanation. First we will solve each inequality for z.

$$
\begin{array}{lcl}
5z + 12 \leq 7 & \text{or} & 3 - 9z < -2 \\
5z \leq -5 & \text{or} & -9z < -5 \\
z \leq -1 & \text{or} & z > \dfrac{5}{9}
\end{array}
$$

The solution set to the compound inequality is:

$$(-\infty, -1] \cup \left(\frac{5}{9}, \infty\right)$$

Example 13.8.29 Three-Part Inequalities. Solve the three-part inequality $-4 \leq 20 - 6x < 32$.

Explanation. This is a three-part inequality. The goal is to isolate x in the middle and whatever you do to one "side," you have to do to the other two "sides."

$$
\begin{aligned}
-4 &\leq 20 - 6x < 32 \\
-4 - 20 &\leq 20 - 6x - 20 < 32 - 20 \\
-24 &\leq -6x < 12 \\
\frac{-24}{-6} &\geq \frac{-6x}{-6} > \frac{12}{-6} \\
4 &\geq x > -2
\end{aligned}
$$

The solutions to the three-part inequality $4 \geq x > -2$ are those numbers that are trapped between -2 and 4, including 4 but not -2. The solution set in interval notation is $(-2, 4]$.

Example 13.8.30 Solving "And" Inequalities. Solve the compound inequality.

$$5 - 3t < 3 \text{ and } 4t + 1 \leq 6$$

Explanation. This is an "and" inequality. We will solve each part of the inequality and then combine the two solutions sets with an intersection.

$5 - 3t < 3$	and	$4t + 1 \leq 6$
$-3t < -2$	and	$4t \leq 5$
$\dfrac{-3t}{-3} > \dfrac{-2}{-3}$	and	$\dfrac{4t}{4} \leq \dfrac{5}{4}$
$t > \dfrac{2}{3}$	and	$t \leq \dfrac{5}{4}$

The solution set to $t > \frac{2}{3}$ is $\left(\frac{2}{3}, \infty\right)$ and the solution set to $t \leq \frac{5}{4}$ is $\left(-\infty, \frac{5}{4}\right]$. Shown is a graph of these solution sets.

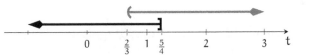

Figure 13.8.31: A number line sketch of $\left(\frac{2}{3}, \infty\right)$ and also $\left(-\infty, \frac{5}{4}\right]$

Recall that an "and" problem finds the intersection of the solution sets. Intersection finds the t-values where the two lines overlap, so the solution to the compound inequality must be

$$\left(\frac{2}{3}, \infty\right) \cap \left(-\infty, \frac{5}{4}\right] = \left(\frac{2}{3}, \frac{5}{4}\right).$$

Example 13.8.32 Application of Compound Inequalities. Mishel wanted to buy some mulch for their spring garden. Each cubic yard of mulch cost \$27 and delivery for any size load was \$40. If they wanted to spend between \$200 and \$300, set up and solve a compound inequality to solve for the number of cubic yards, x, that they could buy.

Explanation. Since the mulch costs \$27 per cubic yard and delivery is \$40, the formula for the cost of x yards of mulch is $27x + 40$. Since Mishel wants to spend between \$200 and \$300, we just trap their cost between these two values.

$$200 < 27x + 40 < 300$$
$$200 - 40 < 27x + 40 - 40 < 300 - 40$$
$$160 < 27x < 260$$
$$\frac{160}{27} < \frac{27x}{27} < \frac{260}{27}$$
$$5.93 < x < 9.63$$

Note: these values are approximate

Most companies will only sell whole number cubic yards of mulch, so we have to round appropriately. Since Mishel wants to spend more than \$200, we have to round our lower value from 5.93 up to 6 cubic yards.

If we round the 9.63 up to 10, then the total cost will be $27 \cdot 10 + 40 = 310$ (which represents \$310), which is more than Mishel wanted to spend. So we actually have to round down to 9cubic yards to stay below the \$300 maximum.

In conclusion, Mishel could buy 6, 7, 8, or 9 cubic yards of mulch to stay between \$200 and \$300.

13.8.7 Solving Inequalities Graphically

Example 13.8.33 Solving Absolute Value Inequalities Graphically. Solve the inequality $|4 - 2x| < 10$ graphically.

Explanation.   To solve the inequality $|4 - 2x| < 10$, we will start by making a graph with both $y = |4 - 2x|$ and $y = 10$.

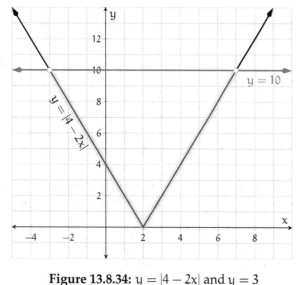

The portion of the graph of $y = |4 - 2x|$ that is below $y = 10$ is highlighted and the x-values of that highlighted region are trapped between -3 and 7: $-3 < x < 7$. That means that the solution set is $(-3, 7)$. Note that we shouldn't include the endpoints of the interval because at those values, the two graphs are *equal* whereas the original inequality was only *less than* and not equal.

Figure 13.8.34: $y = |4 - 2x|$ and $y = 3$

Example 13.8.35 Solving Compound Inequalities Graphically. Figure 13.8.36 shows a graph of $y = G(x)$. Use the graph do the following.

    a. Solve $G(x) < -2$.   b. Solve $G(x) \geq 1$.   c. Solve $-1 \leq G(x) < 1$.

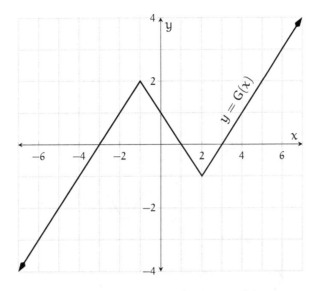

Figure 13.8.36: Graph of $y = G(x)$

Explanation.

a. To solve $G(x) < -2$, we first draw a dotted line (since it's a less-than, not a less-than-or-equal) at $y = -2$. Then we examine the graph to find out where the graph of $y = G(x)$ is underneath the line $y = -2$. Our graph is below the line $y = -2$ for x-values less than -5. So the solution set is $(-\infty, -5)$.

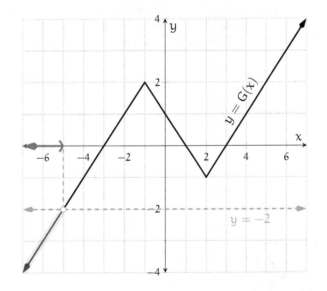

Figure 13.8.37: Graph of $y = G(x)$ and solution set to $G(x) < -2$

b. To solve $G(x) \geq 1$, we first draw a solid line (since it's a greater-than-or-equal) at $y = 1$. Then we examine the graph to find out what parts of the graph of $y = G(x)$ are above the line $y = 1$. Our graph is above (or on) the line $y = 1$ for x-values between -2 and 0 as well as x-values bigger than 4. So the solution set is $[-2, 0] \cup [4, \infty)$.

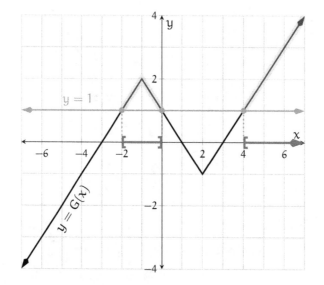

Figure 13.8.38: Graph of $y = G(x)$ and solution set to $G(x) \geq 1$

c. To solve $-1 < G(x) \leq 1$, we first draw a solid line at $y = 1$ and dotted line at $y = -1$. Then we examine the graph to find out what parts of the graph of $y = G(x)$ are trapped between the two lines we just drew. Our graph is between those values for x-values between -4 and -2 as well as x-values between 0 and 2 as well as as well as x-values between 2 and 4. We use the solid and hollow dots on the graph to decide whether or not to include those values. So the solution set is $(-4, -2] \cup [0, 2) \cup (2, 4]$.

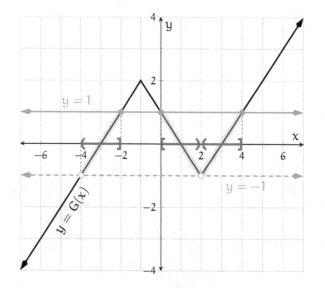

Figure 13.8.39: Graph of $y = G(x)$ and solution set to $-1 < G(x) \leq 1$

13.8.8 Exercises

Overview of Graphing

1. Create a table of ordered pairs and then make a plot of the equation $y = -\frac{2}{5}x - 3$.

2. Create a table of ordered pairs and then make a plot of the equation $y = -\frac{3}{4}x + 2$.

3. Graph the equation $y = \frac{2}{3}x + 4$.

4. Graph the equation $y = \frac{3}{2}x - 5$.

5. Graph the linear equation $y = -\frac{8}{3}(x - 4) - 5$ by identifying the slope and one point on this line.

6. Graph the linear equation $y = \frac{5}{7}(x + 3) + 2$ by identifying the slope and one point on this line.

7. Make a graph of the line $20x - 4y = 8$.

8. Make a graph of the line $3x + 5y = 10$.

9. Create a table of ordered pairs and then make a plot of the equation $y = -3x^2$.

10. Create a table of ordered pairs and then make a plot of the equation $y = -x^2 - 2x - 3$.

Quadratic Graphs and Vertex Form

11. Let $F(x) = 2x^2 - 2x + 3$. Use technology to find the following.

   a. The vertex is

   b. The y-intercept is

   c. The x-intercept(s) is/are

   d. The domain of F is

   e. The range of F is

   f. Calculate F(1).

   g. Solve $F(x) = 6$.

   h. Solve $F(x) \geq 6$.

12. Let $G(x) = -2x^2 + 4x - 1$. Use technology to find the following.

   a. The vertex is

   b. The y-intercept is

   c. The x-intercept(s) is/are

   d. The domain of G is

   e. The range of G is

   f. Calculate G(1).

   g. Solve $G(x) = -6$.

   h. Solve $G(x) < -6$.

13. An object was launched from the top of a hill with an upward vertical velocity of 170 feet per second. The height of the object can be modeled by the function $h(t) = -16t^2 + 170t + 300$, where t represents the number of seconds after the launch. Assume the object landed on the ground at sea level. Find the answer using technology.

    ◻ seconds after its launch, the object reached its maximum height of ◻ feet.

14. An object was launched from the top of a hill with an upward vertical velocity of 180 feet per second. The height of the object can be modeled by the function $h(t) = -16t^2 + 180t + 200$, where t represents the number of seconds after the launch. Assume the object landed on the ground at sea level. Find the answer using technology.

    ◻ seconds after its launch, the object fell to the ground at sea level.

15. Consider the graph of the equation $y = (x - 9)^2 - 7$.
    Compared to the graph of $y = x^2$, the vertex has been shifted ◻ units (◻ left ◻ right) and ◻ units (◻ down ◻ up) .

16. Consider the graph of the equation $y = (x + 8)^2 + 5$.
    Compared to the graph of $y = x^2$, the vertex has been shifted ◻ units (◻ left ◻ right) and ◻ units (◻ down ◻ up) .

17. The quadratic expression $(x - 1)^2$ is written in vertex form.

    a. Write the expression in standard form.

    b. Write the expression in factored form.

18. The quadratic expression $(x - 2)^2 - 9$ is written in vertex form.

    a. Write the expression in standard form.

    b. Write the expression in factored form.

19. The formula for a quadratic function K is $K(x) = (x + 1)(x - 4)$.

    a. The y-intercept is

    ◻ .

    b. The x-intercept(s) is/are

    ◻

20. The formula for a quadratic function h is $h(x) = (x - 1)(x + 2)$.

    a. The y-intercept is

    ◻ .

    b. The x-intercept(s) is/are

    ◻

Completing the Square

21. Solve $r^2 - r - 2 = 0$ by completing the square.

22. Solve $t^2 + 5t - 6 = 0$ by completing the square.

23. Solve $3t^2 - 14t + 15 = 0$ by completing the square.

24. Solve $12t^2 + 20t + 7 = 0$ by completing the square.

25. Complete the square to convert the quadratic function from standard form to vertex form, and use the result to find the function's domain and range.
    $f(x) = -3x^2 - 54x - 240$

26. Complete the square to convert the quadratic function from standard form to vertex form, and use the result to find the function's domain and range.
    $f(x) = -5x^2 - 60x - 184$

27. Graph $f(x) = x^2 - 7x + 12$ by algebraically determining its key features. Then state the domain and range of the function.

28. Graph $f(x) = -x^2 + 4x + 21$ by algebraically determining its key features. Then state the domain and range of the function.

29. Graph $f(x) = x^2 - 8x + 16$ by algebraically determining its key features. Then state the domain and range of the function.

30. Graph $f(x) = x^2 + 6x + 9$ by algebraically determining its key features. Then state the domain and range of the function.

Absolute Value Equations

31. Solve the following equation.
$|4x + 9| = 3$

32. Solve the following equation.
$|5x + 2| = 7$

33. Solve: $\left|\dfrac{2t - 3}{3}\right| = 1$

34. Solve: $\left|\dfrac{2x - 7}{7}\right| = 3$

35. Solve: $\left|\frac{1}{4}x + 7\right| = 5$

36. Solve: $\left|\frac{1}{2}y + 5\right| = 3$

37. Solve: $|5y - 20| + 2 = 2$

38. Solve: $|4a - 4| + 7 = 7$

39. Solve the equation: $|2x - 3| = |7x + 6|$

40. Solve the equation: $|4x - 8| = |3x + 4|$

41. Solve the following equation.
$|3x - 1| = |8x - 10|$

42. Solve the following equation.
$|3x - 8| = |10x + 5|$

Solving Mixed Equations

43. Solve the equation.
$47x^2 + 41 = 0$

44. Solve the equation.
$23x^2 + 47 = 0$

45. Solve: $|y - 1| = 9$

46. Solve: $|y - 5| = 13$

47. Solve the equation.
$2x^2 = -25x - 50$

48. Solve the equation.
$2x^2 = -11x - 5$

49. Solve the equation.
$y = \sqrt{y + 10} + 2$

50. Solve the equation.
$y = \sqrt{y + 8} - 2$

51. Solve the equation.
$\dfrac{8}{r + 1} - \dfrac{7}{r - 6} = \dfrac{5}{r^2 - 5r - 6}$

52. Solve the equation.
$\dfrac{5}{r - 2} - \dfrac{7}{r + 9} = \dfrac{9}{r^2 + 7r - 18}$

53. Solve the equation by completing the square.
$t^2 + 6t = -8$

54. Solve the equation by completing the square.
$t^2 - 16t = -63$

Compound Inequalities Solve the compound inequality algebraically.

55. $-12x - 15 < -6$ or $-8x - 10 > 18$

56. $-10x + 7 < 15$ and $15x + 3 \geq 2$

57. $17x - 17 < 4$ and $-6x + 7 < 18$

58. $3x + 1 < -8$ and $15x + 11 \leq -6$

59. $2x + 10 \geq -19$ and $-11x + 9 < 20$

60. $20x - 5 \geq -20$ or $-9x - 7 \geq 17$

61. $x + 11 < -1$ or $-6x - 19 \leq 3$

62. $16x + 5 > 20$ or $-5x + 1 \geq 11$

63. $18 \leq x + 17 < 23$

64. $20 \leq x + 10 < 25$

65. $3 \leq \dfrac{5}{9}(F - 32) \leq 33$

F is in ⬚

66. $6 \leq \dfrac{5}{9}(F - 32) \leq 46$

F is in ⬚

Solving Inequalities Graphically

67. Solve the equations and inequalities graphically. Use interval notation when applicable.

    a. $\left|\frac{2}{3}x + 2\right| = 4$ b. $\left|\frac{2}{3}x + 2\right| > 4$ c. $\left|\frac{2}{3}x + 2\right| \leq 4$

68. Solve the equations and inequalities graphically. Use interval notation when applicable.

    a. $\left|\frac{11-2x}{5}\right| = 4$ b. $\left|\frac{11-2x}{5}\right| > 4$ c. $\left|\frac{11-2x}{5}\right| \leq 4$

69. The equations $y = \frac{1}{2}x^2 + 2x - 1$ and $y = 5$ are plotted.

70. The equations $y = \frac{1}{3}x^2 - 3x + 3$ and $y = -3$ are plotted.

a. What are the points of intersection?

b. Solve $\frac{1}{2}x^2 + 2x - 1 = 5$.

c. Solve $\frac{1}{2}x^2 + 2x - 1 > 5$.

a. What are the points of intersection?

b. Solve $\frac{1}{3}x^2 - 3x + 3 = -3$.

c. Solve $\frac{1}{3}x^2 - 3x + 3 > -3$.

71. The equations $y = \frac{1}{2}x^2 - x - 1$ and $y = -x + 1$ are plotted.

72. The equations $y = \frac{-1}{3}x^2 + 2x + 3$ and $y = x - 3$ are plotted.

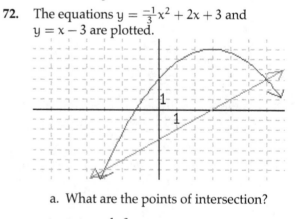

a. What are the points of intersection?

b. Solve $\frac{1}{2}x^2 - x - 1 = -x + 1$.

c. Solve $\frac{1}{2}x^2 - x - 1 > -x + 1$.

a. What are the points of intersection?

b. Solve $\frac{-1}{3}x^2 + 2x + 3 = x - 3$.

c. Solve $\frac{-1}{3}x^2 + 2x + 3 > x - 3$.

73. The equations $y = x - 2$ and
$y = |x + |x - 3| - 4|$ are plotted.

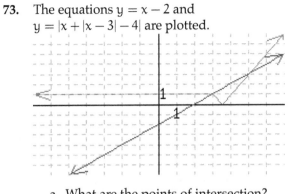

a. What are the points of intersection?

b. Solve $x - 2 = |x + |x - 3| - 4|$.

c. Solve $x - 2 > |x + |x - 3| - 4|$.

74. Use graphing technology to solve the
inequality $\frac{3}{4}x \geq \frac{1}{4}x^2 - 3x$. State the solution
set using interval notation, and
approximate if necessary.

A graph of f is given. Use the graph alone to solve the compound inequalities.

75.

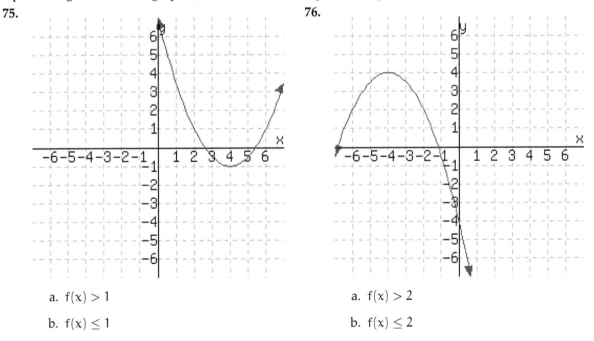

a. $f(x) > 1$

b. $f(x) \leq 1$

76.

a. $f(x) > 2$

b. $f(x) \leq 2$

Appendix B

Unit Conversions

Units of Length in the US/Imperial System	Units of Length in the Metric System	System to System Length Conversions
1 foot (ft) = 12 inches (in)	1 meter (m) = 1000 millimeters (mm)	1 inch (in) = 2.54 centimeters (cm)
1 yard (yd) = 3 feet (ft)	1 meter (m) = 100 centimeters (cm)	1 meter (m) $\approx$ 3.281 feet (ft)
1 yard (yd) = 36 inches (in)	1 meter (m) = 10 decimeters (dm)	1 meter (m) $\approx$ 1.094 yard (yd)
1 mile (mi) = 5280 feet (ft)	1 dekameter (dam) = 10 meters (m)	1 mile (mi) $\approx$ 1.609 kilometer (km)
	1 hectometer (hm) = 100 meters (m)	
	1 kilometer (km) = 1000 meters (m)	

Table B.0.1: Length Unit Conversion Factors

Units of Area in the US/Imperial System	Units of Area in the Metric System	System to System Area Conversions
1 acre = 43560 square feet (ft^2)	1 hectare (ha) = 10000 square meters (m^2)	1 hectare (ha) $\approx$ 2.471 acres
640 acres = 1 square mile (mi^2)	100 hectares (ha) = 1 square kilometer (km^2)	

Table B.0.2: Area Unit Conversion Factors

Units of Volume in the US/Imperial System	Units of Volume in the Metric System	System to System Volume Conversions
1 tablespoon (tbsp) = 3 teaspoon (tsp)	1 cubic centimeter (cc) = 1 cubic centimeter (cm^3)	1 cubic inch (in^3) $\approx$ 16.39 milliliters (mL)
1 fluid ounce (fl oz) = 2 tablespoons (tbsp)	1 milliliter (mL) = 1 cubic centimeter (cm^3)	1 fluid ounce (fl oz) $\approx$ 29.57 milliliters (mL)
1 cup (c) = 8 fluid ounces (fl oz)	1 liter (L) = 1000 milliliters (mL)	1 liter (L) $\approx$ 1.057 quarts (qt)
1 pint (pt) = 2 cups (c)	1 liter (L) = 1000 cubic centimeters (cm^3)	1 gallon (gal) $\approx$ 3.785 liters (L)
1 quart (qt) = 2 pints (pt)		
1 gallon (gal) = 4 quarts (qt)		
1 gallon (gal) = 231 cubic inches (in^3)		

Table B.0.3: Volume Unit Conversion Factors

Units of Mass/Weight in the US/Imperial System	Units of Mass/Weight in the Metric System	System to System Mass/Weight Conversions
1 pound (lb) = 16 ounces (oz)	1 gram (g) = 1000 milligrams (mg)	1 ounce (oz) $\approx$ 28.35 grams (g)
1 ton (T) = 2000 pounds (lb)	1 gram (g) = 1000 kilograms (kg)	1 kilogram (kg) $\approx$ 2.205 pounds (lb)
	1 metric ton (t) = 1000 kilograms (kg)	

Table B.0.4: Weight/Mass Unit Conversion Factors

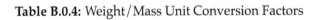

Precise Units of Time	Imprecise Units of Time	Units of Time in the Metric System
1 week (wk) = 7 days (d)	1 year (yr) ≈ 12 months (mo)	1 second (s) = 1000 milliseconds (ms)
1 day (d) = 24 hours (h)	1 year (yr) ≈ 52 weeks (wk)	1 second (s) = 10^6 microseconds (μs)
1 hour (h) = 60 minutes (min)	1 year (yr) ≈ 365 days (d)	1 second (s) = 10^9 nanoseconds (ns)
1 minute (min) = 60 seconds (s)	1 month (mo) ≈ 30 days (d)	

Table B.0.5: Time Unit Conversion Factors

1 byte (B) = 8 bits (b)	1 kilobit (kb) = 1024 bits (b)
1 kilobyte (kB) = 1024 bytes (B)	1 megabit (Mb) = 1024 kilobits (kb)
1 megabyte (MB) = 1024 kilobytes (kB)	
1 gigabyte (GB) = 1024 megabytes (MB)	
1 terabyte (TB) = 1024 gigabytes (GB)	

Table B.0.6: Computer Storage/Memory Conversion Factors

Index